ISBN 978-1-334-26704-8
PIBN 10749774

1 MONTH OF
FREE
READING

at

www.ForgottenBooks.com

By purchasing this book you are eligible for one month membership to ForgottenBooks.com, giving you unlimited access to our entire collection of over 1,000,000 titles via our web site and mobile apps.

To claim your free month visit:

www.forgottenbooks.com/free749774

English
Français
Deutsche
Italiano
Español
Português

www.forgottenbooks.com

Mythology Photography **Fiction**
Fishing Christianity **Art** Cooking
Essays Buddhism Freemasonry
Medicine **Biology** Music **Ancient
Egypt** Evolution Carpentry Physics
Dance Geology **Mathematics** Fitness
Shakespeare **Folklore** Yoga Marketing
Confidence Immortality Biographies
Poetry **Psychology** Witchcraft
Electronics Chemistry History **Law**
Accounting **Philosophy** Anthropology
Alchemy Drama Quantum Mechanics
Atheism Sexual Health **Ancient History**
Entrepreneurship Languages Sport
Paleontology Needlework Islam
Metaphysics Investment Archaeology
Parenting Statistics Criminology
Motivational

Historic, archived document

Do not assume content reflects current
scientific knowledge, policies, or practices.

| VAGABOND PRINCE | MARY SHARY | DR. F. E. BENNETT | MAID OF ORLEANS | BEACON |

Vaughan's Famous Rainbow Garden of Gladioli

Eighty flowering size bulbs, ten each of the eight outstanding varieties illustrated on this page. Each variety separately bagged and labeled. Prepaid 600 miles for . . . **$2.00**

Half Portion, 40 bulbs, 5 each of same 8 varieties, prepaid 600 miles for $1.00.

The reproductions on this page are made, not of exceptional specimens, but of average flowers, reproduced on the same scale of reduction exactly one-fifth life size. For price and description of each variety see Gladiolus Pages.

IN every garden, including Victory gardens, gladioli should be grown. Most beautiful of summer flowers, they are at the same time the easiest to grow. As a border for the vegetable plot, or planted in a row beside the vegetables, they will thrive under the same cultivation and not only decorate the garden, but provide beautiful cut flowers for the home, or other purposes.

bulb of any one of these varieties would have cost a short time ago, you will have a gladiolus garden which few can equal.

The bulbs in this collection are not first size, but they are of flowering size, such as we use for growing exhibition flowers. They take a little longer to bloom than larger

| MINUET | SHIRLEY TEMPLE | PICARDY |

As the largest growers of gladioli in the world, we take pride in making this collection the outstanding value in the gladiolus field, in spite of the handicaps imposed by war conditions, which have seriously advanced costs and reduced production.

Each of the eight varieties is recognized by fanciers as among the finest in its color. With this collection, for a fraction of what a single

bulbs, but the size and quality of flowers are equal to the products of larger bulbs, and the crop of bulbs for next year's planting is likely to be greater.

Vaughan's gladiolus farms are centered at Ovid, Mich., on Michigan Route 21, 13 miles west of Owosso. The farms begin to show flowers about July 15 and from then until October are a sight worth seeing. Visitors are welcome during the flowering season.

EVERBLOOMING HYBRID TEA ROSES

5 for $4 25

ROSE POINSETTIA

ALL these Roses will bloom in your garden this summer, if planted according to simple directions furnished with the plants. Before winter comes they should have borne for you hundreds of lovely blossoms, beginning in June and continuing without interruption until killing frosts. Our plants are finest two year budded plants that are produced. The varieties are of the newest type, some of the very latest to make their debuts. Plant dormant Rose bushes as soon as the soil thaws and dries out enough to be prepared properly. As soon as dormant Roses are properly pruned and planted, hill them up with 3 or 4 inches of moist soil. This keeps the wind from drying the plants and helps them to leaf out more quickly. Remove the soil gradually as the plants begin to grow.

---

5 Hybrid Tea Rose Plants 2 YEAR DORMANT, Our Selection (Value $5.25). By Express Collect **$4 25**

10 Hybrid Tea Roses, 2 YEAR DORMANT, one each as listed (Value $10.25). By Express Collect **$7 95**

20 Hybrid Tea Roses, 2 YEAR DORMANT, two each as listed (Val. $20.50). By Express Collect **$15 00**

Christopher Stone. Classed with Etoile De Holland and Crimson Glory as one of the three finest red Roses in existence. The plants grow well, have heavy foliage, and all season they produce quantities of brilliant, glowing, velvety scarlet blooms of good form. Delicious Old Rose fragrance. Rated by the American Rose Society as being one of the 10 best Roses introduced in the last 10 years. Dormant plants, $1.00.

Duquesa de Penaranda. This glorious Rose produces two distinct types of flowers. In summer the pointed buds are apricot-orange and dark pink opening to splendid blooms of coppery apricot. In autumn great brownish buds open slowly to finely formed flowers of a luscious cinnamon-peach color. Dormant plants $1.00.

Girona. Here is one of the most fragrant Roses in existence and one of the best of all garden Roses for cutting. Very strong growing, with good foliage, and superb blooms of a beautiful red and yellow combination. Dormant plants, $1.00.

McGredy's Ivory. "The perfect white Rose." Its long pointed, perfectly-shaped, ivory-white buds open into magnificent blooms of breath-taking loveliness. The plants are vigorous, have good foliage and produce quantities of long-lasting, moderately fragrant, perfect Roses. Dormant plants, $1.00.

After April 15th it may be necessary to change this collection. See Pages 97-99 for Complete List of Roses, including New Patented Varieties, Climbers and Floribundas. See Page 102 for Rugosa Roses.

McGredy's Yellow. Beautifully formed buds of pure, light buttercup yellow; open flowers cup-shaped with a mass of gold anthers glorifying the center. Plants vigorous and free blooming, with dark glossy, holly-like foliage. Dormant plants, $1.00.

Mme. Joseph Perraud. One of the most gorgeous Roses in existence with enormous, perfectly formed Nasturtium-orange buds, which open to sweetly fragrant flowers of a charming Nasturtium buff, straying to a lovely shade of shell pink. An excellent flower for both garden and exhibition purposes. Rated by the American Rose Society as being one of the 10 best Roses introduced in the last 10 years. Dormant plants, $1.00.

Poinsettia. Here is a rose that will be the sensation of your garden for it is the most dazzling red rose we have ever seen. The buds are ideal in form, long and pointed, and open into large, beautiful Poinsettia-scarlet blooms, with large well-shaped petals. The plants are good and the blooms are produced profusely during the whole season. Poinsettia just lacked 2 votes to be rated as one of the 10 best Roses introduced in the last 10 years. Dormant plants, $1.00.

President Macia. A superb variety that really performs. Extra long, pointed buds of rich carmine-pink, opening into great big blooms, often 5 inches across, of soft flesh-pink, brightened by a yellow flush at the base. Vigorous grower with long stems. Dormant plants, $1.25.

Southport. Fine flowers of an exceedingly brilliant scarlet which is unaffected by the weather. Very showy, probably the most brilliant of all scarlet Roses. Fine buds of lovely form on long stems. Blooms very freely, producing more flowers than any other Hybrid Tea Rose in our collection. Dormant plants, $1.00.

The Doctor. The most glorious pink Rose we have ever seen. The buds are long and pointed and expand to simply enormous blooms of beautiful, glowing rosy pink with satiny pink edges. Intensely fragrant; excellent for cutting. Rated by the American Rose Society as being one of the 10 best Roses introduced in the last 10 years. Dormant plants, $1.00.

Quantity Prices as Follows:	Each	Three	Doz.
	$1.00	2.50	10.00
	1.25	3.50	12.50

1

You Can Grow Giant

CHEROKEE BRAVE

DAHLIAS

CHAMPION VARIETIES OF RAINBOW COLORS

One Each of These Eight Varieties, Value $8.25. (Prepaid 300 Miles), For $6.50

GIANT dahlias are ideal flowers to grow in Victory Gardens. A row of these huge blossoms with their gay colors will decorate your vegetable plot and add to the enjoyment of your daily garden hour.

New varieties in this year's collections bring them up-to-date. All these varieties have stood the test and won places as proven champions. Besides giant size and fine coloring, they have the qualities of vigorous growth and free flowering. There will be no difficulty about growing them if you follow the simple directions which we furnish with each order.

AMERICAN PURITY. (S.C.) Color a large full and glistening white with petals beautifully quilled at the tips. Excellent stems. Price each $1.00.

CHEROKEE BRAVE. (I.D.) Ox-blood red that holds its color in the sun. Long stiff stems. Good grower. Price each $1.00.

EVENTIDE. (I.D.) True purplish shadings. Unusual production of large blooms. Excellent stems and vigorous habit of growth. Price each $1.50.

HUNT'S VELVET WONDER. (I.D.) Color is a rich violet purple. The huge blooms can be grown to immense size. Price each 75c.

KATIE K. (I.D.) A clear pink of large size on long stems. A strong grower. A good exhibition variety. Price each $1.00.

MRS. JAMES ALBIN. (F.D.) A soft pleasing yellow with fine formal blooms carried on straight stiff stems. Good grower and free branching. Price each $1.00.

MONARCH OF THE EAST. (F.D.) Color is a golden yellow bronze with a coral red reverse. It is a big bold bloom, a real giant in the Dahlia world. Price each $1.00.

SON OF SATAN. (S.C.) Bright scarlet blooms on excellent stems. One of the largest and brightest of its type. A winner in any show. Price each $1.00.

ON BLANK

NAME Mrs. ....
E   Miss .... Write very plainly

Post Office .... State ....

Street, P. O. Box
H   or Rural Delivery ....

or { If   different }
'fice { from P. O. } .... Forward Goods by ....
                                                        (Parcel Post, Express, Freight)

CASH OR CURRENCY UNLESS REGISTERED)   Make Money Orders or Checks Payable to Vaughan's Seed Store

T ENCLOSED $ .... ☐ Money Order   ☐ Draft or Check   ☐ Postage Stamps   ☐ Cash
More order blanks will be sent upon request. Always write letters on a separate sheet from your order.

Flower ☐	Veg. 1 ☐	Veg. 2 ☐	Grass ☐	Bulb ☐	Sup. ☐	Fert. ☐	Re-Check

NAME OF ARTICLE	PRICE DOLS.	CTS.
m for Cash Mail Orders Received Before March 1st		
ASH MAIL ORDER for SEEDS AND BULBS, totaling $2 or over, received on this order		
re March 1, 1944, we will send gladiolus bulbs of our selection, to the value of 10		
the order. Premium bulbs will be mailed after March 1. This offer does not apply		
es at stores, or to mail orders for items other than Seeds and Bulbs.		
IN MAKING YOUR ORDER, PLEASE GIVE THE SIZES AND PRICES TO AVOID DELAY AND ERRORS. CARRIED FORWARD	$	

DOMESTIC PARCEL POST RATES On Seeds, Plants, Bulbs, Roots, Books, Tools, etc. within the U. S. and Possessions. Effective Oct. 1, 1932.	First pound or fraction	Each additional pound or fraction	
Local—Chicago or New York City	7c.	1c. (2 lbs.)	A fraction of a cent in the total amount of postage on any parcel shall be counted as a full cent.
First and Second Zone within 150 miles of either	8c.	1.1c.	
Third Zone within 150 to 300 miles	9c.	2c.	
Fourth Zone within 300 to 600 miles	10c.	3.5c.	
Fifth Zone within 600 to 1000 miles	11c.	5.3c.	
Sixth Zone within 1000 to 1400 miles	12c.	7c.	
Seventh Zone within 1400 to 1800 miles	14c.	9c.	
Eighth Zone all over 1800 miles	15c.	11c.	

Filled by_____ Checked by_____ Packed by_____

Shipped by_____ Style of Package_____

Date_____ Book_____ Weight_____

KEEP YOUR LAWN Beautiful

Vaughan's CHICAGO PARKS LAWN SEED

DO not let enthusiasm for Victory gardens cause you to neglect your lawn.' National leaders urge that lawns and landscape beauty shall be maintained wherever possible without handicap to food production.

Without reseeding, fertilizing and good care, your lawn will suffer injury which will take both time and money to repair when peace returns.

Well advised lawn makers will avoid sowing the cheap mixtures which flood the market adulterated with quick show grasses such as timothy, a hay seed whose coarse stems ruin the lawn. Buy only seed on the quality of which you can depend.

The basis of VAUGHAN'S "CHICAGO PARKS" lawn seed is a large amount of the finest Kentucky blue grass, which is combined with other suitable grasses in the proper proportions to produce a fine permanent turf. Needless to say, it does not contain timothy, which is a hay grass and does not belong in a lawn; none of Vaughan's formulas include this unsuitable grass.

Price, ½ lb., 35c; 1 lb., 60c; 2 lbs., $1.20; 3 lbs., $1.75; 5 lbs., $2.85; 10 lbs., $5.50; 15 lbs., $8.15; 20 lbs., $10.75; 25 lbs., $13.25; 100 lbs., $49.00.

We offer this mixture without clover under the name "Vaughan's Fairway Formula"—Prices same as "Chicago Parks."

Vaughan's Special Purpose Mixtures

We recommend our lawn mixtures, composed of suitable varieties of grass seed, because results are more satisfactory from a correct combination of grasses than from a variety sown alone. Our grass seed division has long been known as an authority on growing fine turf, and for the guidance of our customers we send our booklet on lawn-making upon request and without charge. A copy of this booklet is enclosed in every carton and bag of Vaughan's lawn seed mixtures.

For Your Protection—Always remember that we neither buy nor sell seeds that are not tested in our own officially recognized laboratory for purity, germination, identity and freedom from weeds.

Vaughan's "Columbian"
Formula for Shady Lawns or Sandy Soil

In making a lawn on sandy soil or in partial shade, conditions are met which require the use of a special grass seed blend. Vaughan's "Columbian" is the correct blend for such locations.

Price, ½ lb., 40c; 1 lb., 65c; 2 lbs., $1.30; 3 lbs., $1.90; 5 lbs., $3.10; 10 lbs., $6.00; 15 lbs., $8.90; 20 lbs., $11.75; 25 lbs., $14.50; 100 lbs., $54.00.

Vaughan's Dense Shade Formula
(Containing Creeping Red Fescue)

An exceptional formula which is particularly adapted to heavily shaded areas and will also do well in lighter shade. We have spared no care or expense to make this lawn seed the best obtainable for the purpose. Follow instructions in our lawn booklet for growing grass in the shade. Does not contain clover.

Price, ½ lb., 45c; 1 lb., 75c; 2 lbs., $1.50; 3 lbs., $2.20; 5 lbs., $3.60; 10 lbs., $7.00; 15 lbs., $10.40; 20 lbs., $13.75; 25 lbs., $17.00; 100 lbs., $64.00.

Quantity to Use—On new lawns, use 1 lb. for every 300 square feet; 5 lbs. for 1500 square feet; 135 to 150 lbs. for one acre. To replenish lawns where turf is thin, use half quantity.

VAUGHAN'S No. 25 LAWN FORMULA

An economy blend for new seedings and quick results which should be followed by reseeding with a more permanent blend like our "Chicago Parks." In spite of its low price, this blend does not contain timothy. Sow at the rate of 1 lb. to every 200 sq. ft. Begin cutting when grass is 3 to 4 inches high and continue to cut regularly to keep turf fine. Price, 1 lb., 40c; 2 lbs., 80c; 3 lbs., $1.15; 5 lbs., $1.85; 10 lbs., $3.50; 15 lbs., $5.10; 20 lbs., $6.75; 25 lbs., $8.25; 100 lbs., $29.00.

Vaughan's "Private Estate" Bent Formula
FOR LAWNS "DE LUXE"

For those interested in a de luxe mixture we highly recommend our Private Estate Formula—This formula contains over 98% pure seed and is free of all noxious weeds.

In addition to Kentucky Blue Grass of the highest quality, to insure a durable and resistant foundation for your lawn, Private Estate formula includes an important proportion of Certified Bent. It produces a heavy turf of very fine texture.

This mixture is equal or better in purity to the highest priced mixtures on the market and most important, contains more bent seed. It is the best value on the market.

Price, 1 lb., 70c; 2 lbs., $1.40; 3 lbs., $2.05; 5 lbs., $3.35; 10 lbs., $6.50; 15 lbs., $9.65; 20 lbs., $12.75; 25 lbs., $15.75; 100 lbs., $59.00.

Bent Lawns from Certified Seed

Ask for Our Bent Leaflet

Bent grasses are increasingly popular for lawns, especially in cities where lawns are small in area and extra care is not burdensome.

Seed at the rate of 3 to 4 lbs. per 1,000 sq. ft.

ASTORIA BENT. Astoria Bent is identified by its numerous rootstocks which spread underground and throw up new shoots, making a very thick turf, and by the presence of runners above ground in the early stages of development. This Bent has a good color and is excellent as both a lawn and putting green grass. It does not require as much cutting as Creeping Bent. We highly recommend this type.

SEASIDE BENT. This is a true unmixed Creeping Bent grass seed which spreads by surface runners instead of by the underground root stalks which characterize the Astoria Bent.

Our Bent Leaflet Is Included in Each Bag

ASTORIA BENT GRASS. Price, ¼ lb., 45c; ½ lb., 80c; 1 lb., $1.45; 2 lbs., $2.90; 3 lbs., $4.30; 5 lbs., $7.00; 10 lbs., $13.75; 15 lbs., $20.25; 25 lbs., $32.50.

SEASIDE CREEPING BENT GRASS. Price, ¼ lb., 40c; ½ lb., 75c; 1 lb., $1.35; 2 lbs., $2.70; 3 lbs., $4.00; 5 lbs., $6.50; 10 lbs., $12.75; 15 lbs., $18.75; 20 lbs., $24.50; 25 lbs., $30.00.

SEE PAGE 116 FOR PRICES ON OTHER GRASSES AND FIELD SEEDS

All Lawn Seed prepaid anywhere in U. S. A. On Parcel Post C. O. D. Orders there is a postal charge for C. O. D. delivery. 5

Newer Vegetables

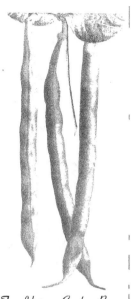

It Has What Cauliflower Lacks

Broccoli, Italian Green Sprouting. 70 days. Though like cauliflower in flavor (many think it superior) this fine vegetable is unlike it in every way that makes cauliflower difficult in the home garden. It survives hot weather, bears a continuous harvest until frozen, and above all is one of the vegetables richest in the vitamins that cauliflower lacks. Pkt., 25c; ½ oz., 45c; oz., 85c; ¼ lb., $2.50.

Top Victory Garden Bean

Bush Bean Tendergreen. 52 days. For a long harvest of tender, brittle, stringless round pods, we recommend this among the many fine beans, for Victory Gardens. Pkt., 15c; ½ lb., 30c; lb., 50c; 2 lbs., 90c; 3 lbs., $1.25.

Hybrid Sweet Corn Our Choice. 68 days. One of the earliest hybrids, it is the sweetest we know, bearing 12-row ears for a heavy yield. Pkt., 15c; ½ lb., 35c; lb., 65c; 2 lbs., $1.20.

Hybrid Sweet Corn Lee. 73 days. A second early, bearing larger ears with deeper kernels, this variety is high in quality and completely resistant. Pkt., 15c; ½ lb., 35c; lb., 65c; 2 lbs., $1.20.

Hybrid Sweet Corn Golden Cross. 79 days. It has the quality of Golden Bantam and yields larger ears more abundantly; completely resistant. Pkt., 15c; ½ lb., 35c; lb., 65c; 2 lbs., $1.20.

Hybrid Sweet Corn Ioana. 83 days. It endures mid-summer and drouth, while maturing heavy crop of 12-14 row ears, 7½ to 8 inches long. Pkt., 15c; ½ lb., 35c; lb., 65c; 2 lbs., $1.20.

Hybrid Sweet Corn Team. To produce a long harvest of heavy-yielding hybrid sweet corn in the Victory Garden, we recommend that the four varieties illustrated above, which vary in season from 68 to 83 days, be planted at the same time. Later varieties will give a longer harvest and heavier yield than earlier; and the four together will provide sweet corn all summer. 2 oz. of each variety in separate packets, totalling ½ lb., 45c.

Finest Early Cucumber

Cucumber Mandarin. 45 days. There is aristocratic Chinese blood in this variety, which we consider the best, early or late, for Victory gardens. Its 12-inch fruits are slender, dark green, appetizing. Pkt., 10c; oz., 40c; ¼ lb., $1.10; lb., $3.20.

At Last, Hot Weather Head Lettuce

Lettuce Great Lakes. 75 days. Of the Iceberg type, bred to make tight heads in hot weather, this variety is actually too good. So reluctant is it to run to seed that almost no seed was produced to sell this year, when it won top place, with a bronze medal in the All-America trials for new varieties. What little seed there is naturally is high priced. Offered only in packets. Pkt., 40c.

The Quality Carrot

Carrot Touchon. 70 days. From the time it is finger size and thinned out of the row in early spring, until it reaches full growth in the autumn, this variety excels in flavor, tenderness, even in yield, for home gardens. Its slender shape permits growing closer than thicker types, and decreases the core which all carrots have even though you may not see it. Its flesh is fine grained, sweet and has bright orange coloring. Pkt., 20c; ½ oz., 45c; oz., 85c; ¼ lb., $2.50.

BIBB LETTUCE, CROSS SECTION

A Lettuce for Connoisseurs

Lettuce Bibb (Limestone). 57 days. This dark green, tender, brittle lettuce, which quickly makes loose heads as big as your fist, is becoming well known to chefs of luxury hotels and to high priced food shops. Some say it was once known as "Half-Century," others that it was bred by Maj. John Bibb, of Kentucky, born in 1789. It is making a comeback and we can promise you a fine spring crop, but must warn that it goes to seed quickly in hot weather. Pkt., 20c; ½ oz., 30c; oz., 45c.

Popular from Coast to Coast

Lettuce Oak Leaf. 40 days. The popularity of this tender, heat-resistant leaf lettuce has spread from coast to coast, and the Massachusetts Horticultural Society last year gave it an award of merit. For vitamins and Victory Gardens, it is our first choice. Pkt., 20c; ½ oz., 35c; 1 oz., 60c.

HEAD OF BIBB LETTUCE

7

Bright Orange Tomato

Tomato Orange King. 66 days. Because of sweet flavor, with a minimum of acidity, and solid flesh, with small seed cavities, yellow and orange tomatoes are growing in popularity. This is the smoothest, heaviest yielding and highest quality variety of the small vine type yet produced. Skin and flesh are a deep orange, giving proof of high Vitamin C content, making its juice an excellent substitute for orange juice in the diet. It is not suitable for pruning, and staking. Pkt., 15c; ½ oz., 30c; oz., 50c.

Orange Colored Pepper

Pepper Oshkosh. 70 days. Color conscious hostesses attach importance to the color scheme of salads. This sweet pepper ripens to a vivid orange hue. The fruits measure 3 by 4 inches, are borne on upright bushes, and have top quality. Pkt., 15c; ¼ oz., 40c; oz., 75c.

Giant Spanish Onion

Onion Valencia Sweet Spanish. 110 days. Any well fertilized Victory garden can grow these huge, sweet Spanish onions. From seed, onions weighing a pound may be produced in the northern states; if started in the hotbed, two-pound specimens can be grown. Our strain is selected for good results in the midwest. Pkt., 20c; ½ oz., 65c; oz., $1.20; ¼ lb., $3.65.

New Type of Squash

Squash Butternut. 100 days. All the seed of this squash is contained in a small cavity at the lower end; so that ninety percent of its heavy fruit (12 inches long) is exceedingly sweet, firm, orange flesh. Pkt., 35c.

ALL AMERICA WINNERS

Cucumber Cubit. Awarded bronze medal in All-America trials for 1944. Dark green, cylindrical fruits with rounded ends, giving heavy early yield. Fruits are 6 to 8 inches, and quality good. Pkt., 25c.

Bean Keystonian Greenpod. Awarded Honorable Mention in 1944 All-America trials. A stringless, round-pod green bean which is compared with Tendergreen for quality, and said to yield more heavily. Pkt., 25c.

Basic War Garden $1.

THIS collection provides the minimum planting of protective foods which should be made for a family of four. It includes the vegetables which combine highest nutritive values with ease of culture, except tomatoes, for which plants started early under protection may usually be obtained at planting time. Each of these vegetables SHOULD BE GROWN AND EATEN to maintain health, and all surplus should be preserved for winter WHILE IT IS YOUNG, FRESH and DELICIOUS. With each collection will be sent a suggested planting plan to give all-season yield.

11 Items, as follows, value $1.40, prepaid $1:

	Catalogue Value
½ lb. Green Pod Bush Beans	30c
1 pkt. Swiss Chard	10c
1 pkt. Leaf Lettuce	10c
1 pkt. Carrots	15c
1 pkt. Parsley	10c
1 pkt. Beets	10c
1 pkt. Radish Mixture	10c
1 pkt. Wax Beans	10c
1 pkt. Turnips	10c
1 pkt. Onion	15c
1 pkt. Bush Lima Beans	10c
Catalogue Value	$1.40
Collection prepaid in U. S. A. for	$1.00

VEGETABLE GARDEN BOOK, PREPAID, 30c.

We recommend the "Pocket Book of Vegetable Gardening," by Charles H. Nissley, a book of 245 pages giving all necessary information on vegetable gardening. Ceiling prices, by mail, 30c, over the counter, 25c.

The vegetables illustrated in the decoration on this page are: Streamliner Green Pod Beans; Tendersweet Beet; Scarlet Globe Radish, on the left; and Gold Standard Wax Pod Beans, Carrot Touchon, and Oak Leaf Lettuce on the right.

New Flowers and Specialties - 1944

Blue and Pink Ageratums ☐

Culture: A, B, D or E, Page 65

214 Fairy Pink. A compact dwarf of delightful soft salmon rose pink. It begins to flower when not more than 1½ to 2 inches high and grows to 5 inches, forming a compact mass of blooms. Pkt. 25c.

195 Midget Blue. Three inch globular plants are smothered with Ageratum blue flowers. Most uniform in habit, truest in color yet produced. The best we know for narrow ribbon planting. Pkt. 25c.

221 Golden Ageratum. 12 in. Fluffy, golden ball flowers, resemble the so-called perennial ageratum. This is an annual. Lonas Inodora. Pkt. 25c.

204 Swiss Blue. 10 in. Even, compact growth, with clear blue flower heads covering the entire plant. In our trials this proved to be the best of all Dwarf Ageratums, both as to habit, size of flower and uniformity. Pkt., 25c.

195 AGERATUM Midget Blue. Pkt., 25c.

Red, White and Blue

MORNING GLORIES

Scarlett O'Hara, Pearly Gates (White), and Heavenly Blue Giant Flowered Morning Glories draped thousand of walls and arbors last summer. Thousands more will wish thus to display our national colors in 1944. We offer true strains of each variety, in separate packets, or in a balanced mixture.

2940 Red, White and Blue Collection. One packet each of Scarlett O'Hara, Heavenly Blue and Pearly Gates Morning Glory (value 60c), for 40c.

2935 Red, White and Blue Mixture. A balanced mixture of the above. Pkt., 25c.

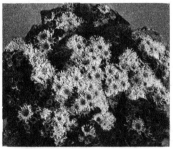

214 AGERATUM Fairy Pink. Pkt., 25c.

Aster

Culture: A, B, D or E, Page 65

576 Extra Early Giant Crego Navy Blue. First of a new race of large flowered, early Asters, this is of that color rare in flowers, a true navy blue. While not wilt-resistant, it has fair growth, 4-inch flowers on strong cutting stems. Pkt., 35c.

2935 RED, WHITE AND BLUE. Morning Glory Mixture. Pkt., 25c.

Varieties judged best of 1944 introductions, after testing in trial gardens in all parts of the country

3960 Petunia Cheerful. Received Bronze Medal in the All America Selection of 1944. The clear salmon pink flowers have a deeper rose veining toward the throat. The growth is low spreading close to the ground, later the plants form a mound 10-12 in. high with a spread of 2 ft. Growth is densely compact and the plants are studded from early summer until frost with flowers 2½ in. across. Pkt., 25c.

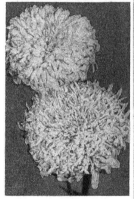

3151 Marigold Mammoth "Mum." 30 in. ☐ Honorable mention in the All America Selection of 1944. Blooms early. The flowers are fluffy ball-like, light sulphur yellow in color. The flowers are 3½ in. across and 2 in. deep and develop into the largest chrysanthemum-flowered Marigold. Pkt., 25c.

On Our Back Cover

VAUGHAN'S SALPIGLOSSIS

Culture: A, B, Page 65

1. Violet and Gold
2. Velvety Red
3. Golden Yellow
4. Rose, Crimson and Gold
5. Purple and Gold
6. Scarlet and Gold
7. Rose and Gold

Each of above 10c per packet

4631 Cover Collection. One packet each above 7 packets, 60c.

4630 Vaughan's Special Mixture of Salpiglossis. Pkt., 15c; ⅛ oz., 30c.

10

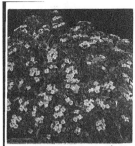

259 **ALYSSUM** Violet Queen. Pkt., **15c.**

True Violet Sweet Alyssum

Culture: A, B, D or E, Page 65

59 **Alyssum Violet Queen.** A beautiful, fragrant sweet Alyssum, of bright clear violet hue, holding its colors through the hottest, driest summer. Can be sheared like white Alyssum and grows luxuriantly covered with bloom, from early summer to freezing. It flowers in 45 days from seed sown in the open ground. After its second year in our test garden we like it better than ever. ⅛ oz., 35c; ¼ oz., 60c; oz., $2.00; pkt. 15c.

Crimson Snapdragon

Culture: A, B, D or E, Page 65

149 **Antirrhinum Large Flowered Rust Resistant Padre.** A glistening crimson, rich and beautiful; an excellent grower with uniformly compact contrasting foliage. One of the best. Pkg. 25c.

1197A **CALENDULA** Orange Beauty. Pkt., **25c.**

New Calendulas

Culture: A or B, D or E, Page 65

Calendulas are at their best in cool autumn days. Sow a second crop in early summer, for fall cutting.

187 **Glowing Gold.** 2½ ft. Vivid color, coming between gold and orange which does not fade. Flowers are fully double, 4 in. across, with loose and fluffy petals that give the appearance of a golden ball. Long, wiry stems. Pkt., 25c.

188 **Orange Fluffy.** 2 ft. Bright orange-yellow, intensified by a jet-black eye. Flowers 3½ inches, semi-double, with petals increasingly erect towards the center. Flowers profusely on long, strong stems. Pkt., 25c.

1197A **Orange Beauty.** 2 ft. Blooms are 3½ in. and more across of curved loose petal formation on long stems. The color is bright, deep orange slightly suffused with yellow at the base of the florets, the inner petals gracefully curling in. Pkt., 25c.

1351 **CARNATION** J. M. Bridgeford. Pk., **50c.**

Carnations

Culture: D, E, A or B, Page 65

1351 **J. M. Bridgeford. (Malmaison.)** 1½ ft. ☐ From seed sown indoors (or outdoors) bears in 90 days on long stems, lovely fully double Carnations, 3 to 4 inches across, of all Carnation colors, including yellow. Flowers throughout the summer. Pkt., 50c.

Culture: B, D or E, Page 65

7411 **Prof. Malmgreen.** A new early flowering, valuable bedding variety of the Vienna Dwarf-Double type with gay brick red flowers. Blooming first year from seed if sown early. Pkt., 50c.

1436 **CELOSIA** Gilbert's Maple Gold. Pkt., **25c.**

Golden Coxcomb

1436 **Celosia Gilbert's Maple Gold.** ☐ The heads of this crested type coxcomb are almost globular, and the dominant color is a golden maple, with some flowers varying toward rose or pink. The plants grow to three feet and bear eight to twelve heads, which can be increased if the center stem is pinched back. Do not feed the plants. Pkt., 25c.

1617 **CHRYSANTHEMUM** Goldwings. Pkt., **25c.**

1621 **CHRYSANTHEMUM** Korean Hybrids. Pkt., **50c.**

Korean Mums From Seed

Culture: A, B, D or E, Page 65

1621 **Chrysanthemum Korean Hybrids.** These large, single flowers of many lovely colors can be flowered from seed the first year. The hardy Korean species is crossed with garden varieties. Pkt. 50c.

1696 **CHRYSANTHEMUM** Vaughan's Rainbow Mixed. Pkt., **25c.**

Novel Annual Mums

Culture: A, B, D or E, Page 65

1696 **Carinatum Vaughan's Rainbow Mixture.** This wonderful new strain of Carinatum Hybrids contains a very wide range of various tones running through purple, scarlet, orange, salmon rose, yellow, white, which are all beautifully zoned round the dark disc with small yellow edges. Pkt., 25c.

7452 **Chrysanthemum September Jewels.** ☐ They are easy to grow from seed, start to bloom two to four weeks ahead of any other type and have many beautiful colors. The plants grow 1 to 2 feet tall and flowers 2½ inches in diameter. Pkt., 25c.

1617 **Goldwings.** ☐ 36 in. Large daisy flowers with long feathery petals of gleaming yellow. A mass of flowers all season. Pkt. 25c.

7464 **GIANT DOUBLE SHASTA** Daisy. G. Marconi. Pkt.,(35 seeds)50c. Plants, 3 for **$1.25.**

Giant Double Shastas ①

Culture: B, D or E, Page 65

7464 **Diener's New Giant Double Ever-Flowering Shasta Daisy G. Marconi.** The largest Shasta Daisy today, the flowers are around seven inches in diameter and stems 2½ to 3 ft. long Pkt., (35 seeds) 50c. Plants, 3 for $1.25; doz, $3.7 , ea. 50c.

7463 **Diener's Fancy Chiffon Shasta Daisy Glendale.** The 2 inch flowers have fringed and laciniated petals, interlaced. Pkt. (35 seeds) 50c.

7504 **Giant Double Shasta Daisy.** While first year flowers of this perennial have many singles, in the second year they are almost 100% double, with flowers up to 6-inches, and a long flowering season. Pkt., 35c. Plants; 3 for $1.25; doz., $3.75; ea. 50c.

1980 **COSMOS** Yellow Flare. Pkt., **25c.**

Early Yellow Cosmos

Culture: A, B, D or E, Page 65

1980 **Cosmos Yellow Flare.** ☐ At last the yellow cosmos Klondike, so late in season it has been grown only in the deep south, has an early flowering counterpart, which will blossom in July in northern gardens. It grows 3 to 4 feet tall and has the same freedom of bloom, on long wiry stems. It is excellent for border effect, and as a cut flower. Pkt., 25c.

1982 **Cosmos Semi-Double Orange Ruffles.** Vivid golden orange, the two or three extra rows of petals lend an airy butterfly-like beauty to the richly colored blossoms. Extremely free blooming, flower 10 days to 2 weeks before Orange Flare and remain in flower six weeks. Pkt., 25c.

1803 **CLEOME** Pink Queen. Pkt., **25c.**

Two New "Spider-Plants"

Culture: D or E, Page 65

1803 **Cleome Pink Queen.** ☐ Huge heads of delightful and refreshing true pink. The large flower bracts turn to white before falling, giving the suggestion of a white collar with a pink cap. Reaches over 4 feet, well branched, airy foliage, blooming from June until frost. This is an excellent background subject to plant in the rear of the flower border, in bold groups, which will provide interesting sky-line color. Pkt., 25c.

1802 **Golden Cleome.** ☐ A new color, rich gold approaching orange, on stems which will grow 8 feet. Crowd plants to keep them low. Fine for border gaps and background. Attractive to bees. Likes full sun and sandy soil. Pkt., 25c.

2318 **DIMORPHOTHECA** Glistening White. Pkt., **25c.**

White-Enamel African Daisy

Culture: A, B or E, Page 65 ☐

2318 **Dimorphotheca Glistening White.** 6 to 8 in. The petals of the daisy-like flowers 4 inches in diameter, glisten like white enamel. They are borne freely on low, spreading plants. like hot sun and dry weather, and flower long after frost. Pkt. 25c.

7659 **DIANTHUS** Barbatus Homeland. Pkt., **35c.**

New Sweet Williams

DIANTHUS BARBATUS ①

Culture: B, D or E, Page 65

7688 **Midget Single Mixed.** 3-4 in. Alpine Sweet William, uniform habit. The color range is from white, chamois, salmon, scarlet, brick red to maroon, with most blooms tri-colored. Pkt., 25c.

7711 **Midget Double Dwarf Mixed.** An attractive double form of the above, 3 to 4 in. tall in a bewildering color range. Pkt., 15c.

7659 **Homeland.** In June, when summer flowers are not yet in bloom and there is little in the garden available for cut flowers, the Sweet William is the most welcome. "Homeland" is dark red with large sharply defined, clear white center. Pkt. 35c.

7650 **Giant White "Special."** Pure white flower clusters, ⅓ larger with strong wiry stem from ⅓ to ½ longer than ordinary. In growth it resembles the Perennial Phlox and is a splendid cut flower. The individual florets average from ⅜ to ⅝ of an inch in diameter, their size depending somewhat on the culture. The flower clusters range from 4 to 7 inches. Sown from May to July will bloom next June. Pkt (75 seeds), 25c.

7523 **DELPHINIUM** Chinese Blue Mirror. **35c.**

TRUE NAVY BLUE DELPHINIUM ☐ ①

Culture: A or B, D or E, Page 65

7523 **Delphinium Chinese Blue Mirror.** 1½-2 ft. One of the few true bright navy-blue flowers. May be cultivated as an annual as well as perennial, and is suited for cutting or border. When grown in massesit makes an overwhelming impression. Pkt.,35c.

2259 DIANTHUS Heddewigii Gaiety. Pkt., 25c.

3170A MARIGOLD Spry. Pkt., 25c.

Color Carnival in New Dianthus Strain

Culture: A or B, Page 65

2259 Dianthus Heddewigii Gaiety. The large fringed flowers have a bewildering variety of pink, white, red and maroon coloring, in decorative patterns, and borne freely on dwarf plants. There are numerous double and semi-double forms. The many blossoms, borne for a long season, will cover a bed of these plants with a fascinating display of brilliant colors. Pkt., 25c.

2820 Gaillardia Sungod. ① The full circular flowers are of a rich golden yellow without a trace of any other color. The large self-colored blooms supported by stout stems above the pale green foliage continue from early summer until late in fall. Pkt. 25c.

2491 Geranium Flowerland Strain. Improved single large-flowered seed saved from name varieties. Include seed of Fiat, White Beauty, Alice of Vincennes, Madam Kovelesky and others which will provide a wide range of colors. This seed will germinate irregularly in from 14 days to two months. The plants may be lifted as they reach suitable size, but the seed box should not be disturbed until germination has ceased. Pkt. (50 seeds), 35c.

7978 HOLLYHOCK Orange Prince. 25c.

Double Hollyhock ①

Culture: B, D or E, Page 65

7978 Orange Prince. Growing 6 to 8 feet, this magnificent perennial bears giant double yellow flowers, fiery orange center, likes rich soil. Pkt., 25c.

2144 Lobelia Cardinalis Special Selection. ① A perennial for moist partially shaded border.. Rich fiery cardinal flowers. Plants often produce 4 to 6 spikes 24 to 30 inches long. Pkt., 25c.

2159 Lily Creole X White Queen Hybrid. A lovely addition to this popular family. The flowers are pure white, longer and larger trumpets of much more substance than White Queen. Lilies are easily raised from seed with care and patience. We supply leaflet on culture if asked for at time of ordering. Pkt. (25 seeds), 50c.

BRILLIANT SUNFLOWER

Culture: A, B, D or E. Page 65

2713 Helianthus Sun Gold. ☐ 4 ft. This sunflower makes a brilliant sea of color as all the plants burst into bloom on the same day. May planting will flower in early August. Blooms are all double. Pkt. 15c.

Glowing Red Marigold

3169A Marigold Scarlet Glow. In the sun this flower does glow and seems redder than any other Marigold. A well fixed Dwarf French double, compact 1-ft. bushes, color a deep maroon. Pkt., 25c.

3159 Honeycomb. 15-in. ☐ This odorless deep orange belongs to the Double Dwarf African type. Peculiar and unusual petal formation makes it a distinct variety. Pkt., 25c.

3165 Sunkist Orange. ☐ All-America Silver Medal 1943. It is a dwarf, compact, very early, continuous blooming, dwarf double, 6 to 12 inches tall, flowers 1 ¾ inches across. Companion variety for the already popular Butterball. Pkt., 25c.

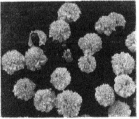

3164A Marigold Dwarf French Double Butterball. The name fits this pretty edging marigold of canary yellow. As the illustration shows, it grows 10 inches tall, in a mound covered with 1 ¾-inch globular blossoms. Early and continuous flowering, excellent for ribbon planting or pot plants. Pkt., 25c.

A Miniature Harmony

3170A Marigold Spry. This is a miniature version of Harmony, growing in compact, 9-inch bushes, producing freely flowers less than half the size of the popular variety Harmony. It is uniform and fine for ribbon planting. Pkt., 25c.

3169A MARIGOLD Scarlet Glow. Pkt., 25c.

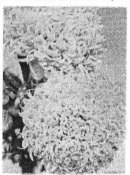

Like Yellow Chrysanthemums

Culture: A, B, C, D or E, Page 65

3132 Marigold Mission Giant Yellowstone. A sister of Goldsmith, 1941 winner, which was orange, this is golden yellow, of incurved, globular form. 2 ½-inch flowers, rather late, plants 3 to 5 ft. Pkt., 25c.

3932 PETUNIA All Double America. Pkt., 50c.

3177 MARIGOLD Gigantea Pot-o-Gold. Pkt. 25c.

Giant Marigolds
Culture: A, B, D or E, Page 65

3177 Dwarf Gigantea Pot O'Gold. 12 inch. Plants are compact, well branched, bearing large blooms of bright deep orange. The flowers are somewhat loosely formed, with broad heavy petals, gracefully overlapping. Blooms early. Pkt., 25c.

3153 Goldsmith. The best version of the Chrysanthemum flowered Marigold which blossoms early enough for northern gardens. Globular flower with incurved petals, borne on long base branching stems, 3 feet tall. Pkt., 25c.

3127 Limelight. A pale primrose yellow or deep cream, in the incurved Chrysanthemum-flowered type. Early-flowering, 1½-2½ inches in diameter, free-flowering and coming quite true. Pkt., 15c.

3163B Yellow Pygmy. 8 in. Light lemon-yellow, Lilliput French double. Small, 1¼ in. blooms, rather free and exciting for edging beds. Use in front of calendulas or combine with the deep blue of ageratum Cardinal Mundelein (plants only). Pkt., 15c.

New Petunias
Culture: A, B, D or E, Page 65

3932 Petunia All Double America. Distinctly different from all Double Petunias and 100% true for doubleness. The first double ever created in America. Branching erect, the plants develop into trim little plants 1 ft. high and 18 in wide. Graceful fully double rose pink flowers up to 2¼ in. Leaves smaller than other varieties with almost entire lack of stickiness. Pkt. (100 seeds); 50c; 2 pkts. for 90c; 1,000 seeds. $3.50.

Racine, Wisconsin, August 16, 1943
"I would like to tell you that the All America Double Petunia I raised from seed from you look like little rose bushes, everyone admires them so."—R. W. S.

3982 Petunia English Violet. This rosy mauve-violet or purple-violet, medium-sized, compact variety brings a distinct new color to its class. With the habit of Blue Bedder, this very free-flowering plant of 12 to 15 inches is true and uniform. Pkt., 25c.

4083 Petunia Blushing Maid. Its single flowers are of largest size, deeply fringed and ruffled, of a rosy pink and white with yellow veins and throat. One of the loveliest giant singles. Pkt., 35c.

4022 King Henry. Compact, globular habit, large blooms of a velvety blood red color on short stems. A dwarf Flaming Velvet. Pkt.,25c.

3973 Petunia Igloo. All-America Bronze Medal 1943. The most uniform, free-blooming, dwarf white Petunia so far developed. Plants are true, very uniform and compact growing. 12 to 15 inches tall. The small, 1½-inch, creamy white single flowers with yellowish throats, cover the plants in a sheet of bloom from early to late. Excellent and very showy for bed or border. Pkt., 25c.

Sister of Heavenly Blue
Culture: A or B, D or E, Page 65

2943 Morning Glory Improved Pearly Gates. This is a white sport of the lovely Heavenly Blue morning glory, and is similar in size, vigor of growth and abundant bloom, to that unsurpassed climber; but the color is satiny white with cream throat. It is effective in combination with blue and red morning glories. Pkt., 25c.

2938 Morning Glory Columbia. □ The vines grow about 10 ft. high and are covered with attractive foliage and produce many 3 in. trumpets of blue, edged bluish white with a reddish star. Pkt., 25c.

4054 **Petunia Golden Jubilee.** □ A most attractive variety with its fringed, 3½-inch flowers of bright carmine, tinged scarlet, with golden throat. Pkt., 35c.

Deep Violet Nierembergia
Culture: D or E, Page 65

3412 Nierembergia Coerulea Purple Robe. This is like the pale lavender hippomanica, in its compact growth, completely covered with bloom, but its flowers are of deep violet, unfading in the hot sun, where hippomanica would bleach to almost white. Blooms in 15 weeks from sowing, prefers sandy soil and full sun, a splendid bedding and edging subject. Pkt., 25c.

3412 NIEREMBERGIA Purple Robe. Pkt.,25c.

4083 PETUNIA Blushing Maid, Pkt., 35c.

3934 **PETUNIA** Dwarf All-Double Victorious Mixed.
Pkt. (100 seeds), **50c.**

4426 **PORTULACA** Jewel. Pkt., **25c.**

All Double Petunias

Since the outbreak of war, no all-double petunia seed has been imported into the United States, and except for one variety none is produced here. The only seed available has been in stocks on hand which has rapidly decreased. Our own stocks were large, but we have reached the point where we are unable to offer named varieties, but we can supply our excellent Victorious mixture, in which all the colors of this well balanced strain, as illustrated, are included.

Seeds should be sown indoors early in the season, taking care to sow thinly enough to avoid crowding, so that every seedling can be raised.

3934 Dwarf Giant Fringed Mixed (Victorious). The flowers are very large, exquisitely ruffled and fringed and contain a good range of brilliant colors. Pkt. (100 seeds), 50c.

Best Small-Flowered Blue

3996 Admiral. ☐ In uniform growth, and unvarying clear dark blue coloring of its abundant blossoms, this excels all other small-flowered blue Petunias. Pkt., 50c.

Red, White and Blue

Many will wish to plant beds or border combinations of red, white and blue flowers this spring, and there are no flowers better suited to this purpose than the small flowered petunias. In the illustration are shown 4007 Snow Queen, pkt., 25c; 4008 Topaz Queen, pkt., 25c; 3992 Blue Bird, pkt., 25c.
3993 Red, White and Blue Collection. 1 pkt. each of above three varieties (value 75c), 60c.
3994 Red, White and Blue Petunia Mixture, a blend of the above three varieties. Pkt., 25c.

3994 **PETUNIA** Red, White and Blue, Mixed. Pkt., **25c.**

4081 Windmiller Pink. The growth is very compact and branching; attaining at maturity height of 10-12 in. and a spread of 15-18 in., at no time does the plant became "leggy" but always presents a solid mass of green foliage studded with blooms. The 2-inch flowers have slightly frilled edges and are brilliant rose, with a flush of scarlet radiating from a small yellow throat. Pkt., 25c.

4062 Theodosia. Large flowering single fringed rosy pink with a clearly defined golden center with minute stripes. Highly recommended at Wisley England trials of the Royal Horticultural Society. Pkt., 35c.

Best Dwarf White

4011 White Perfection. Best dwarf white Petunia. Grows about 10 inches in height. Flowers pure white of fine size and cover the plant. Pkt., 25c.

A Floral Jewel

4426 Portulaca Single Jewel. No one who has in mind the usual portulaca flower can imagine the beauty of this new variety, which is four times as large, and of a brilliant deep crimson coloring. One of the most popular of annuals, the portulaca is so easy to grow in dry, sunny places, that its beauty is often overlooked; but here is a new member of the family that will attract surprised attention in any company. It is as free flowering as the smaller flowered varieties. Pkt., 25c.

8418 Primula Polyanthus (Veris) Pink Shades. ① A selection from the Giant strain of this wonderful hardy Primrose. The flowers, which often open up to 2½ inches in diameter, are borne on stiff stems well above the foliage. These primroses require a semi-shaded position. Pkt. (50 seeds), 25c.

Giant Annual Phlox ☐
Culture: A, B, D or E, Page 65

4104A Gigantea, Red Glory. The richest bright red, with contrasting white eye. Its color is the same as Scarlet Flax; a free, continuous bloomer. Pkt., 25c.

4103A Gigantea Rosy Morn. A gay combination of rose pink with a white eye, a color that will not fade in the strong sun. Pkt., 25c.

4104 Gigantea Salmon Glory. Florets measuring 1½ inches, of pure salmon pink. They not only register well in border clumps and bedding masses, but are useful cut flowers, all summer. Pkt., 20c.

4103 Gigantea Art Shades. A new strain with flowers 1½ inches in diameter, in a remarkable variety of soft color tones, which blend delightfully. ⅛ oz., 35c; ⅓ oz., 60c; pkt., 25c.

4104 **PHLOX** Gigantea Salmon Glory. **20c.**

4620 SALPIGLOSSIS Dwarf Giant-Flowered Mixed. Pkt., 20c.

New Giant Salpiglossis ☐

Culture: A or B, Page 65

4620 Dwarf Giant Flowered Salpiglossis Mixed. Giant flowers of all the delightful colors of this gold-veined trumpet flower are borne on low growing plants of compact habit, and will cover the low bed or border with glowing color. Many consider this the best of all summer cut flowers. Pkt., 20c.

4621 Tall Giant Flowered Salpiglossis Mixed. This is a family that thrives in a hot and dry climate and it is one of the few annuals which will bloom during the heat of summer. The large flowers in their many attractive warm colors appear in full open clusters at the top of the plant and make wonderful cutting material. Pkt., 25c.

5788A VIOLA Blue Elf. Pkt., 25c.

4731 SCABIOSA Blue Moon. Pkt., 15c.

Sky Blue Scabiosa

Culture: A, B, D or E, Page 65

4731 Scabiosa Blue Moon. 4 ft. Large blossoms of conical shape of sky-blue tinged with lavender, borne on long, strong stems, ideal for cutting. Pkt., 15c.

New Blue Viola ☐

Culture: A or B, Page 65

5788A Comuta Blue Elf. 9 in. The upper petals are deep violet blue, lower petals light violet blue with gold eye and black lines radiating from center. Flowers ¾-in. in diameter, small dark green foliage. A perennial best treated as an annual. Seed sown in March will begin blooming in June and continue all summer. Pkt., 25c.

VIOLA CORNUTA ☐ ①

Culture: A or B, Page 65

5787A Bizarre. A new and extraordinary color combination in this family; the two upper petals being a pure violet purple and the lower three clear apricot. It is a combination of the richest and gayest colors. Pkt., 25c.

5790A Chinese Blue. A round-faced type such as Jersey Gem, Chantreyland, or Blue Perfection. Chinese Blue, according to the Royal Horticultural Chart, is French Blue. It is the nearest substitute to the famous Viola Maggie Mott. Pkt., 25c.

5802A King Henry (Purple King). Flowers 1-inch in diameter cover bushy plants 6 inches tall, during a long season. A deep purple violet with lighter center and yellow eye, an effective contrast. Violas have a much longer flowering season than Pansies, and will flower all summer if the faded blossoms are picked off. Pkt., 25c.

5793 Wedgwood. Wonderfully hardy and freer blooming, the flowers are deep, clear Wedgwood blue, and shaped like pansies. This is one of the most charming Violas you can grow. Pkt., 25c.

8582 Super Large Flowering Scotch. The Scotch have been great fanciers of Violas and this is a strain they have greatly improved. The flowers are large, all two toned without blotches and have a complete color range from white through all intermediate shades of bronze rose, light and dark blue to black. Violas are better bedding subjects than Pansies. Pkt., 25c.

Pink Perennial

8351 Physostegia Virginica Vivid. ① A perennial that grows only 20 in. tall, a great improvement on the original type. It blooms three weeks later, flowers are a deeper pink and are much larger and better, lasting a long time when cut. Pkt., 25c.

8351 PHYSOSTEGIA Virginica Vivid. Pkt., 25c.

4667 SALVIA Masterpiece. Pkt., 25c.

Salvia ☐

Culture: D or E, A or B, Page 65

4667 Vaughan's Masterpiece. Of all the Scarlet Sages, this best combines dwarf and uniform habits with vivid scarlet coloring unfading in the sun. Blooms early, and remains in perfect condition until killing frost. Pkt., 25c.

5648 Tritoma Miracle Mixed. ① Showy border plants. Flowers borne in compact form on stout 3 and 4 ft. stems. This mixture is made up from twelve to fifteen different colors from named varieties. Require protection during winter, unless in a very sheltered position. Pkt., 25c.

8570A Veronica Spicata Blue Fay. ① Is larger growing than ordinary Spicata, being sort of midway between that and Longifolia subsessilis. It has the shiny foliage instead of glaucus and the color is a good bright blue, and good spikes. Pkt., 25c.

6050 ZINNIA Lilliput Tom Thumb Mixed. 15c.

Tom Thumb Zinnias ☐

Culture: A, B, D or E, Page 65

6050 Zinnia Lilliput Tom Thumb Mixture. Small double flowers cover the plants which grow 6 inches tall. Red, orange, pink, yellow and white pastels. Delightful for low bowls. ¼ oz., 50c; pkt., 15c.

LARGEST OF ALL ZINNIAS

5902 Burpee's Super Giant Zinnias. 3 ft. Flowers are 5½ to 6½ inches across and of a wide diversity of colors and forms. Striking in the garden; excellent for cutting. Rare and unusual shades of cream, buff, apricot, salmon, rose and orange predominate, with yellow, white, scarlet and crimson, and many two and three-tone effects. Pkt., 25c.

4577 Rosy Wings (Othake or Polypteris). 18-24 in. Its leaves are narrow and somewhat silvery, and the flowers are about an inch in width, in clusters. Each flower has a very double center surrounded by petals in wing-like form, all of a pleasing rose color. Othake should be sown where it is to stand. It will grow in almost any kind of soil, and blooms from June till October. Pkt., 25c.

Vaughan's Annual Flower Seeds

COMPLETE LIST OF STANDARD VARIETIES

Surprise Garden Mixture

80 Different Annual Flowers
Growing 1 to 3½ Feet Tall, Oz. 25c

5848 Vaughan's Surprise Garden of Annuals is a "garden lover's dream come true." From early Spring until killing frost there is a procession of color. It is not a collection of leftovers; but a carefully prepared formula of more than eighty different annual flowers, many of which you have never seen. We want you to know them, and you will be delighted to make their acquaintance and probably will want to order separately another year. Furnishes an unending amount of cutting material and a daily surprise to see what will appear next. This mixture does not contain seeds of vines, nasturtium, etc. Allow plenty of space to avoid crowding, keep watered and weeded, and remove faded flowers. Use these packets (1 oz., each 25c) for friends on their birthdays. **Oz., 25c; ¼ lb., 90c; 1 lb., $3.35**

West Chicago, Ill. July 20, 1943
"I ordered your "Surprise Collection" of flower seeds this spring and I want to tell you how happy I am over them. I want you to share with me the admiration I have received from friends and people who pass by them. They are everything you say they are and every week is a new variety of color. Thank you." Mrs. F. V.

5848 SURPRISE GARDEN MIXTURE. Oz., 25c.

Ageratums for All-Summer Blue

Culture: A, B, D or E, Page 65

Most popular summer blooming annuals supplying, during the season, dense heads of fluffy flowers in tones of blue and lavender, which are so necessary to balance the color effect in a garden.

180 Tall Blue. 18 in. Soft lavender-blue. Try this in the garden with Zinnia Pumila Pinkie for charming effect. Pkt., 10c.

185 Tall White. 18 in. Pkt., 10c.   **190 Tall Sorts Mixed.** Pkt., 10c.

197 Blue Ball Improved. Compact, six inches high, uniform. Broad green foliage is almost smothered with flowers of deep periwinkle blue. Pkt., 25c.

200 Blue Cap Improved. 4 in. Definitely more dwarf than Blue Ball, more compact in habit. Bright, deep, lavender blue. ☆ oz., 50c; pkt., 15c.

221 Golden Ageratum. See Novelties. Pkt., 25c.

202 Imperial Dwarf Blue. 6 in. Compact growth covered with heads of feathery flowers of deep lavender. Pkt., 10c.

214 Fairy Pink. See Novelties. Pkt., 25c.

220 Lasseauxi. 1 ft. Clear pink, excellent cut-flower. Pkt., 15c.

217 Little Blue Star. 4 in. Flower opens light blue with purple center and develops to a bright blue self. Pkt., 15c.

195 Midget Blue. See Novelties. Pkt., 25c.

187 Purple Perfection. 8 in. (Improved Blue Perfection). Vivid dark purple. Compact plant bearing large flowers, freely produced. Fine for ribbons, and edging. Pkt., 15c.

215 Venus. 1 ft. Forms a dense bush which is profusely covered with flowers. The buds are red, the petals are white and the center of the flower red; a plant in full bloom is very charming. Pkt., 15c.

200 AGERATUM Blue Cap Improved. 15c.

Abronia (Sand Verbena) □

Culture: A, B, D or E, Page 65

100 X 10 in. A trailing, succulent plant for light sandy soil, with Verbena-like flowers of bright rose with white center in late summer and fall. Pkt., 10c.

Abrus □ 7 ft.

Culture: A, B, or D, Page 65

105 Precatorius (Weather Plant). Beautiful prayer beans. Seeds resemble coral beads; may be used for necklaces. Soak seed in warm water before sowing. Flowers light purple. Pkt., 10c.

Adonis □

Culture: A or B, Page 65

171 Autumnalis (Red Chamomile). 2 ft. Of somewhat straggly growth with finely divided foliage, its flowers are rich scarlet freely produced in summer and autumn. Pkt., 10c.

170 Aestivalis (Pheasant Eye). 1 ft. Early blooming annual with deep crimson flowers and feathery foliage. Sow where plants remain. Pkt., 10c.

166 ACROCLINIUM Sensation Double Giant Mixture. Pkt., 15c.

Acroclinium (Everlasting) □

Culture: A, B, D or E, Page 65

Its graceful, Daisy-like flowers, with strawy petals of silky appearance when cut in the bud state, can be dried for winter bouquets. It blooms in 6 weeks from time of sowing. Probably the daintiest, both in form and coloring, of all the everlasting flowers. Height, 20 inches.

150 Double Pink. 10c. **155 Double White.** 10c.

166 Sensation Double Giant Mixture. This large-flowering type is twice the size of the preceding one, with long, stiff stems; flowers are double and semi-double; white, chamois, flesh color and bright rose. Pkt., 15c.

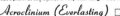

17

Sweet Alyssum
Ideal for Edging □

255 Ribbon Planting of Vaughan's ALYSSUM
Little Gem. Pkt., 10c.

Culture: A, B, D or E, Page 65

IT IS truly queen of edging plants whether grown in a continuous ribbon or alternated with Violet Queen, yellow Signata Marigold, or dwarf Ageratum. Its white flowers never fail; it is amazingly vigorous and hardy, and exceptionally uniform.

255 Vaughan's Little Gem (White Carpet). 4 in. The plants are so completely covered with snow-white blossoms they create the impression of a beautiful white carpet. Sweet Alyssum puts a lace frill to any garden and enhances the colors of every flower. 1 oz., $1.40; ½ oz., 75c; ¼ oz., 40c; pkt., 10c.

250 Maritimum (Sweet Alyssum). 10 in. Flowers white and honey-scented, produced from early in the season, until freezing. Mix the seed with sand to prevent sowing too thickly. 1 oz., 60c; ½ oz., 35c; pkt., 10c.

259 Violet Queen.—See Novelties. Pkt., 15c.

261 Lutescens. 8 in. Dwarf, cream or straw color. Pkt., 10c.

See also Perennial Pages.

241. ALONSOA Miniata. One of the brightest scarlet annuals. Fine compact habit and very free-flowering. Pkt., 15c.

490 ASPERULA Azurea Setosa. Pkt., 10c.

Amaranthus □
Culture: A, B, D or E, Page 65

Tall, vigorous ornamental foliage plants, with showy flower clusters, which attain their finest coloring in hot, sunny locations. Rich soil increases the size of leaves at the expense of their color. Give plenty of room.

267 Caudatus (Love Lies Bleeding). 3 ft. Drooping red spikes. Pkt., 10c.

275 Tricolor (Joseph's Coat). 2½ ft. The inner foliage is of blackest bronze, tipped with green, the outer bright scarlet and gold. Pkt., 10c.

285 Vaughan's Special Mixture. A well balanced mixture of the above and others. Pkt., 10c.

Amberboa □
Culture: A, B, D or E, Page 65

294 Muricata (Star of the Desert). A most pleasing annual flower, easy to grow, long blooming season, fine for cutting, and the garden. Flowers are 3 inch fringed lace-edged stars of tyrian purple with lighter cushion centers. Good foliage. Drought resistant and hardy. Pkt., 15c.

Anagallis (Pimpernel) □
(Poor man's Weather Glass)
Culture: A, B, D or E, Page 65

307 Coerulea. 11 in. One of the most conspicuous low growing blue flowers, but must have a sunny place to do well. The plants spread rapidly and bloom freely. Real turquoise-blue. ½ oz., 25c; pkt., 10c.

309 Terra Cotta Red. 11 in. New, vivid. Pkt., 15c.

305 Mixed. 11 in. Blue and scarlet flowers, effective as edgings, also charming on rockwork and in pots. ½ oz., 25c; pkt., 10c.

307 ANAGALLIS Coerulea. Pkt., 10c.

Anoda Mexican Cup □ 4 ft.
Culture: A or D, Page 65

3223 The Opal Cup. Luxuriantly growing plant bearing cup-shaped flowers 2½ inches across, of changeable coloring, blue lavender in shadow, pink in sun. Flowers in five weeks from seed and continues until frost, forming bush a yard in circumference. Pkt., 25c.

ASPARAGUS— See page 64.

Asperula (Blue Brocade)
Culture: A or B, D or E, Page 65

490 Azurea Setosa. 1 ft. A dainty little annual producing terminal clusters of gray-blue flowers from June until August according to the time seeds are sown. The best results follow early sowing. A shade-loving plant. Pkt., 10c.

Asclepias Curassavica
Culture: A, B, D or E, Page 65

473 A quick flowering tender perennial from Brazil that may be handled as a highly satisfactory garden annual. From seeds sown in early spring, there will be glorious bloom from July to November. The flower corolla is a brilliant orange scarlet; the hood, rich golden buff. Almost as showy are the buds, of a burnished coral. Makes a splendid pot plant, too, for any sunny window, being then in flower most of the year. Pkt., 25c.

ANGEL'S BREATH See Gypsophila Elegans Grand Alba.

Anchusa
Blue Bird □ 2 ft.

311 ANCHUSA Blue-Bird. Pkt., 15c.

Culture: A, B, D or E, Page 65

311 Blue Bird. □ 2 ft. Compact habit and bearing its flowers in a luxuriant bouquet at the top of the plant. Flowers are of an intense blue with a distinct white eye. Blooms all summer. One of the best blue annuals. Try it with Cacalia. You will enjoy the blue of the Anchusa with the yellow and henna shades of the Cacalia. ½ oz., 25c; pkt., 15c.

For others see Perennial Pages.

Arctotis
African Daisy □
Culture: A, B, D or E, Page 65

449 Breviscapa Aurantiaca. 6 in. Deep shade of orange yellow with purple disk. A deep and most attractive shade. Pkt., 25c.

450 Grandis (Blue-Eyed African Daisy). 3 ft. It forms bushes bearing 3 inch daisy flowers of pearly white with a gold band surrounding a delicate mauve center. It closes at evening and displays its lilac tinted undersides. Foliage gray green. Especially good cut flower. ½ oz., 30c; pkt., 10c.

451 New Hybrids. 8-12 inches. A new race resembling the famous Gerberas, but much easier to grow in the garden. Flower 2½ to 3 inches; likes a dry, sunny location. Excellent as a border plant and fine for cutting. Pkt., 25c.

450 ARCTOTIS Blue-Eyed African Daisy. 10c.

Best New Snapdragons

Culture: A or B, D or E, Page 65

425 Vaughan's Special Mixture of Snapdragons. (Antirrhinums). Includes all the varieties, providing a never ending color feast of long stemmed cut flowers. ¼ oz., 60c; ⅛ oz., 35c. **Pkt., 15c.**

Rust-Resistant

If you have found Snapdragons difficult to grow, rust is probably responsible. Rust is a widespread disease which discolors the leaves and saps the vitality. Growing the Rust-resistant strain, difficulties disappear. Seeds germinate better, plants are more vigorous, the foliage clean, flowers large and of fine color and the flowering season prolonged.

Rust-Resistant Maximum

Giant Flowered. Spikes 32 inches tall, and blooms 2 to 2½ inches across.

These have huge individual flowers and flower spikes.

341 Maximum Alaska. White.
342 —Autumn Glow. Copper shades.
343 —Campfire. Pure luminous scarlet.
344 —Canary. Yellow.
343A —Copper King. Burnished copper.
341C —Crimson. Fiery crimson.
344C —Daffodil. Beautiful two-tone yellow.
345 —Fair Lady. Silver pink with white tube and yellow tip on lip.
424 —Golden Rod. The most rugged and most rust-resistant of all Snapdragons. Spikes stand up like rods. Plants are base branching, 26 in. tall with many unusually thick, erect, well-filled spikes of large, bright golden yellow flowers, the edges of which are delicately waved and crinkled.
342A —Golden Glory. The deepest yellow.
343B —Indian Summer. Coppery orange-scarlet.
346 —Loveliness. Pure soft rose-pink.
419 —Pink Sensation. Pure pink.
347 —Red Cross. Deep rich crimson, white tubes.
341A —Swing Time. Loveliest rose-pink, a bright yellow lip and white tube.

Each of above maximum type, Pkt., 20c; any 3 pkts., 50c.

> **348 All the above Rust-resistant Maximum Snapdragons Mixed. Pkt., 25c; 3 pkts., 65c.**

MAJUS GRANDIFLORUM—Large Flowering. 2½ in.
344A Grandiflorum Brilliant Rose. True rose pink.
344B —Daintiness. (Pink Domino). Rose pink, white tube.
348A —Orange Shades.
349 —Padre—See Novelties. Pkt., 25c.
345A —Reveille. Softly tinted by the golden rays of an early sunrise, Reveille is a deep luminous yellow with the upper lip of each floret toning to a lighter lemon yellow.
336 —Rosalie. A rich deep rose with underlying tone of topaz or amber. The tube and lip are the same color, which greatly intensifies the depth and richness of color. Plants base branching and produce 6 to 8 huge flowering spikes on which the florets are decidedly well arranged.
337 —Salmon Pink.
338 —Shasta. Pure white.
353 —Stoplight. Copper scarlet.
352 —Yellow Jacket. A clear deep yellow.
Each of above, pkt., 20c; any 3 pkts., 50c.

355 Majus Grandiflorum Mixed. Pkt., 20c.

SUPER-MAJESTIC TYPE—Semi-tall Giant Flowered
327 Orange Shades. Marvelous shades of rose deeply overlaid tangetine or golden orange.
326A Rose Sensation. Richest rose pink with a slight touch of salmon.
329 Royal Crimson. Garnet crimson.
831 Silver Pink. Lovely deep pink with a white blotch on the lower lip.
332 Super-Majestic Type Mixed.
Each of Super-Majestic type, pkt., 20c; any 3 pkts. for 50c.

Not-Resistant

Semi-Tall Sorts, 18 to 20 inches.

These are recommended for most beds and borders as they require no staking. The flowers have many new shades and tints.

368 Black Prince. Nearly black, small dark leaves.
379 Empress. Rich crimson.
384 Flame. Brilliant orange-scarlet.
390 Golden Queen. Rich yellow.
398 Nelrose. Old rose, shaded blush.
404 Prima Donna. Terra-cotta pink.
404B Red Emperor. Rich deep scarlet, compact habit.
404C Royal Rose. Rich deep rose.
358A St. George. Rich deep rose.
Each of the Semi-Tall sorts, pkt., 10c; 3 for 25c.
409 Semi-Tall Mixed Majus Nanum. ¼ oz., 45c; pkt., 10c.
See Also Novelties.

Baileya
Culture: A or B, Page 65

2117 Multiradiata. (Desert Sunray) Charming flowers, with a thrifty, cultivated appearance like that of a garden flower. The plant is a foot tall with grayish-green woolly stems and foliage, and the handsome flower is an inch and a half across, with a fine ruffle of many bright yellow rays, prettily scalloped, and a yellow center, rather deeper in color. Pkt. 35c.

BABY'S BREATH, See Gypsophila Paniculata.

Balloon Vine (Love in a Puff) ☐ =
Culture: D or E, Page 65

995 A clean, free-growing vine reaching 10 to 15 feet, bearing delicate clusters of bloom and numbers of large, round, inflated seed-pods resembling miniature balloons. Pkt., 10c.

English Daisy ① ☐

1131 BELLIS. Monstrosa Double Mixed. 15c.

BELLIS PERENNIS (6 to 8 inches)
Culture: C, Page 65

Double Giant Daisies of robust habit. Remarkably fine effects are obtained when associated with Pansies or Forget-me-nots in beds or borders.

1119 Monstrosa Alba. Large white. Pkt., 15c.
1121 —Red. Pkt., 15c.
1123 —Rosea. Light rose. Pkt., 15c.
1135 —Mixed. Pkt., 15c.

Typical Florets of Vaughan's Giant Rust-Resistant Snapdragons

Left side, reading down.		Right side, reading down.	
341A	Swing Time	343	Campfire
344	Canary	346	Loveliness
343B	Indian Summer	347	Red Cross
336	Rosalie	424	Golden Rod
338	Shasta	329	Royal Crimson

Each of above, pkts., 20c; any 3 for 50c.

Miniature Snapdragons

ROCK HYBRIDS ×

A delightful new strain forming compact tufts 4 to 6 inches high, covered with miniature flowers. Excellent for rockeries, small beds and edgings.

433 Baby Rose. Very free flowering, compact plants covered with flowers of a deep pink self tint. Much deeper in color than Magic Carpet. Pkt., 20c.

432 Magic Carpet. A Snapdragon of almost creeping habit, covered with soft pink flowers. Pkt., 25c.

ASTERS, Giant Branching, Wilt Resistant. Top, 929, Heart of France (red.) Middle, 901, White. Bottom, 905a, Blue. Each pkt., **15c.** Special Offer 20, 1 pkt. each of above (3 pkts.) **40c.**

Wilt Resistant Asters

Culture: A, B, D or E, Page 65

If YOU should have any trouble raising Asters — TRY OUR WILT RESISTANT STRAINS. Perhaps your soil is infested with Aster wilt but even if not, you will find the Resistant Asters much more vigorous and productive While not immune from the Yellows disease, which is insect-borne and distinct from the Wilt, they are far less susceptible to infection and injury from it Where we offer the Wilt Resistant Strain of a variety, we have omitted the ordinary strain from our list.

VAUGHAN'S SPECIAL WILT RESISTANT

915 Mixed. A specially prepared mixture containing in balanced proportion all the wilt resistant varieties we offer. An outstanding value for the cutting garden, or mixed bed or border. ⅛ oz., 40c; pkt., 15c.

946 Pink Shades Mixed.   **947 Light Blue Shades Mixed.**
948 Dark Blue Shades Mixed.
Each of above, pkt., 15c; 3 pkts. for 40c.

Early Beauty 2 to 3 ft.

Attains a height of 2 to 3 feet of branching habit. Flowers large, borne on long stout stems. Bloom at same time with Crego and Giant Branching.

527 Azure Blue.   **531 Purple.**   **533 White.**
528 Black Prince.   **532 September Beauty,**
536 Carmine Rose.   flesh pink.
529 Crimson.   Each of above, pkt., 15c; 3 pkts. for 40c.
534 Mixed. ⅛ oz., 35c; pkt., 15c

Early Giant 1½ to 2 ft.

An exceptional new class. The flowers are full petaled with broad, graceful petals, daintily plumed and intertwined, very large, 4 to 5 inches across. There are practically no laterals or side branches. Four to six weeks earlier than the Giants of California.

541 Light Blue. A big lacy flower. **542 Peachblossom.** White flushed pink
543 Rose Marie. Rich, lively shade of rose.
Each of above, Pkt., 25c; any 3 pkts. for 65c.
544 Mixed. All three colors. ⅛ oz., 50c; pkt., 25c.

Giant Branching 2 to 3 ft.

The branching habit is accompanied by vigor of growth and profusion of bloom. The flowers are large, very double, stems long and colors vivid.

905 Azure Blue, dark lavender.
905A Blue.   **904 Crimson.**   **902 Shell Pink.**
903 Deep Rose.   **908 Sensation (Scarlet)**   **901 White.**
Each of above, pkt., 15c; any 3 pkts., 40c.
898 Mixed. ¼ oz., 35c; pkt.,15c.

Giant Crego — Ostrich Feather — 24 inches

The flowers are immense on stems. The petals are curled and twisted, plants branching. Flowers in abundance from late August until frost.

559 Azure Blue.   **561 Crimson.**   **565 Pink.**
560 Blue Flame,   **563 Deep Rose.**   **566 Purple.**
     navy blue.   **564 Lavender.**   **568 Violet.**
560A Cattleya fascinating shade of orchid.   **569 White.**
Each of above, Pkt., 15c; any 3 pkts., 40c.
575 Mixed. ¼ oz., 35c; pkt., 15c.

Princess—New Crested

Princess asters have a full crested center surrounded by several rows of strong guard petals. Flowers are fine keepers. Early and free bloomers. 18 in. to 24.

625 Princess Anne. Delicate pink turning to rose pink as they mature.
626 Princess Bonnie: A beautiful soft salmon rose with center of rich gold.
627 Princess Marsha. A strong, vibrant cinnabar scarlet, with rich gold center.
Each of above, pkt., 25c; any three pkts. for 65c.

937A Giant Mammoth Peony-Flowered Silvery Rose 2½ to 3 ft. Immense, fully double flowers resembling the Beauty type, borne on long, stout non-lateral stems. An attractive variety with its rich rose silver tipped flowers. Pkt., 25c.

Golden Sheaf 2 ft.

556 The deepest yellow Aster yet offered and the only one that is Wilt Resistant. The flowers are fully double with an attractive crest-like center of good substance and fine depth of petal. Pkt., 15c.

624 King Mixed 2½ ft. Medium sized pretty flowers with long quill-like petals. Upright grower. Early mid-season bloom. Pkt., 15c.

Heart of France

929 Opens red as the purest ruby, deepens with age and retains its remarkable color to the very end. The petals show now a glow and sheen, now a soft warm velvety texture. 18 to 24 inches. ⅛ oz., 45c; pkt., 15c.

Improved Giants of California Curled and Interlaced

The flowers are large and full, of the well-known Crego type, with broad graceful petals, borne on long heavy non-lateral stems. The plants reach a height of 3 feet, blooming from late summer until frost. A fine cut flower type.

577 Dark Purple. Pkt., 15c.

Finest Giant Sorts Mixed

628 A mixture of giant sorts which we offered last year to out store customers alone. It was so popular we decided to list it in our 1944 catalog. It contains complete color range in all Giant sorts. Large pkt., 25c.

WILT RESISTANT ASTERS—Continued

Queen of the Market (Early Flowering) 16 inches

The favorite early Aster, usually in full bloom two weeks before most others begin to blossom. Of graceful spreading habit.

921 Crimson.   **925** Light Blue.   **925C** Rose.   **924** White.
922 Flesh Pink.   **923** Purple, dark blue. **926** Scarlet.
Each of above, pkt., 15c; 3 pkts. for 40c.
928 Mixed. ⅛ oz., 35c; pkt., 15c.

Royal Early-Flowering Branching 2 ft.

This type fills a gap between the Queen of the Market and the Late-Flowering Branching Asters.

929A Dark Lavender   **930** Rose-Pink
929B Peachblossom   **930A** Shell Pink
929C Purple   **930B** White
Each of the above, pkt., 15c; 3 pkts. for 40c.
930C Mixed. ⅛ oz., 35c; pkt; 15c.

SINGLE GIANTS OF CALIFORNIA 2 to 3 ft.

The flowers are 3 to 4 inches with broad petals closely placed around the large center. Plants with few lateral branches. Mid-season.

871 Mixed. ⅛ oz., 35c; pkt., 15c.

Giant Non-Resistant Varieties

California Giants 2 ft.

California Giants combine the fluffy or feathered type of flower with the long, straight stems of the Beauty class. The large, double flowers with long, attractively curled petals, grow 5 in. and more in diameter, on stems 1½ to 2 ft. long.

594 Appleblossom, shell pink.   **604** Peachblossom, opens white
596 Crimson.   flushes lavender pink.
601 Deep Rose.   **600** White.
602 Dark Purple.
603 Light Blue.   Each of the above, Pkt., 15c; 3 pkts. for 40c.
610 Mixed. ¼ oz., 40c; pkt., 15c.

Giant Mammoth Peony Flowered 2½ to 3 ft.

The flowers are immense, very double, borne on long, stout stems, free from laterals. Splendid for cutting as they keep longer than any other variety.

931 Azure Fairy. Clear azure blue.   **937** Rosebud. A clear, deep rose
935 Maiden's Blush. Delicate flesh.   **934** Swan's Down. Pure white.
933 Purple Robe. Rich purple blue.
Each of the above, Pkt., 20c; 3 pkts. for 50c.
938 Mixed. ⅛ oz., 40c; pkt., 15c.

Super-Giants, Largest of All

Largest and most fully double Asters, with flowers from 6 to 8 inches across, plants 2½ ft. tall, with six to eight long stems. Early flowering.

943 El Monte. Like Los Angeles in size, and form, but of a deep glowing crimson. Blooms early and remains in flower for a long season. ⅛ oz., 50c; pkt., 20c.
942 Los Angeles. Pure shell pink, with huge flowers, but of charming form, with curling, interlaced petals, giving a feathery effect. ⅛ oz., 50c; pkt., 20c.

> ### Vaughan's Excelsior Mixture of Tall Asters, All Types
> **990** A mixture of the most beautiful, tall-growing Asters, Wilt Resistant and Non-Resistant, including the varieties listed and others. ⅛ oz., 50c; large pkt., 25c; pkt., 15c.

Imbricated Pompon 20 in.

Flowers very freely produced, often as many as 20 to a plant. Blooms very early. The small round Pompon blossoms have an outside row of short guard petals.

587 White. Pkt., 15c.

Giant California Sunshine 3 ft.

The flowers are large, with loosely placed outer petals contrasting with the creamy yellow or blue centers, giving a lacy effect which is quite delightful.

887 Finest Mixed. ¼ oz., 50c; pkt., 25c.

Giant Harmony

Fine new cutflower type, long stems, basal branching 4 to 4½ in. flowers with quilled centers.

792 Moonlight. Azure blue. Pkt., 25c.
ASTER Extra Early Crego Navy Blue.—See Novelty Pages.

> ### ANNUALS FOR ROCK GARDENS FOR SUMMER COLOR
> *Culture: A or B, Page 67*
> **4574** Rock Garden Annuals, Vaughan's Special Mixture. A carefully prepared mixture of low growing, many colored, free flowering annuals, which will supply color in your rock garden all summer. ¼ oz., 50c; pkt., 25c.

ASTERS, Giant Crego—Ostrich Feather—Wilt Resistant. Top, 561, Crimson. Middle, 569, White. Bottom, 560, Blue Flame. Each, pkt., 15c. Special Offer 21, 1 pkt. each of the above (3 pkts.) 40c.

Type of BUSH BALSAM
1052 Pink. 1051 Mixed.
Each, Pkt., **25c.**

Bush Balsam □ 1½ to 2 ft.

Gardenia Flowered
Culture: A, B, D or E, Page 65
Free-flowering double Balsam of bushy growth, flowers appear in clusters on the top of stems instead of hidden on side of stems. It is a fine border plant. One of our customers wrote us this year: "My Dwarf Bush Balsams looked exactly like little rose bushes."

1052 **Pink.**   1055 **White Reflected Rose.**
1054 **White.**   1056 **Rose.**
1057 **Torch.** Vermilion red, rich in color, vigorous and free flowering.
Each of above, pkt., 25c; any 3 pkts. for 65c.
1051 **Mixed.** ¼ oz., 50c; pkt., 25c.

Balsam (Lady Slipper) □
An old favorite producing double flowers clustered in the axils of the leaves on short stems. The plants like hot sun, rich soil and plenty of water.
1040 **Double Rose and Camellia-flowered Mixed.** ⅛ oz., 25c; pkt., 10
1045 **Vaughan's Invincible Balsams, Mixed.** Includes the old-fashioned favorite with flowers up and down the stems besides—some of the Bush Balsams which flower on top of stems ⅛ oz., 25c; pkt., 10c.

Balsam Apple and Pear 10 ft. □ =
Culture: A or B, Page 65
1008 **Mixed** Ornamental and quick-growing climber. Excellent in covering unsightly places. Flowers are followed by ornamental fruits Pkt., 10c.

BEGONIA   See page 64—House Plants from seed.
BLANKET FLOWER. See Gaillardia

1168 .BUTTER DAISIES   Pkt., 15c
(Verbesina Encelioides)

22   INDEX ON FINAL PAGES

Irish Green Bellflower □
Culture: D, E, A or B, Page 65
1138 **Bell of Ireland.** Graceful 2-foot branching stems are so surrounded by 2-inch flowers there is little room for leaves. The bell-shaped calyx of the flower is green and delicately veined, containing the white corolla. Both curious and beautiful. Pkt., 25c.

1138   BELL OF IRELAND.   Pkt., 25c.

1155 BROWALLIA Speciosa Major.
Pkt., 25c.

Browallia □
Culture: A or B, Page 65
Profusely blooming bedding plant, covered during summer and autumn with flowers of a rare shade of intense blue, grows freely in any rich soil; blooms well in the winter if lifted and cut back. In the garden they grow with 12 inch stems and make fine cut flowers.
1157 **Blue.** Pkt., 10c.
1156 **White.** Pkt., 10c.
1160 **Mixed.** Blue and white. Pkt., 10c.
1161 **Sapphire.** Flowers of intense blue, white eye; like large lobelia. Pkt., 25c.
1155 **Speciosa Major.** Brilliant ultramarine blue, a rare color; for border or hanging baskets. Pkt., 25c.

Bartonia (Blazing Star) □ 2 ft.
Culture: A, Page 65
1070 **Aurea.** Showy golden-yellow flowers above its gray and downy thistle-like foliage, exceedingly brilliant in the sunshine. Sow where it is to remain, as it does not bear transplanting. Pkt., 10c.

Showy Butter Daisies
Culture: A or B, Page 65
1168 **Verbesina Encelioides.** □ 40 in. A showy easily grown annual bearing 1⅜ inch flowers continuously throughout the summer. Good cut flower or border annual. Pkt., 15c.

BURNING BUSH   See Kochia and Dictamnus.
BUSH ESCHOLTZIA   See Hunnemannia.
BUTTERFLY FLOWER   See Schizanthus.
BUTTERFLY WEED   See Asclepias Tuberosa.

1146   BRACHYCOME Mixed.   Pkt., 10c.

Brachycome
(Swan River Daisy) □
Culture: A, B, D or E, Page 65
A free-flowering, dwarf-growing annual, 12 inches tall, covered during the greater part of the summer with a profusion of dainty flowers which resemble small Cinerarias, suitable for edgings, small beds or pot culture.
1146 **Mixed.** All colors. ⅛ oz., 25c; pkt., 10c.

BIDENS Humilis   See Cosmos Miniature Golden.
BLACK-EYED SUSAN   See Rudbeckia (Perennial seeds) and Thunbergia (annual seeds).

Grow Cacti from Seed
Culture: C, D or E, Page 65.
Growing Cacti from seed is easy and interesting, each miniature plant being perfect. The seeds germinate irregularly over a period of 14 to 40 days.
1251 **Cacti.** All kinds and forms mixed.
Pkt. (50 seeds), 25c; 5 pkts. for $1.00.

Cacalia (Tassel Flower) □ 2 ft.
Culture: A only, Page 65
This "perky" little annual blooms in a few weeks from seed. The flowers of scarlet or gold on branching stems look exactly as the name indicates, fluffy tassels, less than half an inch in diameter. Blooms until heavy frost. Try these in a copper bowl with the Castor Bean (Ricinus) seed pods and leaves for a lovely effect.
1170 **Mixed.** Scarlet and yellow. Pkt., 10c.

1170 CACALIA (Tassel Flower.) Pkt., 10c.

Calandrinia
Culture: B, D or E, Page 65
1174 **Umbellata Amaranth.** 3 in. A sun loving dry weather perennial rock plant that blooms from seed the first year if sown early. Vivid purple flowers make a rich display from July through September. Member of Portulaca family. Pkt., 25c.
Calceolaria— See page 64—House Plants from seed.

1194 CALENDULA. Ball Gold. Pkt., 15c.   1198 CALENDULA. Apricot. Pkt., 10c.   CALENDULA. Campfire. Pkt., 15c.

New Giant Calendulas □

Culture: A, B, D or E, Page 65

Calendula is one of the best annuals for the garden or greenhouse, being equally at home in either place. Vast improvements in size, shape and color of late years have changed the original "Pot Marigold Cinderella" into a Royal Princess. Keep the flowers cut for continuous blooming.

During warm weather the flowers may single out but will return to full doubles when the weather turns cool. Make a late sowing in early July for flowers in cool weather; they stand heavy frosts, and are last to die.

1198 Apricot. A flat petaled variety of a bright apricot shade, deepening towards the center. Pkt., 10c.

1194 Ball Gold. Extra long stemmed, large deep golden yellow. Pkt., 15c.

1194A Ball Lemon Queen. Deep lemon yellow with attractive brown eye. Pkt., 15c.

1191 Ball Orange. It has fine stems and immense double flowers of a brilliant glistening orange. Pkt., 15c.

1200 Campfire (Sensation). Flowers grow 4 inches wide, completely double, are of a deep orange. It grows vigorously with exceptionally strong, heavy stems. Especially selected stock. ½ oz., 50c; pkt., 15c.

1189 Yellow Sunshine. Large, double flowers on long, stout stems, petals broad and drooping, giving the flower a globular form. A pleasing buttercup-yellow color, free from Calendula odor and keeps well in water. Pkt., 10c.

1192 Masterpiece. Extra long-stemmed deep orange with brown center. Pkt., 15c.

1197 Moonlight. A beautiful soft cream yellow, with petals of the Chrysanthemum type, nearest approach to white of all Calendulas. The soft pale yellow harmonizes with anything, especially with the blue of the Centaureas. Pkt., 15c.

1190 Orange King. 18 in. Outer petals are slightly imbricated, while the centers are incurved. A glowing orange. Pkt., 10c.

1203 Orange Shaggy. 18 in. Long fringed petals overlapping form a flower resembling some Chrysanthemums. Deep orange turning lighter at the center gives a two-tone effect. Long stems. Pkt., 10c.

1200B Yellow Colossal. 18 in. Most profuse blooming of all bearing 4½-inch fully double flowers of a clear, bright yellow. Pkt., 10c.

1202 Pastel Bedding Mixture. A balanced selection of dwarf varieties, in light apricot, salmon, orange, lemon and cream. Pkt., 10c.

1205 Mixed, all colors. For woodlands and perennial borders. ¼ oz., 20c; pkt., 10c.

1206 CALENDULA Vaughan's Special Mixture. Besides listed varieties, this mixture includes many others, giving a delightful collection for cut flower use or exhibition. Prepared by a formula which assures balanced representation of colors and types. ¼ oz., 50c; pkt. **15c**

Annual Canterbury Bells □

Culture: D or E, Page 65

Annual varieties of this splendid flower family bloom in about six months from seed, growing to 2½ ft., and bearing six to eight spikes of bloom. A splendid late summer border flower.

1305 Mixed. Contains all the colors so far developed of the annual strain including dark and light blue, pink, rose and white. Pkt., 10c.

CARDINAL FLOWER—See Lobelia Cardinalis in Perennial pages.

CASTOR OIL BEAN —See Ricinus

Gay Calliopsis Clan □

Culture: A, Page 65

The annual Coreopsis, its flowers are similar in form, but many are marked with bands or centers of contrasting tones. Colors include variations of yellow and orange including brown, maroon and almost crimson. They are thrifty, vigorous, bloom throughout the summer and often self seed.

1211 Crimson King. This is a tall variety with rich dark crimson flowers. Pkt., 10c.

1220 Golden Crown. A rich orange-yellow. It has a pleasing fragrance and is nice for cutting, with 12-inch wiry stems. Pkt., 10c.

1217 Nigra Speciosa. 3 ft. Rich maroon. Pkt., 10c.

1235 Dwarf Varieties, Mixed. Valuable for small mixed beds and borders. Pkt., 10c.

1221 Tall All-Double Mixed. 3 ft. The best strain of double flowering Calliopsis. Flowers are semi-double and double, 1 to 1½ inches across. Our mixture contains all colors. Pkt., 15c.

1245 CALLIOPSIS Vaughan's Special Mixture. It contains all the desirable types and colors of these beautiful flowers. A great number of kinds have been especially selected for it. ¼ oz., 30c; pkt **10c**

1220 CALLIOPSIS Golden Crown. Pkt., 10c.

1290 CANDYTUFT Dwarf Hybrids Mixed. Pkt., 10c.

Candytuft (Iberis) □

Culture: A, B, D or E, Page 65

Successive plantings give flowers all summer. May be sown late in Fall in Tulip beds.

1260 Giant Hyacinth-Flowered White. 1 ft. Large, bold spikes of snowy white flowers, habit sturdy and compact. This is an especially select stock. ¼ oz., 40c; pkt., 10c.

Umbellata 1 ft. Flowers in umbrella form.

1275 Alba. White.   **1277 Flesh.**

1276 Carmine.   **1282 Rose Pink.**

1279 Crimson.   **1287 Mixed.** ¼ oz., 25c.

1286 Lilac. Each of the above, pkt., 10c; 3 pkts. for 25c.

1290 Dwarf Hybrids Mixed. 6 in. Compact plants covered with large flowers, rose, salmon, coral-pink to lilac and purple-crimson. ¼ oz., 25c; pkt., 10c.

1291 Dwarf White.   **1294 Dwarf Crimson.**

1293 Dwarf Rose.   A rich reddish purple.

1295 Dwarf Lilac.

Each of above, pkt., 10c; 3 pkts., 25c.

1289 Little Prince. 6 in. Immense spikes of snowy white flowers, borne in great profusion on dwarf sturdy plants. Pkt., 10c.

Coix □ 2 to 4 ft.

Culture: A or B, Page 65

1850 Lachrymae (Job's Tears). An ornamental grass with curious seeds which may be used as beads. Pkt., 10c.

CHINESE BELL FLOWER—See Platycodon.

Vaughan's Seed Store 23

1390 **CARNATION** Vaughan's Special Mixture (100 Seeds), **25c.**

Giant Carnations □

Culture: A or B, D or E, Page 65

Who doesn't love the spicy odor of the Carnation? Its beautiful blossoms may be grown from seed if sown inside and transplanted outside by the end of May. Plants lifted in fall, cut back will bloom again indoors.

1390 CARNATION Vaughan's Special Mixture. This is a mixture of the best strains. The plants will bloom the first summer and will produce many flowers equal to the best florist's Carnation. They may be lifted in September, potted and will bloom in the house. Pkt. (100 seeds). **25c**

Giant Enfant de Nice Carnations. They are of compact growth with extremely stiff stems bearing flowers 2¼ to 2¾ inches without disbudding. The colors come about 75% true from seeds and give about 90% of plants with double flowers.

1325 **White.**   1327 **Rose.**
1326 **Salmon.**   1328 **Red.**
1329 **Mixed** from varieties noted above.
Each of above, pkt. (100 seeds), 35c.

Improved Early Flowering Perpetual. Plants bloom in five months and continue all summer. The flowers are very double, clove scented of large size, on stiff stems 15 to 18 inches high. Our strain will produce 90% double flowers and true color.

1336 **White.**   1340 **Scarlet.**
1337 **Yellow.**   1341 **Maroon.**
1338 **Rose Pink.**   1342 **Salmon Rose.**
1339 **Flesh Pink.**   1343 **Mixed all colors.**
Each of the above, pkt., 25c; any 3 pkts. for 65c.

1350 **Giant Margaret Mixed.** Flowers measuring 3 in. or more; colors include white, pink, crimson and striped. Upright growth. Pkt. 15c.

See Novelties and Perennials.

CHILEAN BELLFLOWER—See Nolana.
CHIMNEY BELLFLOWER—See Campanula Pyramidalis.

1472 **CELOSIA** Royal Velvet. Pkt., **25c.**

Celosia (Cockscomb) □

Culture: A, B, D or E, Page 65

THE name Cockscomb is derived from the resemblance of the flower heads of the crested type to a cock's comb in form, though in texture they are like plush or chenille. The crested type thrive in light soil. Easily dried for winter use.

Crested Dwarf Sorts 8 to 10 in.

1410 **President Thiers.** Fine dwarf habit with bronzy foliage and large, velvety crimson combs.
1415 **Empress.** Blood-red combs and brown foliage.
1420 **Aurea.** Golden yellow combs.
1421 **Rose.**   1430 **Dwarf Mixed.**
Each of above, pkt., 15c.

Crested Tall Sorts 18 to 24 in.

1432 **Crimson.** Pkt., 15c.
1435 **Tall Mixed.** Pkt., 10c.

1463 **CELOSIA** Flame of Fire. Pkt., **25c.**

Ostrich Plume Sorts

They generally form pyramidal bushes branching out in candelabra shape, and the numerous massive plumes which resemble ostrich feathers wave gracefully above the foliage. 2 to 3 ft.

1440 **Aurea.** Orange.   1447 **Scarlet.**
1445 **Coccinea.** Crimson.   1450 **Mixed.**
Each of above, pkt., 10c.

1455 **Thompsoni Magnifica.** Mixed. 2-3 ft. A choice strain of the Ostrich Plume Celosias. Pkt., 10c.

1475 **Dwarf Ostrich Plume Varieties Mixed.** 15 in. Good for pots and beds. Pkt., 25c.

1472 **Royal Velvet.** 2 ft. Produces center and numerous long-stemmed plumy heads of richest crimson, on basal branches. Foliage bronzy green with reddish margins. Pkt. 25c.

1463 **Flame of Fire.** 18-20 in. Perfect pyramidal habit with center head and many side branches of a lush green. The branches terminate in circular feathery combs of fiery scarlet. Pkt., 25c.

1465 **CELOSIA** Chinese Woolflower Crimson. Pkt., 15c.

Other Celosias

1465 **Chinese Woolflower, Crimson.** Grows 2 to 3 feet high with many branches terminating in a flower head resembling a ball of scarlet wool.
1466 **Chinese Woolflower Deep Rose.**
1467 **Chinese Woolflower Yellow.**
1468 **Chinese Woolflower Mixed.**
Each of above Chinese Woolflower, per pkt., 15c; 2 for 25c.

1454 **Miracle Cockscomb Mixed.** Grows 2-3 ft. without branches terminated with enormous Cockscombs. September until frost. Pkt., 25c.

1456 **Parrot's Feather.** The stocky, branched plant bears terminal flower heads of fantastic shapes and varied coloring including silvery pink and salmon, red, maroon, yellow and orange. Pkt., 10c.

1460 **Pride of Castle Gould.** Compact pyramidal plants produce immense flower heads, resembling willow plumes in many shades. Pkt., 25c.

1470 **Spicata.** 3 feet. Round, pointed bloom, 3 to 4 inches in length. At first a soft bright rose, changing to silver-white. Pkt., 15c.

Lilliput

The plants attain the height of 12 inches, consisting of 15 to 20 branches of even length all terminated by brilliant feathery cockscombs.

1476 **Fire Feather.** Red. Pkt., 25c.
1477 **Golden Feather.** Yellow. Pkt., 25c.
See also Novelties.

Cardinal Climber □ = 25 *ft.*

Culture: A or B, D or E, Page 65

1320 This is a very attractive, strong and rapid grower, attaining a height of 25 feet, with beautiful fern-like laciniated foliage and literally covered with a blaze of fiery cardinal-red flowers from mid-summer to frost. The flowers are about 1 inch in diameter and are borne in clusters five to seven blooms each. Like all Ipomoeas it delights in a warm, sunny situation and good, rich soil. The seed should be soaked in water a few hours before sowing and not planted outside until about May 1st. The vines are a favorite playground of dainty humming birds. Pkt., 10c; 3 pkts., for 25c.

1320 **CARDINAL CLIMBER.** Pkt., 10c.

The Popular Centaureas

Culture: A, B, D or E. Page 65

Bachelor Buttons □
Centaurea-Cyanus Super Double

A perfected strain of this popular hardy annual, which very one can grow in any garden soil. They have larger flowers, more double, with more vivid coloring and long, wiry stems, making fine cut flowers. If the faded flowers are kept cut, the plants will blossom continuously throughout the summer.

- **505 Black Boy.** Blackish maroon.
- **506 Blue Boy.** The true cornflower blue.
- **507 Pinkia.** Lovely true pink.
- **508 Red Boy.** Deep glowing red.
- **509 Snowman.** Pure white.

Each of above, ⅛ oz., 30c; pkt., 15c; any 2 pkts. for 25c.

522 Vaughan's Special Super Double Mixed. Pkt., 15c; ¼ oz., 25c; ½ oz., 40c.

504 Jubilee Gem. A dwarf variety, making a compact plant covered with double dark blue flowers. Foliage forms a tufted mass of bright green. 12 inches in height. ¼ oz., 50c; pkt., 15c.

~ "The Victory Flower Garden" ~

Culture: A, B, C or D, Page 65

1517 Centaurea Cyanus Super Double. Red, White and Blue Mixed. Everyone will want flowers in our national colors this year. Here in a balanced mixture are giant Bachelor Buttons, Blue Boy, Snowman and Red Boy which most nearly approximate the hues of Old Glory. In the garden, in arrangements, and for men's button holes, they give just the right patriotic accent. Oz., $1.00; ¼ oz., 30c; pkt., 15c.

- **1506 Blue Boy.** **1509 Snowman.**
- **1508 Red Boy.**

Each of the above, ¼ oz., 30c; pkt., 15c; 3 pkts., 40c.

Various Centaureas

1480 Americana (Basket Flower). 3 ft. A splendid native variety; bears immense thistle-like blooms of rosy lavender color. Pkt., 10c.

Combine the above with those of Salvia Indian Purple for unique arrangement.

1485 Americana Alba (Star Thistle). 2½ ft. Immense heads of double fluffy blooms, almost pure white. Pkt., 10c.

1580 Suaveolens. 2 ft. (Yellow Sweet Sultan or Grecian Cornflower.) Very showy, large, bright yellow flowers sweetly scented and a popular sort for cutting; lasting well. Pkt., 10c.

1570 CENTAUREA Imperialis Mixed. (Sweet Sultan). Pkt., **10c.**

1590 VAUGHAN'S SPECIAL MIXTURE OF CENTAUREAS. Includes all the annual Centaureas, and a packet will produce cut flowers all summer. ¼ oz., 25c; pkt., 10c.

For other varieties, see Perennial Pages.

1580 CENTAUREA Suaveolens Yellow (Sweet Sultan.) Pkt., **10c.**

Giant Sweet Sultans
Imperialis 2½ ft.

Finest of all Sweet Sultans for cut flower purposes. The beautiful, artistic shaped flowers are borne on long, strong stems when cut and put in water will last for several days in good condition. They have a soft fragrance and add beauty to the garden picture.

- **1566 Amaranth.** **1550 Brilliant Rose.** Rich plum color.
- **1545 Delicate Lilac.** **1565 Deep Lavender.**
- **1560 Purple Crimson.** **1540 White.**

Each of the above, pkt., 10c; 3 pkts. for 25c.

1570 Imperialis, Mixed. ¼ oz., 25c; pkt., 10c.

White Leaved (Dusty Millers)

Culture: A, B, D or E, Page 65

All gardens need a few plants with gray foliage to tone down the brilliant colors. Sow early.

1595 Candidissima. 10 in. Thick silvery white leaves. Should be sown early. Pkt., 15c.

1600 Gymnocarpa. 1½ to 2 ft. Foliage finely cut of silvery gray color. Pkt., 10c.

1731 CINERARIA Maritima Candidissima. 1½ ft. is also known as Dusty Miller. Pkt., 10c.

Cheiranthus □

Culture: A or C, Page 65

A hardy perennial which blossoms the first year from seed. Sow in late summer, autumn or spring.

1607 Allioni (Siberian Wallflower). 1 ft. Dazzling fiery orange flowers, on stems about a foot high. Blooms from seed the first year. Pkt., 10c.

1608 Golden Bedder. Fragrant golden yellow flowers, larger than Allioni, are borne for a long season, if faded blossoms are kept picked. Pkt., 15c.

CENTRANTHUS — See Valeriana.

CHINESE FORGET-ME-NOT— See Cynoglossum Amabile.

CHINESE LANTERN PLANT—See Physalis Franchetti.

CHINESE MONEY PLANT—See Lunaria.

CHINESE WOOL FLOWER—See Celosia Childsii.

1607 CHEIRANTHUS Allioni. Pkt., **10c.** (Siberian Wallflower)

Chrysanthemums □

ANNUAL SUMMER "MUMS" OR PAINTED DAISIES

Single Flowering Varieties 20 in.

Culture: A, B, D or E, Page 65

Of the easiest culture; flower profusely during the summer and fall. They are showy in the garden and fine for cutting. Prefer heavy soil. All types should be pinched back to encourage branching.

1635 Burridgeanum. Pure white petals with zone of rich brownish red and inner zone of yellow surrounding the dark brown disc. Pkt., 10c.

1638 Eastern Star. Primrose, yellow, disc, brown eye. Pkt., 10c.

1637 Eldorado. Bright canary, dark mahogany disc. Pkt., 10c.

1650 Northern Star. White, lemon yellow ring, dark eye. Pkt., 10c.

1620 Morning Star. Petals primrose-yellow with halo of deeper yellow; dark yellow disc. Pkt., 10c.

1645 The Sultan. Rich wallflower-red with a narrow yellow zone around the brown disc. Pkt., 10c.

1627 W. E. Gladstone. Rich velvety purple, yellow ring. Pkt., 10c.

1655 Vaughan's Special Single Mixed. Showy flowers of bright colors. Pkt., 10c.

1700 CHRYSANTHEMUM Vaughan's Special Single and Double Annual Mixed. Pkt., 10c.

Double Flowering Varieties 2 ft.

1695 Vaughan's Special Mixture of Double Chrysanthemums. Pkt., 10c.

1647 Double Fringed. Improved Hybrids, choice mixed, rich colors, special selection. Pkt., 20c.

1700 Vaughan's Special Mixture. Single and Double sorts in finest mixture, including many varieties not catalogued. Pkt., 10c.

See Novelty Pages for Korean Hybrids.

1820 COBAEA Scandens. Pkt., 10c.

Cobaea (Cathedral Bells)

Culture: A, B, D or E, Page 65 □ = 30 ft.

1820 Scandens. One of the handsomest rapid growing climbers. The bell-shaped flowers turn lilac. Seed should be sown edgewise. Very vigorous and prolific bloomer. ¼ oz., 25c; pkt., 10c.

1825 White. **1830 Mixed.** White and blue. Each of the above, pkt., 10c.

Double Clarkia □ 2 ft.

Culture: A, B, D or E, Page 65

The lovely Clarkias are effective in the garden or as cut flowers in the home. Great spikes of double and semi-double flowers in the daintiest colors are produced from the poorest soil. Plant in shade. If the roots are confined by growing in small pots, they will bloom earlier.

1735 Albatross. Pure white of upright growth.

1743 Brilliant. Bright carmine.

1749 Firebrand. Brilliant scarlet.

1746 Illumination. Orange mingled with rose. One of the most beautiful.

1750 La France. A wonderful salmon pink.

1747 May Blossom. Pure glowing rose which deepens to pink.

1751 Purple Prince. Rosy purple.

1755 Queen Mary. Bright-carmine.

1761 Salmonea Perfecta. True salmon.

1762 Scarlet Queen. Glowing scarlet.
Each of above, pkt., 10c; any 3 pkts. for 25c.

1790 Vaughan's Special Mixture. Made up especially from the above named varieties. ¼ oz., 25c; pkt., 10c.

Coleus □ 2 ft.

Culture: D or E, Page 65

Very handsome and decorative plants with foliage of brilliant varied colors, many having fantastic markings. Plant in full sun for complete development of color.

1855 Vaughan's Rainbow Mixture. The handsomest foliage plant obtained from seed. The leaves often measure 8x10 inches; their color combinations are remarkably rich. Pkt., 35c.

1864 Glory. A mixture of bronze, pink, apricot, cream, etc. A remarkably fine strain; unequaled for the beautiful form and coloring of its large leaves. Pkt. 50c

1860 Fine Mixed. Pkt., 25c.

CLEOME PUNGENS (Spider Plant)—Pink Queen and Golden. See Novelties.

CORNFLOWER ASTER—See Stokesia.

CORNFLOWER—See Centaurea.

CORN ORNAMENTAL SQUAW — See Gourd page.

COREOPSIS — See perennial pages.

COLUMBINE—See Aquilegia in perennials.

CONEFLOWER—See Rudbeckia.

CONVOLVULUS, Morning Glory—See Page 36.

CORAL BELLS—See Heuchera in perennials

CLOVE PINK—See Dianthus Plumarius.

1790 CLARKIA Vaughan's Special Mixture. Pkt., 10c.

Cyperus □

Culture: A or B, Page 65

2030 Alternifolius (Umbrella Plant) + 1¾ ft. Grows finely in water with rich soil or mud, throwing up long spikes with narrow green leaves umbrella shape. Pkt., 10c.

Cuphea, Firecracker Plant □

Culture: A or B, Page 65

1998A Avalon Hybrids. Compact plants seeming to be covered with fluttering, bright-hued butterflies. In lavender, lilac, pure pink, rose-purple crimson, fire-scarlet and vermilion. Pkt., 25c.

1999 Firefly. 10 inches. A colorful border or edging plant, dwarf, compact, neat in habit, and showy. Small, delicate butterfly-like flowers of fiery red are freely produced. In full bloom it resembles a brightly decorated Christmas bush. Excellent for window box, flower pot, and rockery. Flowers in 12 to 14 weeks from seed and blooms continuously The Des Moines, Iowa, Park used it in the window boxes around the City Hall and wrote on Sept. 1 the plants were still in full bloom. Pkt., 25c.

CYCLAMEN—See page 64.

1999 CUPHEA Firefly. Pkt., 25c.

Cosmidium Orange Crown □ 2 ft

Culture: D or E, Page 65

1930 The flowers are golden yellow with a broad circle of a rich orange around the center disc Bloom all summer. Pkt., 10c.

1855 COLEUS Vaughan's Rainbow Mixed. Pkt., 25c.

Cosmos from July to Frost □

Culture: A, B, D or E, Page 65

Plants of graceful beauty, fine feathery foliage and large flowers. While the early varieties begin blooming in July, the Cosmos reaches the height of its beauty in the autumn. The new giant early varieties are wonderful cut flowers, holding in good condition for 10 days after cutting. We list only the early flowering varieties, as the late varieties are so apt to be taken by early frosts. Try the effect of Cosmos Sensation Pink with White Nicotiana Affinis in a low bowl for a lovely fairy-like combination.

COSMOS Sensation, New Giant Early Strain

Early flowering blooming in about 12 weeks from sowing. The flowers are very large, 4 to 5 inches across, with heavy fluted petals. Height about 4 feet. By disbudding, enormous flowers can be obtained.

1964 **Dazzler.** Very rich, deep amaranth crimson.
1968 **Pink.** A delightful rose-pink selection.
1967 **Purity.** A white with satin sheen.
1966 **Sensation Special Mixed.**
Each of above, Large pkt., 25c; 3 packets for 65c.

Single Early Flowering Mammoth. 3 ft.

1935 **White.**   1945 **Crimson.**   1940 **Pink.**
Each of the above, pkt., 10c; 3 pkts. for 25c.
1950 **Early Flowering Mammoth Mixed,** all colors. ¼ oz., 20c; pkt., 10c.

Double Early Flowering 3 ft.

Forms a perfect bush, massed with bloom, bearing beautiful flowers of good size, on long stems, about 65 per cent coming double.

1990 **Pink.**   1991 **White.**   1992 **Crimson.**
Each of the above, pkt., 25c; 3 pkts. for 65c.
1994 **Mixed.** Above 3 colors. ⅛ oz., 35c; pkt., 25c.

COSMOS Sensation. 1967, Purity, White. 1968, Pink.
1964 Dazzler, Crimson. Pkt., each, 25c. Three pkts. for 65c,

1979 **Orange Flare.** Well-branched plants, 3 ft. tall, covered with showy golden orange, flowers in about 3 months from seed, and blooms with increasing freedom until killing frost. Sow outdoors when soil is warm, or indoors with bottom heat of 70 degrees. Give full sun. Does not need staking. Pkt., 15c.
1980 **Yellow Flare.** See novelty pages. Pkt. 25c.
1982 **Semi-Double Orange Ruffles.** Pkt., 25c.
See Novelty Pages
1954 **Miniature Golden** (Bidens Humilis). 18 in. The rich, yellow, star-like flowers are very attractive on the deep olive green finely cut foliage. They form neat and compact bushes and bloom very freely. Excellent cut flower or edging plant. Pkt., 10c.

Cynoglossum □ 18 to 24 in.

Culture: A, B, D or B, Page 65

2015 **Amabile, Blue Bird Chinese Forget-Me-Not.** Produces long sprays of brilliant blue Forget-Me-Not like flowers. Grows easily and blooms for a long season. A most delightful addition to our list of blue flowers. ⅛ oz., 25c; pkt., 10c.
2017 **—Pink.** Similar to the above but having lovely bright pink blooms. Pkt., 15c.
2018 **—Fairy Blue.** 2 ft. Flowers of bright Cambridge or sky blue tone. Pkt., 15c.
2020 **Firmament.** It is dwarf, free-blooming over a long season; flowers a bright indigo blue. It is to be recommended for growing in dry, even poor soil. 1⅓ ft. Pkt., 10c.

1979 **COSMOS Orange Flare.** Pkt., 15c.

Cypress Vine □ = 10 ft.

Culture: A, B, D or E, Page 65

A graceful, twining annual climber with fernlike foliage and star-shaped blossoms. Sow in May, first soaking seeds in warm water.

2040 **Mixed.** Scarlet and white. Pkt., 10c.

2015 **CYNOGLOSSUM** Blue Bird. Pkt., 10c.

Special Mixture of Annuals for Cut Flowers

Culture: A or B, Page 65

No. 1400 The forty or more varieties in this blend are chosen for their value as cut flowers. They are the long stemmed brightly colored flowers that go so well in vases and baskets. This will produce a glorious variety of flowers for cutting. We suggest planting in rows in the vegetable garden where the plants may be cultivated and the blossoms kept cut close so the production of flowers will be encouraged, as the more one cuts the more one has, the secret being not to allow any seed pods to form. ¼ lb., $1.50; oz., 50c; ½ oz., 30c; pkt., 15c.

1994 **COSMOS Double Mixed.** Pkt., 25c.

1954 **COSMOS Miniature Golden.** Pkt., 10c.

Daisy Corner for Your Garden

2050 **Vaughan's Mixture of Annual Daisies.** These simple flowers have a charm of their own. We have a mixture of the most popular sorts. They will add a definite touch to your garden besides good cutting material for the home. Pkt., 25c.

2110 **DATURA** Double White. Pkt., 10c.

Datura (Angel's Trumpet) ☐ 3 ft.
Culture: A, B, D or E, Page 65
Handsome subtropical plants for summer bedding, having large trumpet-shaped fragrant flowers. Seed must be planted indoors early to bloom in September. They should be given a light soil and sun.
2110 Double White Pkt., 10c.

Dahlborg Daisy ☐ 8 in.
Culture: A or B, Page 65
2047 The thrifty little plants grow about 8 inches high and a foot wide, and are quite covered wth small yellow Daisy-like flowers. Absolute uniformity and early and continuous flowering to frost. Pkt., 25c.

2310 **DIDISCUS** Lavender Lace Flower. 10c.

Didiscus ☐ 3 ft.
Culture: A, B, D or E, Page 65
2310 Coeruleus (Lavender Lace Flower). Charming blue annual, with dainty lavender and blue flowers which resemble Queen Anne's Lace of our roadsides. Excellent cut flower. ⅛ oz., 25c. Pkt., 10c.

Send a packet of seed of their favorite flowers instead of a card to your gardening friends on their birthdays. Seeds will produce plants followed by flowers, which, long after the natal day is passed, will be a constant reminder of a friend. Cards are destroyed at once and soon forgotten. A packet of seed is secured for 10c—the better sorts for 25c and a few very select at 50c, same price as cards which are perishable. When you place your general seed order have this thought in mind and buy in anticipation of the birthdays to come. Nearly all of our packets are attractively colored.

Dahlias from Seed in 60 Days
2086 UNWIN'S DWARF HYBRIDS. This remarkable strain produces branching plants 2 to 3 feet tall bearing semi-double flowers 3 inches in diameter, of lovely soft pink, lavender, red, orange, yellow and maroon. They are as easily grown from seed as zinnias, and blossom in sixty days from seed sown in the garden row. Sow after the ground warms up and danger of frost is over, and give each plant at least one foot in the row. They give a striking effect in the border and are unsurpassed as cut flowers. They flower until frost kills the plants and produce tubers which can be saved. Pinched back, they make fine pot plants. ¼ oz., $1.00; ⅛ oz., 60c; pkt... **25c**

2086 **DAHLIA** Unwin's Dwarf Hybrids. Pkt., **25c**.

Grow Giant Dahlias from Seed ☐
Culture: D or E, A or B. Page 67

It is easy, most interesting and fascinating to grow Dahlias from seed and enjoy the surprise of new colors and forms. If the seed is started early, plants will bloom the same season. Sow in a shallow box or pan in March or early April, transplant them carefully as their growth demands, and keep the soil moderately moist. When all danger from frost is over, plant in the garden.

The varied forms, from the giant Salbach varieties, to the single Coltness and the Unwin varieties, supply a great range of form and color.

2090 DAHLIA Vaughan's Special Mixture. This mixture contains seed from the best collections in America and embraces all the various strains of double-flowering Dahlias, such as Show, and Cactus varieties, also the single flowering sorts. Pkt., (60 seeds)................. **35c**

Double Dahlias
2080 Double Best Mixed; 3 ft. Saved from show and fancy sorts. Pkt., 25c.
2075 Double Cactus Flowered Mixed. 3 ft. With twisted and curled petals. From a specialist's collection including unusual colors. Pkt., (60 seeds), 25c.
2081 Selecta Extra Double Giant Flowered. A most beautiful mixture of the very best new double dahlias, with flowers on stiff, erect stems. There is nothing better. Dahlias will bloom the first year from seed. Pkt. (50 seeds), 50c.
2083 Salbach Choice Mixed. 4 ft. If you want giant show flowers try this. 25 seeds, 35c; 100 seeds, $1.00.
2084 Salbach Selected Mixed. 4 ft. 25 seeds, 75c; 100 seeds, $2.50.

2090 **DAHLIA** Vaughan's Special Mixture Pkt., **35c**.

2087 Unwin's Ideal Bedding Mixed. The flower petals are nearly all twisted. Double and semi-double in many charming colors. excellent for cutting. Pkt., 25c.
2091 Zulu Strain. Dark bronzy leaved plants of the Unwin type, with semi-double flowers of crimson and scarlet. Pkt. (50 seeds), 35c.

Single Flowering
2056 Coltness Hybrids. 18 in. Habit neat and compact, blooms from July until frost. The flowers have either flat or slightly fluted petals, nearly all 3 in. in diameter. Pkt., 25c.
2057 Coltness Gem. 18 in. Bright scarlet, varies. Pkt., 25c. }
2058 Coltness Yellow. 18 in. Good clear yellow. Pkt., 25c. } Any three packets of Coltness for 60c.
2060 Coltness White Gem. The best selection of white. Pkt., 25c. }
2065 Giant Perfection Mixed. 4 ft. The plants are of strong, robust habit, and produce in great abundance flowers of immense size, of the most bewildering variety of color. Pkt., 10c.
2088 Dobbie's Orchid Flowered Mixed. Petals twisted and curled, in a variety of colors. It comes 90 percent true from seed. Pkt., 25c.

Dracocephalum ☐ 18 in.
Culture: A or B, Page 65
2355 Moldavicum (Dragon's Head). A native of Siberia, has lace-shaped leaves, and fragrant bluish-violet flowers borne in long nodding racemes from July to October. A good honey plant. Pkt., 10c.

Echium ☐ 12 to 18 in.
Culture: A or B, Page 65
2358 Blue Bedder. Deep bright blue bell flowers in compact bushy plant. Flowers freely in hot, dry weather all season long. Pkt., 15c.

Golden African Daisy

DIMORPHOTHECA □
Culture: A, B, D or E, Page 65

Showy annuals from South Africa, about 1 ft. tall with gorgeous, Daisy-like blooms during summer and fall. Easy culture in well-drained soil, sunny exposure.

2320 Aurantiaca. 1 ft. A rich orange gold, which is rendered more conspicuous by dark center disc.

2321 —Golden West. Bright golden yellow.

2322 —Salmon Beauty. Soft salmon pink.

2324 —White Beauty. A pure, glistening white.

2325 —Hybrids. They vary in color from pure white to red and blush including sulphur, lemon and bright golden yellow, light orange, reddish yellow and pale salmon-rose.
Each of the above, pkt., **10c.**

2326 Ecklonis. 3 ft. White 3 inch. blossoms of velvety texture marked with a rich blue or purple eye; are produced on bushes with branching stems from August, surviving light frosts. Pkt., 15c.

2318 Glistening White—See Novelty pages. 25c

2325 DIMORPHOTHECA Aurantiaca Hybrids. Pkt., **10c.**

Dolichos □ = 10 ft.
Culture: A, B, D or E, Page 65

If you have a wire fence which you want covered, we know of no plant more decorative than this. The flowers stand upright like Hyacinth flowers and are followed by attractive seed pods.

2330 Princess Helen (Daylight). Snow-white flowers, silvery seed pods. Pkt., 10c.

2335 Purple Souden (Darkness). Rose-violet flowers, ruby-purple seed pods. Pkt., 10c.

2340 Mixed. Pkt., 10c.

2345 Lignosus (Australian Pea Vine). A rapid-growing evergreen climber, flowering freely in clusters of rose pea-shaped flowers. Pkt., 10c.

2340 DOLICHOS Mixed. Pkt., **10c.**

DIGITALIS (Foxglove)—See Perennial Pages.

EVENING GLORY—See Ipomoea Bona Nox.

EVENING PRIMROSE—See Oenothera in Perennial pages.

2301 DIANTHUS Vaughan's Special Mixture of Single and Double. Pkt., **20c.**

Brilliant Annual Pinks

DIANTHUS 1 ft.
Culture: A or B, D or E, Page 65

A magnificent family producing their gay, sweet scented flowers in great profusion. They embrace a great variety of forms and come in a remarkably wide range of beautiful and rich color combinations.

2301 Vaughan's Special Mixture of Double and Single Pinks. This magnificent mixture contains the cream of of the annual pinks, both single and double. ¼ oz., 50c; pkt., 20c.

2251 Double Sweet Wivelsfield. The original single was a cross of the Dianthus Allwoodi and Sweet William. This has the same characteristics only the flowers are double. Brilliant colors, some with honey fragrance. Pkt., 25c.

2250 Single Sweet Wivelsfield, Mixed Colors. A cross of Dianthus Plumarius and Sweet William blooming the first year from seed. The flower heads resemble Sweet William in an almost unbelievable range of colors. Pkt., 15c.

2237 Heddewigii Chabaud Hybrid, Salmon Shades. The plants branch from the base and throw up sturdy stems 12 to 16 inches high, crowned by large double flowers 2½ to 5 inches across in various beautiful shades of salmon. Pkt., 20c.

Double Flowering

2257 Chinese Double Mixed. Handsome clusters of very double flowers; many bright colors. ¼ oz., 25c; pkt., 10c.

2258 Heddewigii Double Mixed. A fine mixture of colors, varying from the richest crimson to delicate rose.

2298 Diadem Double Mixed.

2290 Fireball. Large, double; rich, blood-red.

2280 Lucifer. Orange.

2285 Mourning Cloak. Black purple, white margin.

2295 Rosalind. Rose.

2239 Salmon King. Pink.

2293 Snowdrift. Giant, fringed white flowers.
Each of the above, pkt., 10c; any 3 for 25c.

Single Flowering

2236 Heddewigii Large Flowered Single Pinks. Flowers 2 to 3 inches in diameter, borne profusely. Colors include pink, rose and white, and many marked with rose and red centers.

2238 Crimson Bell. Dark red.

2240 Laciniatus Splendens. Flowers of brilliant crimson, over 2 inches across, with fringed petals, have a boldly contrasting white center.

2196 Salmon Queen. Salmon scarlet.

2241 Vesuvius. Scarlet.
Each of the above, pkt., 10c; any 3 for 25c.

2245 Vaughan's Special Mixture, Single Pinks. The flowers are extraordinarily large and embrace colors ranging from white to pink and deep crimson. ¼ oz., 30c; pkt., 10c.

2300 DIANTHUS Vaughan's Special Mixture of Double Pinks. Pkt., **10c.**

2300 DIANTHUS Vaughan's Special Mixture of Double Pinks. Selection o f the best double pinks in cultivation, ranging in color through all the most brilliant shades. ¼ oz., 30c; pkt., 10c.

Everlastinys Annual
For Winter Bouquets
Culture: A, B, D or E, Page 65

150 Acroclinium Roseum. Double. 2 ft., 10c.

2525 Gomphrena. Mixed, all colors. Pkt., 10c

2810 Helichrysum. Vaughan's Special Mixed. Pkt., 15c.

4683 Salvia Farinacea Blue Bedder. Pkt., 20c.

4795 Statice Russian (Suworowii). Pkt., 10c.

4800 —Bonduellii Superba. Yellow. Pkt., 10c.

4801 —Sinuata Rosea Superba. Pkt., 10c .

4803 —Kampf's Improved True Blue. Pkt., 15c.

5852 Xeranthemum Superbissima Dbl. Mxd. Pkt., 20c.

2440 Everlastings Mixed. 1 to 2 ft. A mixture of all varieties we list. Pkt., 15c.

Vaughan's Seed Store 29

2415 **ESCHOLTZIA** Vaughan's Special Mixture. Pkt., 10c.

California Poppy

ESCHOLTZIA ☐ 12 in.

Culture: A, B, D or E, Page 65

Dainty free flowering plants of easiest culture with gaily colored Poppy-like flowers with a satiny finish. Plants of low spreading growth with finely cut silvery foliage. Do well in any well drained, loose soil and sunny position. Blooms early and continues until frost.

Dwarf Erect Varieties 1 ft. (Californica).

2396 Ramona. Frilled edges give it the appearance of a semi-double. Golden-bronze within and coppery-rose outside.

2414 Ramona Hybrids, Finest Mixed. The flowers are beautifully frilled and fluted, the petals incurving to form a flower which at first glance appears to be double. The plants are dwarf and compact and do not make a profuse foliage.

2399 Tango. Bronzy red overlaid terra cotta.

Spreading Varieties 1 ft. (Californica).

2370 Carmine King. Deep carmine.

2376 Chrome Queen. Soft amber buff.

2385 Golden West. Bright yellow, orange center.

2387 Mandarin. Inside orange, outside scarlet.

2404 Sunlight. A lovely canary yellow.

2398 The Geisha. Brilliant gold inside, orange-crimson outside; fluted.

2405 Vesuvius. Rich wallflower red.

Double and Semi-double Varieties.

2395 Robert Gardiner. Deep orange.

2410 Double and Semi-double Mixed.

Each of the above, pkt., 10c.

2389 Monarch Art Shades. A compact strain of large-flowering California Poppies in mixture distinct from other types. Flowers are semi-double, the colors ranging through light rose to deep rose and carmine, and from deep golden yellow to orange and scarlet. Pkt., 10c.

2415 Vaughan's Special Mixture. This mixture includes all the varieties here catalogued of the double and single sorts and is the most complete mixture of these charming annuals in existence. ¼ oz., 30c. Pkt., 10c.

FEVERFEW—See Matricaria, page 34.

2435 **EUPHORBIA** Variegata (Snow on the Mountain). Pkt., 10c.

2471 **GAILLARDIA** Indian Chief. Pkt., 10c.

Gaillardia ☐

Culture: A, B, D or E, Page 65

One of the most profuse bloomers of the flower garden. Gaillardias grow best in full sunlight. The double varieties are among finest of annuals for cut flowers and deserve to be included in every list. 18 in.

2475 Lorenziana Double Mixed. ¼ oz., 25c; pkt., 10c.

2476 Sunshine. Harmonious blend, ranging from almost self red with yellow tips, until some flowers are pure self yellow. Fully double blooms, 2½ to 3 in. across on stiff stems, 2½ ft. tall. Pkt., 25c.

2471 Picta Indian Chief. 1 ft. Attractive flowers of deep coppery scarlet, accentuated by a dark brown center. Dense bushy plants. Pkt., 10c.

2470 —Single Mixed. Pkt., 10c.

See also Perennial Pages.

Godetia (Satin Flower) ☐

Culture: A, B, D or E, Page 65

Attractive, bushy plants with masses of large, colorful blooms during the summer and fall. Thrive best in a cool, moist soil and half-shady situation.

Upright Growth, Single Flowers. 1½ ft.

2571 Duke of York. Rich scarlet on white.

2574 Kelvedon Glory. 16 in. Glowing salmon orange, of exceptional brilliance, robust and free.

Each of the above, pkt., 10c.

Upright Growth, Double Flower. 2 ft.

2591 Gladiolus Flowered, Mixed. Different from others, producing flowerspikes much like a Gladiolus, which are closely set by double flowers in bright attractive colors. Pkt., 10c.

Compact Dwarf Growth, Single Flowers.

2573 Gloriosa. 10 in. Dark glowing red.

2576 Rosamunde. 8 in. Vivid rose with white.

2586 White Swan. 1 ft. Purest satiny white.

2569 Single Dwarf Mixed.

Each of the above, pkt., 10c.

Dwarf Double Azalea Flowered.

2577 Sweetheart. 12 in. Pink, cream overlay. Pkt., 10c.

2581 Sybil Sherwood Double. The flowers completely hide the foliage beneath a canopy of beautiful bright salmon pink, white edged flowers. Pkt., 10c.

Euphorbia ☐ 2 ft.

Culture: A, B, D or E, Page 65

2430 Annual Poinsettia, or Mexican Fire Plant. Resembling in habit and color the beautiful hot-house Poinsettia. About mid-summer the center top leaves of each branch turn orange-scarlet. Pkt., 10c.

2435 Variegata (Snow on the Mountain or Mountain Spurge). 2 ft. Remarkably distinct plant; very showy with its foliage edged white and green. ¼ oz., 25c; pkt., 10c.

2532 **GILIA** Capitata. Pkt., 10c.

Blue Gilia ☐

Culture: A, B, D or E, Page 65

2532 Capitata (Blue Thimble Flower). 2 ft. Bushy plant of erect habit with fine feathery foliage covered all summer with rich lavender-blue flowers, 1 inch across. Makes a good cut flower as the blooms last well. May also be used as everlasting, retaining their color when dried. ¼ oz., 25c. Pkt., 10c.

2530 Mixed. 1 ft. Exceedingly graceful, early flowers and valuable for bees. Charming in the flower border and for cutting in spring and summer. Pkt., 10c.

2476 **GAILLARDIA** Sunshine. Pkt., 10c.

Flowering Kale

2458 Flowering Kale. Although belonging to the Cabbage or Kale family, this Flowering Kale is entirely different as to its appearance. In young stage its leaves are green just like ordinary Kale, but in autumn as the season advances remarkably beautiful colors begin to appear and paint whole plant self colors or mixed colors.; The colors range from white, cream, pink, rose, magenta, etc., on dark green ground. As the plants grow, the colors become more brilliant. Pkt., 25c.

GOURDS, Varieties Illustrated are, 1. Bottle Miniature (2607); 2. Ornamental Pomegranate (2630); 3. Large Dipper (2610); 4. Bird's Nest (2603); 5. Hercules' Club (2618); 6. Turk's Turban (2645); 7. Spoon (2643); 8. Warted (2646); 9. We Cannot Supply; 10. Apple-Shaped (2600); 11. Sugar Trough (2640); 12. Orange (2627); 13. Calabash (2608); 14. Nest Egg (2625); 15. Pear-Shaped (2635). Each, Pkt., 10c.

Gourds □

Culture: A, B, D or E, Page 65

Large Gourd fruits make attractive decorations at harvest festivals. The small ones may be placed in bowls for table decorations. Bird houses, dippers, bowls, and toys are made of others. Leaflet on culture sent free if asked for with order.

Crown of Thorns Gourd

2609 Also known as Finger Gourd, Holy Gourd, Gourd of the Ten Commandments and Sugar Bowl. Ten prongs extend from the ridges or angles, standing free from the front part of the fruit. The fingers are hollow when inside pulp or fiber dries away. The shell is hard and durable. Base of the Gourd, about the stem, shows the ten customary main grooves. It is white or ivory-white. Pkt., 25c.

LARGE FRUITED GOURDS

2603 Bird's Nest (4). For bird houses.
2605 Bottle. Large. The original Thermos bottle. Makes fine bird-houses.
2608 Calabash Pipe (13). Powder Horn or Penguin Gourd. Odd-shaped fruit which is used in making pipes.
2610 Dipper (3). Fruit makes an excellent dipper and may be used for birds' nests.
2615 Dishcloth. Fruit is made up of a spongy-like porous pulp, which may be dried and used as a sponge with excellent results. The fruit is eaten when young, being cooked like squash. Many women prefer a dishcloth made of it. To speed up germination of Dishcloth Gourd, pour very hot water over seed and allow to stand for 12 hours. Plant immediately.
2617 Green Snake.
2618 Hercules' Club (5). Fruit grows 3 to 4 ft. long.
2622 Maranka (Cave Man Club or Dolphin). Knobby club shaped, dark green.
2640 Sugar Trough (11). Thick shells, very durable.
2645 Turk's Turban (6). Odd brightly colored fruit. Intermediate in size.
Each of above, pkt., 10c; any 3 pkts. for 25c.
2651 Large-Fruited Sorts. Mixed. Oz., 40c; ½ oz., 25c. Pkt., 10c.

SMALL FRUITED GOURDS

2600 Apple-Shaped (10). Small fruits.
2607 Bottle Miniature (1).
2625 Nest Egg (14). Practical nest eggs.
2627 Orange (12). The well known Mock Orange.
2630 Ornamental Pomegranate (2). or Queen's Sweet Pocket Melon. Fruit deliciously perfumed and may be carried in the pocket or laid among linens.
2634 Pear Bicolor. Green and white.
2635 Pear-Shaped (15). Striped yellow and green.
2636 Pear-Shaped White.
2643 Spoon (7). Small ball-shaped fruit with slender necks, deep orange. By slicing off a side a satisfactory spoon is made.

GOURDS—Continued

2646 Warted Sorts (8). Mixed.
Each of the preceding, pkt., 10c; any 3 pkts. for 25c.
2650 Small Fruited Varieties Mixed. Oz., 40c; ½ oz., 25c; pkt., 10c.

2660 Vaughan's Special Mixture. All shapes and sizes of these interesting fruits, so fashionable for ornaments, bird houses, and utensils, are included in this mixture. A bonanza for collectors. 1 oz., 60c; ½ oz., 35c; pkt. **15c**

Sow with Gourds for Decorative Effect:

1927 CORN Ornamental Indian or Squaw. The ears are used in making charm or Patio strings combined with the small gourd fruits. The kernels are of various bright colors. Pkt., 10c.
3211 MARTYNIA Proboscidea (Unicorn Plant). Tall, bushy heavy leaves, medium green. Fragrant creamy white flowers, producing fruits like unicorn or curved horn tapering to the blossom end. 18 to 24 in. Pkt., 15c.

Gypsophila □

Culture: A, Page 65

Graceful plants of light fairy-like growth. The misty bloom adds interest to a bouquet.

2681 Elegans Grandiflora Alba Special Selection. This is extremely free blooming, and petals considerably broader, making the flowers nice and round, without the usual cartwheel effect. About 10% will be the smaller flowered type. Oz., 60c; ½ oz., 40c; ¼ oz., 25c; pkt., 15c.
2682 Elegans Vivid Rose. Pkt., 10c.
2683 —Crimson. Pkt., 10c.
2686 —Mixed. ¼ oz., 25c; pkt., 10c.
See also Perennial Pages.

2681 GYPSOPHILA Elegans Grd. Alba. 15c

Helichrysum □ 3 ft.

Culture: A or B, D or E, Page 65

For winter bouquets, Straw Flowers should be cut before the centers open, and be hung upside down in a cool, dark place to dry. The foliage should be stripped off, and if it is desired, a fairly stiff wire may be twined about each stem to make them easier to handle in arranging them in bouquets. To grow large flowers, disbud, allowing only one bud to remain on each stem.
2775 Fire Ball.   **2770 Silver Ball.**
2780 Golden Ball.   **2771 Silvery Pink.**
2785 Rose Queen.   **2795 Violet Queen.**
2790 Salmon Queen.
Each of the above, pkt., 10c; any 3 pkts., 25c.

2810 HELICHRYSUM Vaughan's Special Mixture of Helichrysums. This is a balanced blend of the varieties listed and many other color tones in large flowered strains, giving an amazing collection of flowers for winter bouquets. It will produce material for many novel and attractive combinations for decorating the home. ⅛ oz., 35c. Pkt.............. **15c**

Gomphrena (Globe Amaranth)

Culture: A, B, D or E, Page 65. 18 in. □
A showy annual everlasting with clover-like heads.
2525 Mixed, all colors. Pkt., 10c.
2520 Orange. Blossoms resemble a ripe strawberry in color and markings. Start in sandy soil in gentle bottom heat. Pkt., 10c.

Grasses Ornamental

Culture: A or B, Page 65
2670 Ornamental Mixed. □ 2 to 5 ft. These are most useful for winter bouquets when combined with Everlasting flowers. Pkt., 10c.

Vaughan's Seed Store   **31**

Fragrant Heliotrope ☐ 2 ft.

Culture: A or B, D or E, Page 65

Heliotrope is a universal favorite on account of its delightful fragrance and duration of bloom, flowering equally well as bedding plants in summer, or as pot plants in the house during the winter. Seeds sown in the spring make fine plants for bedding out, and are as easily grown as Verbenas. It is to be regretted, however, seedlings tend to lose their rich fragrance. In fact none today is as heavy as in the past.

2820 Mammoth Mixed. Large flowers ranging from dark blue to lilac Pkt., 15c.

Hollyhocks (Annual) ☐ 5 ft.

Culture: A or B, D or E, Page 65

These annual kinds bloom the first year and will live over winter and last for several years, if sown in the open ground in April, they will be in flower in August, but if started indoors and set out in May, they will bloom in July. Very striking planted near hemlocks or used for roadside planting for decorative effect.

2842 HOLLYHOCK Indian Spring. Pkt., **15c.**

2845 Everblooming Double Mixed. Double and semi-double. ¼ oz., 35c; pkt., 10c.

2840 Everblooming Single Mixed. Large single flowers, exhibiting every shade known in Hollyhocks. ½ oz., 25c; pkt., 10c.

2842 Indian Spring. If sown in February it will bloom freely in early August, producing flowers of varying attractive bright rose and rosy-carmine semi-double. It grows a central stem which may attain six feet in height. Flowering branches are produced freely. Both stem and branches bear flowers. Pkt., 15c.

(For others, see Perennial Pages).

2861 HUNNEMANNIA Sunlite. Pkt., **15c.**

2820 HELIOTROPE Mammoth Mixed. **15c.**

A Fragrant Garden

Fragrance in gardens is a charming attribute we often talk about, but too seldom find. Just why this should be true is one of those mysteries of current fashion, which is hard to explain. We find the modern gardener in a frenzied effort to create the perfect color setting, and in his haste forgetting to include those sweet-scented subjects which give such a delightful perfume to summer evenings.

Some of this neglect may be due to the homely dress of some of the old-fashioned fragrant flowers. For example the even-scented stocks (Matthiola bicornis), which give such an abundance of perfume they may well be grown for that alone. But many fragrant flowers have been highly developed by modern plant breeding and may be planted for color and beauty as well.

250	**Alyssum.** Sweet. Pkt., 10c.
1287	**Candytuft.** Mixed. Pkt., 10c.
1350	**Carnation.** Giant Margaret Mixed. Pkt., 15c.
1570	**Centaurea.** Imperealis Mixed. Pkt., 10c.
2820	**Heliotrope.** Mammoth Mixed. Pkt., 15c.
3212	**Mathiola.** Bicornis. Pkt., 10c.
3245	**Mignonette.** Machet. Pkt., 10c.
3735	**Nasturtium.** Double Golden Gleam. Pkt., 10c.
3390	**Nicotiana.** Affinis. Pkt., 10c.
4025	**Petunia.** Special Mixture, Small Flowering. Pkt., 25c.
4740	**Scabiosa.** Vaughan's Special Mixture. Pkt., 10c.
4865	**Stocks.** 10 Weeks Best Mixed. Pkt., 10c.
5590	**Sweet Peas.** Fragrant varieties Mixed. Pkt., 25c.
7683	**Sweet William.** Single Giant Flowered Mixed Pkt., 10c.
8561	**Valeriana.** Mixed (Garden Heliotrope). Pkt., 10c.
5835	**Wallflower.** Single Annual Mixed. Pkt., 10c.
2457	**Special Mixture of the above Fragrant Varieties.** Large Pkt., 25c

Hunnemannia ☐ 1½ ft.

Culture: A or B, D or E, Page 65

2860 (Bush Escholtzia, or Santa Barbara Poppy). The plants grow into shrubby bushes, producing their large cup shaped flowers 3 in. across on stems 12 in. long. The petals are broad and crinkled. Does best in well limed sandy soil. Soak seeds overnight before sowing. ¼ oz., 25c; pkt., 10c.

2861 Sunlite. Gorgeous, semi-double, clear canary-yellow blooms. The extra rows of short petals are on the outside instead of the inside of the Tulip-shaped flowers. Light gray-green foliage. Flowers last two to three days as a cut flower. ¼ oz., 50c; pkt 15c.

JOB'S TEARS—See Coix Lachrymae.

KUDZU VINE—See Pueraria in Perennials.

Annual Hibiscus ☐

Culture: A or B, Page 65

2836 Trionum. The plants are uniform, stiff and rugged, requiring no staking, and bloom from June to frost-time. The flowers are three inches across, of cream with a center of dark purple, dotted with orange stamens. Pkt., 15c.

For other varieties, see Perennial Pages.

Quick Flowering Leptosyne ☐

Culture: A or B, Page 65

3010 Stillmanii. 1½ ft. One of the quickest flowering annuals blooming in five weeks and the Cosmos-like flowers continue for a long period. Pkt., 10c.

Jewel Flower ☐ 5 in.

Culture: A or B, Page 65

2961 Leptosiphon French Hybrids. Charming little plants, covered during the summer with small star-like blooms in many attractive shades. Pkt., 10c.

Kochia—Burning Bush ☐ 2½ ft.

Annual Hedge Plant

Culture: A or B, D or E, Page 65

2965 Childsii. It resembles a close-clipped ornamental Evergreen. The pyramidal bushes are close and compact and of a pleasing light green. The plant may be grown singly or in the form of a hedge or background and may be clipped to form a perfect hedge, an excellent substitute for boxwood to edge beds. In early autumn the whole bush becomes carmine or blood-red. Flowers small and numerous, but not conspicuous. Oz., 50c; ½ oz., 25c; pkt., 10c

2965 KOCHIA Childsii (Burning Bush) Pkt., **10c.**

Lantana + 1 ft.

Culture: D or E, Page 65

2980 Dwarf Hybrids Mixed. Plant with Verbena-like flowers in shades of white, red and yellow. May be grown in pots or set out in summer; remains in bloom late in autumn. They have an aromatic perfume. Pkt., 15c.

LAVENDER LACE FLOWER—See Didiscus Coeruleus.

Lavatera—Annual Mallows ☐

Culture: A or B, Page 65

Showy plants, covered with large flowers. 2½ ft.

2985 Splendens Alba. Silky, pure white. pkt., 10c.

2991 —Mixed. Pkt., 10c.

2989 —Loveliness. Rich rose pink flowers. Very effective as a garden plant. The bronzy foliage and stems making a fine foil to the flowers. Pkt., 15c.

2989 LAVATERA Loveliness. Pkt., **15c.**

Annual Larkspurs

ANNUAL Larkspurs give fine spikes of bloom that are exceedingly graceful and attractive. Real treasures for cutting. Perfectly hardy. Sow very early in spring, thin out the seedlings as necessary and give each plant room for development. Seed may also be sown in late fall for early flowers the following spring. In the summer germination is improved by chilling the seed several days in the refrigerator.

Culture: A or B, D or E, Page 65

Double Giant Imperial (Base Branching). ☐ 3 to 4 ft.
These Larkspurs are ideal for cut flowers as the flower stems, three to four feet long, branch from the base of the plants.

2151 Blue Bell. Is a fine medium blue larkspur, deeper than sky blue, yet much lighter than lilac.

2166 Blue Spire. Deep Oxford blue.

2152 Carmine King. Deep carmine rose.

2171 Coral King. Blush pink with a strong suffusion of coral which grows deeper.

2153 Daintiness. Delicate lavender.

2172 Dazzler. A rich scarlet base.

2155 Exquisite Pink Improved. Soft pink shaded salmon.
Each of the above, pkt., 15c; any 3 pkts. for 35c; any 6 pkts. for 60c.

2173 Gloria Improved. A rich deep rose-salmon.

2160 Lilac King.

2167 Lilac Spire. Lilac.

2156 Los Angeles. A shade between salmon and rosy scarlet.

2157 Miss Califomia. Deep pink shaded salmon.

2162 Pink Perfection. Lively light pink, large double florets, excellent upright habit.

2175 White King. Pure glistening white with rounded broad petals. The florets are 2 inches across.

2159 Giant Imperial Mixed. The above and others. Oz., $1.40; ¼ oz., 40c; Pkt., 15c.

Double Stock Flowered ☐ 3 to 4 ft.

2120 Dark Blue.

2131 Lilac Supreme. Deep lilac.

2138 Rosamond. A pure rose color.

2145 White.
Each of the above, pkt., 10c. Any 3 pkts. for 25c.

2150 Stock Flowered Mixed. All colors. Oz., $1.00; ¼ oz., 30c; pkt., 10c.

Super Majestic 5 ft.
The double large flowers are closely set on tall 5-foot spikes and the vigorous growth and abundance of bloom make this new strain especially useful for cut flowers and border backgrounds.

2179 Lavender. Fine lavender.

2180 Rose. An attractive salmon rose.

2181 White. Pure glistening white.
Each of the above, pkt., 25c. 1 pkt. each, 3 varieties, 65c.

2165 Empress Rose Bud. 33 in. Plants are bushy, semi-dwarf; bearing heavy trusses of deep salmon pink double flowers. Pkt., 25c.

2119 Paniculatum. ½-2 ft. An annual, making strong bushy plants, the stems splitting themselves up in manner of Gypsophila Paniculata, but the habit more upright. Leaves small and narrow flowers about ¾ in. in diameter, intense blue, are produced freely on top of plants. Pkt., 25c.

CHINESE LARKSPUR (Delphinium Chinensis). ☐ ①
The Chinese Delphinium blooms from seed the first year if sown early and may be treated as an annual; though it is a hardy perennial and plants will last many years. Fine for beds and border masses. Rarely needs staking and is covered with flowers all summer and fall.

7510 Chinese Blue Butterfly. 18 in. Deepest blue. Pkt., 15c.

7520 —Blue. 2-3 ft. Pure blue. Pkt., 10c.

7525 —Album. 2-3 ft. Pure white. Pkt., 10c.

7522 —Cambridge Blue. 2 to 3 ft. This variety is a really good light blue, far surpassing Belladonna in brilliancy. Pkt., 25c.

7530 —Mixed. Pkt., 10c.
Chinese Larkspur Blue Mirror. See Novelty pages.

2159 LARKSPUR, Giant Imperial Mixed. Pkt., **15c.**

Blue Lobelias ☐
Culture: D or E, A or B, Page 65

Dwarf Varieties
The compact class form bushy plants fairly sheeted with bloom throughout the season. Highly desirable for edgings, ribbon bedding and garden decoration.

3040 Bedding Queen. 4 in. Dwarfest, best for ribbon bedding. Flowers deep purplish-violet, with clear white eye. Pkt., 10c.

3041 Blue Gown. Clear deep blue, without eye, fine compact habit. Pkt., 25c.

3042 Blue Stone Re-Selected. Compact habit, large flowers of brilliant mid-blue. 4 in. Pkt., 25c.

3053 Cambridge Beauty. Large light blue flowers, green foliage. Pkt., 25c.

3145 Crystal Palace Compacta. 4 in. Deepest blue, dark foliage. Pkt., 10c.

3050 Emperor William. Gentian blue flowers, light foliage, one of the best and most popular sorts. 4 in. Pkt., 10c.

3056 Snowball. White. Pkt., 10c.

3070 Mixed Colors. Pkt., 10c.

3067 Tenuior. 15 in. Upright habit, large flowers of rich cobalt blue with white eye. Pkt., 15c.

2170 LARKSPURS Vaughan's Special Annual Mixture. Charming mixture containing all the bright and delicate shades, makes wonderful cut flower material and should be planted generously. They should be grown in good rich well-manured soil, and in a full sunny position. The plants, moreover, should be given plenty of room in order to allow them to branch out freely, and make handsome specimens. 1 oz., $1.00; ¼ oz., 30c; pkt............. **10c**

Trailing Lobelias
The following varieties are especially effective in hanging baskets or window boxes, where a long drooping effect is desired.

3061 Hamburgia. Sky blue with white eye. Pkt., 15c.

3065 Sapphire. Large, deep blue flowers, with a pure white eye. Pkt., 15c.

3060 Speciosa. 10 in. Dark blue, dark foliage. Pkt., 10c.

Lobelia Cardinalis and Lobelia Syphilitica. —See Perennial Pages.

3040 LOBELIA Bedding Queen. Pkt., 10c.

3105 **LUPINUS** Tall Annual Mixed. Pkt., **10c.**

3290 **MARVEL OF PERU** (Four o'Clocks) Mixed. Pkt., **10c.**

3314 **MICROSPERMA** "Golden Tassel." **25c.**

Annual Lupines ☐

Culture: A or B, D or E, Page 65

Free flowering, easily grown annuals, with long, graceful spikes, pea-shaped flowers. The fine, dark, glossy foliage makes an admirable foil for the long spikes of bloom; prefers a little shade.

3091 Hartwegii, White. Pure white flowers.
3085 —Cambridge Blue. Sky blue.
3080 —Oxford Blue. Dark blue.
3088 —Rose.

King or Giant Hartwegii. 3 to 4 ft Base branching plants, each bearing six to eight large flowers.
3076 King Dark Blue.   **3077 King White.**
3078 —Sky Blue.   **3079 —Mixed.**
3100 Subcarnosus (Texas Bluebonnet). 15 in. The flowers are of a delightful blue, with blotch of deep rosy flesh.

Each of the above, pkt., 10c; any 3 pkts., 25c.

3105 Tall Annual Sorts, Mixed. Oz., 30c; pkt., 10c.

Linarias (Baby Snaps)
12 to 18 in. ☐
Culture: A or B, Page 65

Also known as miniature snapdragons, are very charming free flowering border plants in bright and pastel tones. To get best results thin to 18 inches.

3031 Golden Gem. Pkt., 10c.
3033 Snow White. This is very lovely. Pkt., 10c.
3039 Fairy Bouquet. 8 in. A new strain greatly improved by more compact growth, and with large flowers of rose, yellow, pink, lavender, carmine, red, violet, white and salmon. ½ oz., 30c; pkt., 15c.
3034 Maroccana Hybrida Excelsior, Mixed. Colors range through crimson and gold, pink, mauve, dark blue, chamois, rose, and lighter art shades. Pkt., 10c.

Linum—Annual Flax ☐
Culture: A or B, Page 65

Round 1 inch flowers last one day, new blooms appear every morning. Plants come into bloom very quickly.
3020 Grandiflorum Rubrum (Crimson Flax). 2 ft. Brilliantly glowing crimson-rose. May be had in bloom from May to October by successive sowings. Pkt., 10c.

Marvel of Peru or Four O'Clocks ☐
Culture: A or B, D or E, Page 65

Showy summer and fall blooming plants that do well everywhere. Flowers open in the afternoon and all day if it is cloudy. It is little known that roots may be lifted in the fall and stored like Dahlias to be replanted in spring. It will result in larger plants, stronger, with more flowers.

3290 Mixed Colors. Lb., $2.80; ¼ lb., 80c; 1 oz., 25c; pkt., 10c.
3297 Dwarf Mixed. Pkt., 10c.

Sow For Fragrance
EVENING SCENTED STOCK or PERFUME PLANT
Culture: A or B, Page 65

3212 Matthiola Bicornis. ☐ 15 in. Lilac flowers which in the morning, evening and after a shower emit a delicious perfume perceptible at a distance. ¼ oz., 25c; pkt., 10c.

Mignonette (Reseda) ☐
Culture: A or B, Page 65

A well-known, old-fashioned flower of no great beauty, but highly prized for its fragrance, either in the garden or in mixed bouquets. The plants resent moving and seed should be sown where they are to bloom, thinning them to a foot or more apart.

3225 Bismarck. 1 ft. The red flowers are large, the spikes dense, foliage wrinkly, while its powerful fragrance is delicious. Pkt., 10c.
3235 Goliath Red. 2 ft. Giant red flowering variety. Very fragrant. Pkt., 10c.
3234 Golden Goliath. Deep golden yellow flowers Pkt., 15c.
3245 Machet. 15 in. It is the best Mignonette for all purposes, either outside or inside. It is an everbloomer, the flowers lasting until late in the fall. ½ oz., 25c; pkt., 10c.
3260 Mixed. Also many shades and types. ½ oz., 25c; pkt., 10c.

3039 **LINARIA** Fairy Bouquet Mixed. Pkt., **15c.**

Microsperma ☐ 8 to 9 in.
Culture: A, B or D, Page 65

3314 "Golden Tassel." It forms a compact plant strikingly like a Chinese Primula. The upright flowers, 2 inches across, are adorned with a multitude of stamens, which add greatly to their beauty. Sowings should be made in heat about the end of February to March, the seedlings repotted and put out of doors at the end of May. Pkt., 25c.

Mimosa (Sensitive Plant) ☐ 1 ft.
Culture: D or E, A or B, Page 65

3270 A pretty and curious foliage plant with leaves like those of the Acacia. They are very sensitive and close up immediately if touched or shaken. Pinkish white flowers. Pkt., 10c.

Mesembryanthemum (Ice Plant) ☐
Culture: A, B, D or E, Page 65

2870 Crystallinum (Fig Marigold) or Ice Plant. 8 in. Foliage glitters, being covered with ice-like globules; flowers, small, pinkish-white. A valuable plant for dry, sandy spots on banks, rockwork and sunny borders. Pkt., 10c.
2869 Criniflorum (Livingstone Daisy). Plants of slightly spreading Daisy-like flowers. 2 inches, pure white edged with rose, crimson, pink and buff; and self colors. Will grow in crevices of paving or old walls and thrives in poor soil. Pkt., 25c.

Mimulus ☐
Culture: D or E, Page 65

3275 Moschatus (Musk Plant). 10 in. Trailing plant for damp, shady places. Small yellow flowers, without odor. Fine for the rock garden. Pkt., 25c.
3280 Tigrinus (Monkey Flower) Queen's Prize, Single Mixed. 1 ft. Dwarf bushy plants, with large Gloxinia-like flowers. Pkt., 10c.

Matricaria ☐
Culture: D or E, A or B, Page 65

3205 Capensis Fl. Pl. (Feverfew). 3 ft. Neat, small, double white flowers, well adapted for borders, beds and cutting. They are perennial, but may be treated as annuals. Pkt., 10c.
3206 Capensis Improved. Select flat petaled type. snow-white flowers. Pkt., 35c.
3908 Golden Ball. 1 ft. Of compact habit, with very striking double yellow flowers. Pkt., 10c.
3209 Snowball. 10 in. Profuse blooming bedding plant, double white flowers. Pkt., 10c.

3245 **MIGNONETTE** Machet. Pkt., **10c.**

3152 Orange Supreme. Pkt., **25c**   3129 California Gold. Pkt., **15c**   3123 Guinea Gold. Pkt., **10c**   3142 Sunset Giants. Pkt., **15c**

Carnation Flowered

3129 California Gold. 2½ ft. Attractive deep orange flowers, with long loose petals artistically arranged, without the disagreeable Marigold odor of the foliage. Blooms in less than four months from seed. Flowers 2½ in. across on good wiry stems. Pkt., 15c.

3152 Orange Supreme. Except for its deep orange coloring, this is a twin for Yellow Supreme, which can pass for a Carnation in table arrangements, and is conceded to be best of its class. Flowers reach 4 to 5 inches, on long stems, plants 3 feet tall. Pkt., 25c.

3124 Yellow Supreme. A large bloom of honey fragrance, with broad, loose, frilled petals of a rich lemon-yellow, largest of true "Carnation flowered" type. Plants are vigorous, with foliage practically free from Marigold odor. Pkt., 10c.

3123 Guinea Gold. 2 to 2½ ft. The original Carnation-flowered type, producing flowers 2 to 2½ inches across, of brilliant orange flushed with gold. Practically 100% double. This is an early flowering sort. ⅛ oz., 25c; pkt., 10c.

Chrysanthemum Flowered

3128 Golden Glow. Somewhat resembles Rudbeckia Golden Glow. Petals are straight, sharply pointed and rather flat. Blooms about 2½ inches across and are borne in clusters. Pkt., 15c.

3153 Goldsmith—See Novelties. Pkt., 25c.

3127 Limelight—See Novelties. Pkt., 15c.

3132 Mission Yellowstone—See Novelties. 25c.

3140 Vaughan's Chrysanthemum Flowered Hybrids. 3 ft. An early flowering strain, bearing flowers of several distinct types, and tones of orange and yellow. Some have quilled and incurved petals, others flat Carnation-type flowers. Pkt., 15c.

Gigantea or Dahlia Flowered

3141A Orange Suncet. Giant deep orange. 15c.

3142 Sunset Giants. 3½ to 4 ft. Flowers 7½ inches in diameter are sometimes produced by plants of this giant strain, largest of all Marigolds. The average size is less, but still exceptionally large. Color varies, yellow and orange. Plants vigorous, heavy stems, 60% double. Pkt., 15c.

3177 Dwarf Pot of Gold—See Novelties. 25c.

3155 Tall Mixed. All large flowered sorts. Pkt., 25c.

Miscellaneous

3141 Crown of Gold. The first known Marigold with odorless foliage. Flower centers are of short curled, quilled petals with a collar of flat guard petals on outside. Color is orange. 2½-inch flowers, fragrant, 2½ feet tall. Pkt., 20c.

3154 Vaughan's Treasure Chest. 2½ to 3 ft. Colors run from deepest orange through golden orange, golden, golden yellow, lemon-yellow, buff-yellow to lightest primrose. Some Chrysanthemum-like but mostly of the Carnation and Peony-flowered forms, many 3 in. across. Some begin to bloom early, some midseason, and others late, which makes for a long flowering season. Pkt., 15c.

New Marigolds

Culture: A or B, D or E, Page 65

3175 Vaughan's Special Mixture of Dwarf Double and Single Varieties. These dwarf, compact strains are very attractive, each plant being covered with hundreds of small bright flowers, including listed varieties and many others of charming variations. ¼ oz., 25c; pkt., **10c**

3150 Vaughan's Special Tall Mixture. This mixture includes all the African sorts, including this year's novelties. A packet will give you flowers of enormous size in a wonderful assortment of color.
¼ oz., 50c; pkt.................... **15c**

Double Dwarf French Harmony Type

A selection of new strains and varieties in the popular Harmony, crested center, type of Dwarf French Marigold, 12 in. to 14 in.

3164A Butterball—See Novelty Pages. Pkt., 25c.

3174 Harmony. Dwarf, compact, early, golden yellow bordered, maroon red. ¼ oz., 60c; ⅛ oz., 35c; pkt., 15c.

3168A Melody. Excellent rich orange, compact, dwarf. Pkt., 25c.

3169 Spotlight. Rich yellow bordered mahogany red, 1¾ inch, very early flowering, 100% All Double. Pkt., 25c.

3170A Spry. Dwarf compact, yellow bordered mahogany—see Novelty Pages. Pkt., 25c.

3165 Sunkist Orange. Bright golden orange—See Novelty Pages. Pkt., 25c.

3170 Harmony Hybrids. Wide and varied range striking color combinations, 1¾ inch flowers with crested center and flanking guard petals, early, 100% All Double. Pkt., 25c.

Dwarf French Double Sorts 10 in.

3167 Gold Ball.   **3168** Lemon.

3166 Robert Beist. A warm shade of shining purple scarlet. Each of the above, pkt., 10c.

3171 Monarch Strain of Dwarf French, Double Mixed. Symmetrical compact habit, including orange, bronze and mahogany. ¼ oz., 35c; ⅛ oz., 25c; pkt., 10c.

3172 Monarch Strain Re-Selected Golden Ball. It has exceptionally large flowers for a French variety; double and deepest orange. Pkt., 15c.

3158 Dwarf French All Double Early Flowering Mixed. Pkt., 15c.

3161 Double Dwarf French Early Flowering, All Double Striped. Pkt., 10c.

3181 Dwarf Royal Scot All Double. 10 in. Dwarf bushy growth. Mahogany and gold. Pkt., 15c.

Single Dwarf Varieties

3178 Fire Cross (Improved Legion of Honor). Each deep orange-yellow petal carries a large crimson-maroon blotch. Pkt., 10c.

3180 Gilt Edge. 8 in. Maroon, edged yellow. Pkt., 10c.

Single Tall French

3156 Wildfire. 18 in. This seed bearing hybrid between French and African varieties, bears single flowers which sometimes reach 3 inches in diameter, varying in color and markings on the same plant. Blooms in eight weeks from sowing, flowering until frost comes Pkt., 10c.

3184 Ferdinand. 20 to 24 in. Harmony type. Round center of tubular florets of golden yellow surrounded by a single row of broad, mahogany-red guard petals. Flowers 1½ to 1¾ inches. Pkt., 15c.

3186 Flaming Fire. 2½ ft. The long stemmed, brightly colored, large single flowers, 2 in. across, at times are flaming red, at other times red and yellow. Plants bloom in about 12 weeks. Pkt., 15c.

3170 **MARIGOLD** Harmony and Its Hybrids. Pkt., **25c**

First Tall Red Marigold

3173A Idabelle Firestone. Tall double flowering Hybrid of the African and French species has 2½-inch mahogany red flowers on vigorous 3-foot bushes, taller and much larger than any previous double red marigold. It is a distinct and lovely innovation, fine for cutting and for the border. Pkt., 25c.

3173 Red and Gold Hybrids. Hybrid of French and African species which bears no seed, so whether you pick the flowers or not, it just keeps producing, on bushy 2-foot plants, large, double red and gold flowers, twice the size of most French varieties, so beautiful and plentiful that many good judges think it the finest of all border marigolds. Pkt., 20c.

Double Tall African 30 in.

3134 Alldouble Orange. Exactly like tall African Orange Queen in size and color and comes about 90% double from seed. Pkt., 15c.

3133 Alldouble Lemon. Yellow, same as preceding only the color is light yellow, about 90% double. Pkt., 15c.

Double Tall French 24 in.

3147 Striped (Royal Scot). 24 to 30 in. The double flowers are mahogany and gold in symmetrical stripes which radiate from the center of the flower. Pkt., 10c.

3148 Double Tall French, Mixed. Pkt., 10c.

A Golden Shower

3203 Mexican Marigold (Signata Pumila). 10 in. A miniature type forming compact plants completely covered with bright yellow flowers with brown stripe down the center of each petal. Pkt., 10c.

3149 Tom Thumb Golden Crown. 10 in. A dwarf form of Guinea Gold. Golden yellow flowers, of the same Carnation type and firm substance, are produced in great abundance, often 25 to 30 on a plant. Fine for front row of border. Pkt., 15c.

3174A Dwarf Chrysanthemum-flowered, Golden Bedder. Earliest of all, uniform, covered with golden orange flowers of chrysanthemum type. Pkt., 25c.

1922 MORNING GLORY. Royal Ensign. Pkt., 20c.

Morning Glories and Moonflowers

Culture: A or B, D or E, Page 65

If sown outdoors, do not sow until the ground is warm and summer established. Give plants full sun and do not overfeed, as this may limit flowers.

Heavenly Blue Morning Glory

2942 Heavenly Blue Improved. Similar to Heavenly Blue, from which it was developed, this improved strain is in all respects superior to the old. The color is a deep sky blue, shading lighter toward the center; the flowers are large and freely produced, and the plants flower early and continue throughout the summer. It is also much earlier flowering and the flowers remain open to six o'clock in the evening on cloudy days. Oz., $1.00; ¼ oz., 30c; pkt., 15c.

2941 Clark's Early Flowering. There are few flowers which have a more universal appeal than the giant sky-blue trumpets of this Morning Glory, and the flowering period ends only when frost kills the plants. Flowers measure 3½ to 4 inches across. To sow indoors, nick through hard outer shell of seed with knife or file. Then sow in flower pot, in good friable soil, and place where bottom heat of at least 70 degrees is provided. Keep indoors until weather is warm. Oz. $1.00; ¼ oz., 30c; pkt., 15c

2938 Columbia—See Novelties. Pkt., 25c.

2943 Pearly Gates. See Novelty Pages. Pkt., 25c.

2942 MORNING GLORY. Heavenly Blue Improved. Pkt., 15c.

Day Flowering Ipomoeas

2925 IMPERIAL MORNING GLORIES Vaughan's Special Mixture. The colors run from snow-white through all tones of blue, red, and purple. Sun-loving plants do best when protected from north and west wind. 1 oz., 75c; ½ oz., 40c; ¼ oz., 25c; pkt **10c**

2950 Setosa (Brazilian Morning Glory). Leaves are 9 inches across; flowers 2 inches, tinted pink with a star of satiny pink. Curious seed pods. Pkt., 10c.

2937 Alamo or Mile-A-Minute Vine. Fast growing delicate foliage, vine, excellent cover for fences or trellises, flowers 1½ in., creamy white, center deep wine red, open late morning and afternoon. Pkt., 10c.

Night Flowering

IPOMOEA (Moonflower) ☐ = 20 ft.

2895 Bona Nox (Evening Glory). Violet. Pkt., 10c.

2905 Mexicana Grandiflora Alba (White Moonflower). Covered with large white flowers every evening and cloudy day. Pkt., 10c.

2910 Giant Pink. Soft lilac-pink flowers. Pkt . 10c.

2901 Giant Cornell

The flowers, as large as Heavenly Blue, are an intense carnelian red with pure white border, reproducing the colors of Cornell University, presenting a very gay appearance. Growth is rapid and flowers come early, when vine is two feet tall, increasing in number until killing frosts arrive ¼ oz., 50c ; pkt. **20c**

2901 MORNING GLORY. Giant Cornell. Pkt., 20c.

2948 MORNING GLORY Scarlett O'Hara. Pkt., 20c.

2948 Scarlett O'Hara. A sensational climber, stunning 3½-in. flowers of a soft velvety scarlet. The bright color is carried well down the throat, borne in profusion from July until frost. The flowers stay open longer in the day than other sorts and the foliage is quite distinct. ¼ oz., 50c; pkt., 20c.

1908 Crimson Rambler. A Morning Glory of bright ruby red, member of the Convolvulus family, which flowers with all the well-known vigor of its race, and will clamber over an arbor in record time ¼ oz., 25c; pkt., 10c.

2911 Purple. Interesting large flowers of rich velvety purple cover the vines all summer. Pkt., 15c.

2945 Double Rose Marie. We are not surprised by Morning Glories which belong to the Moonflower family (Ipomoeas) but a double Morning Glory is something to talk about. It grows well and produces freely its lovely double flowers. Pkt., 15c.

CONVOLVULUS (Morning Glory)

Culture: A or B, D or E, Page 65

1900 Tall Mixed, all colors. 1 oz., 15c; pkt., 10c.

DWARF MORNING GLORY 1 ft.

Showy hardy annuals for beds and borders, also rockwork; they bloom for a long period and delight in sun.

1923 Dwarf Lavender Rosette. An ideal rockery plant with deep lavender flowers. Given enough moisture it will develop a mass of flowerheads from June to mid-August. Pkt., 25c.

1921 Dwarf Rose. Exactly like above but a lovely rose color. Pkt., 10c.

1922 Dwarf Royal Ensign. A deep bright ultramarine; the deepest and brightest of all blue annuals, with a white halo and gold throat. The plants are covered with their attractive blossoms all summer. Use for edging and borders. Pkt., 20c.

1920 Dwarf Mixed, all colors. Pkt., 10c.

MOSS ROSES—See Portulaca

Fragrant Nasturtiums □

Culture: A or B, D, or E, Page 65

ASTURTIUMS will really grow on soils incapable of supporting any other plants, and are most useful on dry, sandy, or gravely banks.
eaves of Nasturtiums may be used for sandwich fillings and salads and the green ed pods may be used in pickles.

phis on Nasturtiums. One of our friends writes in "Horticulture": "I am not troubled with aphis if I sprinkle moth balls on the ground quite close to the stems of the plants. Red Arrow is also recommended.

Tall, Double, Glorious Gleam Varieties

733 Fire Gleam. Bright scarlet. Pkt., 10c.
735 Golden Gleam. The large double, golden yellow flowers on long stems are borne profusely well above the bright green foliage. Oz., 25c; pkt., 10c.
732 Indian Chief. It has dark foliage and vivid scarlet flowers. Oz. 25c; pkt., 15c.
737 Orange Gleam. Clear deep orange colored flowers. Oz., 25c; pkt., 10c.
734 Salmon Gleam. Delicate golden salmon Pkt., 10c.
738 Salmon Cerise. Pkt., 10c.
736 Scarlet Gleam. The flowers are a fiery orange-scarlet three inches across. Oz. 40c; ½ oz., 25c; pkt., 10c.
729 Sun Gleam. Brilliant lemon yellow, large blooms, the most sweetly scented of all semi-double Nasturtiums. Pkt., 15c.

Dwarf, Double Fragrant Varieties

540 Cherry Rose. Bright shades of cherry rose. Pkt., 15c.
541 Firebrand. Brilliant cerise scarlet, dark foliage. Pkt., 15c.
561 Globe of Fire. Flowers of flaming red, contrasting vividly with the dark green leaves, are borne in great abundance upon a compact dwarf plant. Pkt., 15c.
558 Golden Globe. Identical in color with Golden Gleam, but making bushy plants which the freely produced blossoms convert into mounds of gold. Oz., 25c; pkt., 10c.
542 Mahogany Gem. The darkest colored Nasturtium we have ever seen; the velvety, brilliant flowers are rich, deep mahogany. Red wallflower color. Pkt., 15c.
3543 Orange Glory. The large flowers are bright orange; the base of each of the upper petals and most of the inside of the throat are painted with deep garnet-brown. Narrow lines of this latter color radiate like a fan over the upper petals, but disappear in an overlay of orange-chrome. Petals are wonderfully fluted and crinkled. Pkt., 15c.
3545 Ruby Gem. Dwarf, compact, globe-shaped plants covered with large double, semi-bright ruby colored flowers. Pkt., 15c.
3546 Salmon Gem. Soft golden salmon. Pkt., 15c.
3547 Scarlet Empress. Deep scarlet flowers, very dark foliage. Pkt., 15c.
3560 Dwarf Double Gem Mixed. Ideal for edging beds and window boxes. It produces an evenly balanced range of bright colors. ¼ lb., 90c; oz., 30c; pkt., 10c.

> **3570 Vaughan's Special Mixture of Dwarf Nasturtiums.** This mixture is put up by ourselves from named sorts of the single and double varieties which have the richest and most varied combination of colors. ¼ lb., 55c; 1 oz., 15c; pkt., 10c.

Myosotis Forget-Me-Nots □ 1 ft.

Culture: A, B, or C, Page 65

Will bloom the first year from seed, so treat as annuals. If wintered over, Alpestris varieties will bloom in early spring; they delight in well-drained soil in a sunny location. Other varieties listed will bloom from May until frost and prefer cool, moist loam and half-shade. For beds, borders, rock gardens, pots and cutting.

3321 Alpestris Blue Eyes. Bright blue with white eye, large, early. Pkt., 15c.
3328 —Indigo (Sutton's Royal Blue). Pkt., 10c.
3330 —Rosea. Pink. Pkt., 10c.
The Bouquet type is a compact upright grower of the pillar or column type, blooms so freely the plants are completely smothered with flowers. 1 ft.
3350 Blue Bouquet. Royal blue. Pkt., 15c.
3356 Vaughan's Early and Late Flowering Blue Bird. 1 ft. A beautiful deep blue variety. A perennial which blooms from seed if sown early the first year. Pkt., 25c.

Dwarf Forget-Me-Nots

Victoria 8 in. Dwarf globular plants, completely covered with bloom, best variety for borders and pots.
3340 Victoria Azure Blue, with yellow center. Pkt., 15c.
3341 —Indigo Blue. Pkt., 15c.

Rockford, Illinois April 8, 1943
The giant double climbing Nasturtium seed I purchased from you last year grew the prettiest vines I've seen. Some of the blooms were 3¾ inches across, and double, and had 18½ inch stems. And such large vines! The ground was one mass of bloom. I picked nine to twelve bouquets a day. All the neighbors enjoyed them. Mrs. H. J.

Rothschild, Wis.
I ordered a packet of Double Glorious Gleam Hybrid Nasturtiums this year and I wish to tell you that I've never seen such beautiful Nasturtiums. Each day I pick a huge bouquet and the colors are so wonderful. Mrs. M. A. B.

3739 Vaughan's Double Glorious Gleam Hybrids. Colors never seen before in a double Nasturtium abound in profusion — salmon, golden yellow, orange scarlet, cerise, cream yellow, orange, crimson, and gold flushed scarlet combine with the foliage of fresh green. ¼ lb., 80c; oz., 25c; pkt., 10c.

3404 NICOTIANA Orange Blossom. **25c.**

Nicotiana □ 2 ft.

Sweet-Scented Tobacco Plant
Culture: A or B, D or E, Page 65

Their long tubular flowers close in midday, but open as evening approaches and give forth a rich perfume.

3390 Affinis. One of the most delightfully fragrant flowers, giving a continuous display of waxy white flowers right through the summer and autumn. The plants are of branching, bushy habit, carrying their flowers in clusters. ⅛ oz., 25c; pkt., 10c.

3392 Affinis Hybrids. Splendid hybrids in blue, red and rose shades. ⅛ oz., 25c; pkt., 10c.

3393—Crimson Bedder. The flowers are of a rich deep crimson. 15 in. Pkt., 15c.

3391—Crimson Flame. Petunia-like flowers form five pointed red stars, very fragrant. Pkt., 25c.

3404 Orange Blossom (Miniature White). 18 in. An elegant small-flowered pure white species; delightfully scented; even, upright growth. Daintier than the Affinis or Sanderae Hybrids. Pkt.25c.

3396 Sanderae Crimson King. Dark velvety crimson-red flowers. Pkt., 10c.

3397 Sanderae Hybrids. Pkt., 10c.

3405 Sylvestris. 4 ft. Pyramidal habit, with long, tubular, pure white flowers, in panicles. Pkt., 10c.

Nemesia □
Culture: D or E, Page 65

The orchid-like flowers range from rose to yellow-orange and blue. It should have an early start in greenhouse or hotbed, so it can flower before mid-summer.

3365 Dwarf Blue Gem. 7 inches. One of the best blue annuals for bedding. Pkt., 15c.

3364 Dwarf White Gem (Edelweiss). 7 in. Perfect bushes smothered with white flowers. Pkt., 15c.

3360 Large Flowered Mixed. 1 ft. Is the finest strain for size and richness and variety of colors. Pkt., 15c.

3359 Triumph Hybrids. A splendid race of these popular annuals. The plants grow 6 to 8 inches high, in bushy form, and bear continuously, myriads of brilliantly colored flowers; cream, orange, yellow, crimson, rose, scarlet, etc., tipped with other colors. Pkt., 15c.

Nicandra
Culture: A or B, Page 65

3389 Physaloides. Apple of Peru or Shoofly Plant. A strong spreading annual, 3-4 ft. high, grown for the showy blue flowers and odd fruits. It is an old-fashioned garden annual now rarely seen. Pkt., 10c.

WHITE FLOWERS are especially refreshing to the eye in the hot weather. Put them in a clear glass vase to add to the cooling appearance.

Nigella (Love-in-the-Mist) □
Culture: A or B, D or E, Page 65

3420 Miss Jekyll Dark Blue. A lovely variety, bearing on long stems, large semi-double flowers of a charming intense dark blue nestling in fine feathery foliage. Pkt., 10c.

3422 Miss Jekyll White. Pkt., 10c.

3415 Mixed Blue and White. 8 in. Pkt., 10c.

3417 Hispanica Dragon Fly. This is quite distinct from the Miss Jekyll type. The flower is single with thick fleshy petals and sturdy stem. 15 inches in height—branches well. The flowers are rich dark blue. Pkt., 10c.

3393 NICOTIANA Affinis Crimson Bedder. Pkt., **15c.**

3359 NEMESIA Triumph Hybrids. Pkt., **15c.**

3926 PENTSTEMON Sensation Mixed. **25c.**

3420 NIGELLA Miss Jekyll. Pkt., **10c.**

Nierembergia □

Sheets of Lavender Bloom
Culture: D or E, Page 65

3411 Hippomanica Coerulea. Grows not more than 4 to 6 inches high, forms a cushion of elegant light green foliage from which emerge corymbs of salver shaped flowers of a delicate lavender hue, 1 to 1¼ inches across. Blooms the entire summer. Pkt., 25c. See Novelties.

Nemophila (Baby Eyes) □ 6 in.
Culture: A or B, D or E, Page 65

Hardiest of annuals, and of the easiest culture.

3376 Insignis, Blue. Lovely cup-shaped, sky blue flowers with white center. Pkt., 10c.

3380 Mixed, all colors. Cup-shaped flowers in many bright colors, the blue shades being particularly attractive. Pkt., 10c.

Nolana (Chilean Bellflower) □
Culture: A, Page 65

3387 Blue Ensign. Native Chilean Bellflower. In pots it will grow 12 inches high, outdoors it spreads a little and throws up large ultramarine-blue flowers on stems 5 or 6 inches high. In shape these resemble an Ipomoea, enhanced by the large pure white center. Sow outdoors in May where the plants are to bloom. Fragrant. Pkt., 25c.

Oenothera □ 1½ to 2 ft.
Culture: A, Page 65

The evening primrose is noted for its heavy scent given off during the evening hours. Its yellow flowers attractive during the daytime, seem to reflect the moon at night.

3439 Lamarckiana (Evening Primrose). Yellow. Pkt., 10c.

Oxalis □
Culture: D or E, Page 65

3445 Rosea. An excellent little plant for edging or rock gardens. Blooms all summer in the greatest profusion; flowers dark rose and delicate pink. Pkt., 25c.

Passiflora
Culture: A or B, D or E, Page 65

3910 Coerulea Grandiflora (Passion Flower). Slender but strong grower. Flowers 2½ to 3½ inches across, slightly fragrant, greenish white; the corona is blue at the tip, white in the middle and purple at the base. Pkt., 10c.

Pentstemon
Culture: D or E, Page 65

3926 Sensation Mixture. If sown in heat in February or March, they will flower freely the first year, producing large spikes of handsome Gloxinia-like flowers. Often 2 in. across and in the most brilliant and varied colors, many of which are beautifully edged with a fine contrasting color. 2 ft. Pkt., 25c. See Perennial Pages for other varieties.

Night Garden. Plant white flowers. "These add to the pleasure and enjoyment of a garden in mid-summer as they are the only ones to appear to an advantage in the moonlight."

3894 PANSIES Vaughan's Super Swiss Giants Mixed. Pkt, **35c.**

Giant Pansies

Culture: A, B or C, Page 65

Pansies have long been a specialty with us. We introduced the Swiss Giants to American gardens and named and introduced the lovely Canadian variety Maple Leaf. Leaflet on culture will be supplied if asked for when ordering seed.

GIANT SWISS VARIETIES

3892 Swiss Alpenglow. Rich wine-red shades. Pkt., 25c.

3896 Swiss Berna. Dark violet blue. 25c.

3891 Swiss Blue (Ullswater) (Thuner Sea). Deep blue flower with blue-black blotches. Pkt., 25c.

3920 Swiss Coronation Gold. The largest pure gold self. Pkt., 50c.

3897 Swsss Delft Blue. A delightful tone of translucent blue. Pkt., 25c.

3862 Swiss Fire Beacon. Bright wallflower red with a touch of orange. Pkt., 50c.

3895 Swiss Luna. Light straw yellow. Pkt., 50c.

3900 Swiss Pure White. Pkt., 50c.

3893 Swiss Yellow (Rheingold). Rich yellow with blotches on the three lower petals. Pkt., 25c.

3894 Vaughan's Super Swiss Giant Mixture. The flowers are gigantic and exhibit shades previously unknown in this family. They bloom early, continuing all summer until late in fall. ⅛ oz., $1.25. Pkt.......... 35c

3786 Masterpiece (Frilled Pansy). A remarkable type, each petal being conspicuously curled or waved. Color range extensive, rich, dark, velvety shades predominating. Pkt., 25c.

3840 Trimardeau Mixture. It has a complete color range, but lacks the newer varieties. Pkt., 15c.

3881 Engelmann's Giant. A special strain selected and developed by an English grower. The plants are dwarf and compact and the huge flowers, in many dark and light tones, appear early. Pkt., 50c. For Viola Cornuta see page 47.

Clinton, Michigan February 23, 1943
For years I have raised a few pansies for pleasure, but feel that I should let you know about the pansies raised from your seed last year. Some blossoms measured 3¼ inches across and with stems seven inches long. They were of a very thick lusty texture and gorgeous coloring. They blossomed from August first to late fall. Mrs H. B.

3794 Pansies Vaughan's Super Maple Leaf Giant Mixture. (Canadian Giants) Pkt., **50c.**

Westfield, Wisconsin June 24, 1943
My Pansies this year are beautiful from the seed I got from you last fall. I never saw such large ones and my friends all think your Pansies are wonderful. Mrs. S. H. McW.

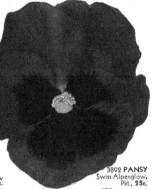

3892 PANSY Swiss Alpenglow. Pkt., **25c.**

Baby Pansies Bloom in 70 days from Seed

3761 Baby Delight. An ideal Pansy for spring blooming. Makes dwarf but compact bushy growth with a height of not more than 8 in. The flower is lovely light blue, with a pleasing "face" about 1 inch in diameter. 20c.

3762 Mrs. A. H. Scott. Another of the "baby group," top petals white, lower ones violet purple. A brilliant combination Pkt., 20c.

3761 PANSY Baby Delight. Pkt., **20c.**

4023 **PETUNIA** Salmon Supreme.
Pkt., **25c.**

Single Dwarf Small Flowering Petunias 12 to 15 in.

3997 Alderman. Deep violet blue. Pkt., 10c.

4017 Celestial Rose. Improvement on Rose of Heaven. More compact in growth and deeper in color. A beautiful rich satiny rose. Pkt., 25c.

3999 Cockatoo. Velvety deep violet-purple with irregular-sized white spots and stars. Pkt., 25c.

4003 Cream Star. Covered all summer with small flowers of soft creamy white, with deeper cream throat. Gives effect of white in the garden. Plant in shade. Pkt., 25c.

W. Walker

3990 **PETUNIA** Violet Queen. Pkt., **25c.**
4018 **PETUNIA** Rose of Heaven Select.
Pkt., **25c.**

4002 Crimson. Pkt., 10c.

4001 Heavenly Blue Re-Selected. A silvery light-blue. Varies about 10% in shade. Pkt., 25c.

4005 Improved Rosy Morn. An improved strain of the clear pink bedding variety. Of deeper coloring, more compact growth, and freer flowering with the same white throat. ⅛ oz., 50c; pkt., 15c.

4079 Martha Washington. 9 in. Blush pink deepening to dark violet throat; ruffled flowers. Pkt., 25c.

3989 Radiance. A cerise rose with enough under-lying salmon to remove harshness. The throat is golden yellow. Pkt., 25c.

4018 Rose of Heaven Select. Rich brilliant rose, with inconspicuous white throat, darker than Rosy Morn. ⅛ oz., $1.00; pkt., 25c.

4023 Salmon Supreme. 12 in. Distinct light salmon color. Flowers 1¾ in.; white throat, Pkt., 25c.

4082 Scarlet Glory. Very bushy, covered with rich scarlet flowers. The result of breeding from the popular Queen of the Market, from which it secured its brilliant color. Pkt., 25c.

4020 Snowball. Pure satiny white. ⅛ oz., 35c; pkt., 10c.

Small Flowering Single Petunias ☐
Culture: A or B, D or E, Page 65

4003 **PETUNIA** Cream Star, Pkt., **25c.**

4008 Topaz Queen. Its scarlet-rose coloring is deeper and richer than Celestial Rose, and does not fade in the sun. Its habit is uniformly compact, flowers larger and borne freely throughout the summer. It is especially recommended for locations where the hot sunshine tends to pale the color of other varieties. Pkt., 25c.

4021 Twinkles. Masses of small brilliant rose flowers with well-defined pure white star. Free blooming. Pkt., 20c.

3990 Violet Queen (Improved Blue Bird). Rich violet, compact and dwarf, best strain. Pkt., 25c.

For **White Perfection** and **Igloo** see Novelties. Special Offer—Any of the 25c packets, 3 pkts. for 65c.

4025 Vaughan's Special Mixture of Dwarf Small Flowering Varieties includes all the varieties listed and many others, and will be a revelation to those who plant a packet, in furnishing an unending supply of flowers in a most bewildering combination of colors. ¼ oz., 85c; ⅛ oz., 50c; pkt., 25c.

4008 **PETUNIA** Topaz Queen. Pkt., **25c.**

Spokane, Washington
May 26, 1943

"Thank you very much for your extra packages of gift seeds and I will say I have wonderful success with all the seeds I got from you."
Mrs. E. R. S.

3972 **PETUNIA** Hollywood Star. Pkt., **25c.**

Single Small Flowering Petunias 18 to 24 in.

4006 Flaming Velvet. A rich velvety crimson, best of its color in this class. Pkt., 15c.

3972 Hollywood Star. The blossoms are of unique shape, the petals being pointed and forming a five pointed star. The color is a lovely deep rose, with yellow throat, making a pleasing combination. It is early and free flowering. Pkt., 25c.

3975 Howard's Star Improved. Red purple with white star. Pkt., 10c.

4025 **PETUNIA** Vaughan's Dwarf Small Flowering Mixed. Includes all colors in this type. Pkt., **25c.**

3971 Norma. Blue with white star. Pkt., 10c.

3980 White King. Showy clear snow white flowers. Pkt., 25c.

3995 Finest Mixed. ⅛ oz., 25c; pkt., 10c.

Miniature 6 in.

A new strain of dwarf compact miniature Petunias.

4027 Rose Gem. Deep rich rose.

4023A Violet Gem. Rich violet blue.

4029 White Gem. New, pure white.

Each of above, per pkt., 15c; 3 pkts. for 40c.

4026 Gem Mixed. This includes white, violet, rose and pink starred white. Pkt., 15c.

See also Novelties.

SOWING FINE FLOWER SEEDS

One garden enthusiast mixes her fine seeds, such as Petunia, Poppy, etc., with ten times their bulk of dry sand, puts them into a salt shaker and sifts them over the beds or borders firming them with a board. A very practical idea. Try it.

Large Flowering Petunias □

Culture: D or E, Page 65

...dry season or wet, the Petunia is the most adaptable, long flowering and colorful of the garden annuals. ...here is an almost complete color range from the pure white to delicate yellow, through many shades to red ...d rich purple, veined or blotched with plain or frilled edges. There are small, large single, and double ...wered. Every gardener's desire may be gratified. Petunias make good cut flower material. We supply a ...flet on culture with order.

4055 Snow Storm. Large Flowered White. Pkt., **35c.**

Large Single Fringed Flowering

049 **Dainty Lady.** A large flowering single fringed variety of delicate golden yellow, the first really yellow Petunia. The plants are semi-dwarf and free-flowering. Plant in shade. Pkt., 35c.

044 **Gaiety.** Plants are bushy, 8 to 12 in. high, and are covered with large, daintily fringed rose and white blooms. Pkt., 25c.

053 **Lace Veil.** 12 in. Large pure white flowers with fringed petals, many waved. Pkt., 25c.

047 **Purple Beauty.** 16 in. A large flower beautifully frilled, the best blue fringed Petunia. 50c.

079 **Setting Sun.** Forms compact bushes 12 inches high, covered with fringed blossoms of rose pink, measuring 3 inches across. Pkt., 35c.

062 **Theodosia.** 20 in. Fringed rosy pink with a clearly defined golden center. Excellent for porch boxes. Pkt., 35c.

059 **White Beauty.** Fringed pure white. 25c.

Large Single Flowering 12 to 16 in.

The flowers of this type average 3 to 4 inches across.

073 **Blue Beauty.** A late flowering, clear, deep blue. Flowers of extra large size on plants of vigorous growth. Extremely free flowering. Pkt., 35c.

057 **Burgundy.** Rich wine red with a contrasting white throat. Pkt., 25c.

058 **Elk's Pride. Reselected.** Velvety black-purple, best of all dark blues. Pkt., 25c.

048 **Queen of The Market.** Best single red. Pkt., 25c.

4077 **PETUNIA** Salmon Beauty. (Giant Flowered) Pkt., **25c.**

4055 **Snow Storm.** Glistening white, shadowing yellow in the throat. An improvement on White Cloud. 4 to 5 in. flowers. Pkt., 35c.

4067 **White Cloud.** Fine compact bushes only 12 inches high, richly covered with pure white blooms 3 to 3½ inches in diameter. Pkt., 35c.

Double Flowering Petunias

3935 **Vaughan's Special Mixture of Double Petunias.** This is a mixture of the best large flowering and fringed double Petunias. Of course, only a certain percentage of double flowers may be expected from seed, but our mixture will produce from 60 to 80 per cent of doubles, while the remainder will be choice, large single flowers. The weaker seedlings should be carefully saved, as those invariably produce the finest double flowers. Pkt. (200 seeds), 50c.

All Double Petunias. See Novelty Pages.

4066 **PETUNIA** Type of Dwarf California Giant Mixed. Pkt., **50c.**

4066 **Dwarf California Giants Mixed.** The habit of the plant is very dwarf, flowers very large and of the finest substance. All with open veined throats of the Superbissima type. Pkt., 250 seeds, 50c; 500 seeds, 90c.

4076 **Fluffy Ruffles Mixed.** The flowers are so ruffled and frilled they have the appearance of being double. The flowers are very large with large throat. It is a well balanced mixture of pink, white, salmon, deep rose crimson, and light blue. about 75% will be ruffled. Pkt........ **35c**

Giant Single Flowering 18 in.

The flowers of this strain average 5 to 7 inches across.

4071 **Copper Red.** Enormous flowers with a dark throat, deeply veined. Pkt., 25c.

4070 **Empress.** Lilac blue with purple veins, one of the most free flowering and out-standing varieties. Pkt., 25c.

4090 **Prince of Wurttemberg.** Rich dark red with a dark throat. Darkest of all Petunias. Pkt., 25c.

4077 **Salmon Beauty.** True salmon pink, one of the outstanding varieties in our trials. Pkt., 25c.

4075 **White.** Yellow throat. Pkt., 25c.

4078 **PETUNIA** Setting Sun. Pkt., **35c.**

4100 **Vaughan's Best Mixture Large Flowering Single.** Includes Giant Ruffled, all colors of large flowering and fringed sorts, and the unsurpassed Superbissima varieties, with their delicately veined throats and mammoth flowers. Pkt. (300 seeds) **25c**

4065 **Giants of California Mixed.** A well balanced mixture containing a remarkably fine variety of colors, in blends of crimson, white, violet, lavender and pink. Large flowers freely produced. Pkt......... **25c**

Balcony Type Petunias 18 to 24 in.

Single large flowering sorts, trailing habit.

4037 **Balcony Black Prince.** Dark crimson, rich and velvety.

4036 **Balcony Cornflower Blue.** Rich blue.

4030 **Balcony Queen.** Rich velvety violet with white star.

4034 **Balcony Red.**

4041 **Balcony Rose.**

4040 **Balcony Rosy Morn.** Rose with white throat.

4035 **Balcony White.**

4039 **Balcony Star of California.** Violet crimson with white star.

Each of the above, pkt., 25c; any 3 for 65c.

4042 **Balcony Mixed.** ⅛ oz., 60c; pkt., 25c.

4037 **PETUNIA** Balcony Black Prince. Pkt., **25c.**

Phlox, the Gayest Annual

Culture: A or B, D or E, Page 65

PLANT a bed of these gorgeous annuals this year. If your favorite colors are the delicate shades, buy the Gigantea Art Shades (see Novelty pages); if you want a brilliant kaleidoscopic display, plant our Vaughan's Special Mixture. It has a complete color range of the delicate and brilliant shades. Seed may be sown in the open as soon as frost danger has passed, and flowers will appear in a few weeks. If faded flowers are removed they bloom until late frost. Sow where the plants are to flower as they do not like to be transplanted. 12 inch.

4175 PHLOX STAR. Mixed. Pkt., 15c.

Grandiflora Varieties ☐

This section has beautiful, round-petaled flowers, which overlap each other.

4113 **Brilliant.** Rose with dark eye.

4140 **Buff Yellow.**

4116 **Cinnabar Scarlet.** The brightest red in this gay family.

4120 **Chamois Rose.**

4137 **Dark Blue.** True blue.

4125 **Fiery Scarlet.**

4126 **Flaming Velvet.** Rich deep reddish purple.

4155 **Rose Pink.**

4105 **Pure White.**

4150 **Scarlet with White Eye.**

4160 **Violet with White Eye.**

4107 **White with Dark Eye.**
Each of the above, pkt., 15c; 3 pkts., 40c.

4165 **Splendid Mixture.**
⅛ oz., 40c; ¼ oz., 75c pkt., 10c.

4175 **Cuspidata or Star Mixed.**
Quaint and unusual flower formation. Pkt., 15c.

Phlox Nana Compacta Dwarf

These make symmetrical bushes, covered with flowers during the whole summer and fall. 8 in.

4183 **Fireball.** Blood-red.

4192 **Isabellina.** Buff yellow.

4200 **Salmon Pink.**

4189 **Snowball.** Pure white.
Each of the above, pkt., 20c; any 3 pkts. for 50c.

4205 **Nana Compacta Mixed.** All colors. ⅛ oz., 75c; pkt., 20c.

See also Novelties.

HARDY PHLOX—See Perennial Pages.

4220 PHLOX Vaughan's Special Mixture. Pkt., 15

Ricinus (Castor Bean) ☐

Culture: A or B, D or E, Page 65

Giant, strong growing plants, with ornamental foliage. These plants drive away moles from a garden.

4547 **Borboniensis Arboreus.** 15 ft. Immense plant with green foliage. Oz., 25c; pkt., 10c.

4546 **Crimson Spire.** 6 ft. Large purplish leaves changing to bronzy green. Stems, stalks and veins are rich red; seed spikes and seed pods are brilliant rosy crimson. Most showy of all. Oz., 50c; ¼ oz., 30c; pkt. 10c.

4555 **Sanguineus.** 7 ft. Whole plant reddish purple, very effective. Oz., 20c; pkt., 10c.

4570 **Mixed.** Many sorts. 1 oz., 25c; pkt., 10c.

4565 **Zanzibar Enormis.** 1 oz., 50c; ½ oz., 30 pkt., 10c.

4560 **Zanzibar Mixed.** 10 to 12 ft. The ornamental leaves, beautifully lobed, are 2½ to 4 ft. across. Each plant a perfect pyramid. Oz., 25c; pkt. 10

Periwinkle—See Vinca.

4370 POPPY Shirley Vaughan's Special Mixture. Pkt., 10c.

Shirley Poppies 2ft.

Culture: A, Page 65

Sow them early—since they defy frosts—and where they are to bloom, as they dislike transplanting. This flower in a few weeks from seed. Successive sowings should be made to provide continuous flowering. Mix the seeds with sand to scatter them, and thin out to 8 inches apart.

(SILK OR GHOST)

These have beautiful satiny flowers of various colors, all with white centers. Foliage is hairy and finely cut.

4277 **American Legion.** A dazzling orange-scarlet of enormous size. ¼ oz., 25c; pkt., 10c.

4296 **Dazzler.** All double orange scarlet. Pkt., 10c.

4238 **Double Begonia Flowered Sweet Briar.** Sweet Briar is a delightful shade of deep rose-pink. The blossoms are full double. Pkt., 10c.

4239 **Double Begonia Flowered Mixed.** The flowers resemble the double tuberous rooted Begonias in form, and contain an assortment of lovely light shades. Pkt., 10c.

4368 **Double Shirley Ryburgh Hybrids.** Beautiful double satiny flowers in shades of white, pink and old rose with white center. Pkt., 10c.

4295 **Eldorado Salmon Shades.** 2 ft. Pkt., 10c.

4280 **Wild Rose Shirley.** 20 in. Shades of rose and pink. Pkt., 10c.

4281 **White Shirley.** White flowers are very popular, they neutralize the effect of the brighter colors in a garden. Pkt., 10c.

4370 **Vaughan's Special Mixture of Shirley Poppies.** Lovely and dainty shades, many edged and shaded with other colors. 1 oz., 75c; ⅛ oz., 40c; ¼ oz., 25c; pkt., 10c.

4277 POPPY American Legion. Pkt., 10c.

4560 RICINUS Zanzibar Mixed. 10c.

4430 **PORTULACA** Single Mixed. Pkt., **10c.**

4455 **PORTULACA** Double Best Mixed. **15c.**

Portulaca ☐

Culture: A, D, Page 65

Moss Rose For Hot, Dry Places

Portulaca makes a brilliant carpet for a sunny spot where a ground cover is needed. Flowers like little Roses. In sowing, mix the seed with many times its bulk in dry sand. Sow in May, when the ground is thoroughly warmed. Easily transplanted. Fine for ground covers after bulbs have died down.

Large Flowering Single

4426 **Jewell.** See novelty pages for illustration and description. Pkt., 25c.

4430 **Single Mixed.** ¼ oz., 90c; ⅛ oz., 50c; pkt., 10c.

Large Flowering Double

A certain amount will produce single flowers.

4455 **Double Best Mixture.** Extra selected true double. 1 oz., $4.00; ¼ oz., $1.25; ⅛ oz., 75c; pkt., 15c.

Phacelia ☐ 8 in.

Culture: A, B, D or E, Page 65

4101 **Campanularia.** Sow where they are to grow. Dwarf plants bearing terminal racemes of gentian-blue flowers with conspicuous white anthers. Pkt., 10c.

4515 **PYRETHRUM Aureum Golden Feather.**

Culture: A or B, D or E, Page 65 ☐

6 in. Edging plant grown for its beautiful yellow foliage. Pkt., 10c.

Salpiglossis

See Salpiglossis in color on back page with collection offer on page 10.

Culture: A or B, Page 65

ONE of the easiest of annuals to grow, the Salpiglossis is rich in deep color tones rare in the floral world, which are set off by veins of gold, marking every flower. Its blossoms, similar in shape to a Petunia, on strong stems are borne profusely until frosts kill the plants. 30 inches.

4611 **Blue and Gold.**
4590 **Bright Crimson.**
4591 **Brown and Gold.**
4592 **Chamois.**
4600 **Rose and Gold.**
4613 **Scarlet and Gold.**
4614 **Velvety Red.**
4595 **Faust. Black.**
4610 **Golden Yellow.**
4598 **Purple.**
4599 **Purple and Gold.**
4605 **Velvety Violet.**
4616 **White and Gold.**
4617 **Violet and Gold.**

4601 **Rose Crimson and Gold.** Definitely a new color in Salpiglossis of English origin. The rich colored blooms are half again as large as the ordinary type.

Each of the above, pkt., 10c; any 3 pkts., for 25c.

4625 **Emperor Mixed.** Large improved strain. Complete range of colors. ⅛ oz., 25c; pkt., 10c.

4615 **Gloxiniaflora Mixed.** A special selection of the Painted Tube Tongue. Flowers large and fancifully veined in contrasting colors. Pkt., 10c.

> 4630 **Vaughan's Special Mixture.** This mixture is put up by ourselves of separate varieties and is without doubt the best mixture obtainable. ⅛ oz., 30c; pkt., 15c.

4620 **Dwarf Giant Flowered Salpiglossis.** See novelty page 16. Pkt., 20c.

Rudbeckia

Culture: A or B, D or E, Page 65

4581 **Indian Maid.** 4 in. Flowers, with rich brown center through artistic coppershades to golden tips. Some few semi-double or double rows of petals. Sown March 1, bloomed in 3½ months. Vigorous habit. Excellent for cutting. 30 in. Pkt., 25c.

8465 **Herbstwald Autumn Tints.** 2 ft. A perennial which blooms the first year from seed sown in March, furnishes starflowers of fiery autumn coloring called "Gerberas of the North." Pkt., 25c.

8467 **Double Kelvedon Star.** A double and semi-double form of Kelvedon Star. The lively shades golden yellow and mahogany are very attractive. Pkt., 20c.

4582 **My Joy.** Giant Black-Eyed Susans. Flowers very large, some over five inches in diameter, of an orange-yellow with rather small cone. Pkt., 15c.

4584 **Starlight.** Large-flowered, semi-double selection of Kelvedon Star, a free bloomer. Color from primrose yellow to mahogany and bicolors with mahogany centers. About 3 feet tall. Pkt., 25c.

4691 **SAPONARIA** Vaccaria Rose. Pkt., **10c.**

4630 **SALPIGLOSSIS** Vaughan's Special Mixture. Pkt., **15c.**

4690 **SANVITALIA** (Creeping Miniature Zinnia) Pkt., **10c.**

Sanvitalia ☐ 6 in.

Creeping Miniature Zinnia

Culture: A or B, D or E, Page 65

4690 **Procumbens.** Like tiny Zinnias, golden with purple centers, single and double. The plants creep over the soil. June until frost. ⅛ oz., 25c; pkt., 10c.

Saponaria (Soapwort)

Culture: A or B, D or E, Page 65

4693 **Vaccaria Alba.** White.

4691 **—Rose.** 2 ft. Light graceful sprays of glistening pink flowers, somewhat like a "glorified" Gypsophila, produced in profusion.

4692 **—Mixed.** **Each of the above, pkt., 10c.**

Scarlet Runner Emperor ☐

Culture: A, D or E, Page 65

4766 A stunning annual climber with sprays of brilliant red flowers like pea blossoms. The pods are edible. Good for arbors and fences. Pkt., 10c.

ANNUALS AND PERENNIALS For Semi-Shaded Locations

Anchusa Italica	Linaria
Antirrhinum	Linum
Aquilegia	Lobelia
Asperula	Lupin
Balloon Vine	Mimulus
Balsam	Myosotis
Begonia	Nasturtium
Bellis Perennis	Nicotiana
Campanula	Nemophila
Centaurea	Pansy
Clarkia	Platycodon
Coleus	Poppies
Cynoglossum	Schizanthus
Delphinium	Stocks
Digitalis	Sweet William
Geum	Torenia
Godetia	Violas

4746 **Annuals for Shade or Semi-Shade Mixed.** Pkt., 25c.

4747 **Perennials for Shade or Semi-Shade Mixed.** Pkt., 25c

4737 VAUGHAN'S Mixture of Super Scabiosa. Pkt, 25c.

Scabiosa (Mourning Bride)

Culture: A or B, D or E, Page 65

Sweet scabiosas have a soft fragrance and add beauty to the garden picture. They are fast growing annuals and one of the most important for cut flowers. Blooms on long, slender stems, which are exceedingly graceful; known as the Pincushion Flower because the stamens of some varieties are light in color and stick out so that they resemble pins stuck in a cushion.

COCKADE TYPE, 3 Ft.

Has conical form with attractive depth of flower.

4703 **Blue Cockade.** Pure deep azure.
4706 **Royal Cockade.** Salvia blue.

Each of above, pkt., 20c.

DOUBLE LARGE FLOWERING, 3 Ft. SPECIAL STRAIN

4715 **Azure Fairy.** Azure blue.
4727 **Loveliness.** Salmon rose shades.
4729 **Peachblossom.** Peachblossom pink.
4732 **Rosetté.** Deep rose suffused salmon.
4734 **Salmon Beauty.** Pure salmon.
4728 **Shasta Improved.** Enormous white.

Each of above, pkt., 15c; 3 pkts. for 40c.

4737 **Vaughan's Mixture of Super Scabiosa.** The above and other charming varieties. ¼ oz., 60c; pkt., 25c.

4731 **Blue Moon.** See novelties. Pkt., 15c.

STANDARD DOUBLE VARIETIES 2½ Ft.

4725 **Black Prince.** Black purple.
4720 **Cherry Red.** Crimson.
4742 **Coral Rose.** Rich pink.
4700 **Golden Yellow.** Sulphur yellow.
4710 **Fiery Scarlet.**
4735 **Pompadour.** Black purple, white tips.
4730 **Rose.** Bright rose.

Each of above, pkt., 10c; 3 pkts. for 25c.

DOUBLE DWARF VARIETIES

4744 **Heavenly Blue.** A lovely azure-blue very early. Plants are dwarf, 18 in., bushy, suitable for bedding. Pkt., 25c.

4738 **Peace.** Flowers are 2 in. across, almost spherical; pure white. 2-ft. Pkt., 25c.

4743 **Dwarf Double Mixed.** 1½ ft. Various colors. Do not require staking and are desirable for planting in front of the taller sorts. ⅛ oz., 25c; pkt., 10c.

See also Perennial Pages.

4740 **SCABIOSA** **Vaughan's Special Mixture.** Many new colors have been purchased for this and we are sure the delicate and soft colors will be admired by all our friends who plant a packet of this seed. ¼ oz., 35c; pkt. **10c**

Salvias

Culture: D or E, A or B, Page 65

The brilliant scarlet Salvia Splendens, so highly valued in summer beds, borders, window boxes and as cutflowers, is by no means the only worthy member of this family. The rich Wedgwood blue Salvia Farinacea Blue Bedder is increasingly popular in summer borders and the Indian Purple, a true violet purple, is most effective with Centauren Americana.

Splendens Type

4640 **America, or Globe of Fire.** 16 in. Freest and most continuous bloomer; also the most uniform in habit, which makes it particularly valuable for bedding or ribbon planting. Pkt., 25c.

4646 **Blaze of Fire.** 12 in. Earliest of all. The compact plants are mounds of brilliant scarlet, starting to bloom when only a few inches tall and continuing in bloom until late fall. Pkt., 25c.

4655 **Clara Bedman or Bonfire.** 2 ft. The spikes grow erect above the foliage forming handsome globular bushes. ⅛ oz., 75c; pkt., 25c.

4662 **Harbinger.** The plants are dwarf and compact and dark foliage is very effective against the vivid scarlet of the flowers; seeded indoors in February, will begin to flower in June and maintain a blaze of color until frost. Pkt., 25c.

4640 SALVIA SPLENDENS America. Pkt., 25c.

4683 SALVIA Farinacea Blue Bedder (in Background). Pkt., 20c.
5770 VINCA White (in Foreground). Pkt., 10c.

SALVIA—Continued.

4665 **Indian Purple.** A true-violet purple, similar in habit to Scarlet Sage, holding its color and flowers through the hottest summer. Gives striking effects in combination planting. Pkt., 25c.

4669 **St. John's Fire.** Brilliant scarlet spikes in profusion. Dwarf, early and continuous bloomer. Pkt., 25c.

4671 **Splendens.** The well known popular scarlet sage. ⅛ oz., 50c; ¼ oz., 85c; pkt., 20c.

4675 **Mixed.** All red varieties. Pkt., 10c.

Other Salvias

Cultures: A or B, D or E, Page 65

4683 **Farinacea Blue Bedder.** 2½-3 ft. A true Wedgwood blue. It makes a splendid background for all other colors in the border, and can be dried as an Everlasting. Is especially handsome when grown behind a line of pink Petunias or used as a cutflower with Marigold Yellow Supreme. Pkt., 20c.

4685 **Royal Blue.** Upright growth and of more intense color than Blue Bedder. Fine bushy plants, nice long spikes for cutting, and true. Pkt., 20c.

See also Novelty and Perennial Pages.

Schizanthus

Butterfly Flower or Poorman's Orchid

Culture: A or B, D or E, Page 65

Beautiful bushy plants covered with dainty flowers handsomely marked with contrasting colors.

4754 **Pansy Flowered (Danbury Park strain).** Large blooms of Pansy shape, in rich pink, crimson, mauve, purple and white. Pkt., 35c.

4755 **Dr. Badger's Hybrids.** An extraordinary strain in many beautiful colors. Pkt., 25c.

4762 **Retusus Mixed.** Pkt., 10c.

4757 **Vaughan's Excelsior Hybrids.** A choice strain with very large flowers with handsome markings on white, buff, brilliant rose, blue and purple ground. Pkt., 25c.

4753 **Vaughan's Dwarf "Masterpiece."** This is to our knowledge the best strain of Schizanthus in existence. The plants grow dwarf and compact, making them most suitable for pot culture. The flowers vary from light pink to dark violet, all with conspicuous blotches. Pkt. (100 seeds), 50c.

SENSITIVE PLANT—See Mimosa Pudica.

GIFT CERTIFICATES

Vaughan's Gift Certificates are available in any amount and redeemable at any time for our Merchandise.

4757 SCHIZANTHUS Vaughan's Excelsior Hybrids. Pkt., 25c.

4805 STATICE Sinuata Mixed. Pkt., 10c.

Statice □

For Winter Bouquets
Culture: D or E, Page 65

Our annual Statice is not only a beautiful flower in the border, but dries retaining its true colors, and is indispensable in making winter bouquets.

4800 Bonduelli Superba. 3 ft. Producing numerous heads of bright yellow flowers. Pkt., 10c.
4793 Puberula. 4-6 in. Flowers 5 months after sowing; magnificent dark violet blooms. Pkt., 25c.
4795 Russian (Suworowii or Rat Tail). 30 in. Flowers bright rose color. Dries well and can be used as an everlasting. ¼ oz., 25c; pkt., 10c.
4801 Sinuata Rosea Superba. 3 ft. Pkt., 10c.
4808 —Lavender Queen. Clear bright lavender. Pkt., 10c.
4806 —New Hybrids. One of our growers has selected Art Shades, which we offer in a mixture for the garden and winter bouquets. Pkt., 15c.
4803 —True Blue (Kampf's Improved). Pkt., 15c.
4804 —Pure White. 3 ft. Pkt., 10c.
4805 —Mixed. 3 ft. Pkt., 10c.

4795 RUSSIAN STATICE. Pkt., 10c.

4820 STAR OF TEXAS. Pkt., 25c.

Stocks □
Culture: A or B, D or E, Page 65

STURDY flower spikes covered with rosette blossoms in soft colors of an exceptional tone range. Stocks require a rich soil of a sandy, well manured loam. Only 60 per cent will come double. Sow seed early in the house and transplant outside when all danger of frost is over. Stocks are a cool temperature crop.

Column—Non Branching

An excellent new class producing one stem 2½ ft. thickly set with large, double flowers. The first flowers appear when the plant is about 14 inches high.

4950 **Ball Blue.** Dark lilac blue.
4951 **Chamois Pink.** 4956 **Silvery Lilac.**
4961 **Yellow Wonder.** Best yellow.
4960 **Rose Pink.** 4957 **White.**
4955 **Ruby.** 4958 **Mixed.**
4953 **Moonlight.** Light yellow.
Price, each of the above, pkt., 25c.

4865 STOCKS Best Mixed. Pkt., 10c.

4952 Double Giant Column Gardenia. Shimmering, glistening white, the flowers are the purest snow white of any stock variety yet introduced. Producing generally only one flower spike to a plant, this spike will however be of enormous size, 12" to 15" of florets and nearly 3 feet in length, and 4" or even 4½" in depth, with the individual florets closely and compactly placed on the stem. Pkt., 50c.

Bismarck or Giant Imperial

If sufficient room is given, the plants develop to enormous dimensions, forming magnificent bushes with long and thick flower stalks. The best variety for greenhouse use. 2½ ft.

4921 **Buttercup.** Yellow. 4946 **Chamois.**
4945 **Blood Red.** 4931 **Dark Blue.**
4944 **Elk's Pride.** Royal Purple
4947 **Flesh.** 4930 **Lilac.**
4948 **Golden Rose.** 4929 **Old Rose.**
4932 **Lavender.** 4925 **Shasta.** White.
Price, each of the above, pkt., 15c.
4949 **Bismarck Mixed.** ⅛ oz., 50c; pkt., 15c.

Dwarf Large-Flowering Double Ten Weeks Stock, 12 in.

4845 **Blood Red.** 4850 **Light Blue.**
4835 **Canary Yellow.** 4841 **Rose Pink.**
4856 **Dark Blue.** 4830 **White.**
Each of the above, pkt., 10c; any 3 pkts. for 25c.
4865 **Best Mixed.** ⅛ oz., 50c; pkt., 10c.

Pretty Star from Texas □
Culture: A, B, D or E, Page 65

4820 Star of Texas (Xanthisma Texanum). Bushy, 18-inch plants bear these bright yellow Daisies on wiry stems. Sow early in the open, plants bloom freely and like dry, sunny places. Pkt., 25c.

Runnerless Strawberry

4828 Baron Solemacher. This wonderful novelty has the largest berries in this strain. It makes no runners; flowers in eight weeks and produces quantities of fruit. Wash the berries, sprinkle with sugar several hours before using. The berries will almost float in juice. This brings out the flavor. Pkt., 25c.

5645 TORENIA Fournieri. Pkt., 15c.

Torenia (Wishbone Flower) □
Culture: D or E, A or B, Page 65

5645 Fournieri. Bushy globular plants literally covered with the lovely, richly-colored Snapdragon-like flowers of a delightful sky-blue with a touch of gold on the lip. Grown in southern states instead of Pansies, they flowered freely and grew vigorously during a hot and dry season in our Trial Grounds. Excellent for rock gardens, pots and hanging baskets. Pkt., 15c.

Annual Sunflowers

HELIANTHUS Large Flowered □
Culture: A or B, D or E. Page 65

2700 Gaillardia-flowered or Red Sunflower. 4 to 8 ft. Some flowers of a rich chestnut-red, others tipped with yellow, still others slightly washed with red. Pkt., 10c.
2709 Chrysanthemum Flowered Double. 3 to 4 ft. Select double golden yellow flowers. Pkt., 10c.
2703 Maroon Prince. Single best red. Pkt., 15c.
2713 Sun Gold. See novelty pages for illustration and description. Pkt., 15c.
2715 Double Mixed. Pkt., 10c.
2725 Russian Mammoth. 8 ft. Single, of gigantic dimensions. The Kansas Sunflower. Some of our friends grow these for support for their pole beans. Lb., 40c; ½ lb., 30c; ¼ lb., 20c; 1 oz., 10c.

Miniature-Flowered

2750 Cucumerifolius Stella. Purest golden yellow flowers, the petals of which are slightly twisted. Pkt., 10c.
2755 —Vaughan's Special Mixture. Includes many cucumerifolius sorts not listed. Pkt., 10c.

> **2760 Vaughan's Special Mixture.** Of all the single and double Sunflowers we list and several varieties we buy especially for this mixture. ½ oz., 25c; pkt., 10c.

Tahoka Daisy □ 20 in.
Culture: A or B, D or E. Page 65

5635 A beautiful lavender-blue Daisy with fern like foliage. Carried on good long stems, the flowers are tinted with rose as they fade, center deep yellow. Under open ground culture the plants are in bloom by middle of June and flower until October. Excellent for cutting. To get an even and quick germination, keep seed in refrigerator two weeks. Pkt., 25c.

Golden Flower of the Incas
TITHONIA □ 8 ft.
Culture: D or E, Page 65

5642 Avalon Earliest. The blossoms range from orange topaz through tangerine. Sow where the plants are to stand, after the soil is warm. By mid-July the plants will be in bloom. Pkt., 25c.

Trachelium □ 1 to 3 ft.
Culture: D or E, Page 65

5656 Coeruleum. Large cloudlike heads of tiny flowers resembling the Gypsophila produced in the fall from spring-sown seeds. Heliotrope blue in color, borne freely on branching stems, the flowers can be increased by pinching back the stems, making a fine pot plant. Pkt., 25c.

VIOLA CORNUTA. 5805 Yellow Gem Pkt. **20c.** 5806 White Perfection **10c.** 5804 Chantreyland Pkt. **25c.**

Thunbergia (Golden Glory Vine)

Culture: D or E. A or B, Page 65 □ 5 ft.
Germination 3-4 Weeks.

5640 Alata, Mixed (Black-Eyed Susan). A lovely plant with large showy flowers. Forming a dense mat of foliage and flowers. Colors range through yellow, orange, buff, to pure white, mostly with jet-black centers, or eyes. Seed germinates slowly. ¼ oz., 30c; pkt., 10c.

5639 Gibsoni. Glistening green ivy foliage and flowers of glowing orange. Pkt. (15 seeds) 35c.

5655 TRITOMA Hybrida Mirabilis (Red Hot Poker Plant). A perennial that blooms the first year. Pkt., 15c.

Texas Queen Anne's Lace □

Culture: A or B, Page 65.

5638. Large heads of tiny white flowers of lacelike appearance. Resembles Queen Anne's Lace of our roadsides, but more refined. Grows 3 to 5 ft. tall. Pkt., 10c.

THIMBLE FLOWER— See Gilia Capitata.

Viscaria □

Culture: D or E, Page 65

Very showy and effective garden annual, producing freely throughout the summer large single flowers in red, white and blue shades. Very bright and effective for beds and useful for cutting.

5776 Blue Bouquet. 1 ft. Large blue. Pkt., 10c.

5782 Blue Pearl. This is a distinct variety, differing from all other blue Viscarias, and entirely without an "eye." It is a pure lavender blue, the flowers borne in abundance. Pkt., 10c.

5784 Dwarf Fiery Red. A very showy and effective dwarf garden annual producing freely throughout the summer. Large single bright red flowers. Pkt., 15c.

5778 Mixed. 1 ft. Pkt., 10c.

5779 Dwarf Mixed. 8 in. Pkt., 10c.

Free Flowering Violas □

Culture: A or B, Page 67

BECAUSE of their free flowering habit and long season of bloom, Violas are becoming rapidly more popular for use in the foreground of the border, in small beds, and in rockeries, where their dwarf spreading habit is welcomed. They continue flowering all summer.

CORNUTA TYPE

5790 Blue Perfection. Light blue. Pkt., 10c.

5804 Chantreyland. Apricot, very free flowering. See illustration in color. Pkt., 25c.

5809 Ilona. Wine red. Pkt., 25c.

5796 Jersey Gem. Flowers of rich pure violet, large, fragrant, flowering persistently all summer. Pkt., 25c.

5806 White Perfection. Finest white. See illustration in color. Pkt., 25c.

5795 Nosegay. A blend of bright gay colors, red, yellow, blue and apricot, combined with many blotched combinations. Pkt., 25c.

Miscellaneous Violas

5797 Johnny-Jump-Up or Viola Tricolor. Also known as "Ladies' Delight" and "None so Pretty" of our grandmother's garden. It is a precious possession even if we have to weed out the plants when they get too ambitious and crowd out more delicate kinds. They are more hardy than their relative the Violas and if allowed to seed will carpet a rose or iris bed with a mass of flowers early in May. They bloom all season. Purple, blue and yellow are the three colors that give them their name-and the combinations are variable—sometimes there will be a yellow blossom and below it on the same stalk one of yellow and blue. Pkt., 25c.

5811A Nigra or Black Imp. Quaint little flowers that might have been snipped from black velvet, come true from seed. Maybe naturalized effectively. Blooms quickly first year from seed. Pkt., 25c.

5805 Yellow Gem. Free flowering clear yellow of compact habit, reproduced nearly true from seed. See illustration in color. Pkt., 20c.

CORNUTA HYBRIDS (Large Flowers)

5786 Apricot. Beautiful rich apricot shade, tinged orange towards the center. Pkt., 25c.

5787 Arkwright Ruby. Bright ruby crimson shaded terra-cotta; fragrant. Pkt., 25c.

5789 Blue Butterfly. Vivid mid-blue shading to white in the upper petals. Pkt., 25c.

5798 Lutea Splendens. 8 in. Bright yellow. 10c.

5813 VIOLA Vaughan's Special Mixture. A charming and delightful mixture of these bright and everblooming Violas in a complete color range, shading from pale lavender to rich purple-black, yellow, white, terra-cotta, apricot and rose. Pkt. **25c**

See Novelties.

Auburn, New York   March 15, 1943
I raised some Johnny Jump Ups last year and they were grand. Everyone admired them.
                                             J. M. R.

Venidium □

Culture: D or E, Page 65

5658 Fastuosum. 2 to 3 ft. Above the grayish silky foliage rise numerous orange flowers marked with a purple-black zone averaging four to five inches across. Treat as a half-hardy annual, sowing in March or April, as germination is difficult earlier. Plant in sunny position. Pkt., 25c.

5658A Fastuosum Hybrids. 2-3 ft. A race with colors from pure white through ivory, yellow and buff, set off by glistening black centers with maroon markings at base of petals. Pkt., 25c.

VERBESINA ENCELIOIDES—See Butter Daisies

Vinca Rosea (Periwinkle) □

Culture: D or E, Page 65

Ornamental free-blooming plants, with dark Laurel-like foliage and handsome pink and white flowers Seed germinates slowly but if sown early plants will bloom the first summer. They can be taken up in the fall, potted, and kept in bloom for the winter. 1 ft.

5770 White.   **5772 White with Eye.**

5771 Delicata. Soft pink. **5773 Pink.**

5774 Kermesina. Bright red, dark green leaves with red stems.

Each of the above, pkt., 10c.

5769 Twinkles. Large flowers of an unusual soft blush pink with a bright red eye. Pkt., 15c.

5775 Mixed. Pkt., 10c.

5775 **VINCA** Rosea Mixed. Pkt., **10c.**

Early Spencer Sweet Peas

Culture: D or E, Page 65

RACE of Sweet Peas, having the large waved flowers of the Spencer type but flowering fully one month earlier, and for a much longer period. This class is recommended for all sections where spring is late, as they give flowers before the summer heat arrives. ★Varieties preceded by star are fragrant.

Collection No. 5600. One Packet Each, Sweet Peas, Early Flowering Spencer

Amethyst, Daphne, Fiesta, Laddie Improved, Mrs. Herbert Hoover, Orange King, Sequoia, White Champion, Tahoe and Twilight for **75c**

Any of the packets below, 10c each; 3 packets for 25c.

343 **American Beauty.** Crimson-rose on white.

345 **★Amethyst.** Royal purple.

346 **Apollo.** Soft salmon cerise.

353 **Bacchus.** Rich red maroon.

354 **★Blue Bird.** Violet-blue.

352 **Boon.** Deep salmon-pink.

347 **Bridesmaid.** Silvery pink.

348 **Burpee's White.**

361 **Celestial.** Soft warm shade of cerise and salmon rose.

362 **Coquette.** Coral pink with amber and salmon shadings on duplexed flowers.

367 **Daphne.** Soft salmon-pink on cream ground.

411 **★Fragrance.** Large frilled lavender.

408 **Fiesta.** Almost deep enough to be an orange scarlet, definitely sun-proof.

415 **★Gardenia.** Fragrant white.

416 **★Giant Rose.** Extremely large rose-pink.

430 **Grenadier.** Dazzling scarlet.

438 **★Harmony.** Lavender.

470 **★Laddie Improved.** Light rose-pink.

485 **Miss Liberty.** Rose carmine on white ground.

488 **Mrs. Calvin Coolidge.** Rich salmon-pink.

495 **★Mrs. Herbert Hoover.** Clear deep blue.

5500 **Orange King.** Glowing orange.

5501 **Oriental.** Deep cream, black seeded.

5522 **Redwood.** Bright rich crimson.

5521 **Rhapsody.** Deep lavender base color that is enlivened by dainty rose pink tints.

5526 **Rhumba.** A glistening golden cerise, deeply duplexed.

5532 **Sequoia.** Rich golden salmon-cerise.

5539 **Snow Queen.** Pure white, black seeded.

5543 **Sparks.** Bright orange scarlet.

5546 **Tahoe.** Large wavy flowers, chicory blue.

5547 **Tops.** A fine salmon rose. Beautifully duplexed flower.

5552 **Triumph.** Lovely soft lilac mauve.

5554 **Twilight.** Medium clear lavender, large flowered and long stemmed.

5553 **Treasure Island.** A sparkling golden orange.

5555 **Valencia.** Bright orange, sun-proof.

5558 **Vulcan.** Vivid scarlet, sun-proof.

5560 **White Champion.** Long stemmed, pure white flowers.

5561 **★White Harmony.**

Inoculate Sweet Peas with Nitragin. Two garden sizes, 10c and 25c.

For PERENNIAL SWEET PEAS— See Lathyrus Latifolius on Perennial pages.

Heat-Resisting Summer Flowering Spencer

The introduction of these spring flowering or heat resistant varieties greatly prolongs the flowering period of Sweet Peas especially where the summers are very warm. The stems are longer than the early flowering varieties and the flowers come earlier and last longer.

5275 **Blackseeded White Improved**

5278 **Blue**

5276 **Clear Pink**

5279 **Lavender**

5282 **Light Blue**

5280 **Light Lavender**

5281 **Mauve**

5277 **Rose Pink**

Each of above, pkt. 20c; 3 pkts. 50c.

5285 **Mixed Heat Resisting New Early Flowering.** Pkt., 20c; ½ oz., 60c; oz., $1.00.

5285 **SWEET PEAS.** Heat Resisting Summer Flowering Spencer Mixed. Pkt., 20c.

5590 **Fragrant Varieties of Sweet Peas Mixed.** A mixture of the starred varieties noted in text. Large pkt., 25c; oz., 65c.

5595 **Vaughan's Special Mixture, Early Flowering Spencers.** All the varieties listed and many others. 4 oz., $1.50; 2 oz., 90c; oz., 50c; pkt., 15c.

5320 **Vaughan's Special Mixture, Late Spencer.** Named late flowering Spencer, varieties growing wonderful blossoms for a long period ¼ lb., 60c; oz., 25c; pkt., 10c.

5730 **VERBENA** Vaughan's Best Mixture.
Pkt., 15c.

Dwarf Compact Varieties—6 in.

This group is compact in habit, continuous bloomers, adapted for bedding, borders and small gardens.

5748 Blue Sentinel. Rich navy blue. Pkt., 25c.
5732 Chamois. Salmon buff.
5733 Dark Blue.
5735 Fireball.   **5740 White.**
5745 Carmine Ball. Ten inches high and 12 inches across, completely covered with bright carmine flowers.

5747 Splendor. Very compact, scarlet with white eye.
5742 Violet Bouquet. Deep violet with cream eye.

Each of the above, except when noted otherwise, pkt., 15c; any three 15ct. pkts. for 40c.

5789 Red, White and Blue Mixture
A mixture of large flowered Verbenas in red, white and blue are carefully blended in equal proportions. The effect is not only patriotic, but artistic. Pkt......... **15c**

Verbenas □

Culture: D or E, A or B, Page 65

These are colorful annuals for some sunny spot in the border. In bloom continuously. They make gay bouquets for table decorations. Do not sow the seed outdoors until the soil gets warm (May 15th to June 1st). May also be started earlier indoors to advantage. Grows only 6 to 12 inches tall but spreads to 2 feet across.

HYBRIDA Gigantea 1 ft.

A magnificent strain of Verbenas, of robust habit, the individual florets measuring an inch in diameter.

5701 Gigantea Alba. Pure white. Very fragrant.
5698 —Brightness. Bright rosy cerise scarlet, large white eye, semi-compact.
5700A —Brilliant. Rich deep flame rose with white eye. Pkt., 25c.
5702 —Cerise Queen. Salmon cerise.
5722 —Crimson Glow. A pure glowing crimson. Pkt., 25c.
5701A —Etna. Geranium-red, with a cream eye.
5718 —Lavender Glory. A true lavender with a medium-sized, creamy white eye. The color runs about 80% true. It is also distinctly fragrant.
5703 —Lucifer. Vivid scarlet self.
5704 —Luminosa. Luminous flame-pink to salmon.
5709 —Miss Willmott. Salmon-rose, white eye.
5705 —Rose Cardinal. Rose, white eye.
5706 —Rosea Stellata. Pink, white eye.
5719 —Royale. Royal blue, creamy yellow eye.
5710 —Spectrum Red. Intense bright red.
5720 —Spitfire. A strong scarlet rose self, showing only a trace of an eye. The liveliest color in this group: Pkt., 25c.
5717 —Sutton's Giant Pink. Salmon-pink, light eye.
5707 —Violacea Stellata. Deep violet, white eye.

Each of the above, except when noted otherwise, pkt., 15c; any three 15ct. pkts. for 35c.

5708 Gigantea Mixed. A wonderful mixture of large flowering varieties. Pkt., 15c.
5727 Golden Queen. The best yellow so far introduced. Medium sized cream colored flowers. Pkt., 15c.
5711 Beauty of Oxford Hybrids. A beautiful giant strain. Color shades from clear rose-pink to rose-red, making this the brightest rose Verbena ever produced from seed. Florets easily cover a silver half dollar. Pkt., 15c.
5712 Floradale Beauty. Beauty of Oxford type o rose shades, salmon-rose predominating. Pkt., 15c.
5713 Royal Bouquet, Finest Mixed. Upright, large flowers, auricula eyed, brilliant mixed, especially good for pot culture. Pkt., 15c.

5748 VERBENA Vaughan's Special Dwarf Mixture.
A formula mixture of named varieties of compact dwarf varieties of all colors, giving a brilliant effect in mass planting. Excellent for front yard and formal plantings. ⅛ oz., 60c; large pkt., 25c; pkt. ... **15c**

Various Verbenas

Culture: D, E or C, Page 65

5755 Erinoides. 12 in. Moss-like foliage spreads over the ground like a carpet, purplish-blue blossoms in lavish profusion. Blooms until frost. Pkt., 10c.
5751 Fern Leaved (Bipinnatifida). Plants grow 18 inches, spread over two square feet. with ferny, feathery gray-green foliage; covered by clusters of lavender-blue flowers, resembling sprays of lilac Candytuft. Pkt., 25c.
5765 Venosa. 1 ft. Largely used for bedding; covered with bright rosy heliotrope flowers. Sow in March in clear sand for quick germination. Blooms until frost, hardy with protection. An interesting combination when used with Marigold Harmony. Pkt., 10c.
5766 —Lilacina. 1 ft. Resembles Venosa, but with blossoms of lavender-blue. Hardy with protection. Pkt., 25c.
8566A Bonariensis. ① 4 ft. A grand perennial that blooms from seed the first year for the herbaceous border or for cutting. Sweet scented rosy lavender flowers on long stiff stems. Pkt., 15c.
5750 Lemon-Scented. ÷An old favorite with fragrant evergreen leaves. It is a low-growing tender plant and may be grown in the garden in summer and in pots in winter, and the leaves dried and laid among linens. Pkt., 25c.

6126 **ZINNIA**, Vaughan's Midget Mixed, 15c

Midget Zinnias

6196 Vaughan's Mixture of Midget Zinnias. Includes more than fifteen varieties, all delightfully charming in the garden and of just the size to make attractive table arrangements. Many o your friends will never recognize them as Zinnias Easy to grow and always covered with bloom. ⅛ oz., 35c; ¼ oz., 60c; pkt., 15c.
6125 Mexicana Fl. Pl. Hybrids. 16 in. Double flowers in various shades of brown and orange. 10c
6115 Mexicana or Miniature. Flowers small and showy. Daisy-like in form, range in color from yellow to mahogany red, free flowering. Excellent for decorative bowl arrangements. Pkt., 10c.

Wallflower ÷18 in.

Culture: D or E, Page 65

Wallflowers excel in adaptability for pot culture and out-door bedding and their fragrance and oriental coloring, rich reds and yellows. In the Northern state they should be wintered in cold frames.

5820 Single Mixed. Pkt., 10c.
5825 —Annual Blood-Red. Pkt., 10c.
5830 —Annual Golden Gem. Pkt., 10c.
5835 —Annual Mixed. Pkt., 10c.
5832 Annual Double Mixed. A fine pot plant will bloom first year from seed, if sown early. Pkt. 15c.

Wild Cucumber □ =

Culture: A or B, D or E, Page 65

5847 Quickest growing climber on our list. It is thickly dotted over with white fragrant flowers, followed by an abundance of ornamental and prickly seed pods. Sown on banks it will act as soil binder. If sown along a wire fence the vines will soon cover it and the dainty white flowers will make it a lovely sight for a long time. 1 oz., 25c; ½ oz., 15c; pkt., 10c.

Xeranthemum (Everlasting)

□ 2 ft.

Culture: D or E, Page 65

5852 Superbissima. One of the loveliest of the everlastings, with flowers which retain their brilliant colors remarkably well when dried, this double pompon flowered Xeranthemum may also be used as a cut flower when fresh. It makes delightful arrangements in small bowls. Pkt., 20c.

6175 ZEA Japonica Quadricolor Perfecta (Rainbow Corn). Striped and colored foliage; small ears, dark colors. Pkt., 10c.

KEY TO SYMBOLS
□ Annuals.   # Biennials.   ① Perennials.
÷ Greenhouse Plants.   + House Plants.
= Climbing Plants.   × Rock Garden Plants.

Small and Medium Flowered Zinnias □

Culture: A or B, D or E, Page 65

THEY bloom in much greater profusion than the larger types, standing well out above the foliage and registering as a color mass in the picture. They are also excellent for pot plants and cut flowers.

Pumila Double 18 in.
"Cut and Come Again"

On bushy plants 18 inches tall, fully double flowers are borne in abundance. The flowers average two inches across, and are held above the foliage on stout stems. They make fine border plants, registering color well, or excellent plants for large pots and tubs. They are also fine cut flowers.

6080 **Snow Ball.**   6095 **Fire Ball.**
6085 **Golden Ball.**
6097 **Pinkie.** Rose-pink. Plant this with No. 180 Ageratum Tall Blue for a charming effect.
6098 **Spun Gold.** A delicate butter-yellow or deep primrose, fine form.
6100 **Watermelon Pink.** A very pleasing and charming shade of salmon-rose.

Each of above, pkt., 10c; any 3 pkts., 25c.

6105 Pumila Vaughan's Special Mixed. Oz., $1.25; ¼ oz., 35c; pkt., 10c.

Pompon (Lilliput) or Baby Zinnias

The plants form handsome little bushes and fairly bristle with tiny, short-stemmed, very double flowers. They bloom all summer. 12 to 15 in.

6071 **Black Ruby.** Rich deep maroon.
6052 **Bright Pink.**   6064 **Purple.**
6073 **Canary Yellow.**   6065 **Salmon Rose Gem.**
6061 **Crimson Gem.**   6066 **Scarlet Gem.**
6062 **Golden Orange.** 6067 **White Gem.**
6068 **Rose Bud.** Rose-pink.
6069 **Valencia.** A real deep burnt orange.

Each of the above, pkt., 10c; 3 pkts. for 25c.

6075 **Lilliput Vaughan's Special Mixed.** All above and others. Oz., $1.25; ¼ oz., 35c; pkt., 10c.

6076 **Lilliput Pastel Mixture.** 15 in. A carefully chosen mixture of pastel tints of yellow, pink, rose and orchid. They flower in 45 days. Pkt., 15c.

6105 **ZINNIA** Pumila, Vaughan's Special Mixed. Pkt., **10c.**

6110 **ZINNIA** Red Riding Hood. Pkt., **10c**

A Favorite Border Plant

6110 **Red Riding-Hood.** 1 ft. Of compact form, covered the entire season with double scarlet flowers not over an inch across; as a border plant it is highly effective. A customer writes: "Just imagine clumps of little red flowers, with maybe a hundred blooms. They have been in flower all summer through the heat and drought. They make buds as soon as they get started and keep merrily on their way." Oz., $1.30; ¼ oz., 40c; ⅛ oz., 25c; pkt., 10c.

6172 **Navajo Mixed.** 18 in. Flowers abundant, of medium size, scarlet, orange and other hues suggesting Navajo Indian decorations. Pkt., 15c.

6071 **ZINNIA** Pompon Lilliput Black Ruby. Pkt., **10c.**

Cupid Type. The smallest of all. 1 ft.

Compact plants of bushy habit. Each upright stem bears a flower 1 in. in diameter. Ideal for cutting and for use in miniature vases.

6025 **Cupid Mixed.** ¼ oz., 35c; pkt., 10c.

6173 **Vaughan's Novelty Mixture.** All the new forms of the Zinnia, such as the Fantasy, Navajo, Striped and others. We recommend it to all interested in novelties. Pkt., 25c; 3 pkts., 65c.

6127 **ZINNIA** Linearis. Pkt., **15c.**

6127 **Linearis.** 10 in. The flowers, with a single row of petals, are one and one-fourth inches in diameter; at first each golden orange petal carried a greenish stripe down the center and a greenish tip, but as the flower developed, the green turned to light yellow, making a pleasing contrast with the orange of the outer portions. The quarter-inch orange center cushion turned dark as the flower developed. Early flowering. Pkt., 15c.

5896 **Fiesta.** Medium sized flowers are striped red and yellow, suggesting the colors of the Spanish flag so popular in Mexican Fiesta decorations. A gay variety for a sunny planting. Pkt., 25c.

Dahlia Type Zinnias

6171 6 PACKETS, CATALOG VALUE 90c.
One each of Crimson Monarch, Polar Bear, Illumination, Oriole, Royal Purple and Eldorado prepaid.

50c.

Zinnias are heat loving plants, and seed should not be sown until the ground and atmospheric conditions are warm If grown in a sunny spot in well fertilized soil and watered freely, the flowers will be more completely double.

Giant Dahlia Flowered Zinnias 2 to 3 ft. *Culture: A or B, D or E, Page 65*

The broad petals are closely imbricated, sometimes seeming almost to be piled one upon the other, the flowers often 4 inches in depth and 6 inches in diameter, resembling Show Dahlias.

6131 Canary Bird. A delicate shade of primrose.
6133 Crimson Monarch. Rich crimson, largest and best of red shades.
6131A Crown of Gold Desert Gold. Deep golden-yellow at the base of each petal, with light or deeper gold at the tip.
6134 Dream. A fine, deep lavender, turning to purple (Mallow Purple).
6134A Eldorado. Salmon apricot.
6135 Exquisite. Color light rose with center a deep rose.
6137 Golden Dawn. Beautiful shade of golden-yellow with red center.
6136 Golden State. A very rich orange-yellow. Yellow in the bud, turning to an attractive range when in full bloom.
6130 Illumination. A striking self-color of deep rose.
6128 Lemon Beauty. Lemon yellow turning to russet.
6130A Luminosa. Bright deep pink.
6142 Meteor. A rich glowing deep red, darkest of all red shades.
6129 Old Gold. Glowing burnished deep and lighter shades of old gold.
6138 Oriole. An immense orange and gold bicolor.
6139 Polar Bear. A very large pure white, the best white.
6143 Royal Purple. A deep rich reddish purple.
6141 Scarlet Flame. Bright scarlet.
Each of above .... Any four pkts., 50c; pkt., **15c**

6145 Giant Dahlia Flowered, Gold Medal Mixed. All the above and others, including a bewildering variety of delightful colors, all giant flowers. A very charming and delightful surprise will result if you plant this .... Oz., $1.50; ¼ oz., 50c; pkt. **15c**

Giants of New Race

5891 Zinnia David Burpee. 4 ft. This is a distinct strain of giant flowers, which is full of surprises, all of a pleasant nature. While giant flowers of the shaggy Fantasy type are most numerous, other forms are frequent; and colors include cream, chamois, buff, rose, burnt-orange, terra cotta, apricot and some two-toned. All are interesting, some exciting; a "surprise garden mixture" all by itself. Plants grow vigorously and flowers have long, wiry stems. Pkt., 15c.

5891 **ZINNIA**, Giant David Burpee. Pkt., **15c.**

ZINNIAS Giant Dahlia Flowered
6130A - Luminosa. Pkt., **15c.**
6133 Crimson Monarch. Pkt., **15c.**
6135 Exquisite. Pkt., **15c.**

6170 Vaughan's Special Mixture of all Giant sorts including the cream of the Dahlia Flowered and California Giants mixed. Producing a mass of color .... Oz., $2.00; ¼ oz., 60c; pkt. **25c**

California Giants

They are larger than Colossal and a cross between them and the Dahlia Flowered types. They have smaller flat centers with more loosely placed petals. The petals are decidedly imbricated and the flower graceful. Grow 3 to 4 ft. tall.

6161	**Brightness.** A bright, deep rose.	6163	**Miss Willmott.** Soft pink.
6164	**Cherry Queen.** Beautiful orange rose.	6151	**Orange King.** Rich, deep orange.
6161A	**Daffodil.** Canary yellow.	6167	**Pink Profusion.** Delicate shrimp pink.
6162	**Enchantress.** Giant flowers of light rose pink, early.	6153	**Purity.** A clean pure white.
6146	**Grenadier.** A very dark red.	6166	**Rose Queen.** Warm, deep rose, outstanding.
6147	**Lavender Gem.** A good clear lavender.	6154	**Salmon Queen.** Salmon.rose.
6164A	**Lemon Queen.** Lemon orange.	6165	**Scarlet Queen.** Glowing scarlet.
		6149	**Violet Queen.** Deep purple.

Each of the above, pkt., 15c; any 4 pkts. for 50c.

6156 **California Giants Vaughan's Special Mixed.** Made from a carefully prepared formula with due regard to color harmony and will make a gorgeous showing in beds or borders. Oz., $1.50; ¼ oz., 50c; pkt., 15c.

5901 **Super Crown of Gold Pastel Tints.** Strictly a mixture of pastel tints and contains a wide color range including soft yellow, old gold, light pink, apricot pink, various salmon shades, peach, and buff, lively cerise salmon as well as pure white and cream.   All the flowers carry the deep golden yellow base of the Crown of Gold types and the individual color at the tip. Midway between Dahlia Flowered and California Giants as to type. Pkt., 25c.

New Type Zinnias □

6159 **ZINNIA**, Scabiosa Flowered Mixed. Pkt., 15c.

5908 **ZINNIA**, Fantasy Mixed. Pkt., 15c.

New Crested Type

Scabiosa Flowered or Harmony 2 ½ ft.

6159 **Mixed.** On a single corona of outside petals stands a crown of small florets similar in form to the flowers of the Scabiosa. ¼ oz., 60c; pkt., 15c; 3 pkts., 40c.

6160 **Autumn Tints Mixed.** This strain comes true in all the gorgeous autumn tints, including orange to terracotta. Pkt., 15c.

6159A **Campfire.** Vivid intense scarlet. Pkt., 15c.

6160A **Sunburst.** Bright canary yellow. Pkt., 15c.

Fantasy, Shaggy Type

2 ½ ft. Shaggy ray-like petals, like Cactus Dahlia.

5912 **Orange Lady.** Bright deep orange.

5911 **Rosalie.** Intense rose.

5909 **Star Dust.** Deep golden yellow.

5913 **White Light.** Pure white.

5914 **Wildfire.** Rich dazzling scarlet.

Each of the above, pkt., 15c; 2 pkts. for 25c.

5908 **Mixed.** A bright colorful mixture of shaggy petaled double flowers. ¼ oz., 60c; pkt., 15c.

ZINNIAS California Giants

6163	Miss. Wilmott.	**Pkt., 15c.**
6164A	Lemon Queen.	**Pkt., 15c.**
6166	Rose Queen.	**Pkt., 15c.**

Perennial Flower Seeds and Plants

For Additional Perennial Seeds and Plants See Also Pages 57 to 63 Inclusive.

NOTE—All plants are F. O. B. our Greenhouses, Western Springs, Illinois. Postage must be added to cover cost of transportation at rates noted on page 57, or they will be sent express at buyer's expense.

7195 **ARABIS** Alpina Rock Cress. Pkt., 10c.

Arabis (Rock Cress) ①
Culture: D or E, Page 65

Spreading dwarf, spring-flowering plants. They do well in any soil, but need plenty of sun.

7195×**Alpina.** 1 ft. April. Pure white. Pkt., 10c.
7198A—**Snow-cap.** Extremely dwarf and compact habit; really shining, snow-white cushions of flowers. Pkt., 15c.
7197×—**Rosea.** 1 ft. May. Compact rosettes of foliage and pink flowers. Pkt., 35c.

Carnation ①
Culture: B, D or E, Page 65

GRENADIN
A valuable bedding variety with double flowers, blooming first year from seed if sown early. 20 in.

7390 **King of the Blacks.** Darkest red, very fine. Pkt., 25c.
7398 **Golden Sun.** Early flowering, very double, large clear yellow flowers. Pkt., 35c.
7395 **Scarlet.** 25c.   7400 **White.** 25c.
7385 **Triumph, Rose.** 25c.   7401 **Mixed.** 25c.

7401 **CARNATION** Grenadin Mixed. Pkt., **25c.**

Columbines ①
Culture: B, C, D or E, Page 65

ONE of the best-known and best-loved perennials. Dwarf varieties for the rock-garden, tall varieties for the border and for cutting. They are easily grown from seed, prefer light shade, and thrive in any fairly rich soil. These plants covered with dancing, quivering blossoms, add grace and airiness to any garden.

7151 **Dobbie's Imperial Hybrids.** A strain with large, long-spurred flowers in strong, brilliant tones of all colors. Pkt., 25c.

7150 **Mrs. Scott Elliott's Strain of Long-Spurred Hybrids.** The blooms are of large size and the spurs very long. The colors range through shades of lavenders, mauves, blues, purples, whites, creams, yellows, pinks, reds, etc., with soft pastel tones dominating. Pkt., 25c. **Plants, 3 for $1.15; doz., $3.50; ea., 45c.**

7119×**Alpina.** Powder blue. 2 ft. April-July. Pkt., 15c.
7121 **California Hybrids.** 3 ft. Long spurred, dark carmine-lake. Pkt., 20c.
7120 **Canadensis (American Columbine).** 1 to 2 ft. May-July. Scarlet and orange. Pkt., 10c.
7125 **Chrysantha.** 3 to 4 ft. May-August. Yellow, long spurred. Pkt., 15c.
7126 —**Silver Queen.** 3 ft. Long spurred silvery white flowers. Pkt., 25c.
7140 **Coerulea (Rocky Mountain Columbine).** 1 to 2 ft. April-July. One of the most beautiful of native flowers. Sepals, deep blue; petals, white. Pkt., 10c.
7141 —**Mrs. Nicholls.** This is a glorified Rocky Mountain Columbine with larger flowers, long spurs, and strong habit. Pkt., 50c.
7145 —**Rosea (Rose Queen).** 2½ ft. Light to dark rose, white center. Pkt., 25c.
7131 **Clematiflora.** Mixed. Spurless Columbine with beautiful open flowers like Clematis. Contains all lovely pastel shades. Pkt., 25c.
7142 **Colorado Rainbow Hybrids.** Including blue, yellow, white, lavender, orchid, purple, three shades of red, all pink, pink and white, red and white and red and yellow. Pkt., 25c.
7148 **Flabellata Nana Alba.** A charming dwarf variety for the rock garden, perfect foliage and ivory-white flowers, plant 8 to 10 inches. Pkt., 25c.
7143 **Longissima.** A beautiful American species having 4 inch spurs on flowers of a delicate pale yellow. One of the most attractive. Pkt., 50c.
7144 **Longissima Hybrids.** A new race obtained by crossing Mrs. Scott Elliott's with Longissima. All the beautiful hues, in red, blue, white, rose, etc., of the former, long spurs and broader petals. They are hardier and more lasting. Pkt., 50c.
7158 **Long-Spurred Blue.** Splendid selection from light to dark blue. Pkt., 25c.
7156 **Long-Spurred Crimson Star.** The brightest red Columbine, long spurs and outer petals rich crimson, center petals white. Three-inch flowers on 2-foot stems. Pkt., 25c. **Plants, 3 for $1.35; doz., $4.25; each, 55c.**

7156 **COLUMBINE** Long. Spurred Crimson Star. Pkt., **25c.** Plants, 3 for **$1.35;** each, **55c.**

7190 · **AQUILEGIA.** Vaughan's Special Mixture. Pkt., **25c.**

7157 **Long-Spurred Copper Queen.** Lovely deep copper with long spurs of deeper hue, while the inside of the corolla is buff. Pkt., 50c.
7159 **Long-Spurred Orange and Scarlet.** Many unusual tones. Pkt., 35c.
7166 **Suaveolens.** 25 in. A rare perennial from the Himalayan Mountains. Flowers of cream and lilac with rich perfume. Lacy foliage. Pkt., 25c.
7190 **Aquilegia Vaughan's Special Mixture.** Includes a complete collection including the Long Spurred, and the Non-Spurred types, the tall and dwarf sorts. Pkt., 25c. **Plants, 3, $1.15; doz., $3.50; each, 45c.**

Perennial Campanulas ①

Seed sown one year, plants will bloom the next and for several years following, increasing in size each year.

7260 ✕ Carpatica (Harebell) Blue. 9 in. June to Aug. Forms tufts of neat foliage above which are borne cup-shaped, upright blooms of a glistening light violet-blue, freely produced. Splendid for edging. Likes partial shade. Pkt., 10c.

7265 ✕ —Alba. 9 in. July. Pure white. Pkt., 10c.

7331 ✕ Garganica. Beautiful star-shaped sky-blue flowers fairly cover the trailing plants, excellent for rock gardens. Pkt., 15c.

7335 Lactiflora Coerulea. Broad-leaved, 2½-3 ft. July. Light blue. Pkt., 15c.

7344 Persicifolia (Peach Bells). Blue. 2-3 ft. June-July. Fine border plant. Pkt., 25c.

7345 —Alba. White. Pkt., 25c.

7350 —Mixed. Blue and white. Pkt., 25c.

7346 —Telham Beauty. 4 ft. It produces on long stems very large globular open flowers of a lovely china-blue with silvery shading. Pkt., 25c.

7347A—Wedgwood. Large flowers of deep violet blue, good in full sun or partial shade. Pkt., 35c.

7367 Rapunculoides. Spikes of loosely swung bell-blossoms, beauty for months on end. Variable coloring from soft blue to deep violet. A row of it becomes a hedge of bloom, and it has perhaps the longest flowering season of any campanula. Pkt., 20c.

7355 Pyramidalis (Chimney Bellflower). Blue. 5-6 ft. August-Sept. Pkt., 10c.

7365 Pyramidalis Mixed. Pkt., 10c.

7354 Punctata. 28 in. Plants form rambling foliage mats from which arise flower stalks of varying height from which hang big, pendant bells not unlike a Foxglove, which are waxen without, downy within. Colors range from translucent creamy pink, through lilac to purple. Pkt., 20c.

7366 ✕ Rotundifolia (Blue Bells of Scotland). 6-12 in. Matted foliage, slender, branching stems, covered with dainty frail blue flowers. Blooms generously in July and again in fall. Pkt., 15c.

7370 Vaughan's Special Mixture of Campanulas. A grand assortment of all varieties. Fine for cut flowers. Pkt., 25c.

Hardy Pinks

(Dianthus)

Culture: B, D or E, Page 65

In the rockery and in the border the Dianthus family is of value. Most of them grow easily from seed, thrive in ordinary soil which must contain some lime, and should be in a well-drained situation.

7576 ✕ Allwoodi Alpinus. 6 in. Flower first year from seed. It has single and semi-double flowers in all Dianthus colors. Is a perfect gem for the rock garden. Pkt., 50c.

7575 Allwoodi Mixed. The flowers are about 75 percent double and all colors except yellow. The single flowers have the advantage of making large clusters. It is exceptionally hardy and flowers from early spring until fall. Pkt., 25c.

7579 ✕ Arenarius (Sand Pink). 6 in. Flowers white, fringed, fragrant, forming a dense carpet. Pkt., 25c.

7578 ✕ Atro-coccineus (Everblooming Sweet William) Cruentus. 15-18 in. Crimson, semi to full double flowers. Pkt., 10c.

7579A Carthusianorum Giganteus. The tallest Dianthus we know, established plants bearing clustered blossoms of crimson pink opening from varnished mahogany buds on stems fully 40 inches. Pkt., 25c.

7580 ✕ Caesius (Cliff Pink). 1 ft. Flowers delicate rose pink, fragrant. Pkt., 25c.

7580A Delight. 9 in. It has a neat, erect habit of growth, continuously in flower from June until October, producing flowers about an inch in diameter, not in trusses, but in alternating spikes in great profusion. There is a bewildering range of colors from the palest pink to purple. Pkt., 35c.

7582 ✕ Deltoides Brilliant (Maiden Pink). 8 in. Delicate pink blossom carried above fine, feathery foliage. Pkt., 25c.

7588 —Major Stern. A free-flowering form with bright crimson flowers and dark foliage. Pkt., 35c.

7583 ✕ Graniticus. 4 in. Low growing, forming dense carpet covered with crimson flowers in May and June. Pkt., 25c.

7581 Knappii. A yellow "Hardy Pink," unusual color for this family. Clusters of clear golden yellow flowers above grassy green foliage. Pkt., 25c.

7631 Loveliness. The flowers have large laciniated petals of a most exquisite mauve-pink, with delightful fragrance. Pkt., 25c.

7625 **DIANTHUS** Plumarius' Vaughan's Special Mixed. Pkt., **25c.** Plants, 3 for **$1.15.**

HARDY PINKS—Continued

7587 Best Rock Garden Varieties, Mixed. Rock gardens now so popular need the low growing Dianthus to brighten spots and fill in crevices with its attractive flowers. Pkt., 25c.

7592 Winteri. The flowers are of pure colors; habit compact; flowers first year from seed; deliciously scented. Pkt., 50c.

PLUMARIUS (Clove or Grass Pinks)

Plumarius is the old-fashioned, fragrant garden Pink. Fine for perennial border or rockwork.

7591 ✕ Albus Plenus. Double white. Pkt., 25c.

7620 ✕ Double Mixed. Fine for cutting. Pkt., 10c.

7590 Cyclops Red Hybrids. A fine mixture of perpetual flowering red shades. Pkt., 25c.

7585 Highland Hybrids. Tall, strong stemmed pinks in varied colors, beautifully marked and zoned. Pkt., 35c.

7595 Little Jock Hybrids. 6-8 in. Compact plants produce a multitude of fringed flowers, an inch across, in pink, rose and white, 50 per cent double. Pkt., 35c.

7605 ✕ Nanus Fl. Pl. 1 ft. Double dwarf mixed. 15c.

7632 Scoticus Double Special Strain. Self colors of various tints of pink, rose, salmon and white and the same colors in combination with a bright crimson zone. Stems 12 to 15 inches. Blooms 1½ to 2 inches. Free flowering. Pkt., 35c.

7609 ✕ Spring Beauty. Double giant-flowered Grass Pinks, Carnation-like in form and size and with a beautiful range of color. Very fragrant. Pkt., 25c.

7615 ✕ Single Mixed. Delicately fringed. Pkt., 10c.

7625 ✕ Vaughan's Special Mixture. A grand selection of Clove Pinks of the above Plumarius type and others. Pkt., 25c. **Plants,** 3 for $1.15; doz., $3.50; ea. 45c.

Little Joe. The most interesting recent Dianthus introduction. 3 inches high with blue spiney foliage; single, deep crimson flowers. Blooms heavily and continually from spring until frost. Disease resistant. Each, 60c. 3 for $1.50; doz., $4.75.

DIANTHUS Little Joe Plant each 60c.

Hardy Delphiniums ①

Culture: B, D or E. Page 65

Modern hybrid Delphiniums have become the dominant flowers in the perennial border of late June. In deep, rich soil, they grow six feet tall or more, with huge spikes of large flowers, varying in colors from the darkest violet to pale lavender. Lower growing types are also valuable for both border and cut flower use; the Chinese and Butterfly types are fine for bedding.
NOTE—A teaspoonful of sugar in the water will delay shattering of cut Delphiniums two or three days.

Pacific Giant Hybrids

▶ **Illustrated on the left. Top to bottom:**
1 BLUE JAY   3 GALAHAD
2 GUINEVERE   4 SUMMER SKIES
              5 KING ARTHUR

The new strain produces plants that are 60 to 65 per cent mildew resistant. The flowers are of immense size, tightly set on straight stems that are strong and whippy. The flowers do not shatter and represent a truly outstanding addition to the midsummer garden.

7563 Black Knight. Deep midnight violet of beautiful round form and heavy velvety texture.

7559B Blue Bird. Clear medium blue with white eye with huge tall spikes.

7559A Blue Jay. From medium to dark blue with dark bee.

7568A Cameliard Series. Pure lavender self, white bee.

7560 Galahad. Clear glistening white.

PRICE. Each of the above large packet (containing about 200 seeds) $1.00 per packet. Smaller packets (containing about 100 seeds) 50c per packet.

7561 King Arthur. Royal violet, large white bee.

7561A Guinevere. Light pink lavender, white bee.

7562 Summer Skies. Light blue with white bee.

7562A Clear White. Of glistening texture.

7559 Round Table Series Mixture. All the above Knights and their Ladies.

PRICE. Each of the above, large packet (containing about 200 seeds) 75c per packet. Smaller packets (containing about 100 seeds) each 40c per packet.

STANDARD COLORS OF PACIFIC GIANTS
7556 Dark Blue Shades.
7557 Light Blue Shades.
7558 Lavender Pastel. Color range from lavender, generally of two tone combinations, brown or black bees.
7558A Mixed. The three varieties of the above standard sorts.

PRICE, Each of the above, 50c per packet.

Plants of Pacific Giant Delphiniums

Strong 1-yr. plants of Blue Jay, Galahad, Guinevere, Summer Skies or White. 3 for $1.50; doz. $4.75; ea. 60c. Field grown mixed shades 3 for $1.35; doz. $4.25; ea. 55c.

Dianthus Barbatus ①

Single Sweet William
Culture: B, D or E. Page 65

Among the early hardy plants, they are outstanding. They appreciate rich soil. To be sure of large plants and flowers, sow new seed each year. 18-24 inches. May-June.

7670 Atro-sanguineus. Blood-red. Pkt., 10c.
Homeland. See Novelty Pages.
7655 Nigrescens. Dark foliage and flower. Pkt.,10c.
7660 Newport Pink. Salmon-pink. Pkt., 10c.
7661 Purple Beauty. Bright deep purple. Pkt., 10c.
7635 Scarlet Beauty. Vivid orange or salmon scarlet. Pkt., 15c.
7685 Single Giant-Flowered Mixed. Pkt., 10c.

Double Varieties

Seedings of all double Sweet William produce about 40% of single blooming plants.

7703 Nigrescens (Black).   **7700 Blood-Red.**
7705 Mixed.

Each of above, pkt., 10c.

7710 Giant Double Mixed. A decided improvement. The plants are of robust, bushy habit, producing numerous stems surmounted by immense umbels of full, double flowers, many of the individual flowers measuring over one inch in diameter. The colors are extremely varied. Pkt. 10c.

Other Species of Hybrids

7550 Belladonna Improved Cliveden Beauty. 2 ft. June-July. Exquisite turquoise blue. These and Thermopsis Carolina (Yellow) are charming when combined in bouquets. Pkt., 20c. Plants, 3 for $1.15; doz., $3.50; ea. 45c.

7552 Bellamosum Improved. Large deep blue flowers, uniform in color, with a white bee. Blooms 2½ inches across. Pkt., 25c.

7564 Blackmore and Langdon Strain. A famous English strain. All the clear shades of blue, with bees of contrasting colors. Pkt., 35c.

7547 Cardinale. "Scarlet Larkspur," a native California species with long spikes of scarlet flowers, seed germinates slowly. 2-3 ft. Pkt., 25c.

Chinese. See page 33.

7523 Chinese Blue Mirror. See novelty pages. Pkt., 125 seeds. 35c.

7555 Indigo (True Blue). 3 ft. Pure indigo-blue, comes true from seed. Pkt., 35c.

7542 Lamartine. It makes a sturdy, vigorous, healthy plant five feet tall which blooms from June until frost. The flowers are a rich, deep blue with a pure white eye. We have seen flower spikes of these gorgeous flowers over two feet in length. Perfectly hardy, easy to grow and succeeds everywhere. Seeds, pkt., 25c. Plants, 3 for $1.15; doz., $3.50; ea. 45c.

7569 Wrexham Hollyhock-Flowered Strain, Mixed. Giant-flowered strain of superior quality. Flowers in blue, white and pink combinations; many of them bicolor 1½ to 2 inches in diameter, many double.
Mixed Color Seed Pkt., 50c. PLANTS. 3 for $1.25; doz., $3.75; ea. 50c.

7570 Vaughan's Gold Medal Hybrids. This strain is especially grown for us, the seed being saved from selected plants. Many of them are double flowered, and range in color from pale lavender to indigo-blue. Pkt., 25c.

7571 DELPHINIUM Vaughan's Special Mixture. This contains the Elatum varieties, both double and single, the Butterfly, Chinese and all the other various kinds. Pkt., 35c.

Homer, Alaska, July 1943
"Your Surprise Garden sure is a fine mixture of beautiful flowers. We enjoy wonder 'What will it look like.' I have very good luck with your flower seed way up here in Alaska."—Mrs. J. N. F. Sr.

7715 SWEET WILLIAM Vaughan's Special Mixture of all listed and others. Pkt., **25c.**

7775 **DIGITALIS** Vaughan's Special Mixture.
Pkt., **15c.** Plants, 3 for **$1.15;** each, **45c.**

7719 **DICENTRA** Spectabilis.
Pkt., **35c.** Plants, 3 for **$1.75.**

7852 **GEUM** Lady Stratheden. Pkt., **35c.**
7855 **GEUM** Mrs. Bradshaw. Pkt., **25c.**

Digitalis (Foxgloves) ①

Culture: B, D or E, Page 65

These are biennials and should be sown very early in the spring so plants will be large enough to flower the following year. They should be wintered in a cold frame where sub-zero temperatures are common and always in a well drained place, as their crowns remain green all winter. The tall nodding spires of Foxglove are at home in any garden, but they are most effective against a suitable background of foliage.

7745 Gloxiniaeflora Mixed Colors. Pkt., 10c.
7768 —The Shirley Hybrids. 6 to 7 ft. The flower-heads are over 3 ft. long, covered with big bell-shaped blossoms from white and shell-pink to deep-est rose. Pkt., 25c. **Plants,** 3 for $1.15; each, 45c.
7750 Grandiflora or Ambigua. 2 to 3 ft. June-July. Yellowish flowers marked with brown. A true perennial. Pkt., 10c.
7771 Laevigata. A dignified and handsome peren-nial Foxglove. Bronzy yellow flowers with whitish lip. Pkt., 25c.
7769 Lutzii Hybrida. 4 ft. The spikes are strong and heavily laden with salmon-rose bells. Pkt., 20c.
7760 Monstrosa Mixed. Long spikes surmounted by one enormous flower. Pkt., 10c.
7761 Nevadiensis. 40 in. Slender wand-like stems that carry all their length many florets of soft cream. The blooms face one way, and their weight bends the stems, giving a graceful appearance. Cut blooms also lend themselves to effective decorative arrangements. Pkt., 25c.
7770 Orientalis. Blossoms of silvery down, on cream, all overlaid with an even netting of chestnut brown. An odd and attractive species. Pkt., 25c.
7749 Princess, Pastel Mixture. 4 ft. Here is really a new flower for your garden—a Foxglove in dis-tinctly new pastel tints of pink, apricot, buff, rose and heliotrope. Pkt., 15c.
7773 Vaughan's Special Mixture of Digitalis. The above, and other colors. Pkt., 15c. Plants, 3 for $1.15; doz., $3.50; each, 45c.

Dicentra (Dielytra) ①
(Bleeding Heart or Seal Flower)

Culture: B or C, Page 65

Best sown in fall; needs freezing to germinate.
7718 Eximia (Plumy Bleeding Heart). Dwarf; reddish purple. May and June. 12 in. Pkt., 25c.
7719 Spectabilis. Its long racemes of graceful heart-shaped pink flowers are always attractive. Is perfectly at home in any part of the hardy border, especially in the shade. Pkt., 35c. PLANTS, 3 for $1.75; doz., $5.50; each, 65c.

Gaillardias ①

Culture: B, D or E, Page 65

For cheerful, long-lasting garden color, Gaillardias are indispensable. Groupings of them here and there in front of shrubs will provide splotches of color for weeks and weeks. A rich light soil is essential and they require a sunny situation to do well.

7809 Grandiflora Monarch Strain. A robust strain very varied in coloring and with flowers of giant size and perfect form. Pkt., 25c.
7812 —Burgundy. 2 ft. Shining wine-red flowers, 2½ in., from June until fall. Blooms same year, sown early. Pkt., 25c. **Plants,** 3 for $1.15; doz., $3.50.
7811 —Dazzler. Large golden yellow flowers with rich maroon center. Pkt., 25c.
7817 —Goblin. 12-15 in. First real dwarf, cov-ered with showy deep red flowers yellow bordered. Flowers first year from seed. Pkt., 25c.
7836 —Portola Hybrids. 2½-3 ft. The flowers are nearly 4 inches; brilliant scarlet intensified by golden yellow tip. Pkt., 25c.
7831 —Tangerine. Compact grower. Large tan-gerine orange-colored flowers. Pkt., 25c.
7818 —The King. Special strain with enormous flowers, deep red, edged gold. Pkt., 25c.
7819 —Torchlight. Bright golden yellow flower[s] with a rich maroon center. Pkt., 15c.
7810 —Mixed. Composite flowers variegated with shades of red and yellow. Pkt., 10c. **Plants,** 3 for $1.15; doz., $3.50.
7820 Sungod. See Novelties.

Geum ①

Culture: B or C, D or E, Page 65

Geums are showy, producing a wealth of attractive flowers much prized for cutting. Excellent for border.

7851 X Borisii. An evergreen species with foliage rather prostrate and the branching flower stems 8 to 12 in. long. Orange scarlet flowers. Pkt., 25c.
7852 Lady Stratheden (Golden Ball). 2 ft. Flowers loosely double; a delightful shade of golden yellow. Pkt., 35c.
7855 Mrs. Bradshaw. 2 ft. The double orange-scarlet flowers are very large and full. June-Sept. Pkt., 25c.
7853 Orange Queen. 2 ft. Flowers large and semi-double, of a beautiful orange-scarlet. Pkt., 25c.

Hibiscus (Rose Mallow) ①
(3 to 5 Feet)

Culture: B, D or E, Page 65

In the late summer, when perennials are few, well established plants of Mallow bear their beautiful single flowers, 3 to 5 inches, several weeks. Aug.-Sept.

7945 Crimson Eye. Creamy white flowers, large crimson center. Pkt., 10c.
7950 Golden Bowl. Deep cream, with a velvety maroon center. Pkt., 10c.
7946 Jumbo Red. A special selection made to im-prove color and size of the flower of the Mallow Marvels Red. Pkt., 15c. **Plants,** 3 for $1.35; doz., $4.25; each, 55c.
7960 Mallow Marvels, Mixed. Pkt., 10c. **Plants,** 3 for $1.15; doz., $3.50; each, 45c.
7965 —Red. Pkt., 15c.
7966 —Pink. Pkt., 15c.

7960 **HIBISCUS** Mallow Marvels Mixed.
Seeds, pkt., **10c.** Plants, 3 for **$1.15.**

7809 **GAILLARDIA** Monarch Strain. Pkt., **25c.**

7812 **GAILLARDIA** Burgundy. Pkt., **25c.**

Vaughan's Seed Store 55

8015 HOLLYHOCKS Vaughan's Prize Double Mixture. Pkt., 10c. Plants, 3 for **$1.15**.

Hollyhocks ①

Culture: B, D or E. Page 65

Hollyhocks are most decorative and the great spikes of bloom are "Towers of Beauty" to the garden picture. Following Delphiniums in the border show, have a long season of bloom which can be prolonged by picking off faded flowers, and a second crop will come if the first stalks are cut back. Need well drained location.

Hollyhock rust can be overcome by treating the plant as a biennial, sowing the seed early one year for flowering the next, as it is a well known fact rust seldom attacks young plants.

Double Varieties

7971 Colorado Sunset.	7980 Rose.
7995 Crimson.	7990 Salmon.
7972 Deep Salmon Red.	7970 White.
7975 Maroon.	7992 Yellow.
8004 Lilac Beauty.	A clear bright lilac color.
8005 Newport Pink.	The finest pure pink.
8001 Purple Robe.	Deep purple.
8000 Palling Belle.	Lovely silvery pink flowers.

Each of above, pkt., 10c.

PLANTS. Mixed Colors, 3 for **$1.15**; doz., **$3.50**; ea. **45c.**

8008 Begonia Flowered Imperator, Mixed. Flowers with broad collar of frilled and fringed petals and double center rosette. Mixture containing many interesting, attractive combinations of colors. Pkt., 25c.

8015 Vaughan's Prize Double Mixture. Finest shades in perfect flowers. Pkt., 10c; ¼ oz., 50c.

8010 Allegheny Mixed. Flowers come single, semi-double and double, about 5 inches across. Pkt., 10c.

8007 Mixed "Souvenir de Madam Perrin." Semi-double flowers, notched or toothed at the edge in lovely shades of yellow and pink. Pkt., 25c.

8016 Vaughan's Special Mixture. This mixture is composed of all the best double varieties as well as two new French strains, not offered before. A most interesting combination. Pkt., 25c.

Single Varieties

More permanent and hardy than the double and if planted with a deep green background, such as arborvitae hedge, they afford a most striking effect.

8045 White.	8040 Rose.
8051 Yellow.	8020 Red.
8030 Black.	

Each of the above, pkt., 10c

8055 Mixed. ¼ oz., 30c; pkt., 10c.
Annual Hollyhocks—See Page 32.

Plants by Parcel Post

If to be sent by parcel post, add postage for most zones as follows: Single plants, 12c; 3 plants, 16c; 6 plants, 20c. We accept no responsibility for delays or conditions that may prove injurious to the contents.

No C. O. D. Shipments

Perennial Poppies

ICELAND or Nudicaule
12 to 18 in.
Culture: B. Page 65

Cool moist soil is necessary, and light shade preferred. If faded flowers are picked off plants blossom all summer, and they usually bloom the first year from seed. 12 inches.

8289 Coonara Pinks. Lovely flowers; pink, salmon pink and salmon shades. Pkt., 15c.

8272 Cardinal. This is a brilliant cardinal-red on long and strong stems. Cut in bud-stage, the flowers will keep for a long time. Pkt., 25c.

8291 Gartford Giant Art Shades. Exceptionally large flowers, fluted and carried on long wiry stems. The colors include lovely pastels. Pkt., 25c.

8281 Yellow Wonder. Buttercup yellow flowers on stems 25 in. long, heat and drough resisting. Pkt., 25c

8292 Empress. 18-22 in. A companion to Emperor, even more nearly double, with delightful color range of salmon rose and pink tones. Pkt., 25c.

8286 ✕ Sunbeams Mixed. This is a cross between the Shirley and Nudicaule types. The flowers are charming shades of orange, salmon, and other tints. Pkt., 25c.

8279 Vaughan's Special Iceland. Poppy Mixture. We have included in this all the newer varieties and older forms. Pkt. 25c

8270 ✕ Nudicaule Mixed. Pkt., 10c.

8293 POPPY Iceland Emperor. 18-22 in. Finest giant orange variety, of distinct new form, with broad overlapping fluted petals giving effect of semi-doubleness. Blooms freely first year from seed. Pkt., 25c.

ORIENTALE (Oriental Poppy) 3 ft. May-June

The named varieties of Oriental Poppies do not come entirely true from seed.

These gorgeous spring flowers, often six inches across, of vivid coloring, may be left undisturbed for years. They are beautiful with the tall bearded Iris.

8307 Beauty of Livermere. Finest dark crimson. Pkt., 25c.

8309 Mrs. Perry. Delicate salmon-rose, black base. Pkt., 25c.

8305 Princess Victoria Louise. Large flowers, soft lilac-rose color. Pkt., 15c.

8310 Red. Very striking color. Pkt., 10c.

8313 Named New Varieties Mixed. Seed collected from a field of the newer named sorts. Pkt., 25c.

8314 Vaughan's Special Mixture. Pkt., 25c.

ROOTS OF ORIENTAL POPPIES

Shipment made of dormant roots Midsummer only.

Beauty of Livermore Imp. 3 ft. Crimson with dark blotch, stout stems. 3 for $1.50; doz., $4.75; each, 60c.

Helen Elizabeth. One of the best. Clear La France pink. 3 for $1.50; doz., $4.75; each, 60c.

Henri Cayeaux Imp. Large old rose burgundy. Reaches perfection in light shade 3 for $1.50; doz., $4.75; each, 60c.

Jeannie Mawson. 2½ ft. Charming geranium pink, large flowers on stiff stems. 3 for $1.50; doz., $4.75; each, 60c.

Joyce. 4 ft. A charming soft red on long stems. 3 for $1.35; doz., $4.25; each, 55c.

Mrs. Perry Imp. The best known pink poppy. Delicate salmon-rose with black blotches. 3 for $1.35; doz., $4.25; each, 55c.

Salmon Glow. Fine double salmon orange of large size. 3 for $1.75; doz., $5.50; each 65c.

Royal Scarlet. Old-fashioned scarlet Oriental Poppy. Plants, 3 for $1.15; doz, $3.50; each, 45c.

Wunderkind. Enormous carmine pink, vigorous growth. Plants, each, 75c; 3 for $2.00; doz., $6.00.

8313 POPPY Oriental Named New Varieties. Mixed. Pkt., 25c.

8490 SCABIOSA Caucasica Perfecta. Seeds, pkt., **15c.** Plants, 3 for **$1.15.**

8490 Caucasica Perfecta. 18 in. Light blue flowers prettily fringed on long stem; fine for cutting. June-October. Pkt., 15c. Plants, 3 for $1.15; doz., $3.50; ea. 45c.

8491 —Alba. Pure white, comes true. Pkt., 25c

Additional Perennial Seeds and Plants

For Additional Perennial Seeds and Plants See Also Pages 52 to 56 Inclusive, and Back Cover.

OTE—All plants are F. O. B. our Greenhouses, Western Springs, Illinois. Postage must be added to cover cost of transportation at rates noted below, or they will be sent express at buyer's expense.

.7010 ACHILLEA, The Pearl, Pkt., 15c

It is fascinating to grow your own perennials from seed. We recommend sowing perennial seeds in spring. Seed germinates better in the cool weather than in the heat of midsummer, and the long growing season produces larger plants that winter over more successfully. The majority of these perennials bloom the second year from seed, although some, like Coreopsis and Gaillardia, if sown early, bloom the first year. Plants can be raised in beds and transplanted, or the seed may be planted directly in your perennial garden. The great charm of perennials lies in their permanence; once established they are a constant source of pleasure.

Plants by Parcel Post

If to be sent by parcel post, add postage for most zones as follows: Single plants, 12c; 3 plants, 16c; 6 plants, 20c. We accept no responsibility for delays or conditions that may prove injurious to the contents.

No C.O.D. Shipments

Plants by Express

We recommend this mode of transit where quantities are 12 plants or over. We pack carefully, but accept no responsibility for delays over which we have no control that may cause injury to the contents.

7080 ANEMONE, St. Brigid's Strain, Pkt., 20c

Achillea (Yarrow) ①

Culture: B, D or E, Page 65

chilleas grow readily from seed in sunny, well-rained positions, except the varieties marked X, hich should have rock garden conditions. They are ne border flowers, and several are excellent for cutting.

007 X **Agenteum.** 1 to 2 ft. A pretty Alpine of compact habit, with leaves like Ageratum. Yellow, sweet-scented. Pkt., 25c.

008 **Eupatorium Filipendula, Parker's Variety.** 3 to 5 ft. June-Sept. Clear yellow flower-heads. May be dried for winter bouquets. Pkt., 15c.

010 **The Pearl.** 2 ft. June to August. Pure white, double flowers, fine for cutting. Pkt., 15c.

013 X **Tomentosa Aurea.** 8-10 in. A woolly carpet-like plant for rockeries. Pkt., 15c.

Aconitum (Monkshood) ①

Culture: C, Page 65

conitums need rich, acid soil and prefer shade. Seed ay be sown in the fall, as it germinates slowly. They ould not be moved when once established, and require a mulch in winter. The roots are poisonous.

026 **Barker's Variety.** This variety is more vigorous than others, but its outstanding merit is the branching habit of the flower spike. Flowers are amethyst blue, considerably darker than Wilsoni. Pkt., 25c.

025 **Wilsoni.** 6-7 ft. Sept.-Oct. Tall, autumn flowering, mauve, fine for cutting. Pkt., 15c.

037 X **AETHIONEMA Cordifolium** (Lebanon Candytuft). 6-8 in. June. Rosy lilac. Pkt., 50c.

Alyssum (Madwort) ①

Culture: B, D or E, Page 65

howy free flowering spring-blooming plants, valuable for front row in border or rock garden.

054 X **Argenteum.** 1 ft. Dwarf, yellow flowers, leaves silvery underneath. Pkt., 10c.

055 X **Saxatile Compactum (Basket of Gold).** 9 in. Almost as soon as winter is over Alyssum Saxatile Compactum becomes a mass of yellow gold; a fine companion to spring bulb flowers. Pkt., 10c.

056 X —**Compactum Sulphureum.** Lovely pale lemon colored flowers. Very effective with lavender or pink Tulips. Pkt., 15c.

058 **Rostratum.** 20 inches. Flowers deep yellow in dense heads. Pkt., 15c.

059 X **Serpyllifolium (Alpestre)** Thyme-leaved. 3-4 in. Gray leaves, pale yellow flowers, excellent for dry, sunny positions. Pkt., 15c.

Agathea ①

Culture: D, E or C, Page 65

7040 **Coelestis (Blue Daisy).** 1½ ft. June. Flowers sky-blue with yellow disc. Useful in the border, for bedding and as a pot plant; half hardy. Pkt., 10c.

Anemone (Windflower) ①

Culture: B, C, D or E, Page 65

This interesting family furnishes a remarkable variety of showy garden subjects. Seeds germinate slowly. Some varieties flower in the spring, and others are among the most beautiful of fall flowering perennials.

7080 X **Coronaria St. Brigid's Strain.** May-June. Double and single mixed. 12 in. A beautiful selection in a wonderful array of colors. Pkt., 20c.

7077 —**His Excellency.** Large single scarlet. 25c.

7079 —**Syphide Blue.** Light purple. Pkt., 15c.

7090 X **Pulsatilla (Pasque Flower).** 1 ft. April-May. Flowers varying from lilac to purple. Pkt., 10c.

7100 X **Sylvestris (Snowdrop Windflower).** 1 to 1½ ft. Large, nodding, sweet-scented white flowers, tinged lavender. April-May. Pkt., 15c.

Anemone (Windflower). Plants.

Blooms freely from September to severe frosts. One of the most important Fall Garden plants. Requires a fertile and well-drained location in either light shade or sun. Water freely in dry weather. When once established, this should not be disturbed.

Japonica. 2 to 3 ft.

Alba. White, yellow center.

Queen Charlotte. La France Pink, semi-double.

September Charm. Delicate silvery pink, single.

Whirlwind. Full double, white.

Hupehensis. 12 to 14 inches. Earlier than the above, commencing to flower in August. Pleasing mauve-rose color.

Plants, any of above, 3 for $1.35; doz., $4.25; each, 55c.

Anemone Collection No. 57

One plant each of above varieties for $1.90.

Armeria (Thrift, Sea Pink) ①

Culture: B, D or E, Page 65

Dwarf-growing perennials with grassy leaves and a tufted habit of growth. The flowers are borne in globular heads during May and July, and the plants are suitable for edgings to borders.

7205 X **Alpina.** 3 in. July. Deep rose. Pkt., 10c.

7206 **Glory of Holland Giant Pink.** Improved variety bearing clear, deep pink flowers the size of a silver dollar on straight stems of 24 inches height, in large profusion all summer. Fine for cutting. Pkt., 25c.

7218 X **Laucheana.** 6 in. June-Aug. Crimson. Pkt., 10c.

New Hardy Asters ①

Illustrated in Color on Inside Back Cover.

Culture: B, D or E, Page 65

If you have ever seen the glorious effects of a mass planting of these hardy perennial Asters, you will not fail to make a planting of them in your garden. They are among the showiest of our late flowering hardy plants, giving a wealth of bloom in late summer and fall, a season when most other perennials are past blooming. For best effect they should be planted in masses of one color.

Three New Dwarf Asters, $1.15.

One each of the varieties listed below:
Extremely showy in full bloom and a welcome addition.

X **Countess of Dudley.** 1 ft. Oct. Charming clear pink flowers with yellow eye.

X **Niobe.** Dwarf white.

X **Victor.** 6 in. Sept. The flowers are of good size and of a beautiful clear pale lavender blue.

Any of above New Dwarf Asters; **Plants,** 3 for $1.15; doz., $3.50; each, 45c.

DWARF ALPINES

7226A **Alpinus Albus.** Pure white. 1 ft. 25c.

7226 —**Goliath.** Indispensable for the rockery or edge of hardy borders; 6 to 10 inches high, and bears large, showy, bluish purple flowers in May and June. Plant in full sun. Pkt., 25c.

7228A **Wartburg Star (Star of Eisenach).** May. A bright lavender-blue giant-flowered subcoeruleus type. Pkt., 25c.

7229 **Farreri.** June-July. Soft violet-mauve, with large orange center, flowers 2 to 3 inches across. Blooms in June and July. Pkt., 25c.

7225 **Perennial, Large-Flowering Mixed.** 3-5 ft. Sept.-Oct. Various shades of blue. Pkt., 25c.

MICHAELMAS DAISIES—See inside back cover.

7112 ANTHEMIS Santa Johannis, Pkt. 25,

Anthemis (Marguerite) ①

Culture: B, D or E, Page 65

Free-flowering perennials with attractive cut foliage and large Daisy-like flowers. Need full sun.

7110 Kelwayi. 2 ft. Daisy-like lemon-yellow blossoms, all summer. Excellent for cutting. Pkt., 10c.
7112 Sancta Johannis. 1½ ft. Clear golden yellow flowers. Pkt., 25c.
7114 Tinctoria, Perry's Variety. 2 ft. Large lemon-yellow Daisies, in bloom all summer. Pkt., 25c.
Moonlight. Fine pale yellow Anthemis, excellent for cutting. Plants keep within bounds. Plants, 3 for $1.35; doz., $4.25; each, 55c.

Anchusa (African Forget-Me-Not) ④ □

Culture: B, D or E, Page 65

Anchusas provide some of the few really blue flowers of our garden.

They do best in a deep, well drained soil, in a sunny position. All are excellent bee plants.

7070 Italica, Dropmore Variety. 5 ft. June-July. Gentian flowers. Pkt., 15c.
7069 —Lissadell. 6 ft. Large, gentian-blue. 25c.
7071 —Feltham Pride. Bright blue, Pkt., 25c.
7068 —Morning Glory. 5 ft. Buds appear a rosy mauve but turn to clear blue as they open. Pkt., 25c.
7073 × Myosotidiflora. 1 ft. April-May. A lovely perennial which blossoms with the late Tulips, forming a mound of attractive foliage almost hidden by pale blue Forget-me-not blossoms held above the foliage on straight stems. Germination is slow and fall sowing in an open seed bed gets good results. Pkt. (50 seeds), 35c.

Aubrietia ①

Culture: B, D or E, Page 65

One of the daintiest and most delicately beautiful of all dwarf creeping plants for carpeting beds or rockeries, forming brilliant sheets of blue, crimson or rose for many weeks. A gem for planting in crevices of rocks or wall, forming a cataract of color. 6 in.

7231A Deltoidea. Lilac. Pkt., 25c.
7231B Eyrii. Fine large blue. Pkt., 25c.
7232 × Graeca. Light blue, dwarf. Pkt., 25c.
7233 × Leichtlinii. Large-flowered, rosy lilac. 25c.
7233A Rosea Grandiflora. Pkt., 25c.
7230 × Large-Flowered Hybrids, Mixed. A wonderfully fine strain, good range of colors. Pkt., 25c.
7232A New Giant Flowered. Monarch strain. All full petalled types equal to the best named varieties. Vastly superior in size and color range to any other strain raised from seed. Highly recommended. Pkt., 35c.

Asclepias (Butterfly Weed) ①

Culture: B, D or E, Page 65

7220 Tuberosa. 2 ft. One of the showiest of our native perennials, producing from July until frost brilliant orange flowers with purplish stems and hairy leaves. Seed pods if gathered just as they begin to open and brought into the house and placed in a vase, soon open and develop into an attractive everlasting. Pkt., 15c.

Baptisia ①

Culture: B, C, D or E, Page 65

7235 Australis (False Indigo). Forms a spreading bush 3 to 4 ft. high with dark bluish green leaves and Lupin-like blue flowers in June and July. Pkt., 10c.

Blackberry Lily or ①
LEOPARD FLOWER

Culture: B, D or E, Page 65

7243 3 to 4 ft. A perennial of easy culture in rich sandy loam in a sunny spot. Flowers orange spotted red. Seed stalks may be used in winter bouquets, are clusters of shining black seeds. Pkt., 10c.

Boltonia (False Chamomile) ①

Culture: B, D or E, Page 65

They are among the relatively few fall flowering perennials, and are effective as background plants. They bear small star-flowers in large clusters.

7250 Latisquama. 4-5 ft. July-Oct. Delicate pink. Pkt., 15c.

7435 × CERASTIUM Tomentosum ① (Snow in Summer). 4 in. June-July. A low, creeping plant bearing a profusion of white flowers. Pkt., 15c.

Centaurea ③
(Hardheads, Knapweed)

Culture: B, D or E, Page 65

The flower-heads are like showy, ragged Thistle blooms.

7425 Macrocephala. 3 ft. During July and Aug., its stiff upright stalks are topped with radiant yellow Thistle-like blooms. Flowers often 4 in. across. Fine for background. Pkt., 10c.
7430 Montana Blue. 2 ft. June-Sept. Numerous large deep blue flowers somewhat resembling the annual Cornflower. Pkt., 10c.
7428 Hardy Perennial Mixed. A mixture of thirty hardy Centaureas. A real treat is in store for those who plant this mixture, as it will be a means of securing plants of unknown and unlisted sorts of various forms and colors. Pkt., 15c.

Bocconia × ①

Culture: B, D or E, Page 65

7240 Cordata (Plume Poppy). 5 ft. A handsome border plant, having large lobed heart-shaped leaves with silvery under surface and flower plumes of a pretty cream color. Pkt., 10c.

BUDDLEIA (Butterfly Bush). See Page 100.

7220. ASCLEPIAS Tuberosa, Pkt. 15c.

7493 COREOPSIS Double Sunburst, Pkt. 25

Coreopsis ①

Culture: B, D or E, Page 65

A useful and attractive perennial, both for border and cut flowers. They are of easy culture, and flower profusion throughout the summer.

7495 Lanceolata Grandiflora. 2 ft. June-October. Large orange-yellow flowers on long graceful stems. Will flower the first year if sown early. Pkt., 10
7494 Mayfield Giants. Australian origin. It produces a taller and more vigorous plant with long and firmer stems and larger individual blooms which the ray petals are broader. Pkt., 20c.
7493 Double Sunburst. The flowers are double 1½ to 2 inches across, excellent for cutting. the flowers are fine keepers and the plants easy grow. Comes about 80% double. Pkt., 25 Plants, 3 for $1.15; doz., $3.50.

7376 CASSIA Marylandica. ① 4 ft. Yellow. 10
7256 × CALLIRHOE Involucrata ① (Poppy Mallow). Crimson. Pkt., 15c.
CLEMATIS Jackmanii. See Climbing Vines

Cheiranthus ①

Culture: B, D or E, Page 65

A hardy perennial which blossoms the first year fr seed. Sow in late summer, autumn or spring.

1609 Kewensis. Winter-blooming Wallflowe Fragrant flowers, sulphur passing to gold and viol 30 in. Pkt., 10c.
1611 Linifolius. Lilac, 18 in. Pkt., 10c.
For Allioni and Golden Bedder see Annual Pages

Shasta Daisies ①

Culture: B, D or E, Page 65

The name Shasta is now applied not to a single varie but to a class of hardy Daisies, bearing giant flowers, splendid border subjects and easily grown from se

7500 Alaska. 2-2½ feet. Splendid for cutti Pkt., 10c. Plants, 3 for $1.15; doz., $3.50; ea., 4
7464 Diener's New Giant Everblooming Marconi. See Novelty Pages. Pkt. (35 seeds) 5
7463 Diener's Fancy Chiffon Glendale. S Novelty Pages. Pkt. (35 seeds) 50c.
7502 Elder Daisy. 2 ft. May. A popular varie for early cutting and border. Pkt., 15c.
7504 Giant Double. See Novelty Pages. Pkt. 3
7462 Maximum Conqueror. June. 2¾ ft. Lar pure white flowers, five inches in diameter, on lo stiff stems, in profusion. Pkt., 15c. Plants, 3 $1.00; doz., $3.00; 100, $20.00.
7460 —King Edward VII. 2½ feet. Very la flowers on stout stems. Pkt., 10c.
7449 —Fringed Semi-Double and Double. 7 plants are extremely vigorous, producing at time from 25 to 40 feathered fringed blooms. T strong heavy stems support blooms that avera from 5 to 8 inches in diameter. A percentage the plants will produce full double blooms, t balance semi-double and fringed. Pkt., 15c.

Esther Reed. Snow-white flowers, completely double and everblooming in habit. Stiff stems. excellent for border and cutting. Each, 65c; 3 for $1.75; doz., $5.25.

Funkia (Hosta, Day Lily)

Very attractive plants with broad overlapping leaves of various markings; very ornamental, surmounted by dainty Lily-like flowers in terminal racemes, 1½-2 ft., July-Aug. Excellent and effective in front of shrubbery, or any shady position.

Coerulea (Lanceolata). Blue flowers from July to August. 3 for $1.15; doz., $3.50; each, 45c.

Fortunei Robusta. Unusually large blue-green foliage. Flowers are white, shaded a light lilac blue. A novelty of real value. 3 for $1.50; each, 60c.

Japonica Aurea Marginata. Large bi-colored foliage in spring. The flowers are mauve and appear in July. 3 for $1.25; doz., $3.50; each, 50c.

Subcordata Grandiflora. Flowers white; large green leaves. One of the best perennials for shade. 3 for $1.50; doz., $4.75; each, 60c.

Variegata. Beautiful edging plant with white and green foliage. Blue flowers. 3 for $1.15; doz., $3.50; each, 45c.

Gerbera (Transvaal Daisy) ①

Culture: D or E, Page 65

7846 Jamesoni Hybrids (Flowerland Strain). 2 ft. Large Daisy-like blooms on long stems in yellow and red. Seed should be sown singly, point up; cover lightly in greenhouse or hotbed. Transplant when leaves are one inch long. Water sparingly. Give sunny, airy location, protect from rain in summer in the open. Needs protection over winter. Pkt. (25 seeds), 25c.

Gypsophila (Baby's Breath) ①

Culture: A, B, D or E, Page 65

Established plants, which should never be disturbed, produce cloud-like masses of small flowers in the border. They are fine for cutting and dry perfectly for winter bouquets. Dried flowers can be made to look again like fresh ones by wrapping the dried blooms in a moist towel half a day in a cool place.

7864 Acutifolia. 3 ft. Pretty, useful species; flowers pale pink. Pkt., 15c.

7861 Mangini. Wide tangles of large and pretty pink and white flowers valued for misty border effects, also for adding airy grace to cut flower arrangements. Pkt., 15c.

7866 Oldhamiana. 3 ft. The light little buds are first almost white, but open a lively shade of pink that tends to darken as the flowers mature. Each individual flower measures slightly more than one-quarter of an inch in diameter and possesses a white throat. The flowers are fragrant. Pkt., 25c.

7867 Pacifica. 4 ft. Withstands both severe winter and extreme heat. The seedlings form dense bushes with myriads of tiny pink blossoms. Pkt., 25c.

Paniculata Bristol Fairy (Double Baby's Breath). Early double pure white large-flowering perennial Baby's Breath. Produces a second crop of spikes. 3 for $1.75; doz., $5.50; each, 65c.

Rosenschleier (Rosy Veil). A semi-dwarf double pink variety giving two crops of bloom. 3 for $1.50; doz., $4.75; each, 60c.

7860 Paniculata Double Snow White. A great improvement on the single-flowered type and more lasting. 2-3 ft. July-August. Pkt., 25c.

7865 —(Baby's Breath). 2-3 ft. July-Aug. Small single flowers on branched stems, so thick as to give the plant a white lace-like effect. Pkt., 10c.

7863 × Repens Rosea. 6 in. Attractive dwarf pink. Pkt., 15c.

7862 × Repens Dwarf White. Pkt., 15c.

Helianthemum ①

Culture: C (April-July), Page 65. Set out Aug.-Oct.

7906 × Mutabile (Rock Rose). 8-12 in. Low-growing evergreen plants forming large clumps, completely covered with bloom during July and August. Pale rose changing to lilac, then to white. Excellent for rockeries. Mixed colors. Pkt., 15c.

Helenium (Sneezewort) ①

Culture: B, D or E, Page 65

To register masses of color in the border background, the Heleniums and other members of the Sunflower family are most useful. They grow easily from seed and spread rapidly. Autumn-flowering varieties are especially valued for contributing autumn color.

7880 Bigelowi. 2 ft. Light yellow flowers borne from July to September. Pkt., 10c.

7885 Hoopesii. 1½ ft. June. Rich orange-yellow with slightly drooping rays. Pkt., 10c.

7890 Riverton Gem. 2 to 4 ft. Covered from August to October with brilliant old gold, changing later to wallflower-red. Pkt., 25c.

GYPSOPHILA Paniculata Double Baby's Breath

Heliopsis (Orange Sunflower) ①

Culture: A, B, D or E, Page 65

A very brilliant border plant, resembling a double Sunflower; an excellent cut flower.

7909 Lemoine Strain. Double golden yellow. Blooms first year from seed. Pkt., 15c.

7910 Pitcheriana. 3 to 4 ft. high. Golden yellow flowers 2 inches in diameter; blooms all summer. Pkt., 25c.

Heuchera (Coralbells) ①

Culture: B, D or E, Page 65

From a tuft of heart shaped leaves, graceful flower stalks rise, bearing flowers in clusters. Beautiful both in border and in rockery.

7940 Sanguinea. 2 ft. July-Aug. Long stems of large crimson-scarlet flowers. Pkt., 25c.

7943 —New Hybrids Mixed. All shades of red and coral pink. Large flowers and free flowering. Pkt., 25c. Plants, 3, $1.50; doz., $4.50; each 60c.

7944 Hoodacres Hybrids. These are the result of 14 years of selection. Very vigorous and prolific. The bells are much larger than other sorts. The bloom stalks are tall; some have the habit of blooming twice in a season. Wide range of color shades. Pkt., 75c. Plants, 3, $1.50; doz. $4.50; each 60c.

Hesperis Matronalis ①
(Sweet Rocket—Evening Scented Stock)

Culture: B, D or E, Page 65

The fragrant flower-heads of these thrifty flowers somewhat resembling perennial Phlox, make a fine display in the border, or in bits of woodland, for they endure light shade. 2 to 3 feet. June and July.

7930 Purpurea. Lilac. Pkt., 10c.

7935 —Alba. White. 10c. **7936 —Mixed.** 10c.

Iberis (Perennial Candytuft) ①

Culture: A, B, D or E, Page 65

Dwarf evergreen plants, 6 to 10 in. Covered with blooms in spring and early summer. Excellent for rockeries or borders where bright dwarf masses are wanted.

8075 × Gibraltarica. Pinkish white. Pkt., 10c.

8078 Queen of Italy. Dwarf bushes covered with large pink blooms. Pkt., 10c.

8080 × Sempervirens. Sheet of white. Pkt., 25c.

HEMEROCALLIS Yellow Day Lily.

Newest Hemerocallis
(Yellow Day Lily)

New Hybrid Hemerocallis have become dominant summer border flowers. Taller, with larger flowers and new colors, they are as vigorous and free flowering as the older varieties.

5 New Hemerocallis $2.10
(Cat. Value, $3.10)

One each of the following:

Hyperion. Soft canary yellow of immense size. Very vigorous. 3 for $2.00; each, 75c.

Margaret Perry. July. Excellent because of its long flowering season. Orange scarlet lined with yellow. 3 for $2.00; each, 75c.

Mikado. June. Large deep orange with maroon mahogany blotches on three petals. 3 for $2.00; each, 75c.

Mrs. W. H. Wyman. 4 ft. Early August. Lovely lemon yellow. 3 for $1.75; each, 65c.

Ophir. 4 ft. July. Giant golden yellow. Very fragrant. 3 for $1.50; each, 60c.

OTHER VARIETIES

Calypso. 3½ ft. July. Large lemon yellow. 3 for $1.25; each, 50c.

Cinnabar. July-August. Light bronzy red, suffused gold. 3 for $1.50; each, 60c.

Lemona. July-August. Lemon yellow. 3 for $1.25; each, 50c.

Serenade. Pastel shades with crinkled petals. 3 for $1.50; each, 60c.

Sovereign. 2 ft. May-June. Soft chrome-yellow shaded brown on the outside, fragrant. 3 for $1.25; each, 50c.

D. D. Wyman. 2½ ft. July-August. Tawny golden yellow. 3 for $1.50; each, 60c.

SEEDS GERMINATE SLOWLY AND IRREGULARLY

The following varieties and seed bed should be prepared where it will be undisturbed for a year or more.

Aconitum, Anemone, Delphinium Cardinale, Dictamnus, Dielytra, Incarvillea, Iris, Phlox Decussata, Hardy Primulas, Trollius.

Grow Iris From Seed
Culture: A, B or C, Page 65

8090 Kaempferi. These grow easily from seed sown in either the spring or fall. Flowering plants are often produced the first year. They will thrive in well drained soil, but require plenty of water in the flowering season. Pool margins are a good location. Pkt., 25c.

8092 Siberian. This type of Iris resembles the Spanish and English Irises. It makes a bright show in the garden and is excellent for cutting. Seed from our own nursery. Pkt., 15c.
For Iris plants see Page 104.

8091 Dichotoma (August or Vesper Iris.) Fragrant flowers on tall branching sprays, from July to September. Cream to violet-purple markings of various colors. Seed sown in early spring will germinate quickly, and a fair proportion will bloom the first summer. Pkt., 20c.

Isatis ①
(Golden Gypsophila)
Culture: B, or C, Page 65

8094 Glauca. 3 ft. Graceful plant with glaucous green leaves with a white mid-rib. Belongs to Wallflower family, yellow flowers borne in terminal panicles in July and August. Pkt., 10c.

Lathyrus Latifolius ①
(Hardy Sweet Pea)
Culture: B, C, D or E, Page 65

Very decorative climbing vines of the Pea family for growing on fences, trellis, etc., and for cutting. Blooms all summer, if seed pods are removed.

8100 Pink Beauty. Pale pink variety. Pkt., 10c.
8105 Rubra. Bright rosy crimson. Pkt., 10c.
8110 White Pearl. Large white. Pkt., 10c.
8115 Mixed. The above colors. Pkt., 10c.

Lavender (Lavendula) ①
Culture: B, D or E, Page 65

Delightfully fragrant flowers, much used when dry on account of their sweet odor. Prefers warm, dry soil. Favorite for centuries.

8117 ✕ Munstead Strain. 1 ft. A most valuable variety. A month earlier than the common Lavender. Pkt., 25c.

Liatris ①
(Kansas Gay Feather)
Culture: B, D or E, Page 65

8119 Scariosa. Rare North American species. Crowded spikes of rosy purple flowers. Pkt., 15c.

8117B —Alba. 2½ ft. The stems branch freely, and the flowers are attractive white pompons thickly studding each stem. The top buds open first and then the others gradually down the stem. Valuable as garden and cut flower. Pkt., 25c.

8117A —September Glory. A giant 6-foot spike solidly covered with purple flowers from top to bottom. The flowers, unlike the common variety, come into bloom all at the same time, creating a marvelous effect. A splendid improvement over the old variety. Late flowering, September. Pkt. 25c.

Lilies from Seed ①

Many Lilies are easily grown from seed; and seedling Lilies are likely to be more enduring in your garden. A leaflet describing the simple methods which bring success, requiring no skill, but merely care and patience, will be sent free with each order for Lily seed, if requested. You will find it fascinating.

8156C Concolor. Especially adapted to rockeries. Flowers upright, starlike, deep vermilion. July. 6 to 18 inches. Pkt. (50 seeds), 25c.

8158A Longiflorum Praecox White Queen. Produces long trumpet-shaped flowers of clear white. Pkt., 25c.

8162 Regale (The Royal Lily). 3½ ft. The flowers are white, slightly suffused with pink on backs of petals. Fragrant. Blooms out-of-doors early in July, and seedling bulbs will flower the second year. Pkt., 15c.

8163 Tenuifolium (Coral Lily of Siberia). It is a gem, perfectly hardy. One of the earliest to flower. 24 in. high with the flowers up and down on stem. Blooms are deep scarlet and have recurled petals of waxy texture. Pkt., 25c.

8164A Mixture of Hardy Lilies. Pkt., 25c.
For bulbs of varieties of Lilies we can supply see page 96.

Linaria (Toad Flax) ①
Culture: A, B, D or E, Page 65

Showy free-flowering plants of a trailing habit, for borders, window boxes or rockeries.

8121 Macedonica Speciosa. 36 in. Cr white. Pkt., 15c.

Linum (Flax) 12 to 18 in.
Culture: C, Page 65

The foliage and flower present the appearance of a feathery bush. The flowers are borne in great nur from May through September.

8126 ✕ Alpinum. 4 in. Purple, blotched or Pkt., 25c.

8140 Flavum. 1-2 ft. Produces masses of g yellow flowers from June until Sept. Pkt., 2

8141 —Compactum Nanum. A glowing g yellow, blooms for months and if cut back g fall crop. Pkt., 25c.

8127 Narbonense Heavenly Blue. The fl are twice as large as the common Linum Per The color is a luminous ultramarine blue. Bl from seed the first year. Pkt., 25c.

8124 Narbonense. Forms a spreading clum azure-blue flowers with white eye. Pkt., 25c.

8123 Lewisii. 2½ ft. A robust species with ing sprays of fragrant blue flowers with blotches. Pkt., 15c.

8125 Perenne Blue. 2 ft. May-Aug. Has d sky-blue flowers on graceful arching stems. Bl produced continuously in profusion. Pkt.,

Lobelia ①
Culture: B, C, D or E, Page 65

Handsome border plants, thriving in any ord garden soil, but preferring a moist, deep loam.

8145 Cardinalis (Cardinal Flower). 2 ft. Oct. Tufts of bronzy green foliage from arise spikes of fiery scarlet flowers. Pkt.,

8144 —Special Selection—See Novelty P

8146 Syphilitica. 3 ft. Aug.-Sept. Fine of blue flowers. Pkt., 15c.

For Winter Bouquets ①
Culture: B, D or E, Page 65

8150 LUNARIA Biennis Annua (Honesty Peter's Penny). Flowers lilac-purple, follow silvery seed pods, prized for winter bou Biennial but readily self-sows. Pkt., 15c.

8155 —Alba. Flowers white. Pkt., 10c.

Lupinus Polyphyllu
Culture: A, B, D or E, Page 65

Inoculate Lupin seeds with Nitragin. Two ga sizes, 10c and 25c. Chill seed before sowi

8170 Albus. Large, pure white spikes. Pkt

8165 Blue. Stately spikes of blue. Pkt., 10c

8174 Downer's Hybrids. Perpetual flowerin hybrids. Pkt., 25c.

8173 Harkness' Regal Mixture. Charming colors. Pkt., 15c.

8175 Roseus. 4 ft. Light and dark rose. Pkt

8171A "Russell," Re-selected Strain. Th remarkable Lupins are often 3½ ft. in leng The coloring has an enormous range and unid character. Flowers in 4 months from sowi Gold Medal award by the R.H.S. Pkt., 50c.

8171 "Russell" (Grown from originate stock seed). A fine collection. Pkt., 25c.

Famous Russell Strain. Mixed colors, stro blooming size. Plants, 3 for $1.15; doz., $3.

8178 Sunshine (Arboreus or Treety Sweet scented, golden yellow, 30 in. Pkt., 1

8182 Six Hills Scented Mixed. Fragrant, range of color. Pkt., 15c.

8179 Vaughan's Special Mixture. This choice mixture of the best English and Am strains, including recent novelties. Pkt

8220 LYTHRUM Roseum Superbum. ① Rose-pink. Pkt., 10c.

8190- LYCHNIS Chalcedonica, Pkt., 10c

Nepeta (Mauve Catnip) ①

Culture: B, D or E, Page 65
Neat bushes covered with lavender-blue flowers; both foliage and flowers aromatic.
8254×Mussini. 1 ft. May-Sept. Lightblue. Pkt., 25c.

Oenothera (Evening Primrose) ①

Culture: B, D or E, Page 65
Showy plants flowering from June to October.
8261×Missouriensis (Macrocarpa). 1 ft. Long trailing stems with yellow flowers. Pkt., 10c.

Perennial Everlastings ①

For Winter Bouquets

7008	Achillea Filipendula Parker's.	Pkt., 15c.
7788	Echinops Ritro (Globe Thistle).	Pkt., 10c.
7860	Gypsophila Paniculata Fl. Pl.	Pkt., 25c.
8150	Lunaria Biennis or Honesty.	Pkt., 10c.
8345	Physalis Franchetti.	Pkt., 10c.
8520	Statice Latifolia (Sea Lavender).	Pkt., 10c.

For Annual Everlastings, Separate Varieties and Mixed, See Page 29

Pentstemon (Beard Tongue) ①

Culture: B, D or E, Page 65
They are very showy, growing from 2 feet to 4 feet high, are rather bushy and have very long, slender spikes which bear many trumpet-shaped flowers.
8323×Blue Gem. 1 ft. Compact with charming blue flowers. Pkt., 25c.
8335 Digitalis. 2 ft. June-July. White flowers with purple throat. Pkt., 25c.
8326 Grandiflorus. 3 ft. Lavender blue. Long-lasting flower. Pkt., 25c.
8330 Hartwegi. Large Flowering Newest Hybrids. Splendid assortment of colors. Pkt., 15c.
(See Also Page 38 in Annuals.)

Garnet. Large flowering, the plants have a succession of several 12-18 in. spikes, with bell-shaped flowers, rich garnet red in color. The flowers are excellent for cutting. **Plants,** 3 for $1.50; doz., $4.75; each 60c.

Firebird. Very similar to above excepting color, which is ruby-crimson—another excellent cut flower. Plants, 3 for $1.50; doz., $4.75; each 60c.

8327 Ovatus. A particularly fine strain. Base branching plants, with flowers carried in loose clusters well above the foliage. Blossoms of a most attractive lavender, buds a bit deeper color. Foliage is a glorious copper crimson in fall. Pkt., 25c.
8338 Hardy Perennial Blend. Pentstemons are most satisfactory perennials. This mixture contains many varieties not listed separately. Pkt., 25c.

Lychnis ①

Culture: B, D or E, Page 65
A fine old-fashioned flower that livens up the border during summer and early autumn.
8200×Alpina. 4 in. April. Close tufts, olive-green foliage. Clusters of rose flowers. Pkt., 20c.
8189 Arkwrightii. 2 to 3 ft. Magnificent hybrid of Chalcedonica and Haageana. Salmon-rose to flaming scarlet and dark carmine. Pkt., 25c.
8190 Chalcedonica (Maltese Cross). 3 feet. June-Aug. Burning Star. Flowers fiery red in clusters, each blossom forming a Maltese cross. Will bloom from seed the first year. Pkt., 10c.
8196 —Salmon Queen, 3 ft. Salmon-pink. 15c.
8195×Forrestii Hybrids. Showy panicles of carmine, crimson, pink and whiteyflowers, excellent for rock garden and border. 2 ft. Pkt., 35c.
8215×Viscaria Splendens. 1½ ft. Almost evergreen foliage, bright rose flowers. Pkt., 10c.

Monarda (Bergamot)

Close heads of flowers surrounded by colored bracts. Foliage is fragrant.
Didyma Mrs. Perry. — Rose scarlet flowers. 3 for $1.25; doz., $3.75; each, 50c.
Didyma Rosalie.—Soft clear pink. 3 for $1.25; doz., $3.75; each, 50c.

Myosotis (Forget-Me-Not)

×Palustris Semperflorens. Dwarf blue, in flower from early spring until autumn. Thrives in almost any situation and is an ideal variety for rock gardens or edgings. Plants, each, 45c; 3 for $1.15; doz., $3.50.

Native Wild Flowers

7140	Aquilegia Coerulea.	Pkt., 10c.
7120	Aquilegia Canadensis.	Pkt., 10c.
7220	Asclepias Tuberosa.	Pkt., 15c.
7807	Euphorbia Corollata.	Pkt., 25c.
8145	Lobelia Cardinalis.	Pkt., 15c.
8326	Pentstemon Grandiflorus.	Pkt., 25c.
4101	Phacelia Campanularia.	Pkt., 10c.

All the above are perennial except the Phacelia.

8259 Native Wild Flower Mixture.
Seeds of more than 100 different species, carefully collected in the field, are included. All are American, and all are collected in the temperate zone. There are few annuals, the rest hardy perennials. For sowing in woodlands, naturalistic border, and wild flower gardens. ½oz., 50c. Pkt., **25c**

Best New Perennial Phlox ①

8340 PHLOX Decussata Mixed. 2-3 ft. This special mixture comes from a superior collection of large-flowering sorts. We flowered this mixture in our nursery last summer and were greatly pleased with the size of the flowers and flower-heads and colors. Perennial Phlox do not come true from seed and can be had only in mixture. Seed germinates slowly. Pkt., 25c.

Six Perennial Phlox $2.00

One each of varieties in list below. Postage extra.
Africa. Carmine red with dark eye. Large trusses. 3 for $1.25; doz., $3.75; each, 50c.
B. Compte. Rich satiny, amaranth purple. 3 for $1.25; doz., $3.75; each, 50c.
Border Queen. Pure pink. Very large flowers. Plants, 3 for $1.25; doz., $3.75; each, 50c.
Leo Schlageter. Outstanding vivid scarlet or flame red. Good foliage, large blooms. 3 for $1.50; doz., $4.75; each, 60c.
Lillian. Cameo pink, faint blue shading at the center. One of the finest. 3 for $1.25; doz., $3.75; each, 50c.
Mary Louise. Pure white head; extra large. One of the best. 3 for $1.50; doz., $4.75; each, 60c.

NEW AND STANDARD VARIETIES
Appleblossom. Soft pink with large pyramidal spikes. Large florets. Healthy and vigorous. 3 for $1.35; doz., $4.25; each, 55c.
Augusta. U. S. Plant Patent No. 252. Brilliant cherry red. 3 for $1.50; doz., $4.75; each, 60c.
Bridesmaid. Pure white, crimson eye. 3 for $1.15; doz., $3.50; each, 45c.
Chas. Curtis. Brilliant sunset red. A very fine new variety. 3 for $1.50; doz., $4.75; each, 60c.
Columbia. Patented. Cameo pink, faint blue shading at center. 3 for $1.25; doz., $4.00; each, 50c.
Daily Sketch. Big trusses, salmon pink with crimson eye. 3 for $1.35; doz., $4.25; each, 55c.
Dr. Klemm. White with a prominent diffused eye of rich violet. Very distinct. 3 for $1.35; doz., $4.25; each, 55c.
Flash. Carmine crimson with orange center. 3 for $1.35; doz., $4.25; each, 55c.
Frau Alfred Von Mautner. Superb brilliant orange cherry red. Gorgeous new variety. 3 for $1.50; doz., $4.75; each, 60c.
Harvest Fire. Large heads of flaming orange red. 3 for $1.50; doz., $4.75; each, 60c.
Miss Lingard (Suffruticosa). Pure white; the earliest of all. 3 for $1.15; doz., $3.50; each, 45c.
Morgenrood. Deep rose shade of red. Striking. Large florets. 3 for $1.50; doz., $4.75; each, 60c.
Salmon Beauty. A very outstanding variety. Rich, salmon pink with white eye. 3 for $1.35; doz., $4.25; each, 55c.

PHLOX THOR

Sweetheart. Beautiful deep salmon-pink. Dwarf. An excellent new one. 3 for $1.75; doz., $5.50; each, 65c.
Thor. A splendid variety of a lovely shade of deep salmon-pink suffused and overlaid with a scarlet glow. 3 for $1.25; doz., $4.00; each, 50c.
Von Hochberg. Large size blood-red blooms. The best deep red. 3 for $1.50; doz., $4.75; each, 60c.
Mixed. 1-year field-grown plants of a choice mixture of colors. Un-named varieties. Our selection. 3 for $1.15; doz., $3.50; each, 45c.

Dwarf and Subulata Phlox

8341 Divaricata Canadensis. Blooms early April. Fragrant lavender flowers on stems 10 inches high. Prefers shade. Pkt., 20c. 3 for $1.00; doz., $3.00; 100, $20.00; each, 40c.
Dixie Brilliant (Nivalis Sylvestris). Low spreading gray-green foliage, covered in early spring with rosy red flowers. 1 inch diameter. 3 for $1.25; doz., $3.75; each, 50c.
Subulata Vivid. Most profuse bloomer of all. Bright pink eye. 3 for $1.15; doz., $3.50; each, 45c.

8345 PHYSALIS Franchetti, Pkt., 10c

Physalis Franchetti ①

Culture: B, D or E, Page 65

8345 Chinese Lantern Plant. 1¾ ft. Produces balloon-like husks the second year from seed, which turn bright red when ripe and resemble Chinese lanterns, useful in winter bouquets. Pkt., 10c.

8346 Physalis Gigantea. The attractive orange-scarlet balloon-shaped seed pods are very large and will make excellent winter decorations. Pkt., 20c.

Platycodon ①

(Chinese Bell Flower)

Culture: B, D or E, Page 65

They resemble Campanulas, with dainty bell flowers on graceful stems, and are effective in the border foreground. They flower from June to September.

8360 Grandiflorum. 2-3 ft. Large handsome deep blue flowers. Pkt., 10c. Plants, 3 for $1.15; doz., $3.50; each, 45c.

8365 —Album. White. Pkt., 10c. Plants, 3 for $1.15; doz., $3.50; each, 45c.

8361 —Mixture. Pkt., 10c.

8363 —New Giant Early Blue. Oriental Bellflower: Immense blossoms of blue-violet, great bells spread to starry form. Sometimes variants of pure white, or white streaked with azure, will appear. Blooms first year as quickly as an annual. Pkt., 25c.

8364 —New Giant Early White. White form of above. Pkt., 25c.

8370 X Mariesii Blue. 1 ft. Deep blue dwarf. Pkt., 10c.

8375 X —Alba. White. Pkt., 10c.

Plumbago

Larpentae. 8 inches. Dwarf spreading habit covered with deep sky-blue flowers all summer. Rich color and abundance of bloom make ideal edging plant. Plants, 3 for $1.15; doz., $3.50; each, 45c.

Polemonium (Jacob's Ladder) ①

Culture: B, D or E, Page 65

Free-flowering hardy perennial herbs; belong to the Phlox order. They have graceful, pinnate leaves, and bear their flowers in loose heads. Showy plants for the mixed, sunny border, blossoming with the Tulips.

8380 Coeruleum (Greek Valerian). 2 ft. Beautiful sky-blue flowers with golden anthers. April-July. Foliage fern-like. Pkt., 10c.

8381 —Album. White form of the above. Pkt., 10c.

8388 —Richardsoni. 18 in. Large sky-blue flowers with a yellow eye. May to Sept. Pkt., 25c.

8387 X Reptans. 6 in. Flower sprays china-blue Mounds of beautiful blossoms. Pkt., 25c.

Pyrethrum Roseum

(Painted Daisy) May-June

Culture: B, D or E, Page 65

Their large flowers, well named Painted Daisies, blossom with the tall Iris, and continue through June. A second crop will come if the first growth is cut back. They are easily grown from seed. 1 to 2 ft.

Grandiflorum Single Mixed. Plants, 3 for $1.15; doz., $3.50; each, 45c.

8444 Roseum Single Atro-Sanguineum. Blood-red. Pkt., 15c.

8436 James Kelway. Rich velvety blood-red. Pkt., 25c.

8438 Robinson's Hybrids, Mixed. A selection made by an English specialist, with a fine color range of single overlapping petals carried on long stiff stems. Pkt. 25c.

8438A Robinson's Crimson. The best red. Pkt., 25c. Plants, 3 for $1.25; doz., $3.75; each, 50c.

8435 Single Mixed. Pkt., 10c.

Primula ①

There is a growing appreciation of the beauty of the amazingly varied Primrose family. Blossoming in April and May, their brilliant colors have few rivals in plantings along shady paths or in the rock garden. Seed germinates slowly, may be in the ground a year.

Culture: C or B, Page 65

8403A X Auricula Large Flowering Mixed. 6 in. Flowers in early spring in colors of yellow, brown and red. Seeds, Pkt., 25c. Plants, 3 for $1.25; doz., $4.25; each, 55c.

8405 X Bulleisana Hybrids. New hybrids of rose, orange, carmine, light and dark blue. Pkt., 50c.

8405C Cortusoides Rosea. 10 in. A charming variety. Flowers in early summer, deep rose; prefers light, rich, well-drained soil. Pkt., 25c.

8407 Florindae. 3 to 4 ft. It bears from late June to late in August, 60 to 80 fragrant bright yellow pendent flowers at the top of its stem. Does well in full sun—heavy soil; hardy in Illinois. Pkt., 35c.

8410 X Japonica Special Strain. Colors range through white, rose, pink, crimson, mauve and lavender, bright crimson, orange eye, Pkt., 25c.

8412 Sieboldii. A charming variety requiring light woodland conditions, of partial shade and a cool leaf soil, under which conditions they increase vigorously; slight protection is desirable in very cold weather. The large rich green leaves are crinkled and scalloped and the upright stems bear a quantity, of large brightly colored flowers in April and May, 9 in. They also make splendid pot-plants for the cold greenhouse. Pkt., 25c.

Polyantha Type (Bunch Primrose)

These are showy, cluster-flowered, of exceptional size, thriving in rich, moist soil:

8416 X —Grandiflora, Mixed. An extra choice large flowered mixed strain. Pkt., 25c. Plants, 3 for $1.35; doz., $4.25; each, 55c.

8417 X —Munstead Strain. A giant Polyanthus in many charming light shades. Pkt., 35c. Plants, 3 for $1.35; doz., $4.25; each, 55c.

8419 —Kleynii. Lusty growth with many large golden yellow flowers, shaded apricot in center: Pkt. (60 seeds); 25c.

8423 —Red Shades. Pkt., 25c.

8423A —Monarch Strain. Undoubtedly the finest of all strains. Pkt., 25c.

8424 Vulgaris (English Primrose). Pale yellow for wild gardens. Pkt., 25c.

Pueraria (Kudzu Vine) ①

Culture: A, B, D or E, Page 65

8425 Thunbergiana (Jack - and - the - Bean - Stalk). 50 ft. Flourishes where nothing else will grow. The large bold leaves of the brightest green afford a dense shade. Pkt., 15c.

For Roots, see Page 101.

8475 SALVIA Pitcheri, Pkt., 20c

Rose

Culture: B, D or E, Page 65

8452 The Baby Rose. Multitudes of tiny roses in varied lovely colorings, but largely in white, blush or delicate pink. Flowers single to fully double. More or less everblooming. Quick from seed, and from earliest spring sowings, plants will be in flower by June, midgets but four inches high. Height variable, but always low-growing and compact. Though fully winter-hardy the Baby Rose makes a splendid pot plant. Pkt., 25c.

Rudbeckia (Cone Flower) ①

Culture: B, D or E, Page 65

Hardy, free flowering and easily grown perennials belonging to the Daisy order. They are somewhat akin to the Sunflowers in habit. Excellent and showy plants for sunny or partially shaded borders, and for yielding flowers for cutting. Natives of N. America.

Herbstwald Autumn Tints. See Annual Pages.

Indian Maid. See Annual Pages.

Double Kelvedon Star. See Annual Pages.

Purpurea Grandiflora—See Echinacea Purpurea.

"The King." Habit of growth similar to ordinary species but Daisy shape blossoms are larger, petals are held erect and color is distinct wine-red with large brown center cone. Flowers have long life, 3 ft. July-Sept. 3 for $1.25; doz., $3.75; each, 50c.

Salvia ①

Culture: B, D or E, Page 65

Showy, hardy plants of medium growth and of easy cultivation in sunny borders. Grow on dry side and without fertilizer. The flowers are borne in spikes, racemes, or panicles, and are very attractive during the summer months.

8471 Azurea Grandiflora. 4 ft. September-October. Stately willow-like growth, spikes of pale blue flowers in great profusion. Pkt., 15c.

8475 Pitcheri. Delightful flowers of brightest azure blue, carried in long racemes. Foliage is silver dusted. Fully hardy and long lived perennial, that will nevertheless bloom the first year from seed if sown early. Pkt., 20c.

8480 Patens. 2 ft. Large, rich deep blue flowers. Roots can be wintered in cellar. Sept. Pkt., 25c.

Silene (Catchfly) ①

Culture: B, D or E, Page 65

A charming class of plants for the rock garden. They are closely allied to the Pink family and require much the same treatment. They bloom nearly all summer.

8510 Orientalis. 2 ft. Deep rose flowers in terminal umbels. Pkt., 15c.

Saponaria ①

Culture: B, D or E, Page 65

8482 X Ocymoides Splendens. 6 in. A showy dwarf trailing plant, producing a sheet of rose colored flowers. June-August. Pkt., 10c.

Thalictrum (Meadow Rue) ①

Culture: B, D or E, Page 65

Though not of bright and conspicuous color, the feathery flowers of the Thalictrums are decorative and interesting, and their leaves, resembling the maiden-hair fern, are attractive both in the border and when cut. They grow easily from seed.

8545 Dipterocarpum. 4 to 5 ft. Aug.-Sept. Very graceful plumes of rosy-purple flowers with conspicuous yellow anthers. Pkt., 25c.

Thermopsis ①

Culture: B, D or E, Page 65

8548 Caroliniana. 3 to 5 ft. June and July. The long, graceful spikes of yellow Lupin-like flowers blossom with the Delphiniums and provide an excellent foil for their blues. Pkt., 25c.

THRIFT. See Armeria.

Tritoma, Red Hot Poker ①

Culture: B, D or E, Page 65

Very handsome and showy border plants. Flowers borne in compact form on stout 3 and 4 ft. stems, having the appearance at a distance of orange and red colored spear heads. Require protection during winter, unless in a very sheltered position.

8558 Pfitzer's Hybrids. Orange scarlet. Pkt., 15c.

Grandis Pfitzeri. 2-3 ft. Aug.-Oct. The rich orange-scarlet flowers come freely in late summer and often continue till late October. The great waxy flowers make a vivid splash of color and are an excellent cut flower. 3 for $1.25; doz., $3.75; each, 50c.

Trollius (Globe Flower) ①

Culture: C, Page 65

Globe flowers of unique character, of bright orange or yellow, and finely cut leaves, make this a desirable subject for moist, lightly shaded locations or pool sides. Better sown in fall, as seed needs freezing to germinate.

8551 Ledebouri. 2 ft. Orange flowers. Pkt., 50c.

Tunica ①

Culture: B, D or E, Page 65

8559 ✕ Saxifraga. A pretty tufted plant with light pink flowers, produced all summer. Useful either for the rockery or the border. Pkt., 15c.

Verbascum (Mullein) ①

Culture: B, D or E, Page 65

Plants of stately growth. The leaves more or less woolly, and the flowers are borne in branched spikes. Belongs to the Foxglove order.

8569A Harkness Hybrids. 6 ft. Immense spikes well furnished with large pure yellow flowers during the whole summer. Pkt., 25c.

8566 Hybridum, Miss Willmott. The large white flowers are produced in stately spikes, rising 5 to 6 feet. July to frost. Pkt., 15c.

8567 Olympicum. 6 ft. Silvery foliage; golden yellow flowers borne in large pyramidal spikes. June-Sept. Pkt., 25c.

8569 Phoeniceum Hybrids. 2 ft. Bears white, purple, rose or red flowers in erect spikes. Pkt., 25c.

STOKESIA Cyanea

VERONICA (Speedwell)

Valeriana ① (Garden Heliotrope)

Culture: B, D or E, Page 65

8560 Rubra. 2 ft. Showy heads of old rose flowers in umbels on 12 inch stems. Pkt., 10c.

8561 Mixed. Pkt., 10c.

8562 Officinalis. 3 to 4 ft. Produces showy heads of rose-tinted white flowers during June-July with delicious strong Heliotrope odor. Pkt., 25c.

Veronica (Speedwell) ①

Culture: B, D or E, Page 65

Hardy, herbaceous perennials varying in height from a few inches to 3 or 4 ft., and bearing blue or white flowers in terminal spikes or racemes.

8577 ✕ Incana. White woolly plant, numerous blue flowers. 12 in. June-July. Pkt., 25c.

8576 Longifolia. 2½ ft. Spikes of light blue flowers, glaucous blue foliage. July-Sept. Pkt., 15c.

8570 Spicata. Blue. 2 ft. July-August. Flowers violet blue in long spikes. Pkt., 15c.

VERONICA Subsessilis. 2 ft. July-Sept. Conceded to be the best of the Veronicas. It blooms latest of all; the large spikes of dark blue flowers are borne on stiff stems well above the foliage. **Plants,** 3 for $1.25; doz., $3.75; each, 50c.

Vinca Minor (Grave Myrtle) ✕

Valuable for rockeries or makes a fine evergreen carpet under and about shrubs and trees. 4 in. June. Green foliage, large blue flowers.

Bowles Variety. Glossy leaved plant which makes a fine evergreen for shady locations. Flowers are a charming intense blue. **Plants,** 3 for $1.15; doz., $3.50; each, 45c.

PLANTS OF HARDY SWEET VIOLETS

✕ Frey's Fragrant. Large deep purple single blooms, standing well above the heavy foliage. **Plants,** 3 for $1.15; doz., $3.50; each, 45c.

✕ Double Russian. The true hardy double violet. Very double, dark purple flowers, intensely fragrant. Plant in shade and mulch. **Plants,** 3 for $1.25; doz., $3.75; each, 50c.

✕ Rosina. New. This charming variety has an abundance of very fragrant, rose-pink flowers. It also blooms more freely in Autumn than other varieties; very often it will bloom all October. Extremely hardy and a gem for the shady corner. **Plants,** 3 for $1.25; doz., $3.75; each, 50c.

8587 WILD FLOWERS FOR SHADE. A mixture of our native wild flowers which will do well in shaded locations. Some may be annual, some perennial, some easy and some hard to grow, but with patience you should get a wonderful showing. The better your soil is prepared the better will be your stand. Large pkt., 25c.

8589 WISTERIA Chinensis Blue. Climber, purplish pea-shaped flowers. Pkt., 10c.

House Plants from Seed

AGAPANTHUS
Culture: C, B, D or E., Page 65

175 **Umbellatus (Blue Lily of the Nile)** 1 ft. Bright blue flowers produced in clusters on long stems. Does well out of doors in all Southern States. House plant in the North. Pkt., 15c.

ANTIRRHINUM Snapdragon
For Greenhouse Forcing.
Culture: D or E, Page 65
See Also Novelties and General List of Annuals

BRONZE
362 **Afterglow.** Golden bronze.
397 **New Deal.** Early fragrant golden bronze.
400 **Suntan.** Rose shade of tan yellow lip.

LAVENDER
367 **Bertha Bauer.** Standard lavender.

RED
407C **Velvet Beauty.** Rich American Beauty color.

ROSE AND PINK SHADES
375 **Cheviot Maid Supreme.** Deep rose pink.
378A **Daybreak.** Briarcliff shade of pink.
408A **Rose Queen.** Dark pink.

WHITE
395 **Lucky Strike.** Early flowering white.
408 **White Wonder.** Early flowering white.

YELLOW
374 **Cheviot Court.** Dark canary yellow.
409A **Cheviot Maid.** Yellow.
390 **Ethel.** Bright yellow.
405 **VAUGHAN'S MIXTURE OF GREENHOUSE VARIETIES.** A mixture of the forcing varieties we list.

Each of the above, per pkt., 50c; any 3 pkts. for $1.40.

ASPARAGUS
Culture: C. Pot up in fall, force in greenhouse. Page 65
480 **Plumosus Nanus.** + 3 ft. Pkt., 25 seeds, 30c.
485 **Sprengeri.** + Finest material for hanging baskets. Pkt., 25 seeds, 30c.

BEGONIAS
Fibrous-Rooted Ever-Blooming
Culture: B, C, D or E, Page 65
A continuous flowering class of greatest value for bedding; the flowers are of brilliant colors and borne in great profusion from summer to autumn. Seedlings of spring bloom in summer, while seedlings of summer make decorative winter house plants.

Begonia seed is very fine. Open packets carefully over a sheet of white paper.

1071 **Christmas Cheer Red.** The blooms attain a diameter of 2 inches. Dark crimson-scarlet. Pkt., 25c.
1072 **Christmas Pink.** Identical with above variety except the color is warm rose-pink. Pkt., 25c.
1079 **Gracilis Dwarf Luminosa.** Extra dwarf scarlet. Pkt., 25c.
1081 **—Prima Donna.** Rich, clear pink with deep green foliage. Pkt., 25c.
1076 **—White Pearl.** Clear, glistening white. Pkt., 25c.
1084 **Semperflorens Ile de France.** The flowers are 1¼ inches to 1½ inches, pure white, with bright yellow stamens. Foliage light green. Pkt., 35c.
1085 **—King of the Reds.** Dwarf glowing scarlet, foliage green edged bronze. Pkt., 25c.
1087 **—Masterpiece.** Large clear rose-pink flowers. Fairly cover the foliage. Pkt., 50c.
1090 **Semperflorens Special Mixed.** Finely balanced blend of full color range. Pkt., 25c.
The following varieties are strong, vigorous, branching early if pinched back. Excellent as a house plant.
1092 **Vaughan's Rose Bud.** Large rosé colored flowers, green foliage.
1093 **Vaughan's Snow Fairy.** Pure satin white flowers, yellow stamens, green foliage.
1094 **Vaughan's Sweet Heart.** Rich dark crimson flowers, foliage dark green.

Each of above, 3 var. per pkt., 35c; or 3 pkts. for 90c.

2846 **House Plants Mixed.** A mixture of the following: Begonia, Calceolaria, Cineraria, Cyclamen, Primula Malacoides and Obconica mixed and Solanum. Pkt., 50c.

CALCEOLARIA +
Culture: C. Pot up in fall, force in greenhouse. Page 65
1180 **Hybrida Grandiflora Extra Choice Mixed.** 1½ ft. A colorful greenhouse plant bearing a profusion of small, pocket-shaped orange or yellow flowers, many of which are beautifully tigered or spotted. Pkt., 50c.
1179 **Multiflora Nana, Mixed.** The average size of the blooms is only 1½ inch, but the amount of flowers produced is unsurpassed. The color scheme is extraordinarily gay and full of contrast. $1.00.

CINERARIA Hybrida +
Culture: C. Pot up in fall, force in cool greenhouse. Page 65.
1715 **Vaughan's Columbian Mixture.** A mixture of the finest strains; the flowers from 7 to 9 inches in circumference, brilliant colors. Pkt. (75 seeds), 25c.
1716 **Cremer's Prize Mixture.** The petals in most of the blooms of this strain are wide, numerous and overlap well to form attractive heads. The plants can be finished in smaller pots, too, making shapely specimens covered with masses of blooms. Pkt., 50c.
1726 **Multiflora Nana Gold Center.** The golden yellow stamens make a wonderful contrast with the blues, reds and pinks of the flowers. Pkt., 50c.
1718 **Potsdam Strain, Mixed** (Berlin Market or Weissensee). Taller and larger flowered than Cremer's Prize mixture. Pkt., 50c.
1816 **CLITORIA Ternatea.** + Very graceful vine covered with hundreds of fan like flowers of deep blue with soft yellow throat. Outdoor plant in the south; in they north, indoor culture advisable. Pkt., 25c.

CYCLAMEN Persicum Giganteum +
Culture: C. Pot up in fall, force in greenhouse. Page 65
2010 **Mixed.** Colors are vivid and varied. 10 seeds, 25c; 25 seeds, 60c.

DRACAENA Indivisa
Culture: D, E of C (Jan.-July) Page 65.
2350 □ +2 ft. Ornamental leaved plants; long, narrow, green-leaved foliage. Pkt., 10c.

FREESIA
Culture: D, E or C, Page 65
2451 **Dalrymple Special Strain.** Large sweet scented flowers borne on long stems, in blue, lavender and many shades of yellow. Pkt. (50 seeds), 50c.
2452 **Buttercup.** Good yellow. Pkt. (25 seeds), 50c.
2453 **Princess Mary.** Blood red. Pkt. (35 seeds), 25c.

GERANIUM +
Culture: D or E, Page 65
These grow readily from seed the first year and produce blooming plants the first summer.
2490 **Large Flowering. Newest Varieties Mixed.** Pkt. (50 seeds), 25c.
2491 **Flowerland Strain—See Novelties.**

GREVILLEA
Culture: D or E (Jun.-April) Page 65
2675 **Robusta (Silk Oak).** + 1 to 5 ft. Grows rapidly from seed, and is pretty in all stages of growth, with its long, drooping, silky foliage. Pkt., 15c.

GLOXINIA
Culture: D or E, Page 65
2560 **Vaughan's International Mixture.** + 12 in. Magnificent house-blooming plants, with handsome bell-shaped flowers in a diversity of the richest colors. Pkt., 25c.
2562 **Hybrida Grandiflora Mixed.** A brilliantly colored mixture containing many shades in self and bicolors with the popular rich dark red Beacon predominating. Pkt., 35c.

MARIGOLD
Culture: D or E, Page 65
3122 **Lieb's Winter Flowering.** Mahogany brown with golden yellow crested center. Pkt., 25c.
3125 **Lieb's Winter Flowering Sunshine.** Golden orange, yellow center. Pkt., 25c.
3145 **French Tall Double Winter Harmony** Golden orange center, reddish brown guard petals This is an entirely new type for winter flowering in the greenhouse. Very uniform growth, long stems, 2½ inch flowers, and comes 100% double and true to type. Pkt., 25c.

PANSY
Culture: A, B or C, Page 65
3841 **Vaughan's Long Stemmed Winter Flowering Re-selected Mixed.** Vaughan's new winter color range than the original Winter Flowering strain and has an excellent stem length, averaging better than 10 in. The bloom size is from 2½ to 3 in. and the flowers are of very good substance Sow in summer for Midwinter blooming. Pkt., 50c

PRIMULA
Culture: D, C or E, Page 65 +
4465 **Chinese Vaughan's International Mixture.** Our mixture contains all the choicest colors of the single-flowering Primulas in all their dainty shades Pkt. (100 seeds), 35c.

Primula—Various Sorts
Culture: C (May-July). Pot up July-Sept. Page 65
New Giant Malacoides
4469 **Snow Flake.** Has flowers of the purest shimmering snow white one can imagine. 200 seeds, 35c
4470 **Mixture.** Contains a good many varieties still in the developmental stage. 200 seeds, 35c.
4475 **Malacoides.** 10 in. The flowers are of a delicate shade of lavender, produced in whorls on tall graceful spikes in great profusion. Pkt., 25c.
4479 **—Salmon Rose.** True salmon. Pkt., 50c.
4464 **Giorgis.** This is a cross between Primula Malacoides and Chinese fringed varieties. The flower formation is that of the Chinese Primrose while the short compact foliage reveals the Malacoides blood: Finely fringed, double rowed, single flowers 1¼ inches in diameter. Dark green foliage. The color is a strong carmine rose with a strong yellow center. Pkt. (150 seeds), 50c.

Primula Obconica Grandiflora
Culture: D or E (Jan.-April); C (May-July). Winter in greenhouse. Germination 3-4 weeks. Page 65
4487 **Fassbender Red.** Large rich deep red. Pkt (200 seeds), 50c.
4496 **Gigantea. Wyaston Wonder.** The huge heads of bright crimson flowers are carried on strong stems well above the foliage. In spite of the vigorous growth, Wyaston Wonder makes a compact and tidy plant. Pkt. (100 seeds), 50c.
4495 **Obconica Grandiflora Mixed.** Good mixture. Pkt. (200 seeds), 25c.
4493 **Double Portland Beauty.** Ranging in color from light pink to rose-pink. Pkt. (250 seeds), $1.00.

SMILAX 6 ft.
Culture: D or E, Page 65
4780 Makes a fine pot or basket plant. Elegant for table decoration when cut. Pkt., 15c.

SOLANUM
Cultures C or D, Page 65.
4789 **Hlavacek's Masterpiece.** Compact and produces many more cherries than the old type. Pkt., 25c.

STEVIA
Culture: D or E, Page 65
4825 **Serrata.** 2 ft. Free-blooming plants, bearing a multitude of fragrant pure white flowers; suitable for summer or winter blooming and cutting. Pkt., 15c.

| FIRMING THE SOIL | MARKING THE ROWS | SOWING THE SEED | COVERING THE SEED |

SOWING SEEDS IN THE INDOOR BOX

FLOWER SEED CULTURES—HOW TO SOW

IN FIVE paragraphs below, designated A, B, C, D and E, we cover in considerable detail the methods of starting flower seeds which are available to the amateur without a greenhouse, and which cover well the needs of an outdoor garden. In the flower seed section in the case of each flower listed, information is given as to the cultural methods which can be used for that subject.

A Sow in the bed, border or row where the plants are to grow. The soil should be loamy, with well pulverized surface. With heavy soil inclined to cake and crack, it is usually best to grow plants in a seed bed (B) and transplant to the permanent place. Loosen the soil where seeds are to be sown, with the trowel, or hoe, several inches deep. Rake smooth. Broadcast small seeds and cover them lightly four or five times their diameter. Very small seeds may be merely pressed in. Larger seeds may be planted singly, well covered, but more thickly than plants are wanted. Firm the soil well over the seed. Watering now becomes of great importance. At no time should the soil be allowed to become hard and dry, yet excessive watering may cause the seeds to rot, sour the soil, or cause "damping off." When the plants appear, thin them out, allowing each to grow singly, without crowding. The distance between them is governed by their ultimate size and spread. Excess plants may usually be moved to a new location.

B Sow in outdoor seed bed, to be transplanted. The seed bed in the open should be of loose, mellow loam, raised slightly above the surrounding surface, and preferably surrounded by a wooden curb, to prevent rain washing across it. It should not be wider than four feet, so it can be worked easily. Shelter from high winds is valuable, but damp and shady corners are not desirable. Full sun is advisable when seedlings are up, while shade when needed, as in midsummer for perennial seedlings, is best supplied by a lath or cloth canopy, which can be removed in damp and cloudy weather. Sow the seeds in rows which may be as close as five inches. Sowing and watering are the same as described in "A" above. Seedlings may be transplanted when they make true leaves, the second pair of leaves to appear; or they may be left until larger before being moved to their permanent location. Perennials should be moved from the seed bed to a nursery row, to grow until fall before being moved to the border.

C Sow in flat, pot or pan outdoors or in a cold frame. This method is applicable to slow germinating subjects, some of which may take a year to germinate. Fill the receptacle with potting soil as described in "D", firm the soil and broadcast the seed, covering four or five times their diameter. Place the receptacle in a shaded location, where there is free air circulation. During the spring, summer and fall, water often enough to prevent soil from drying out.

While our cultural instructions are definite, detailed and exceptionally thorough, they should be supplemented by reading in good gardening books and by obtaining, at first hand, advice from successful gardeners in your neighborhood. Success in gardening requires study, and the opportunity for enlarging one's information and trying out new things is one of the most fascinating features of gardening.

A mulch of peat moss will help retain moisture. In winter, place in a protected place outdoors and cover with leaves. Have patience with slow germinating subjects; do not disturb too quickly. Any live seed will eventually grow if given time enough, provided soil, moisture supply, etc., are right. When seedlings appear and make true leaves, transplant to pots, nursery row or permanent location. If moss forms on soil surface, sprinkle fresh earth over top.

D Sow indoors in a box, pot or pan. This method may be followed where there is a window facing south, enjoying sunlight most of the day. Use a standard florists' pot or pan (shallow pot) or a "flat", which is a shallow box, with holes bored in the bottom for drainage. Cover the drainage holes in pot or box with broken pottery; fill with potting soil. This is a mixture of half sand and half black loam. It may be obtained from florists. Firm the soil, and sow the seeds in rows, marking each row to identify the sowing. Water by setting the box or pot in water, so that it soaks up from below, or use a fine spray which does not wash the soil. Place in a dark place, covered with a wet newspaper blanket until the seeds sprout. As soon as sprouts appear bring into full light. Cover the box or pot with glass to hold moisture in, but when moisture collects on glass wipe it off, and prop up one end of the glass to allow air to circulate during the sunny part of the day. A temperature not below 50 degrees at night, or 75 degrees by day, is best. Do not allow the soil to dry out. When the seedlings have made true leaves (the second set), they should be transplanted to other flats, giving at least two inches of space apart; or they may be moved to small pots or to an outdoor seed bed or border.

E Sow in a hot bed or cold frame. A cold frame or a hot bed heated by manure or other means may be used. The best method with flower seeds is to sow seeds in flats, which are placed in the frame. With manure heated beds, seeds should not be sown until the temperature of the newly made bed has dropped to 90 degrees. Watering and ventilation are important. On sunny spring days, always prop up one end of the sash to prevent overheating, which may occur quickly and cause spindly growth. Do not allow the soil to dry out. When the seedlings have made true leaves, they should be transplanted to other flats, spaced two inches apart each way; or to the soil in the hot-bed, if late enough.

Victory Garden Guide

TO AVOID waste, save money and work, and reap the greatest harvest possible from your Victory Garden, devote a few hours to making a well considered plan, which will accomplish these things:

1—Grow vegetables your family likes, in quantities which you can use.

2—Provide a continuous harvest through the garden season in your locality, with a substantial surplus for winter canning.

3—Place emphasis on the protective foods, rich in vitamins, which are especially needed under a rationed diet to avoid malnutrition.

Data given on this page, plus the cultural instructions on the pages which follow, provide a complete garden guide, from which your plan may be prepared, and your garden planted and cultivated.

These are the Most Nutritious Vegetables

This table has been prepared from the best authorities available as an approximate guide to the relative value of vegetables as the source of vitamins.

VITAMINS REQUIRED DAILY FOR BUOYANT HEALTH
National Nutrition Conference's Recommendation for Active Adult

A	B1	C	B2 (Riboflavin)
5,000 I.U.	600 I.U.	75 Milligrams	2.7 Milligrams

Vitamin Contents of a 3½-oz. Portion

	A I.U.	B1 I.U.	C Mg.	B2 Mg.		A I.U.	B1 I.U.	C Mg.	B2 Mg.
Beans, Green Stringless	600	20	7	.....	Kale	10,000	59	140	0.50
Beans, Lima	125	100	13	0.25	Lettuce, Green Leaf or				
Beans, Wax Stringless	410	25	...	.....	Cós Varieties	6,000	18.6	4.6	.12
Beet Greens	12,000	15	28	.....	Onions, Spring	6,200	...	...	.....
Beet Root	40	24	10	.....	Parsley	1,000	...	11	.....
Broccoli, Green	4,000	25	50	.....	Parsnips	380	66	38	.....
Brussels Sprouts	1,100	50	90	.....	Peas, Green	530	78	13	.....
Carrots	2,700	32	3	.....	Peppers, Green	660	69	0.12	.....
Celery, Green Stalks	.320	...	2	.....	Peppers, Red	2,200	...	135	.....
Celery, White Stalks	2	5	2	.....	Spinach	14,000	27	13	.....
Chard	9,000	10	21	.....	Spinach, New Zealand	7,500	10	0.45	.....
Chicory					Squash, Summer	1,000	15	...	.....
(Endive or Escarolle)	9,500	12	5	0.022	Squash, Winter	2,900	21	3.5	.....
Collards	7,000	50	22	.....	Tomatoes	3,000	26	25	0.05
Corn, Yellow Sweet	1,250	22	4	.....	Turnip Greens	6,000	35	42	0:25
Corn, White Sweet	125	18	4	0.13	Turnip Roots, White	20	12	30	.....

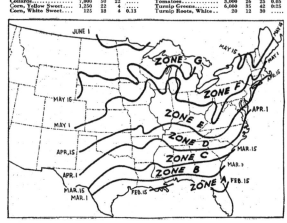

Check Frost-Proof Date in Your Locality

This map shows the average date of the last killing frost in each zone. The latest recorded killing frost will be about thirty days later than the average. From this data, and from neighborhood experience, you can figure the probable frost-proof date in your locality.

One week before frost proof date sow bush beans 2 inches deep, 2-4 inches apart, pole beans 4-6 inches apart. Harvest pods before seeds form. If picked clean, plants will bear until frost; but young plants yield best and succession plantings are advised.

Artichokes

rusalem Artichoke Roots. About five bushels plant an acre, enough to keep 20 to 30 hogs from Oct. to April. Cut and plant like potatoes. In Europe the tubers are baked, like potatoes, and esteemed as food because of their distinctive flavor. Tubers can be supplied in March and April. Lb., 25c; 3 lbs., 50c; 10 lbs., $1.25. Write for quantity prices.

Asparagus

SPARAGUS from the home garden is one of the most delicious and earliest of crops. It may be ›wn in any deep, rich soil, either from seed or roots.

SEED PLANTING — Asparagus may be raised m seed and a crop obtained in three years. e ounce of seed will produce 300 plants.

ROOT PLANTING — A year may be saved by ying the plants and setting them two feet apart in e row, and the rows four feet apart.

ASHINGTON RUST-RESISTANT STRAIN. Developed by the experts of the United States Department of Agriculture, who originated this strain. Rust-proof plants are preferred by commercial growers. The most satisfactory strain is MARY WASHINGTON.

ary Washington. Pkt., 10c; oz., 20c; ¼ lb., 50c.

radise. This is comparatively a new introduction and is claimed to be superior to the Washington strains in the following points: yields heavier, produces a crop one year earlier and has a very mild delicious flavor. It is claimed to produce as much as five tons of cut Asparagus in one season. Pkt., 15c; ½ oz., 25c; oz., 40c.

ASPARAGUS ROOTS

	1-Year Old			2-Year Old		
	Doz.	100	1000	Doz.	100	1000
ary ashington	$.50	$2.50	$20.00	$0.60	$2.75	$25.00

by mail, add postage as follows..........100, 50c.

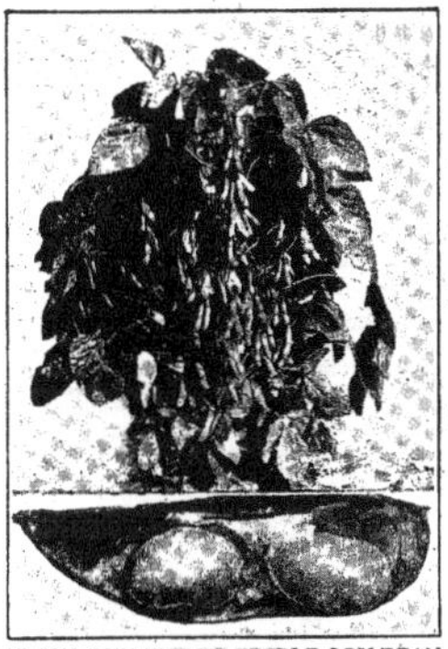

PLANT AND POD OF EDIBLE SOY BEAN

Edible Soy Beans

We offer four strains of edible Soy Beans, differing ıdically from the field varieties, developed to proide a valuable and palatable human food. Soy Beans ave proteins, 36.5%; fats, 17.5%; compared with lavy Beans proteins, 22.7%; fats, 1.5%. They are steemed highly as a food for diabetics. Yield much heavier for same area than Navy Beans. Iniversity of Illinois, Urbana, Ill., will supply on equest "Ways of Using Soy Beans as Food."

ansei. 90 days. 18 to 24 in. tall, the earliest and best in Northern districts. Pods 2½ x ½ x ⅜ pale green turning to pale greenish yellow.

Villomi. 95 days. Plant 3 ft. tall, otherwise similar to Bansei.

ogun. 98 days. Plant 30 in. tall, otherwise similar to Bansei.

Above Soys. Pkt. 10c: ½ lb. 25c: 1 lb., 40c: 2 lbs., 75c.

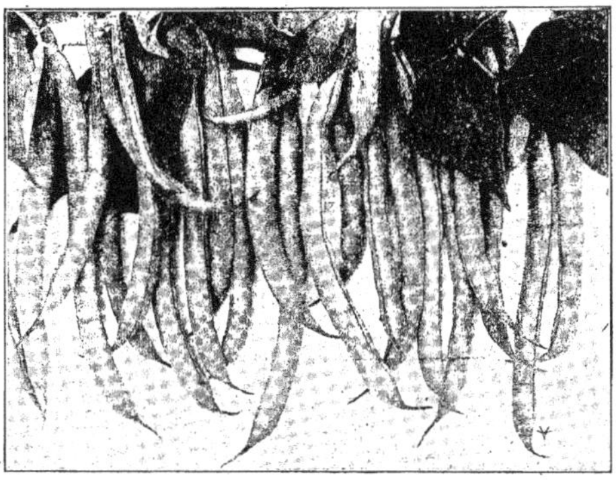

TENDERGREEN BEANS. Pkt, 10c; ½ lb. 30c; lb. 50c; 2 lbs. 90c; 3 lbs. $1.25.

Green Pod Bush Beans

QUALITY in Beans is measured by stringlessness, by tenderness, or the absence of fibre, or "linen" in the pod; by ability to produce well; a long, straight pod being preferred. After the harvest our Beans are hand-picked. The improvement in your crop far outweighs the increased cost.

★Tendergreen. **52 days.** Good sized bush bearing long round pods of excellent color. 6 in. long, ⅜ in. through. Good green color, straight, stringless. Seed: mottled buff and purple. Does best in black loam soil. Pkt., 15c; ½ lb., 30c; lb., 50c; 2 lbs., 90c; 3 lbs., $1.25.

★Streamliner. **55 days.** This is among the most productive of the bush types, a large bush of upright growth, bearing an extra heavy crop of long, straight semi-flat pods, 7 in. long, ½ to 9/16 in. wide and fleshy. For home use it will continue bearing when others have ceased. The quality is excellent; stringless, nearly fiberless, fleshy, round to flat, straight. Seed clear white, kidney shape, excellent as dry bean. Does well in medium heavy soil. Pkt., 10c; ½ lb., 30c; lb., 50c; 2 lbs., 90c; 3 lbs., $1.25.

★Plentiful. **55 days.** Large bush, bearing dark green pods that have a waxy or varnished shade which is not desirable for canning. Pods 6½ in. long, ½ in. wide. Tender, free from fiber, fleshy, straight, stringless, said to be resistant to common rusts. Does best in medium heavy soil. Pkt., 10c; ½ lb., 30c; lb., 50c; 2 lbs., 90c; 3 lbs., $1.25.

★Bountiful. **49 days.** One of the foremost Market Garden types. A sturdy bush, bearing long flat pods, 6½ in. long, ½ in. wide; stringless, straight, medium light green, some fiber but an excellent shipper. One of the fastest picking beans, good flavor. Seed: solid straw color or brownish yellow. Does well in any soil. Pkt., 10c; ½ lb., 30c; lb., 50c; 2 lbs., 90c; 3 lbs., $1.25.

Commodore. **63 days.** This is strictly a Kentucky Wonder Bush bean. Large, sturdy, productive. Very hardy bush type holding its dark green color till late and bearing fresh green beans till frost is kept picked. Pods 8 in. long, 9/16 in. diameter, very fleshy and of a flavor different from other bush beans. Pods round, very heavily dented between beans and usually crooked or moderately so; stringless in early stage of growth. Seed: reddish wine color, long. Does best in loam or medium light soil. Pkt., 15c; ½ lb., 30c; lb., 50c; 2 lbs., 90c; 3 lbs., $1.25.

Giant Stringless Green Pod. **53 days.** Very similar to Landreth's Stringless, but pods a little more curved and more fleshy with more indentation between the beans. Pods 6 in. long, 7/16 in. diameter. Stringless, tender, good flavor, a good canner and home garden sort. Seed: oval and yellowish brown. Does best in heavy soil. Pkt., 10c; ½ lb., 30c; lb., 50c; 2 lbs., 90c; 3 lbs., $1.25.

Black Valentine Stringless. **52 days.** Medium size bush bearing quantity of long fleshy pods, 6 in. long, ⅜ in. wide and from oval to flat, with good green color. Stringless and of good quality, excellent shipper. Seed black, oval. Does best in heavy soil. Pkt., 10c; ¼ lb., 30c; lb., 50c; 2 lbs., 90c; 3 lbs., $1.25.

Red Valentine Stringless. **53 days.** Medium bush, bearing fair crop of round pods 4½ in. long, ⅜ in. diameter, creased back, fleshy, brittle, fine grained, used principally in the south. Seed purplish red splashed with buff. Does best in heavy soil, cold resister. Pkt., 10c; ½ lb., 30c; lb., 50c; 2 lbs., 90c; 3 lbs., $1.25.

Wonderful. **53 days.** The vigorous bush type, resembling Tendergreen in color, having dark foliage, pods averaging 1 inch longer than Bountiful, flat, stringless until mature, slightly curved, excellent quality. This bean was produced by crossing Bountiful and Streamliner. Pkt., 10c; ½ lb., 30c; lb., 50c; 2 lbs., 90c; 3 lbs., $1.25.

Stringless Green Pod. **50 days.** Medium size bush, productive, bearing long, round pods of good color. Pods 5½ in. long, 7/16 in. diameter. Stringless, fleshy, nearly straight. Good quality. Seed: coffee brown. Does best in heavy clay soil. Pkt., 10c; ½ lb., 30c; lb., 50c; 2 lbs., 90c; 3 lbs., $1.25.

NAVY BEANS

Great Northern. **90 days.** Hardier and heavier vine than the navy, having a longer pod and larger beans. Seed a little longer than round, and clear white in color. Pkt., 10c; lb., 35c; 2 lbs., 65c; 3 lbs., 85c.

Improved Navy (White Pea Bean). **85 days.** Medium vine with runners. Pods 4 in. long, nearly round when ripe. Only used as dry bean. Lb., 35c; 2 lbs., 65c; 3 lbs., 85c.

Robust Navy. **100 days.** Selection of White Navy bean bred by the Michigan State Agricultural College, to get resistance to blight. Larger than the Navy which it sometimes outyields. Lb., 35c; 2 lbs., 65c; 3 lbs., 85c.

Inoculate Bean Seed.

To stimulate growth, use culture of nitrogen secreting bacteria. Garden size, sufficient for 5 lbs. of seed of peas, beans, lima beans and sweet peas, 10c.

For Soy Beans, special culture, sufficient for 120 pounds, 30c; for 5 bushels, 55c; for 25 bushels, $2.50.

Wax Pod Bush Beans

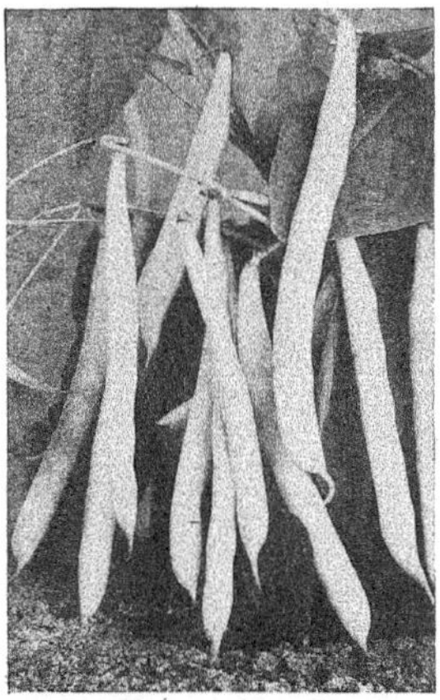

GOLD STANDARD WAX BEAN, Pkt. 10c; ½ lb. 30c; lb. 50c; 2 lbs. 90c; 3 lbs. $1.25.

★Golden Bountiful Wax. **53 days.** Plant large, sturdy, very productive. Pods 6-6½ in. long, ⅜ in. wide. Flat, thick stringless, small amount of fiber, good texture, quality and color. Seeds purplish black, kidney shaped and trifle flattened. Does best in sand loam. Pkt., 10c; ½ lb., 30c; lb., 50c; 2 lbs., 90c; 3 lbs., $1.25.

★Gold Standard Wax. (Davis Stringless) **52 days.** Plant medium large and fairly productive. Pods 6 in. long, ½ in. wide; thick, flat, stringless, straight, some fiber. Well drained soil of any kind is suitable. Good color, and quite hardy. Pkt., 10c; ½ lb., 30c; lb., 50c; 2 lbs., 90c; 3 lbs., $1.25.

New Kidney Wax. **52 days.** Medium large bush and productive. Pods clear yellow waxy color. Pods 6 in. long, ½ in. broad; flat, stringless, fleshy, free of fiber. An excellent table variety or canner. Does best in medium heavy soil. Pkt., 10c; ½ lb., 30c; lb., 50c; 2 lbs., 90c; 3 lbs., $1.25.

Pencil Pod Wax. **52 days.** Plant large, strong and bears an abundance of pods over a long period making it excellent for home garden use. Pods 6 in. long, 7/16 in. broad. Nearly-round, stringless, nearly straight, fleshy, free from fiber and excellent quality. Seed oblong, slightly flattened Does best in black loam soil. Pkt., 10c; ½ lb., 30c; lb., 50c; 2 lbs., 90c; 3 lbs., $1.25.

★Round Pod Kidney Wax. **55 days.** (Brittle Wax.) Very desirable for both home garden and canning trade. Plant medium large, erect, vigorous and productive. Pods waxy light yellow, 5½ in. long, ⅜ in. thick. Round, fleshy, brittle, stringless and without fiber. Seed white; blackish eye, kidney shape. Does best in medium heavy soil. Pkt., 10c; ½ lb., 30c; lb., 50c; 2 lbs., 90c; 3 lbs., $1.25.

Top Notch Golden Wax. **52 days.** A superior type to the old Improved Golden Wax. Very productive and compact plant. Creamy yellow pods that are straight, oval, stringless and brittle. 5 in. long, ½ in. wide. Seed solid white with brown eye. Decidedly the most prolific of the Golden Wax types. Does best in sand loam. Pkt., 10c; ½ lb., 30c; lb., 50c; 2 lbs., 90c; 3 lbs., $1.25.

Unrivalled Wax. **52 days.** Medium size bush of upright growth bearing profusely of rich waxy, yellow pods, 5 in. long, ⅜ in. wide; flat and fleshy, brittle, stringless in early stage. Seed small; long, round, yellowish brown. Does best in medium light soil. Pkt., 10c; ½ lb., 30c; lb., 50c; 2 lbs., 90c; 3 lbs., $1.25.

Wardwells Kidney Wax. **53 days.** Large bush, upright growing, bearing long straight pods 6 in. long, ⅝ in. wide. Fleshy stringless pods though flat. Seed white with brownish eye and markings over the end; flattened kidney shape. Does best in heavy clay soil. Pkt., 10c; ½ lb., 30c; lb., 50c; 2 lbs., 90c; 3 lbs., $1.25.

Two Pounds Prepaid

Catalogue prices of peas, beans and sweet corn include prepayment on lots up to and including 2 pounds. For postage charges on larger lots, see page 120.

LIMAS

One week after frost proof date sow seeds 2 inches deep, and thin plants of small seeded bush and all pole varieties to stand 6 inches apart, all large seeded bush to stand one foot apart. Plants kept picked clean will bear until frost.

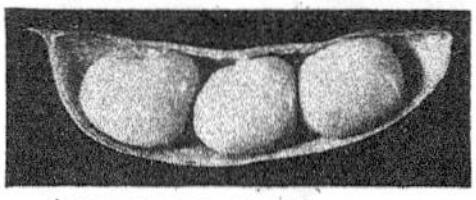

BABY POTATO. Pkt., 10c.

LIMAS should be planted a little later than the other bush Beans, in the most favorable location possible, as they are very late in maturing. Always plant with the eye down. The Bush Lima is more easily grown than the tall, and is earlier and more economical of space but the pole limas yield better.

BUSH

★Fordhook Bush. **78 days.** The highest quality Bush variety, it grows erect, and its large pods contain 4 to 5 large, thick green Beans. Pkt., 10c; ½ lb., 30c; lb., 50c; 2 lbs., 90c; 3 lbs., $1.25.

★USDA 2 Henderson. **About 60 days.** A prolific yielder of small Beans, thriving in ordinary soil. Earlier than standard Henderson and recommended to replace it., Pkt., 10c; ½ lb., 30c; lb., 50c; 2 lbs., 90c; 3 lbs., $1.25.

Baby Potato. **72 days.** It resembles Henderson Bush, but with darker foliage, more productive and averaging more Beans to the pod. Good flavor and excellent for canning or freezing. Pkt., 10c; ½ lb., 30c; lb., 50c; 2 lbs., 90c; 3 lbs., $1.25.

Burpee's Improved Bush. **About 76 days.** This has larger pods and Beans than the original. Pkt., 10c; ½ lb., 30c; lb., 50c; 2 lbs., 90c; 3 lbs., $1.25.

Burpee's Bush. **About 75 days.** Large white seeds; very productive and splendid quality. Pkt., 10c; ½ lb., 30c: lb., 50c; 2 lbs., 90c; 3 lbs., $1.25.

Cangreen. A new green seeded small bush lima of Henderson type. A stronger grower, more prolific, with slightly larger seeds. Pkt., 25c; ½ lb., 40c; lb., 75c; 2 lbs., $1.35.

POLE

Packet plants 15 hills; lb., 100 hills.

★Succulence. **75 days.** Earliest of pole limas. bears Beans slightly larger than Henderson's Bush. It is an exceptional producer and can be grown on a pole or allowed to run on the ground. Pkt., 10c; ½ lb., 30c; lb., 50c; 2 lbs., 90c; 3 lbs., $1.25.

Early Leviathan. **In about 83 days.** Pkt., 10c; ½ lb., 30c; lb., 50c; 2 lbs., 90c; 3 lbs., $1.25.

King of the Garden. **In 85 days.** A large podded, vigorous, immensely productive variety. The numerous pods, 5 to 7 inches long, are well filled with 5 to 6 large Beans of excellent quality. Pkt., 10c; ½ lb., 30c; lb., 50c; 2 lbs., 90c; 3 lbs., $1.25.

Carolina Sieva. **77 days.** Hardy, tall pole type, resembling Henderson Bush in other respects. Pkt., 10c; ½ lb., 30c; lb., 50c; 2 lbs., 90c; 3 lbs, $1.25.

Florida Butter. **78 days.** Similar to Carolina Sieva, except seed instead of white is buff spotted brown. Pkt., 10c; ½ lb., 30c; lb., 50c; 2 lbs. 90c: 3 lbs., $1.25.

Large White Seeded. **About 85 days.** Pkt., 10c; ½ lb., 30c; lb., 50c; 2 lbs., 90c; 3 lbs., $1.25.

BEETS

Sow as soon as soil can be worked in the spring, not over 13 seeds to the inch, in drill half-inch deep. Firm soil well over seed. Thin when roots begin to make globes, to stand 4 inches apart in row. Cook discards with their tops.

Eat Roots and Young Tops

QUALITY in Beets is measured by an even, globular shape, uniformity in size, bright, even color, flavor, fine texture and tenderness. Here, as with all vegetables, the difference between a fine and a mediocre strain of one variety may be as great as between different varieties.

Our best seed is grown only from transplanted roots, which are taken up in the fall, carefully graded, stored over the winter and transplanted again in the spring. Only Beets which conform to the highest quality standards are planted for seed. Thus improvement is shown annually.

While this extra care increases the cost of the seed, the increase is small compared with the added value which improved quality gives to the crop.

Quantity needed to sow: 15 ft. row, 1 pkt.; 60 ft. row, 1 oz.; acre, 7 lbs. (Rows 18 in. apart).

★Perfected Detroit. Matures in about 55 days. In this improved strain of Detroit Dark Red Turnip Beet the fine qualities which have made that variety standard for main crop sowing have been strengthened by careful breeding. It is earlier, and almost spherical in shape. Its small tops are just right for either dry or wet season, heavy or light soil. The color inside and out is a very dark red, and flesh of fine texture, tender and of excellent flavor. Pkt., 15c; ½ oz., 25c; oz., 45c; ¼ lb., $1.25.

★Detroit Dark Red Turnip. Matures in about 55 days. A main crop variety unequaled as a heavy yielder, and having the qualities which are valued for shipping and canning, as well as for the home and market gardens. Tops are uniform, small and erect. Roots are globe shaped, and very dark red, inside and out, with inconspicuous zoning. It is sweet, and remains tender until maturity. Pkt., 10c; ½ oz., 25c; oz., 40c; ¼ lb., $1.10.

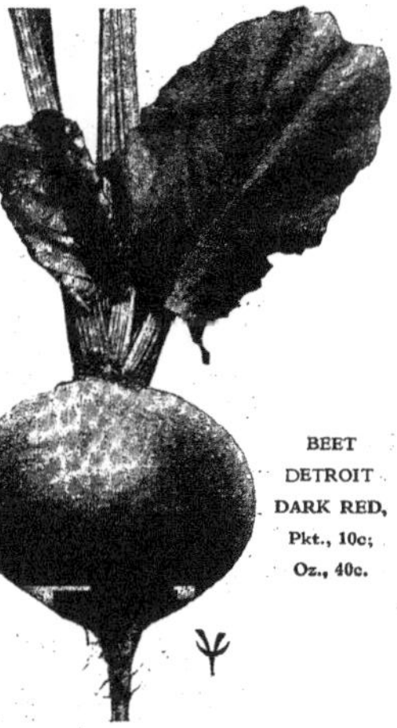

BEET DETROIT DARK RED, Pkt., 10c; Oz., 40c.

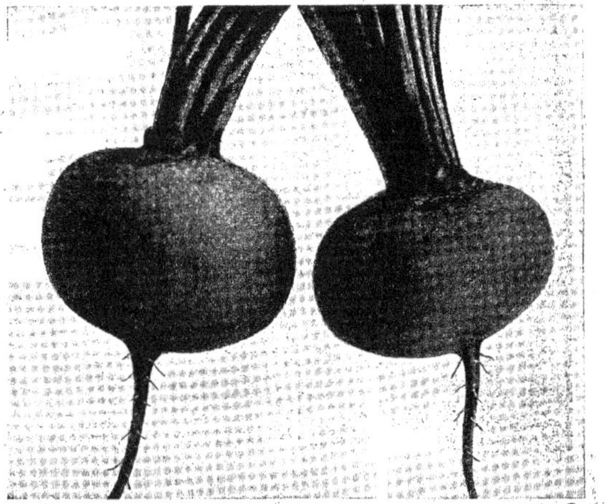

Crosby's Egyptian Beet, Vaughn's Selected Stock. Pkt., 15c; ½ oz., 25c; oz., 40c; ¼ lb., $1.10.

★Crosby's Egyptian. Matures in about 50 days. This early variety has long been a home garden favorite; and our strain has maintained and improved its excellent qualities. It is exceptionally tender and sweet, of a deep red with some light zoning, and fine texture. Tops are of medium size, and the roots of a flattened globe shape, excelling in table quality.
Vaughan's Selected Stock. Pkt., 15c; ½ oz., 25c; oz., 40c; ¼ lb., $1.10.
Standard Stock. Pkt., 10c; ½ oz., 20c; oz., 35c; ¼ lb., 85c.

Early Wonder. Matures in about 50 days. This is a selection of Crosby's Egyptian more nearly globe shaped, and a darker red. The tops are small, making it a fine variety for bunching. Pkt., 10c; ½ oz., 20c; oz., 35c; ¼ lb., 85c.

Good for All. Matures in about 50 days. This is a selection of Detroit, bred to produce uniform roots which can be harvested when 1¼-1½ inches in diameter, especially for canning and pickling. Pkt., 15c; ½ oz., 25c; oz., 40c; ¼ lb., $1.10.

Crimson Globe. In about 60 days. Second early main crop, of medium size. Pkt., 10c; ½ oz., 20c; oz., 35c; ¼ lb., 85c.

Edmand's Blood Turnip. 60 days. Pkt., 10c; ½ oz., 20c; oz., 35c; ¼ lb., $1.00.

Tendersweet. 50 days. Deep red throughout, with almost no zoning, globe shape with tender flesh. Pkt., 15c; ½ oz., 25c; oz., 45c; ½ lb., $1.25.

Winter Keeper or Long Dark Blood. 75 days. Roots long, smooth, dark red, tapering to a point, 7 in. long, remaining tender even in storage. Pkt., 10c; ½ oz., 20c; oz., 30c; ¼ lb., 90c.

Early Blood Turnip. In 55 days. Pkt., 15c; ½ oz., 25c; oz., 45c; ¼ lb., $1.25.

Improved Early Egyptian. About 45 days. The best variety for forcing and first early crop. Roots very dark red, rounded on top, flat beneath, small tops. Pkt., 10c; ½ oz., 25c; oz., 40c; ¼ lb., $1.10.

Mangel Wurzel

Mature in 90 to 120 days.

Mangels are an excellent crop for dairy and poultry farms, giving a crop of good feeding value for both cattle and chickens. Sow in May or June, 6 lbs. to the acre, in rows 2 feet apart, and thin to nine inches.

Barres Sludstrup. This Mangel holds the world's record for dry matter content. It is a long, reddish yellow, ovoid root. Pkt., 10c; oz., 25c; ¼ lb., 75c.

Vaughan's Mammoth Long Red. Largest and heaviest cropper of long red sorts. Pkt., 10c; oz., 25c; ¼ lb., 75c.

Golden Tankard. Pkt., 10c; oz., 25c; ¼ lb., 75c.

Giant Rose Half Sugar. Pkt., 10c; oz., 25c; ¼ lb., 75c.

Sugar Beets

Klein-Wanzleben. Wedge shape tapering to long tail. Pkt., 10c; oz., 25c; ¼ lb., 75c.

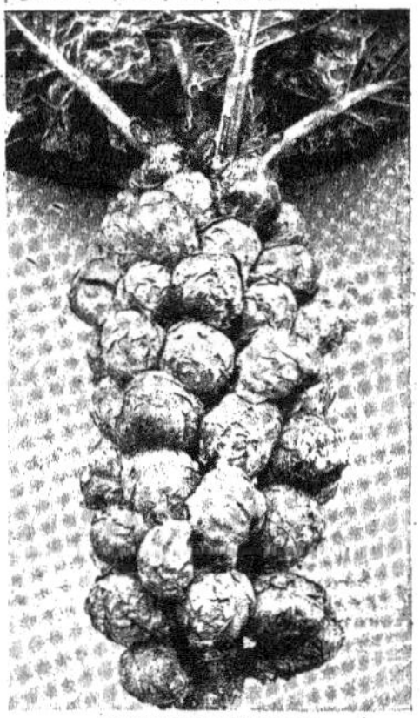

BRUSSELS SPROUTS

Brussels Sprouts

Brussels Sprouts are miniature cabbages formed on a plant stalk. The delicate flavor is improved by a touch of frost. For late use sow seed in June.

Long Island Improved. About 90 days. The most satisfactory Brussels Sprouts for American conditions. Pkt., 15c; ½ oz., 55c; oz., $1.00.

BROCCOLI

Sow outdoors with earliest crops; transplant or thin to stand 18 inches to 2 feet apart. Protect from aphids and cabbage worms. After center heads are cut, each branch will produce a head, harvest lasting until killing frosts.

BROCCOLI ITALIAN GREEN SPROUTING.

Richest of Its Race in Vitamins

Green sprouting broccoli has been given new importance by the disclosure that because of its green coloring it is far richer in vitamins than white cauliflower, which it resembles in flavor. It takes rank as one of the protective foods, which defense authorities urge shall be given precedence in Victory Gardens. It is also a much easier subject for the amateur than cauliflower, and has a much longer season of harvest.

The type which has won greatest popularity produces a terminal head which may be cut, whereupon other heads are produced on lateral branches, which in turn may be harvested. Typical center heads are shown in the illustration. It survives light frosts, and produces well in the cool autumn weather.

★Italian Green Sprouting (Calabrese). Matures in about 70 days. A selected strain of the most popular type from an Italian specialist who has bred it to a high standard of yield, flavor and tenderness. After its large center heads are harvested, smaller heads 2 inches in diameter form at the ends of lateral branches. It continues to bear for eight to ten weeks. Pkt., 25c; ½ oz., 45c; oz., 85c; ¼-lb., $2.50.

LATEST BOOK ON HOME CANNING
The Pocket Book of Home Canning by Elizabeth Beveridge. Complete instructions for: Canning, Preserving, Quick Freezing, Pickling, Storing, Drying. It will tell you how to convert the summer's surplus from garden, field, and orchard into a substantial war-time larder. Describes the A, B, C's, and the X, Y, Z's of canning, preserving, curing and storing. 140 pages illustrated; 30c postpaid; 25c over the counter.

PAOTING. Pkt., 10c. "PE TSAI." Pkt., 15c.
Quantity needed for 30 ft., 1 pkt.; 200 ft., 1 oz.

Chinese or Celery Cabbage

★Celery Cabbage Pe Tsai. The VAUGHAN Strain. This exceptionally fine vegetable is rapidly growing in public favor. Its growth resembles the Cos lettuce, but the outer leaves have the general texture of ordinary cabbage. When the outside leaves are stripped away, the cabbage presents a well nigh irresistible appearance. Our strain of this seed is grown in China by a specialist whose family has raised and selected this particular type for many years. The heads blanch without tying. June is the proper planting time. Pkt., 15c; ½ oz., 35c; oz., 65c; ¼ lb., $2.00.

Celery Cabbage "Paoting." Genuine "WONG BOK" type. Will mature firm heads through the summer months. It has produced heads weighing 15 pounds and stands long before going to seed. It is the largest of the Chinese cabbages. Pkt., 10c; ½ oz., 30c; oz., 50c; ¼ lb., $1.50.

Red Cabbage
Valued for Distinctive Flavor

Mammoth Rock Red. (Long Island strain). In 95 days. The hardiest and largest heading red cabbage. Round, very solid and of a deep red color, often weighing up to 12 pounds each. Pkt., 10c; ½ oz., 45c; oz., 80c; ¼ lb., $2.40.

Red Yellows Resistant. About 100 days. Not as large as Mammoth Rock Red, but darker and more uniform color. Pkt., 20c; ½ oz., 50c; oz., 90c; ¼ lb., $2 65.

VAUGHAN'S SELECT SNOWBALL. Pkt., 35c; ¼ oz., $1.00; ½ oz., $1.75.

Pedigreed Cauliflower

Before war completely shut off communication with Denmark, where our finest strains of cauliflower were grown, we were able to import highly selected stock-seeds with which to start production of the same strains in this country. Tests have shown the excellent quality of the Danish strains to be maintained in crops grown from the American seed, which is produced under climatic conditions similar to those of Denmark.

Home gardeners will find cauliflower not difficult where conditions are right. When plants are set out in June or early July to mature in October, there is seldom any question of getting fine, large heads. Quantity needed for 150 plants, 1 pkt.; for 1,500 to 2,000 plants, 1 oz.

★Vaughan's Select Snowball. Matures in about 55 days. Improved strain of our New Snowball, early, dwarf, compact, producing solid white heads which measure 9 to 10 inches across and have a perfectly white core. Its heads are more uniform in size and there are more leaves, for protection in bleaching. The seeds are about one-third smaller. Pkt., 35c; ¼ oz., $1.00; ½ oz., $1.75.

Vaughan's Earliest Dwarf Erfurt. New Like Snowball, but a few days later. Pkt., 35c; ¼ oz., $1.00; ½ oz., $1.75.

★Vaughan's New Snowball. Matures in about 55 days. A well grown head measures 9 to 10 inches across, with depth in proportion, and a perfectly white core. It is dwarf and compact in growth, and as early as any other. Pkt., 35c; ¼ oz., $1.00; ½ oz., $1.75.

Autumn Giant. Large heading late fall sort. Pkt., 25c; ½ oz., 65c; ¼ oz.-$1.10; oz., $2.00.

Danish Snowball or Dry Weather. Heads larger, snow-white, second early. Pkt., 35c; ¼ oz., $1; ½ oz., $1.75.

★—Varities designated by a star as illustrated above are recommended as of especially fine strains and suited to the home garden.

YOUNG COLLARD PLANT.
Pkt., 10c; oz., 20c.

Collards

This is a relative of the cabbage which produces of green leaves of cabbage flavor, and having a much higher vitamin content. It produces edible leaves in 45 days from sowing, and succession sowings should be made. Though used chiefly in the south, where it is too hot for cabbage, it maybe grown in any part of the U. S. A. and is recommended for home gardens as a protective food. Pkt., 10c; oz., 20c; ¼ lb., 50c; lb., $1.50.

After frost proof date, set out plants which were started indoors four to six weeks previously. Late varieties may be sown outdoors in June. Space small early types 12 inches apart, medium 18 inches, large late 2 feet. Water well and protect from worms and aphids.

Resistant Strains Thrive in Hot Summers

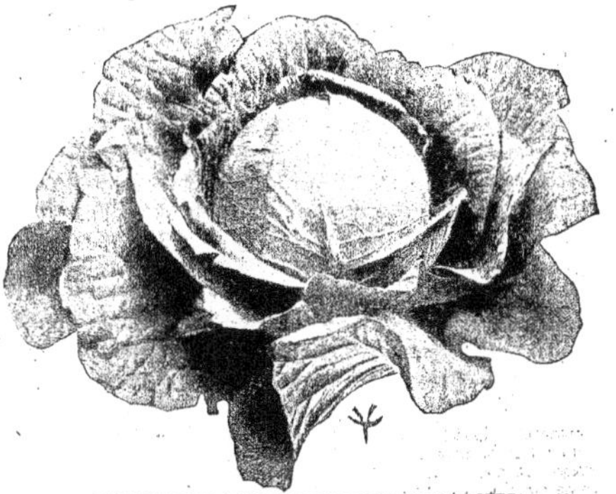

COPENHAGEN MARKET CABBAGE (RESELECTED)
Pkt., 15c; ½ oz., 50c; 1 oz., 95c; ¼ lb., $2.85.

HEREVER the temperature of the soil rises to 90 degrees or higher, there is danger of the yellows disease, and when it strikes, crop failure may result.

In the great cabbage growing district centering around Racine and Kenosha, Wisconsin, an industry has been saved by developing strains of cabbage resistant to yellows. We offer seed of these strains, which have been developed by years of scientific work, and actual growing tests. The uniformity and yield of resistant strains have greatly improved. We recommend their use wherever danger of yellows may exist. If the disease strikes, resistant strains will show slight loss, where non-resistant types would probably be destroyed.

Regular Stock of Yellows Disease-Resistant Varieties

Jersey Queen. 60 days. As near a true Jersey Wakefield as is possible to select in type and earliness. Exceptionally resistant to yellows. This is the first of our resistant strains to mature and is recommended to the home gardener where a cabbage for summer salad use is desired. Pkt., 15c; ½ oz., 40c; oz., 75c; ¼ lb., $2.35.

★Wisconsin Pride (Racine Market) (Early Detroit). 64 days. A round head early of the Golden Acre type. Of dwarf, compact growth with few leaves; of exceptionally uniform size and maturity season. Pkt., 20c; ½ oz., 50c; oz., 95c; ¼ lb., $2.75.

Wisconsin Ballhead. 100 days. Most highly perfected strain of yellows-resistant cabbage yet introduced. It excels in all the qualities that mark a good cabbage, besides being 100 percent resistant. A better keeper, of finer texture and matures earlier than Wisconsin No. 8. We sincerely recommend this for home garden and market growers. Pkt., 15c; ½ oz., 35c; oz., 55c; ¼ lb., $1.65.

★Globe. 75 days. The resistant Glory of Enkhousen is but 3 or 4 days later than Copenhagen, of excellent flavor. You who think that there is no difference in the flavor of cabbage should compare a mature Globe with any other cabbage. Pkt., 15c; ½ oz., 50c; oz., 95c; ¼ lb., $2.75.

★Bugner. 100 days. A winter variety grown in infected soil near Chicago, which is the most popular variety with market growers. Our own strain has been selected for resistant qualities over many years. Pkt., 20c; ½ oz., 70c; oz., $1.30; ¼ lb., $4.15.

Wisconsin All Head Early. In about 80 days. Is the second resistant variety to mature. Will stand for a long time without bursting and is nearly 100% resistant. Large heading general purpose cabbage. Pkt., 15c; ½ oz., 40c; oz., 75c; ¼ lb., $2.35.

Marion Market. In 75 days. The third yellows-resistant cabbage to mature. Of an excellent Copenhagen Market type, though later than select Copenhagen, coming a short time before Glory of Enkhousen. Pkt., 15c; ½ oz., 50c; oz., 90c; ¼ lb., $2.65.

Wisconsin All Seasons. About 90 days. Either a kraut or home variety, but is used more for kraut than any other purposes. Pkt., 15c; ½ oz., 40c; oz., 75c; ¼ lb., $2.35.

Wisconsin No. 8. 110 days. A late winter keeper. Pkt., 15c; ½ oz., 35c; oz., 55c; ¼ lb., $1.65.

SAVOY CABBAGE

RICHER IN NUTRITION

This type of cabbage has leaves which are crumpled or savoyed instead of smooth, as in other types, and do not bleach white, but remain green and retain more vitamin A. The heads are not as tight as the smooth leaved type, but are of superior flavor and are esteemed for table quality.

Improved American Savoy (Long Island strain). The best main crop variety of this type. The vigorous short stemmed plant bears a large, fairly solid head, sweet and tender. Pkt., 15c; ½ oz., 45c; oz., 80c; ¼ lb., $2.40.

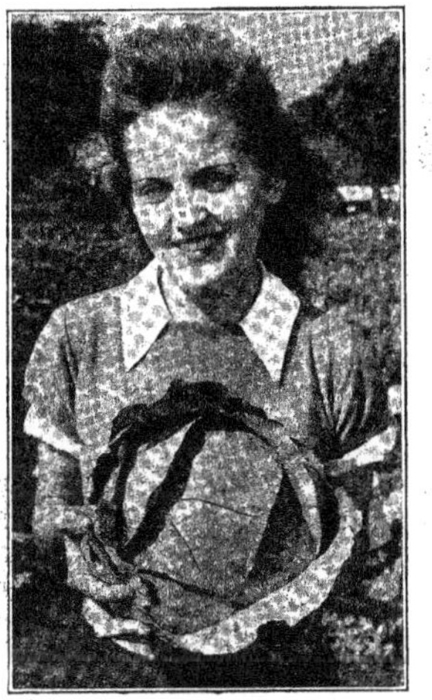

RESISTANT CABBAGE BUGNER. Pkt., 20c.

Standard Cabbages

★Copenhagen Market Extra Early. Matures in about 62 days. Earliest of the large heading cabbages, maturing even before the conical types, this select strain is of unique value both to home and market growers. It is the result of many years' selection by our European grower, and produces heads round as a ball, crisp, tender and of fine texture.

Reselected, 62 days. Pkt., 15c; ½ oz., 50c; oz., 95c; ¼ lb., $2.85.

Standard Stock, 68 days. Pkt., 10c; ½ oz., 45c; oz., 80c; ¼ lb., $2.35.

★—Varieties designated by a star as illustrated above are recommended as of especially fine strains and suited to the home garden.

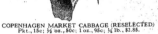

STANDARD CABBAGES—Continued

Daybreak. 60 Days. It bears a round, hard head with short stem and was developed by one of the best growers in Denmark, in whose trials it matured 65% in 60 days, averaging 3 pounds, 12 tons to the acre. Pkt., 15c; ½ oz., 50c; oz., 95c; ¼ lb., $2.85.

★Golden Acre. Matures in about 60 days. Resembles Reselected Early Copenhagen Market in most respects, except that its heads are slightly smaller, 4 to 5 lbs. It is of dwarf, compact growth, with few leaves, so that the plants can be set close together, and is exceptionally uniform in size and maturity date. Pkt., 10c; ½ oz., 40c; oz., 70c; ¼ lb., $2.10.

★Green Acre. 60 days. A round headed variety which instead of bleaching in the hot sun holds its rich green color to the bursting stage. Smooth, solid, of fine texture and flavor; heads weigh 3 to 4 pounds. Pkt., 15c; ½ oz., 50c; oz., 95c; ¼ lb., $2.85.

Glory of Enkhousen. Matures in about 75 days. This globe shaped, medium early variety is of excellent flavor and crispness and produces heads weighing 8 to 10 pounds, and more uniform than the earlier types. Recommended for the main crop in the home gar en. Pkt., 10c; ½ oz., 35c; oz., 60c; ¼ lb., $1.85.d

Penn State Ballhead. About 105 days. A heavy yielding strain of the short stem Danish Ballhead type. Yields as high as 26 tons per acre have been recorded. Pkt., 15c; ½ oz., 45c; oz., 80c; ¼ lb., $2.40.

Vaughan's Select Early Jersey Wakefield. In about 62 days. This extra early conical sha ed head cabbage is a specialty with us. The heads are hardi the outside leaves small, so that close planting s possible. Pkt., 10c; ½ oz., 35c; oz., 60c; ¼ lb., $1.85.

Early Flat Dutch. In 90 days. Sure solid header; weighs 10 to 12 pounds. Pkt., 10c; ½ oz., 30c; oz., 60c; ¼ lb., $1.80.

Charleston Wakefield. About 73 days. Later than "Jersey Wakefield," with heads much larger and uniform. Does well on heavy soil. Pkt., 10c; ½ oz., 35c; oz., 55c; ¼ lb., $1.60.

Vaughan's All Seasons. About 90 days. Suited to every growing season. Even when planted late it keeps well, and is of better quality than big ribbed winter sorts. Pkt., 10c; ½ oz., 35c; oz., 55c; ¼ lb., $1.60.

All Head Early or Faultless. In about 78 days. Matures large, uniform handsome heads of unsurpassed quality. Pkt., 10c; ½ oz., 35c; oz., 55c; ¼ lb., $1.60.

LATE STANDARD VARIETIES

Danish Ballhead Short Stem. Or Dwarf Amager. About 105 days. Ball shaped splended keeper. Very fine 8 lb., heads. Pkt. 10c; ½ oz., 45c; oz., 80c; ¼ lb., $2.40.

Vaughan's Premium Late Flat Dutch. In about 110 days. Seed may be sown in the open ground and plants raised without the use of hotbeds. Pkt., 10c; ½ oz., 30; oz., 50c.

CARROTS

Sow as soon as soil can be prepared, in shallow drills, seeds to the inch. Thin out when of finger size, and serv discards. Carrots will mature well growing close enough t touch, and remain delicious all season; but many prefe them young, and make several sowings.

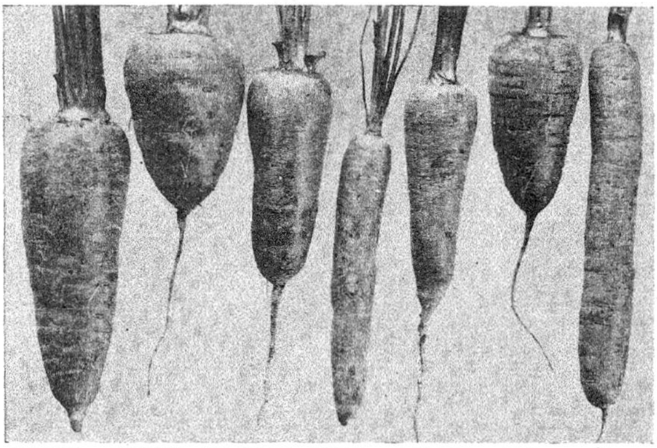

DANVERS OXHEART RED HEART NANTES HALF LONG IMPROVED CHANTENAY DUTCH HORN TOUCHON

Sow Slender, Tender Kinds

CARROTS have been improved in quality at the same time their value as a healt food has been gaining wider recognition In addition to color, size, shape, tops and season of maturity, our special strains ar selected for sweetness, and the tenderness and even texture of the flesh, especially for a minimum of "core." Scientists say the brighte the color, the more Vitamin A in carrots.

★Touchon. **70 days.** Experienced home gardeners know the exquisite flavor o tender young Carrots, not much thicker than you little finger, which contribute one of the early summer's most delicious table treats. Here is a variety which retains when grown to full size the qualities which others lose so quickly as they mature. Pkt., 20c; ½ oz., 45c; oz., 85c; ¼ lb., $2.50

★Redheart. **70 days.** It has no core of the usua sort, but its rich red coloring is ever throughout the flesh. The top is ample for bunching and the foliage is fern-like. The root is of medium length, blunt, smooth and easily prepared for serving. Pkt., 20c; ½ oz., 45c; oz., 85c; ¼ lb., $2.25

★Nantes Half-Long Scarlet. **Matures in about 70 days.** This early variety is not surpassed in tenderness and sweetness. The tops are small, the roots bright orange, smooth and cylindrical, 6 to 7 inches long. There is almost no core. Pkt., 15c; ½ oz., 35c; oz., 65c; ¼ lb., $2.00.

★Table Queen. **Matures in about 70 days.** Half-long type, rich red, tender, crisp and one of the sweetest we know. Pkt., 20c; ½ oz., 45c; oz., 85c; ¼ lb., $2.50.

Vaughan's Select Danvers. **About 75 days.** It is a half-long type, averaging five and one-half inches in length, tapering to a blunt point. Its yield greater per acre than any other. Pkt., 15c; ½ oz., 35c; oz., 60c; ¼ lb., $1.75.

Improved Chantenay. **75 days.** This is a strain of Early Chantenay which resembles the original type in most respects except that it averages 1½ to 2 inches longer and has sloping shoulders. Pkt., 10c; ½ oz., 30c; oz., 50c; ¼ lb., $1.50.

Dutch Horn **In about 65 days.** Larger than French Horn and almost as early, 1½ inches thick, three inches long; fine grain, sweet-flavored, rich orange. Pkt., 15c; ½ oz., 35c; oz., 65c; ¼ lb., $2.00.

Guerande or Oxheart. **In 70 days.** Is a variety of very rapid growth, often attaining a weight of ½ pound. It is thick shouldered, short and top shape; has a good flavor and is tender. A second early. Pkt., 10c; ½ oz., 30c; oz., 50c; ¼ lb., $1.50.

Imperator. **About 77 days.** Has roots 7 to 8 inches long, slightly tapering, and just enough top to bunch well. Color is deep solid orange all-through. It is prolific and of high quality, brittle, tender, sweet. Pkt., 15c; ½ oz., 35c; oz., 60c; ¼ lb., $1.75.

CARROTS FOR STOCK

Improved Long Orange. **About 88 days.** It is a good keeper of fine quality for winter use, and extensively grown for stock feeding. Makes a large tonnage of feed and may be used for cattle or poultry. Pkt., 10c; ½ oz., 30c; oz., 50c; ¼ lb., $1.50.

Green Celery Best for *Vitamins*

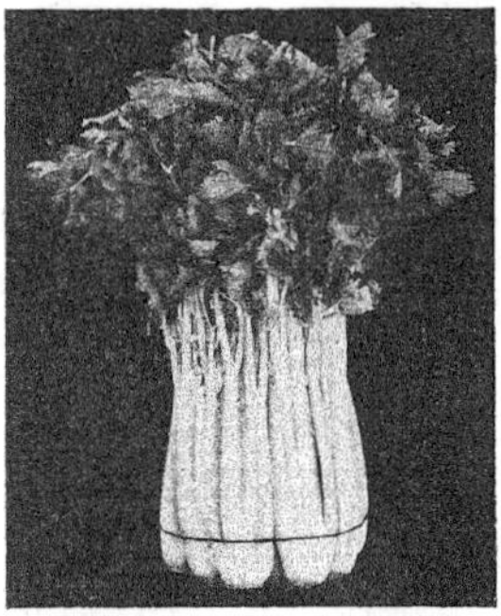

CELERY Salt Lake. Pkt., 25c.

CELERY is often thought to be difficult to grow. Every home gardener whose soil is sufficiently light and rich to produce good Cabbages may easily produce a family supply of this most welcome delicacy. Start the seed indoors and set the plants out around the middle of June. Eight inches apart for the early kinds and a foot for the winter varieties. Do not work over the plants when they are wet with dew or rain.

Vaughan's Celery Seed is of the finest strains in the world and is used by market gardeners selling to the most exacting trade.

Quantity needed for 400 to 500 plants, 1 pkt.; 8,000 plants, 1 oz.

★Salt Lake. Selection from Utah Golden. Large round stalk. Free from string, finest quality, blanches easily. An excellent winter seller. Pkt., 25c; ½ oz., 60c; oz., $1.00.

Salt Lake Special. Utah grown select strain. Pkt., 25c; ¼ oz., 65c; ½ oz., $1.00; oz., $1.75; ¼ lb., $6.00.

★Golden Detroit. The plants are heavy, compact and full hearted. This is a pure line selection of the Dwarf Golden Self-Blanching type which accentuates the good points of that variety. Pkt., 25c; ½ oz., 60c; oz., $1.00.

★Michigan Golden (College Golden). Developed at Michigan State Agricultural College, resistant to "Fusarium Yellows," bred from the tall strain of Golden Self-Blanching. Pkt., 40c; ¼ oz., 75c; ½ oz., $1.40; oz., $2.50.

Golden Plume. A selection from or a cross with the Golden Self-Blanching, it is more vigorous and withstands heat and blight better. It is a beautiful gold in color, brittle and of the highest table quality. **Select.** Pkt., 20c; ½ oz., 70c; oz., $1.35; ¼ lb., $4.00. **Regular.** Pkt., 10c; ¼ oz., 50c; oz., 9 c.

Golden Self-Blanching. Dwarf bunches with broad, heavy stalks, blanch into a rich, appetizing, golden yellow. Though the stalks are heavier than white varieties, its sweetness, tender crispness, delicious flavor and absence of strings make it a favorite. The French originators of this type have introduced a re-selected strain earlier and stronger growing than the older type.

Tall Strain. French type. Pkt., 25c; ½ oz., 75c; oz., $1.50.

Dwarf Strain. American-grown. Pkt., 10c; ½ oz., 60c; oz. $1.00.

Giant Pascal. The stalks are large, light green solid, crisp and of rich nutty flavor. For fall and winter, this is a splendid sort. Pkt., 10c; ¼ oz., 45c; oz., 85c.

Emperor. It is dwarf in type (hence easier to blanch than taller kinds), second early and a good winter keeper. The stems are round. Pkt., 10c; ½ oz., 40c; oz., 75c; ¼ lb., $1.50.

White Plume. It excels in crisp and tender table quality. Its habit of growing is vigorous, stalks are uniformly white and large sized.

Selected Stock. Pkt., 10c; ½ oz., 40c; oz., 75c;

Winter Queen. An excellent winter sort with double the amount of heart of any known celery. Pkt., 10c; ½ oz., 40c; oz., 75c.

Soup Celery or Smallage. Green foliage used for soups. Oz., 50c; ¼ lb., $1.50.

Easy Blanching. Medium dwarf, stalks thick, quality excellent. Pkt., 10c; ½ oz., 35c; oz. 65c;

Celeriac

TURNIP ROOTED CELERY

This vegetable deserves much wider cultivation. Cooked and prepared as a salad, it has a rich celery flavor. The roots keep well in winter—recipes for preparing enclosed upon request.

Large Smooth Prague. **About 120 days.** A main crop variety. Pkt., 10c; ½ oz., 45c; 1 oz., 85c; ¼ lb., $2.50

Cardoon

Main stalks are blanched like Celery; used for salad or in soups. Pkt., 20c; ½ oz., 50c; oz., 95c.

Sow two weeks before frost proof date, seeds 2 inches deep, three inches apart; to be thinned out to six inches; or six seeds to a hill, 2 to 3 feet apart according to variety's height, thinning to three plants per hill. Time succession sowings, two weeks apart.

HYBIRD SWEET CORN IOANA

Hybrids for Heavy Yield

YBRID sweet corn excels in three ways: Heavier yield, more even maturity, and resistance to Stewart's disease, and other troubles. In flavor, which many home gardeners sider the supreme point; the variety Our Choice is equal to Golden Bantam, some think tter. Other hybrids will compare well in flavor with other open pollinated.
Any open pollinated corn will mature unevenly and give edible ears from one planting over onger-period, which some may prefer. Our list has been revised to offer the best of both brid and open pollinated types, as proved by exhaustive tests in our trials.

A packet plants 40 hills; a pound 400 hills; 12 pounds an acre.

HYBRID RESISTANT

Lee. Pkt., 15c; ½ lb., 35c; lb., 65c; 2 lbs., $1.20. See Novelty Page 6 for Description.

olden Pride. 68 days. From Connecticut Experiment Station. Compared with Our Choice, it is longer by one inch, upplies more cut corn, is fully as fine a kernel and as as good or better quality. We recommend it. kt., 15c; ½ lb., 35c; lb., 65c; 2 lbs., $1.20.

Golden Treasure. 66 days. Two weeks am and about five days earlier than Golden Bantam. Of 120 different strains in our trials, this was the earliest of all. It has a larger ear than Golden Bantam, 12 rows of kernels of good, sweet flavor, producing 35% more shaved corn to the ear. Pkt., 15c; ½ lb., 35c; lb., 65c; 2 lbs., $1.20.

Our Choice. 68 days. Maturing two days later than Golden Treasure, this is the sweetest variety we know, not excluding Golden Bantam. It is heavy yielding, with a good size 12 row ear, and completely resistant. For the home garden this would be our choice for an early. Pkt., 15c; ½ lb., 35c; lb., 65c; 2 lbs., $1.20.

Surprise. 64 days. 10 to 12 rows, golden yellow, low, ears 5½ to 6 inches. Stalks 57 to 60 inches tall and bear the ears 12 inches from the ground. We can recommend this for your first early corn of good flavor. Pkt., 15c; ½ lb., 35c; lb., 65c; 2 lbs., $1.20.

olden Nugget. 68 days. An excellent early, 66 inches tall, well filled ear.7¼ inches long, 8 to 12 rows of kernels. The size of the ear recommends it more than the flavor, which is medium. Pkt., 15c; ½ lb., 35c; lb., 65c; 2 lbs., $1.20.

incross (Vaughan's Top Cross Golden Bantam). 76 days. This variety is produced by crossing our Early Golden Bantam with Purdue Bantam. It is earlier than its male parent and not as uniformly eight rowed as its female parent, though it may vary. Pkt., 15c; ½ lb., 35c; lb., 60c; 2 lbs., $1.10.

arcross. 75 days. This is Golden 60-day crossed with Purdue Bantam and has given us a cross that is practically the same as Golden 60-Day. Pkt. 15c; ½ lb., 36¢ lb., 65¢ 2 lbs., $1.20.

hipcross. 75 days. Ten days later than Whipple's Yellow. Pkt.; 15c; ½ lb., 35c; lb., 65c; 2 lbs., $1.20.

arrow Grain Hybrid. 98 days. Same season as Narrow Grain Evergreen. Much more prolific in poor years. Pkt., 15c; ½ lb., 40c; lb., 70c; 2 lbs., $1.35.

untry Gentleman Hybrid. In about 99 days. Same season as Country Gentleman but better yielder. Pkt., 15c; ½ lb., 40c; lb., 70c; 2 lbs., $1.35.

owell's Hybrid. Pkt., 15c; ½ lb., 40c; lb., 70c; 2 lbs., $1.35.

Ioana. 83 days. Productive variety, highly resistant to drought and wilt. Plants tall and sturdy, with broad and numerous leaves. Ears 7½ to 8 in. long, 12-14 rowed, cylindrical; well filled with medium-narrow, light, yellow kernels. Pkt., 15c; ½ lb., 35c; lb., 65c; 2 lbs., $1.20.

Vaughan's Golden Cross Bantam. In about 79 days. Obtained by crossing the two strains produced by G. M. Smith of Purdue. It has the same resistance and will produce a heavier crop of more uniform ears. Pkt., 15c; ½ lb., 35c; lb., 65c; 2 lbs., $1.20.

Pop Corn

Golden Hulless. Pkt., 10c; ½ lb., 25c; 1 lb. 40c; 5 lbs., $1.50.

South American. 110 days. Usually 2 ears to a stalk. Large yellow kernels, 12 to 14 row ear, 6 to 7 inches long, pops to enormous size, no hard center. Pkt., 10c; ½ lb., 25c; 1 lb., 40c; 5 lbs., $1.50.

GOLDEN SWEET   BANTAM EVERGREEN   GOLDEN BANTAM

Sweet Corn All Summer, 25¢

Collection No. 22. One Packet each, Earliest Golden Sweet, Golden Bantam, and Bantam Evergreen, prepaid for 25c. ½ lb. each, 50c; 1 lb. each, 85c.

OPEN POLLINATED YELLOW

Golden Bantam. Matures in about 80 days. The tender sweetness of an ear of true Golden Bantam, picked just after it turns yellow and served in half an hour, has never been excelled. To maintain this supreme quality, however, requires constant vigilance, and there is great variation in the seed sold under this name. Our strain is grown on our Michigan farm, where it is selected for size, uniformity and flavor, and runs much larger than the usual type, and has better flavor. Pkt., 10c; ½ lb., 25c; lb., 45c; 2 lbs., 85c.

Extra Early Golden Bantam. Matures in about 72 days. Same as Golden Bantam.

Earliest Golden Sweet. Matures in about 63 days. To produce an earlier variety with the quality of Golden Bantam we have worked many years, and this is the best of many tested. It gives you Bantam quality twelve days earlier. Pkt., 10c; ½ lb., 25c; lb., 45c; 2 lbs., 85c.

★Vaughan's Bantam Evergreen. 85 days. A product of Golden Bantam crossed with Stowell's Evergreen. It has retained much of the quality of Bantam and has the size and tender skin of Evergreen. Pkt., 10c; ½ lb., 25c; lb., 40c; 2 lbs., 75c.

Whipple's Early Yellow. About 87 days. A 14 rowed ear, 7 to 8 inches in length. Pkt., 10c; ½ lb., 25c; lb., 45c; 2 lbs., 80c.

Golden 60-Day. 68 days. It is bred from 60-Day White crossed with Golden Bantam. Except for color, same as 60-Day. Pkt., 10c; ½ lb., 25c; lb., 45c; 2 lbs., 85c.

Vaughan's Black Sugar or Black Mexican. About 85 days. Selected for large ears and high sugar qualities. Ears 10 rowed, 8 inches long. Pkt., 10c; ½ lb., 25c; lb., 45c; 2 lbs., 85c.

OPEN POLLINATED WHITE

Howling Mob. 83 days. A large-eared fine second early corn. Pkt., 10c, ½ lb., 25c; lb., 45c; 2 lbs., 85c.

Vaughan's Mammoth White Cory. In about 67 days. The ears are long with 10 to 12 rows, usually averaging two ears to the plant. Our seed is grown and bred on our own farms. Pkt., 10c; ½ lb., 25c; lb., 45c; 2 lbs., 85c.

Early Evergreen. About 75 days. It is earlier than Stowell's Evergreen and in northern localities is a surer cropper. Pkt., 10c; ½ lb., 25c; lb., 45c; 2 lbs., 85c.

Country Gentleman. About 95 days. The grain is small and crowded together on the cob, instead of forming in defined rows. Deliciously tender and sweet. Pkt., 10c; ½ lb., 25c; lb., 45c; 2 lbs., 85c.

Stowell's Evergreen. About 95 days. The stand ard main crop variety. The stalks grow 7 to 8 feet high, and bear ears 8 inches long, with 16 or more rows of the finest sugary grains. Vaughan's eastern grown seed develops a larger percentage of sugar than seed grown in the western states. Pkt., 10c; ½ lb., 25c; lb., 45c; 2 lbs., 85c.

Narrow Grain Evergreen. 95 days. Similar to Stowell's Evergreen, but with narrow and smaller kernels. Used mostly by canners. Pkt., 10c; ½ lb., 25c; lb., 45c; 2 lbs., 85c.

60-Day White. 68 days. Height 3 feet, ears 10 to 12 rowed, 6 to 7 inches. Pkt., 10c; ½ lb., 25c; lb., 40c; 2 lbs., 75c.

Two Pounds Prepaid

Catalogue prices of peas, beans and sweet corn include prepayment on lots up to and including 2 pounds. For postage charges on larger lots, see page 120.

CUCUMBERS

Sow in hills three to six feet apart; six seed 1½ inch deep to a hill, thinned to three plants Protect small plants from beetles. Water whe needed, and keep vines picked clean.

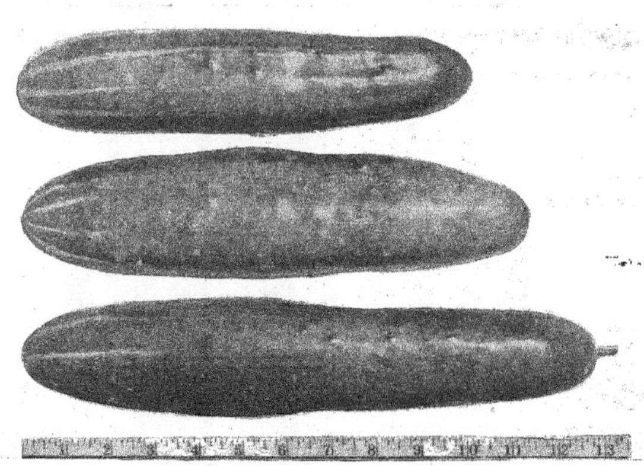

At top, CUCUMBER STRAIGHT EIGHT; In middle, COLORADO or "A and C;" Bottom, THE VAUGHAN. Each variety, Pkt., 10c; oz., 40c.

For Salads and Pickles

TWO distinct types of cucumbers are bred to fill the need for large fruits suitable for slicing to serve in salads, and the smaller, uniform, prolific, pickling varieties. Our special strains in both types are grown with the greatest care to insure that all standards of quality are maintained in your crop. **Quantity needed for 20 hills, 1 pkt.; 80 hills, 1 oz.**

Home gardeners will have no trouble in producing from our strains fruits that excel in table quality. We recommend especially Mandarin, our new Chinese, earliest as well as of the highest quality, and the Vaughan, largest of outdoor varieties.

Cubit. For description, see Novelty page 8. Pkt., 25c; ½ oz., 45c; oz., 85c.

★The Vaughan. Matures in about 74 days. The largest of outdoor cucumbers, it is also of first table quality. Compared to other Long White Spine varieties, it is much darker in color, more uniform in shape and size, thinner, and more prolific. It is the ideal American forcing variety, as well as an outdoor sort. Pkt., 10c; oz., 40c; ¼ lb., $1.10; lb., $3.20.

★Colorado, or "A and C." 68 days. A beautifully long, slender, dark green cucumber of excellent shape and intense dark color which is maintained longer than in any other variety. Fruit is inclined to taper, especially at stem end. Seeds form late in season and are few. Pkt., 10c; oz., 40c; ¼ lb., $1.10; lb., $3.20.

Cucumber, Marketeer. 60 days. An ideal slicer for market and shipping. A dark green cucumber of the white spine type. Smooth uniform. Pkt., 25c; ½ oz., 45c; oz., 80c; ¼ lb., $2.25.

★Straight Eight. 60 days. A white spine which produces a high percentage of fruits perfectly straight and 8 or more inches long. Pkt., 10c; oz., 40c; ¼ lb., $1.10; lb., $3.20.

Mincu. Matures in about 45 days. Its fruits averaging 4½ inches long by 2 inches in diameter are suitable both for salad slicing and pickling. It bears from 8 to 10 fruits within a foot of the hill. Pkt., 10c; oz., 35c; ¼ lb., 95c; lb., $2.70.

Midget or Hill Cucumber. 70 days. Produced by Dr. Yager of the North Dakota Agricultural College and is the true hill type. The cucumber is about 6 in. long and 2½ in. in diameter. Fit for any small home garden. Pkt., 15c; oz., 35c; ¼ lb., 95c.

★Mandarin. Matures in about 45 days. Earliest of any variety we have tried, this new variety, thanks to its Chinese blood, is also supreme in quality. It is 10 to 12 inches long, 1¾ to 1½ inches in diameter, deep green, with the crispness and flavor for which Chinese cucumbers are noted. Pkt., 10c; oz., 40c; ¼ lb., $1.10; lb., $3.20.

Earliest of All. About 60 days. A fair size, dark green White Spine. Of special value for first crop. Pkt., 10c; oz., 35c; ¼ lb., 95c; lb., $2.70.

Vaughan's Improved Arlington White Spine. About 60 days. A heavy yielder; symmetrical, straight, 7 to 10 inches long. A great favorite in the south. Pkt., 10c; oz., 35c; ¼ lb., 95c; lb., $2.70.

Evergreen White Spine. About 60 days. A great blight resister. 8 to 12 inches long. Select stock. Pkt., 10c; oz., 35c; ¼ lb., 95c; lb., $2.70.

Davis Perfect. 65 days. Fine length, slim, dark green and crisp. The best blight resister of long sorts. Pkt., 10c; oz., 35c; ¼ lb., 95c; lb., $2.70.

Deltus. In 72 days. A dark green cucumber nearly free from spine, may be used for forcing out of doors. Pkt., 10c; oz., 35c; ¼ lb., 95c; lb., $2.70.

Early Fortune. In 64 days. Medium length White Spine, much planted in the south. Pkt., 10c; oz., 35c; ¼ lb., 95c; lb., $2.70.

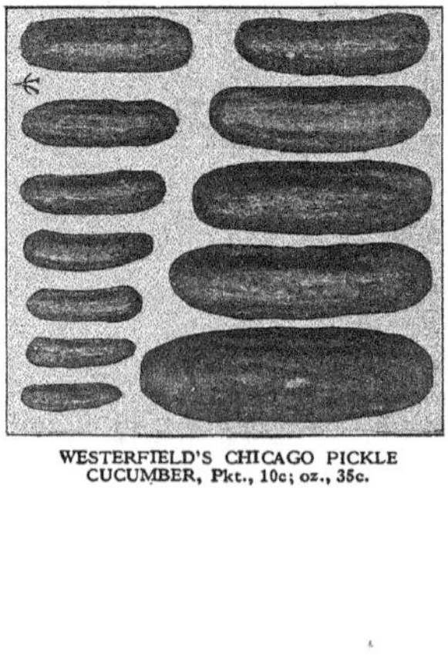

WESTERFIELD'S CHICAGO PICKLE CUCUMBER, Pkt., 10c; oz., 35c.

Climbing. About 68 days. This is quite resistant t disease and insects. It is good quality and of a dar green color. May be grown on a trellis. Pkt., 10 oz., 35c; ¼ lb., 95c; lb., $2.70.

Improved Long Green. In 68 days. Used f yellow chunk pickles. The vines are vigorous an productive; the fruit (12 inches long) has a di tinctive flavor. Pkt., 10c; oz., 40c; ¼ lb., $1.1 lb., $3.20.

White Wonder. 55 days. This variety of fir quality bears fruits 7 to 8 inches long which, whe young, have pure white skin. Pkt., 10c; oz., 35 ¼ lb., 95c; lb., $2.70.

FIRST RESISTANT CUCUMBER

Shamrock Resistant. 65 days. Resistant to Mosai early, uniform and satisfactory as a slicer or sma pickler. A white spine variety 6 to 8 in. long. Pkt 15c; oz., 35c; ¼ lb., 95c; lb., $2.70.

ODD CUCUMBERS

Lemon Cucumber. In 65 days. Not the Garde Lemon, though similar in appearance. It is a re cucumber. Pkt., 10c; oz., 45c.

Serpent or Snake. In 80 days. A curious, twiste cucumber. Pkt., 10c; oz., 45c.

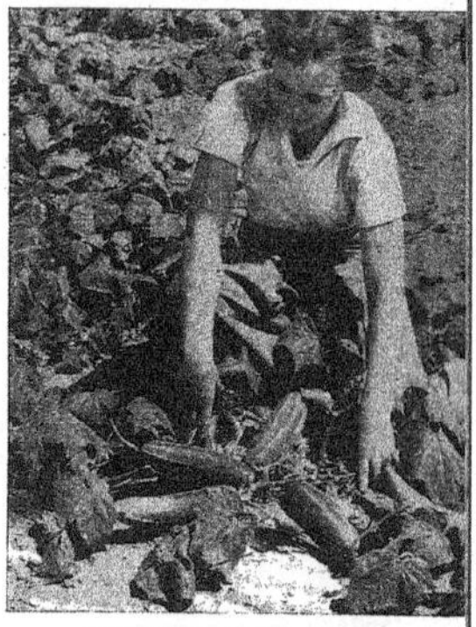

CUCUMBER MINCU. Pkt., 10c.

Pickle Cucumbers

Grow Quick. 48 days. A pickle type simil to Chicago Westerfield in si and shape, but a week or ten days earlier. It usuall matures its crop before the early blight appear. Pkt., 10c; oz., 35c; ¼ lb., 95c; lb., $2.70.

★Westerfield's Chicago Pickle. 58 day Since w first introduced this pickle years ago, it has been distinguished success. When ripe the fruit is m dium size, blunt at both ends, has prominent blac spines. Pkt., 10c; oz., 35c; ¼ lb., 95c; lb., $2.7

West India Gherkin. About 60 days. A very sma oval prickly sort, distinct from all others. It grown for pickles only and must be used whe young. Pkt., 15c; oz., 35c; ¼ lb., 95c.

National. About 56 days. The type is shorter tha the Chicago Pickle and is broad at the stem en tapering slightly to the tip. The fruit being smalle blight does not sap the strength of the vine to th detriment of a crop. We offer a strain of mo carefully selected seeds from fields inspected by u Pkt., 10c; oz., 35c; ¼ lb., 95c; lb., $2.70.

Green Prolific or Boston Pickling. In abou 58 days. Smooth, symmetrical pickle, very earl and productive. Pkt., 10c; oz., 35c; ¼ lb., 95 lb., $2.70.

Early Cluster. 55 days. Similar to Boston Picklin but fruits come more in clusters. Pkt., 10c; oz., 35 ¼ lb., 95c; lb., $2.70.

Essential Foods for Good Nutrition

SPINACH KING OF DENMARK. Pkt., 10c.

Old Dominion. 40 days. The same as Virginia-Blight-Resistant in type and quality. Will eventually take the place of Virginia because of its long standing qualities, which permit early fall planting. Pkt., 10c; oz., 20c; ¼ lb., 50c.

Vaughan's Special. In 43 days. An early, smooth leaved spinach, being more upright in growth than other spinaches and nearly a long standing variety. Pkt., 10c; oz., 25c; ¼ lb., 65c.

Prickly Seeded Hollandia. 43 days. Pkt., 10c; oz., 25c; ¼ lb., 65c.

Bloomsdale or Norfolk Savoy-Leaved. About 40 days. Is a very hardy sort; the leaves are very thick and blistered, making it a fine shipper; it is a good standard size. Pkt., 10c; oz., 20c; ¼ lb., 50c.

NEW ZEALAND SPINACH

Tetragonia Ex-
★**New Zealand Spinach.** pansa. 60 days.
While this is not a member of the Spinach family proper, it furnishes an abundance of delightful "greens" throughout the summer and right up to cold weather. Both the leaves and the stalks of the plant are very fleshy and extremely brittle and of the finest quality when cooked. Do not sow seed until May 1st or when the soil is fairly warm. Plant in rows 3 feet apart and thin the plants to stand 2 feet apart in the rows. Soak the seed before sowing. Pkt., 10c; ½ oz., 25c; oz. 45c; ¼ lb., $1.35.

CUT & COME.   LARGE WHITE RIB.
SWISS CHARD. Pkt., 10c.

Spinach

PINACH delights in cool, moist weather. Seed should be sown at the earliest possible moment spring in rows one foot apart and thinned to six ches in the row. It matures in 45 to 50 days and lickly runs to seed in warm weather. The Antvorgv variety, listed below, is most free from this ndency. Home gardeners have generally adopted riss Chard and New Zealand Spinach as a greens op, as both may be cut many times and will produce a continuous crop until freezing weather in the ll. A fall crop of spinach may be sown in late dly or August and will find the cool, moist autumn ather favorable for growth. The value of spinach in the diet has been scientifically established by e vitamin investigation.

Viking. 45 days. This 1935 All-America winner bears largest leaves of the thick-leaved type, and is almost as long standing as King of Denmark. Its leaves are smooth to slightly crumpled, dark green, and of excellent quality for home and market Pkt., 10c; oz., 20c; ¼ lb., 50c.

ing of Denmark (Antvorskov). 48 days. In our trials this variety has been slower to run to seed than any other sort. Antvorskov forms quite large tufts (or rosettes), compact and low. The numerous leaves are extra large, broad and rounded, exceedingly bushy, slightly crumpled and of a glossy dark green color. Pkt., 10c; oz., 25c; ¼ lb., 65c.

loomsdale Long Standing. 45 days. Latest of the Long Standing Spinach introductions. Improvement was accomplished through the selection of hermaphrodite plants (bisexual), which run to seed much more slowly than the unisexual. This variety is of better quality than the Antvorskov (King of Denmark) having larger, Savoy type leaves. Pkt., 10c; oz., 25c; ¼ lb., 65c.

Nobel Giant Thick Leaved. 45 days. The seed of this thick-leaved variety produces the largest spinach under cultivation. It grows rapidly and remains in good condition a long time. The medium-green leaves are large, rounded, slightly crumpled, succulent and tender. It is an excellent home garden spinach. Pkt., 10c; oz., 20c; ¼ lb., 50c.

oomsdale Dark Green. 43 days. The leaf is savoyed, or rinkled, and of a darker green than Bloomsdale ong Standing. The dark color is preferred in some narkets. Pkt., 10c; oz., 20c; ¼ lb., 50c.

ncess Juliana. In 50 days. This is a new type of "Long Season" Spinach. The leaves are of good size, very dark green, well crumpled and thick. The first plants of Spinach to bolt to seed are the male plants. (Spinach is generally dioecious; i. e., there are male and female plants.) This first bolting seed has been eliminated in this new race by the production of hermaphrodite plants, these plants seeding much later than male plants. Pkt., 10c; oz., 25c; ¼ lb., 65c.

NEW ZEALAND SPINACH. Pkt., 10c.

Garden Sorrel

Is boiled and served like spinach, also delicious for soups. As the hot sun tends to increase its acidity, a northern exposure is advisable. It should be sown in drills 18 inches apart. It is hardy, but should be divided every four years. Pkt., 13c; oz., 75c.

Kale or Borecole

Greens for early fall, winter and spring. Sow seed about middle of June, later transplant to rows 2 to 2½ feet apart. Dwarf sort can be sown later. Frost improves flavor.

Dwarf Green Curled Kale. In about 55 days. Leaves curly as Parsley, tender and very fine flavor. Immense quantities produced in south and ready sales in the north. Pkt., 10c; oz., 50c; ¼ lb., $1.50

Vaughan's Excelsior Moss Curled Kale. Ready in about 55 days. Plants grow 18 to 21 inches high and produce as many as 50 edible leaves to a plant. Leaves very early and unsurpassed in flavor. Pkt., 10c; oz., 50c; ¼ lb., $1.50.

Tall Green Curled. About 60 days. Pkt., 10c; oz., 50c; ¼ lb., $1.50.

Siberian. In 65 days. Plant dwarf, spreading and very hardy. Pkt., 10c; oz., 50c; ¼ lb., $1.50.

Swiss Chard

★**"Cut and Come Again."** 45 days. This vegetable gives maximum returns for little care and space; it yields a constant crop from July to Winter. The leaves are used for greens the same as spinach or beet tops. Sow early in spring, in rows 16 inches apart, and thin out to 6 inches in the rows. The leaves grow very large. Cut the leaves off and new ones grow quickly. As it grows, thin out for use and keep clear of weeds. Leaflet of recipes enclosed upon request. Pkt., 10c; oz., 30c; ¼ lb., 80c.

Lucullus Swiss Chard. About 55 days. A new Moss Curled sort. Very large leaves. Pkt., 10c; oz., 30c; ¼ lb., 80c.

Large White Rib (Dark Green). The leaf is large, smooth, dark green on a long fleshy stem, 1 to 2 inches wide. Pkt., 10c; oz., 30c; ¼ lb., 80c.

Fordhook. This variety resembles Lucullus, but is a darker green. Pkt., 10c; oz., 30c; ¼ lb., 80c.

Rhubarb Chard. A recent introduction having all the chard characteristics excepting color. It has dark green, heavily crumpled leaves and crimson stem and mid rib. Pkt., 25c.

Mustard

Leaves useful as salad or boiled like Spinach. Matures in 30 days.

Chinese Smooth. Large, light green, smooth leaves, borne well above the ground. Pkt., 10c; oz., 30c; ¼ lb., 75c; lb., $2.25.

Florida Broadleaf. Upright growing, deep green leaves, fairly smooth. Desirable for greens because of the ease of preparing and its pleasant pungent flavor. Pkt., 10c; oz., 30c; ¼ lb., 75c; lb., $2.25.

Giant Southern Curled. Large leaves often measure 14 inches; ready for use in about six weeks after sowing. Plants will continue to yield until frosty weather. Leaves boiled like spinach. Pkt., 10c; oz., 30c; ¼ lb., 75c; lb., $2.25.

Improved Ostrich Plume (Fordhook). The handsomest of the mustards. Pkt., 10c; oz., 30c; ¼ lb., 75c; lb., $2.25.

White London. Good for general use. Pkt., 10c; ½ oz., 30c; ¼ lb., 75c; lb., $2.25.

New Fast Grower

Tendergreen. A new variety of greens, producing only a small root, but large dark green leaves having a small rib. It is the only vegetable that is ready for table or market in 21 to 25 days after planting, and will produce 8 to 9 crops a year. An excellent addition to the list of greens. Pkt., 10c; oz., 30c; ¼ lb., 75c; lb., $2.25.

NEW YORK PURPLE   MINNOVAL   BLACK BEAUTY

Egg Plant

EGG plant likes a rich, loamy soil. Plants should be set out in the garden as soon as danger of frost has passed, in rows three feet apart, the plants two feet apart. Our special strains excel in uniformity, flavor and yield.

Florida High Bush. 85 days. Plants are well branched holding their large deeppurple oval fruits well off the ground. Hardy, and resistant to disease. Pkt., 15c; oz., 65c; ½ lb., $2.00.

Black King. 75 days. This new hybrid is a heavy yielder, a vigorous grower and earlier than other varieties. The fruit is about two-thirds as large as Black Beauty and the vines produce as many as thirty fruits. Pkt., 15c; ½ oz., 35c; oz., 65c; ¼ lb., $2.00.

Black Beauty. 80 days. It is oval in shape, uniformly the darkest in color. Perfectly spineless and smooth; has beautiful, rich purple color and handsome lustre. Pkt., 15c; oz., 65c; ¼ lb., $2.00.

Minnoval. 72 days. One of the earliest, it has firm, dark purple oval fruits, 6 x 7 inches, produced abundantly over a long season. Pkt., 20c; ½ oz., 40c; oz., 75c; ¼ lb., $2.25.

Oyster Plant (Salsify)

THOUGH not as generally grown as it should be, this is, when cooked, a really delicious vegetable, surpassing in richness of flavor both carrots and parsnips. It acquires a decided oyster flavor after a good frosting. Roots for winter use should be lifted in the fall, while those for early spring use may be left in the ground over winter.

Improved New York Purple. About 83 days. Plants grow low, stalky and branching, are early and almost continuous bearing; fruits are satiny smooth, rich purple color and large. Pkt., 10c; oz., 65c; ¼ lb., $2.00.

Mammoth Sandwich Island. This variety is much more uniform in growth than the old standard "Long White" variety; it is twice the size and weight; the roots are of superior quality and most delicate flavor. Pkt., 10c; ½ oz. 35c; oz. 60c.

Horseradish Sets

Horseradish. The roots produce good Radish, fit for use in one season's growth. Plant roots in trench, pressing small end down, and cover with 3 to 4 inches of soil. Raise the plant once in the early season, without disturbing the tap root end, and rub off all excess rootlets, recovering the plant as fast as accomplished. Doz., 50c; 100, $3.00; 1,000, $25.00.

GARDEN HUCKLEBERRY

This is a novelty, well described by the above name, which bears racemes or bunches of black berries, tomato-shaped, ½ to ¾ inch in diameter, which make excellent pies and preserves. The bushes are about 3 feet tall. Cultivation is the same as with the tomato, of which this plant is a distant cousin. Pkt., 15c; ½ oz., 30c; oz., 50c.

VIENNA KOHLRABI EARLY WHITE. Pkt., 15c.

Kohlrabi

Sow in April or May, in rows, thin to 8 inches. The globular fruits grow above ground, are stripped and cooked l'ke Turnips, but are much sweeter.

★**Early White Vienna.** 55 days. White and tender. Pkt., 15c; ½ oz., 45c; oz., 85c; ¼ lb., $2.50.

Early Purple Vienna. About 55 days. Pkt., 15c; ½ oz., 45c; oz., 85c.

Martynia

100 days

The tender young seed pods, gathered when half-grown, make excellent pickles. Pkt., 10c

Tobacco Seeds

Big Havana. A hybrid Havana. Pkt., 10c; ½ oz., 25c; oz., 45c; ¼ lb., $1.35; lb., $4.00.

Connecticut Seed Leaf. Best adapted to climate of middle and northern states. Pkt., 10c; ½ oz., 25c; oz., 45c; ¼ lb., $1.35; lb., $4.00.

Burley. The popular Kentucky sort. Pkt., 10c; ½ oz., 25c; oz., 45c; ¼ lb., $1.35; lb., $4.00.

Rhubarb

★**Flare.** A variety of erect, compact habit, medium leaves 23 inches long, with stalks of attractive red extending from base almost to tip. Flesh is of fine texture, tender, juicy and crisp. Pkt., 15c; ½ oz., 30c; oz., 50c.

Vaughan's Mammoth. Vigorous and productive; stalks fifteen inches long. Pkt., 10c; oz., 25c; ¼ lb., 65c; lb., $2.00.

Victoria. A popular red strain. Pkt., 10c; oz., 25c; ¼ lb., 65c; lb., $2.00.

Rhubarb Roots. Set in spring they will furnish leaf stalks the following year. (If wanted by mail, add 10c for 1 or 2 roots, 13c for 10 roots for postage and packing).

Canada Red, Stems dark red clear to heart. Makes a sweet, fine flavored, beautiful red sauce. Divisions, $1.00; 3 for $2.75.

McDonald Crimson, Divisions. Bright red stalks, low acidity, thin skin, fine grain and fruity flavor. Each, 75c; 3 for $2.00.

Victoria, 1 year, 3 for 75c; 10 for $1.50; 2 years, each 60c; 3 for $1.25; 10 for $3.00.

Rutabagas

Mature in 90 days.

★**Vaughan's Improved American Purple Top** is a fine strain of Purple Top. Largest size, best shaped variety, small neck, smooth skin; good cropper and keeper. A heavy yielder. Excellent table quality. Pkt., 10c; oz., 20c; ¼ lb., $1.60.

Canadian Gem. Round medium size, quick growing, purple top, yellow flesh. It resists mildew and is of excellent flavor. Pkt., 10c; oz., 20c; ¼ lb., 60c; lb., $1.60.

ENDIVE

BROAD LEAVED BATAVIAN WHITE ESCAROLLE. Pkt., 10c; oz., 25c; ¼ lb., 65c

ENDIVE is a delightful autumn and winter salad. Sow seed from middle of June to the end of August. Frost improves the flavor.

★**Broadleaved Batavian White Escarol** (Florida Full Heart.) 92 days. Of the straight smooth leaf Batavian type, this variety has largest number of heart leaves and the finest quality of any we have tried. It grows upright, resists drought, and when tied up for bleaching produces a cluster of creamy, tender, spicy leaves which are easily prepared for serving. Pkt., 1 oz., 25c; ¼ lb., 65c.

★**Florida Deep Heart** 95 days. Similar. Full Hearted Escarol. It has a deeper heart and is more easily blanched. Pkt., 10c; oz., 25c; ¼ lb., 65c.

Cos Endive. A new variety worth trying. Pkt., 10c; oz., 25c; ¼ lb., 65c.

Green Curled. In 70 days. Standard variety for fall and winter. Finely divided leaves make plant appear mossy, and when centers are blanched it is most beautiful. Pkt., 10c; oz., 25c; ¼ lb., 65c.

Moss Curled. Pkt., 10c; oz., 25c; ¼ lb., 65c

Rose Ribbed Curled. In 75 days. Has leaf of red. Pkt., 10c; oz., 25c; ¼ lb., 65c.

Ever White Curled. About 75 days. Very cr Pkt., 10c; oz., 25c; ¼ lb., 65c.

Chicory

Witloof (French Endive). In about 150 days European delicacy now standard in all best hotels and restaurants in the U. S. It is easily grown. Sow in spring; store parsnip-like roots in sand until wanted for growing on in winter; directions on packages. Pkt., 10c; ½ oz., 40c; oz., 75c.

Large Rooted Magdeburg. 65 days. Roots cut in thick slices, roasted and used as coffee; spring leaves make good salad. Pkt., 10c; ½ oz., 40c; oz., 75c; ¼ lb., $2.25.

Asparagus Chicory. 55 days. Cultivated for its fresh green shoots, which are boiled in salt water and served hot, or in cold salad. New sprouts continue to spring from the base, to be harvested and enjoyed. Pkt., 10c; ½ oz., 40c; oz., 75c.

ENDIVE GREEN CURLED. Pkt., 10c; oz.,

LETTUCE

Sow as soon as soil can be prepared, in ½-inch drill, 10 seeds to an inch. Feed well, to make it grow fast. Thin out first to stand an inch apart; then use alternate plants until leaf varieties stand 8 inches, heading varieties 12 inches apart. Make succession sowings to prolong harvest.

TASTY bowl salads not only delight the palate, but when made with green leaves, are rich in Vitamin A and other dietary necessities. Home gardeners may plan their sowings so as to have bowl salad materials throughout the season. Besides lettuce, endive of both curly and broad-leaved types (Escarolle) are excellent, as are cress and Finnochio. Heading varieties of lettuce may not head readily in hot weather sections, but they grow rapidly and produce an abundance of leaves. Says Emile Folally, salad chef of the Hotel Sherman's famous College Inn, Chicago: "Leaf lettuce and româine are far more tender and better flavored; and take the salad dressing perfectly, which is important. And the doctors say their green leaves have more vitamins. What a combination!" Quick growth is essential for all leaf crops. Quantity needed to sow: 30 ft., 1 pkt.; 250 ft., 1 oz.

LEAF LETTUCE

★**Lettuce Oak Leaf.** 40 days. This novel variety excels in ability to withstand hot weather without turning bitter. Its leaves are small, tender, and deep green, testifying to their richness in Vitamins. It has the superior butter-type flavor. Pkt., 10c; ½ oz., 35c; oz., 60c.

★**Black Seeded Simpson.** Matures in about 46 days. Its large rich green leaves are thin, tender and crisp, forming a loose head. It is one of the most vigorous varieties in hot weather and slow to run to seed. It is especially adapted to the home garden.
Vaughan's Selected Stock. Pkt., 10c; oz., 30c; ¼ lb., 70c.

Grand Rapids. About 45 days. This home garden favorite, also extensively planted for hotbed or greenhouse growing. The leaves are light green, daintily curled, tender, crisp, delicious. Our selected stock has been bred to a high degree of uniformity in type and season.
Vaughan's Extra Selected Stock. Pkt., 10c; oz., 30c; ¼ lb., 70c.

Early Curled Simpson. About 40 days. A white seeded leaf lettuce of excellent quality. Pkt., 10c; oz., 30c; ¼ lb., 70c.

Prizehead. 45 days. A popular, loose heading sort. Leaves crumpled, shaded brown; crisp, sweet and tender. Pkt., 10c; oz., 30c; ¼ lb., 70c.

Crisp as Ice. 74 days. Small dark green head overlaid with dark brown crumpled leaves, does not get bitter in hot weather. Pkt., 10c; ½ oz., 25c; oz., 40c; ¼ lb., $1.10.

BLACK SEEDED SIMPSON LETTUCE. Pkt., 10c.

EXPRESS COS
Pkt., 10c

ROMAINE OR COS LETTUCE

THIS type of lettuce forms upright loose folding heads, and the inner leaves bleach white. It is usually preferable to tie up the heads to assist bleaching. Esteemed the finest of lettuces in flavor.

Express Cos. In 70 days. A Vaughan introduction. The most dwarf and earliest of all. Delicious flavor. Self-closing. Pkt., 10c; oz., 30c; ¼ lb.

Paris White or Trianon. In 75 days. Grows to large size. Self-closing. Pkt., 10c; oz., 30c; ¼ lb., 80c.

FAST GROWING FOR POULTRY

New Chicken Lettuce. About 48 days. Here is a genuine lettuce which will yield as much or more chicken or rabbit feed as any "greens" plant. When cut it starts at once to grow again. The leaves can be pulled off each stem like a kale. Pkt., 10c; oz., 25c; ¼ lb., 60c.

HEAD OF COSBERG LETTUCE

HEAD LETTUCE

★**Cosberg.** 76 days. Small compact heads, firm, somewhat resistant to blight. Matured tight heads in July, in Chicago last summer. Pkt., 10c; ½ oz., 20c; oz., 35c.; ¼ lb. $1.05.

Cosberg 600. 65 days. This is an early sort heading lettuce under adverse conditions. A smaller head than Hanson or Iceberg. Has light green leaves with no bronzing effect. Pkt., 10c; ½ oz., 25c; oz., 40c; ¼ lb., $1.15.

★**New York No. 12.** Matures in about 80 days. This is the variety grown in California and shipped the year around to eastern markets. It often weighs two pounds, stands hot weather well. We offer the highly selected strain known on the Pacific Coast as No.12. Seed should be started indoors and the seedling plants can be set out when true leaves have been formed, as soon as the soil is prepared. Pkt., 10c; ½ oz., 40c; ¼ lb., $1.15.

★**Iceberg.** Matures in about 84 days. This is the tightest of any variety we know, and it resists hot weather well. It is an excellent home garden variety and entirely distinct from New York, which is sometimes called Iceberg. Pkt., 10c; oz., 30c; ¼ lb., 80c.

New York No. 515. Matures in about 80 days. This is a cross between New York and Iceberg bred for resistance to tip burn. Excellent for the home or market garden. Pkt., 10c; ½ oz., 25c; oz., 40c; ¼ lb., $1.15.

New York P. W. 55. 70 days. A crisp, hard heading, high quality lettuce having considerable resistance to tip burn. Pkt., 10c; ½ oz., 25c.

Improved Hanson. 80 days. This globe-shaped variety excels with vigorous growth in hot weather. It has broad leaves, beautifully crinkled, tender and sweet. The outside leaves are a deep green, and the inner ones almost white. Pkt., 10c; oz., 30c; ¼ lb., 80c.

Great Lakes. See Novelty Page. Pkt., 40c.

Imperial No. 44. 82 days. The latest introduction in blight resistant types. Heads a little earlier than 847 and is a little more curled. Pkt., 15c; ½ oz., 25c; oz., 40c; ¼ lb., $1.15.

Imperial No. 847. 84 days. Pkt., 15c; ½ oz., 25c; oz., 40c; ¼ lb., $1.15.

Vaughan's All Seasons. About 80 days. In 1879 we introduced this distinctive variety. It is still a favorite. Heads are large, solid and handsome. It stands hot weather well and is slow to run to seed. Pkt., 10c; oz., 25c; ¼ lb., 65c.

★**Bibb.** 57 days. Rather small head used as forcing lettuce in the South and shipped to the northern hotels where it has a reputation for its excellent quality. Leaves smooth, dark green, bleaching to a rich yellow. Pkt., 20c; ½ oz., 30c; oz., 45c.

May King. 60 days. Very early variety. The outer leaves are tinged with brown; they fold close, permitting close planting in frames—tender yellow heart. Pkt., 10c; oz., 30c; ¼ lb., 80c.

Vaughan's Big Boston. 75 days. Large heads of bright green leaves, very tender. Pkt., 10c; oz., 25c; ¼ lb., 65c.

California Cream Butter. About 75 days. One of the best summer varieties, large, solid heads, buttery flavor. Pkt., 10c; oz., 30c; ¼ lb., 75c.

Mignonette. In 67 days. A delicious, crisp, solid, small head. Pkt., 10c; ½ oz., 25c; oz., 40c; ¼ lb., $1.15

Cress

Upland Cress. About 65 days. Has highly prized flavor of Water Cress. Green all year; ready for use before any other salad. Pkt., 10c; ½ oz., 30c; oz., 50c.

Curled Garden. About 65 days. Used with Lettuce, it adds an agreeable pungency. Pkt., 10c; oz., 35c; ¼ lb., $1.00.

Dandelion

THICK leaf or cabbage variety. Cultivated for spring greens and salads, is fast gaining favor. Unlike common sorts, almost double usual size. Pkt., 10c; ½ oz., 30c; oz., 50c.

Finnochio

Fennel, Florence. 85 days. It has an enlarged leaf base which should have the dirt drawn up around it when it is the size of a hen's egg. Height of plant, 2 feet. Directions for culture are given with each order. Pkt., 10c; ½ oz., 20c; oz., 30c; ¼ lb., 75c.

MUSKMELON

Grow in light soil, in full sun, where plants can be watered. Sow in hills, five or six feet apart each way, six seeds 1½-inch deep to a hill, thinning out to 3 plants.

TO ONE who has tasted a Vaughan's Milwaukee Market or Hearts of Gold muskmelon ripened on the vine, quality in muskmelons has a new meaning. In no other crop does quality respond more quickly to careful breeding. Our special strains are selected for size, color, flavor, small seed cavity and thick flesh.

Remember, muskmelons must ripen on the vine. Except the Honey Dew, they do not improve after picking. Quantity needed for 20 hills, 1 pkt.; 100 hills, 1 oz.

★**Hearts of Gold.** 80 days. For the home garden, this is our idea of the most delicious variety that can be grown. It has a flavor all its own, and never surpassed. In size it is just right, 5 to 6 inches in diameter, almost a sphere, with small seed cavity, well netted with shallow sutures. Pkt., 15c; oz., 45c; ¼ lb., $1.25.

★**Vaughan's Milwaukee Market.**
Matures in about 80 days. This is a large melon averaging 8 in. in diameter, with a small seed cavity and thick salmon flesh, which has the sweetest, most delicious flavor and the finest texture of any we know. It does not stand shipping. Its original quality has been increased by breeding on our Michigan farms, and has reached its highest point in seed from hand-cut, inspected melons.
Seed from hand-cut, Inspected melons—Pkt., 15c; oz., 45c; ¼ lb., $1.35.
Standard Seed—Pkt., 10c; oz., 35c; ¼ lb., 85c.

Honey Rock (or Sugar Rock). 85 days. A wonderfully sweet melon with thick orange flesh and a distinctive flavor, suggesting the Honey Dew taste. It produces heavily and is the earliest quality variety. Oval fruits of medium size. An excellent home garden variety. Pkt.,15c; oz., 45c; ¼ lb.,$1.25.

Imperial. 85 days. Pale cream color skin with small amount of coarse netting, but looking quite smooth. Yellow flesh and a faint Honey Dew flavor. Season of Milwaukee, very similar to Weaver's Special, but smaller and more subject to cracking. Pkt., 10c; oz., 35c; ¼ lb., 85c.

Bender's Surprise. 90 days. Large, thick-fleshed, heavily netted. Its flavor is wonderfully sweet, with almost no stringiness. An excellent home garden variety. Pkt., 10c; oz., 35c; ¼ lb., 85c.

★**Pride of Wisconsin.** 85 days. This new variety seems to include many of the desirable characteristics of the Honey Rock. The rind is very hard, of a pearly gray color, with but a faint rib, heavily covered with a distinctive netting. The flesh is unusually thick with good flavor. Pkt., 15c; oz.,45c; ¼ lb.,$1.35.

Superb. 90 days. Delicious, thick-fleshed with flavor blending Osage and Honey Rock. Grows 6 to 8 inches long, 5 to 7 inches in diameter. Pkt., 10c; oz., 25c; ¼ lb., 65c.

Golden Marvel. 90 days. (Golden Osage.) A melon varying in shape from round to oblong, with varying netting, small seed cavity and thick flesh of excellent flavor. Pkt., 10c; oz., 25c; ¼ lb., 75c.

Golden Oblong. 87 days. It has the appearance of Honey Rock. 10 inches long, 6 inches in diameter; but superior flavor. George Swissheimer of Muskegon, Mich., says of it: "In the fashionable White Lake and Sylvan Beach, resorters prefer this melon over all others." Pkt., 10c; oz., 25c; ¼ lb., 75c.

Tip Top. 96 days. It is yellow-fleshed, sweet, juicy; of finest flavor. A strong grower and yielder. Pkt., 10c; oz., 35c; ¼ lb., 85c.

Hale's Best No. 36. 86 days. This is the improved Hale's Best type of outstanding merit. It not only is resistant to mildew and the ideal melon for shipping but is rapidly becoming a leader in other sections wherever Hale's Best is grown. The shape is oval, the size is medium with heavy net and a faint stripe which insures earliness. Pkt., 10c; oz., 35c; ¼ lb., 85c.

Vaughan's Select Early Osage. About 84 days. Not as large as Osage, but of equal quality. Pkt., 10c; oz., 35c; ¼ lb., 85c.

Banana. In 98 days. Cucumber shape. Delicious odor. A novelty melon for the home garden. Pkt., 10c; oz., 25c; ¼ lb., 85c.

Emerald Gem. In 87 days. Pkt., 10c; oz., 35c; ¼ lb., 85c.

Mango Melon or Vegetable Peach. In 95 days. Makes splendid mangoes, stuffed like peppers. For sweet pickles, pies and preserving. Cooking directions on packets. Pkt., 10c; oz., 35c; ¼ lb., 85c.

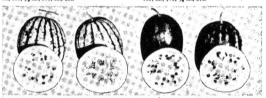

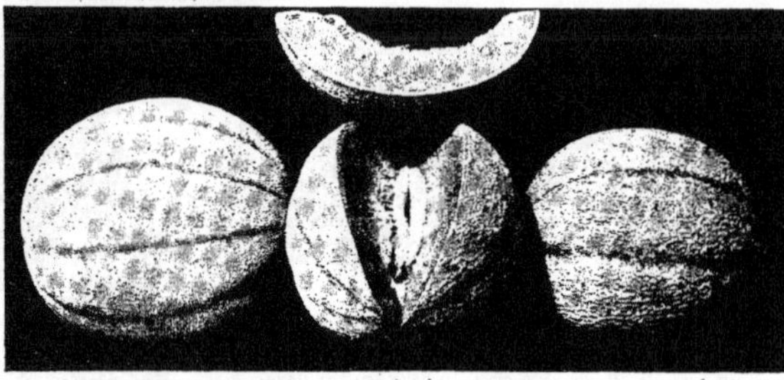

MUSKMELON Milwaukee Market. Inspected Seed. Pkt., 15c; oz., 45c; ¼ lb., $1.35

Persian. About 102 days. Perhaps the largest of all quality melons, but with too long a season to mature in the north. A fruit will weigh 10 lbs., almost spherical in form, heavily netted, with thick pink flesh, fine flavor. Pkt., 15c; oz., 45c; ¼ lb., $1.35.

Honey Dew. 110 days. An old-time French melon imported by Vaughan's Seed Store for a melon specialist in Michigan; later found of good commercial value. Honey Dew is best when quite ripe. Unlike other melons, it grows sweeter after being picked. Pkt., 10c; oz., 35c; ¼ lb., 85c.

Cranshaw—An Earlier and Improved Persian. Pkt., 20c; ½ oz., 35c; oz., 60c.

THE ROCKY FORD TYPE

Rocky Ford Pink Flesh. 95 days. Same as Rocky Ford Netted Gem except pink flesh. Pkt., 10c; oz., 35c; ¼ lb., 85c.

Rocky Ford Netted Gem. About 96 days. Of the green-fleshed muskmelons, Rocky Ford is the recognized standard of excellence. Pkt., 10c; oz., 35c; ¼ lb., 85c.

Pollock, 10-25: About 98 days. Salmon tint. Pkt., 10c; oz., 35c; ¼ lb., 85c.

CUBAN QUEEN   DIXIE QUEEN   OVID   RED RUSSIAN
Each, pkt., 10c; oz., 20; ¼ lb., 50c; One packet of each (4 packets) 25c

Newest Early Watermelons

WATERMELONS may be grown under favorable conditions in the north though they require 100 to 120 days to mature. Soil such as will mature good muskmelons is needed, with plenty of hot weather and no lack of water. Room for the vines to wander is required, preferably 8 to 10 feet between hills both ways. Avoid tilting the vines and use only hand tools in cultivation. Quantity needed for 8 hills, 1 pkt.; 25 to 30 hills, 1 oz.

★**Stone Mountain.** 82 days. A new round melon having red flesh free from stringiness. Very productive and excellent for home use. Pkt., 10c; oz., 25c; ¼ lb., 65c.

★**Stone Mountain Resistant No. 5.** 85 days. Pkt., 10c; oz., 35c; ¼ lb., 85c.

★**Ice Box.** 70 days. It is desirable to have a melon that will go in the ice box without having to be cut. This round melon is about six inches in diameter, is early, hardy and of excellent flavor. Pkt., 10c; oz., 25c; ¼ lb., 65c.

Cole's Early. 80 days. The northern states' favorite. The flesh is rich, deliciously sweet and crisp. It is about 20 inches long, 12 inches through; not a good shipper. Pkt., 10c; oz., 25c; ¼ lb., 65c.

★**Dixie Queen.** 85 days. The latest. It is semi-round, has very thin rind but stands shipping. With white seed and deep red flesh. One of the sweetest. Pkt., 10c; oz., 35c; ¼ lb., 85c.

Cuban Queen. Like Dixie Queen, with black seed. Pkt., 10c; oz., 30c; ¼ lb., 75c.

Early Ovid. 75 days. Very similar to Red Russian, darker green, bright red flesh with black seeds. Pkt., 10c; oz., 25c; ¼ lb., 65c.

Improved Kleckley. About 87 days. Similar to Kleckley's in shape, but larger and has harder rind. Pkt., 10c; oz., 25c; ¼ lb., 65c.

★**Red Russian.** Or Early Kansas. 85 days. Flesh very deep pink, brown seeds, thin rind and very solid center. Pkt., 10c; oz., 30c; ¼ lb., 75c.

Florida Giant (Cannonball). 95 days. The largest melon of good quality, often reaching 50 pounds in weight, good for shipping and for distant gardens where the season is long enough. Dark green, solid pink flesh, seed dark brown to black. Vigorous and productive. Pkt., 20; oz., 35c; ¼ lb., $1.00.

Klondyke. Striped. In 90 days. Known as the best long black watermelon grown in California. The seeds are small, flesh a deep red. It has a remarkable flavor, stands short distance shipping but is more of a home type. Pkt., 10c; oz., 35c; ¼ lb., 85c.

Klondyke Resistant No. 7. 90 days. Pkt., 15; oz., 35c; ¼ lb., $1.00.

Tom Watson. In 92 days. The flesh is rich red; tenderly melting. Pkt., 10c; oz., 30c; ¼ lb., 75c.

Sweet Siberian. In 80 days. A very early variety of medium size, with yellow flesh of superb quality. Pkt., 10c; oz., 35c; ¼ lb., 85c.

Irish Gray. In 90 days. A mottled greenish gray, equal of any. Pkt., 10c; oz., 25c. ¼ lb., 65c.

Wilt Resistant Kleckley's No. 6. 92 days. Pkt., 10c; oz., 30c; ¼ lb., 75c.

Citron. In 90 days. For preserves. Red or green seeded. Pkt.,10c; oz., 30c; ¼ lb., 75c.

Winter Watermelon. 85 days. Like Honey Dew in size and long-keeping qualities. Prolific, and excellent flavor. Pkt., 10c; oz., 35c; ¼ lb., 85c.

OTHER GOOD WATERMELONS

Rattlesnake or Georgia Striped. About 92 days.
Halbert Honey. Matures in about 87 days.
Golden Honey. 90 days.
Any of above, pkt., 10c; oz., 25c; ¼ lb., 65c.

PARSLEY, Champion Moss Curled. Pkt., 10c.

Parsley

PARSLEY should be sown early because it is very slow to germinate; and it is best to use radish seed mixed with the parsley seed to mark the rows.

The rooted parsley provides excellent flavoring for soups and stews. Quantity needed to sow 50 ft., 1 pkt.; 200 ft., 1 oz.

Vaughan's Champion Moss Curled.
In about 70 days. Robust, compact plants; the leaves are so crumpled and curled as to have the appearance of curled moss, with rich, green color; it is quite hardy. Pkt., 10c; oz., 25c; ¼ lb., 65c.

Vaughan's XXX Parsley. In 75 days. Curled
leaves of delicate green, appetizingly fresh and beautiful, add zest and richness to substantial or delicate viands. It grows very dwarf in the garden—many of our customers plant it as a border. Vaughan's XXX Parsley was chosen after many trials and a careful inspection trip through Europe. Pkt., 10c; oz., 25c; ¼ lb., 65c.

Plain or Italian. In 72
days. Not curled. However, the flavor is excellent and plant is very hardy. Pkt., 10c; oz., 25c; ¼ lb., 65c.

Double Curled. 70 days.
Dwarf, handsome green, curled variety. Pkt., 10c; oz., 25c; ¼ lb., 65c.

Hamburg Rooted. 90
days. Resembles a small parsnip. Used for flavoring soups. Our strain is exceptional. Pkt., 10c; oz., 25c; ¼ lb., 65c.

Evergreen. In 80 days.
Darkest green curled. All-America award. Pkt., 10c; oz., 25c; ¼ lb., 65c.

Hamburg Rooted Parsley. Pkt., 10c.

Parsnips

PARSNIPS may be harvested at times when the garden has little else to offer. Let them remain in the ground over winter, and dig them during a thaw or when the spring thaw comes—they will be as sweet and tender as ever. A freeze is required to sweeten them. For the best results deep soil is needed, and fresh manure should not be used as it will cause the roots to divide. Quantity needed to sow 25 ft., 1 pkt.; 150 ft., 1 oz.

★Vaughan's Marrowfat. In 95 days. The
illustration tells the story of uniform good size, fine shape, clean, smooth skin. In richness of flavor it is unequaled. For exhibition it is a winner. Pkt., 10c; oz., ¼ lb., 75c.

Hollow Crown, Long Smooth. About 95 days.
Tender and sugary; one of the best. Our strain is a good selection. Pkt., 10c; oz., 40c; ¼ lb., 75c.

Improved Guernsey. 98 days. An improvement
over the parent, "Hollow Crown," but it is much larger in diameter, though not so long. The roots are more easily gathered. This sort gives general satisfaction. Of excellent sugary flavor. Pkt., 10c; oz., 40c; ¼ lb., 75c.

Ideal (All-America). About 95 days. Shorter than
Hollow Crown and freer from side roots; tender, uniform and slightly hollowed neck. Washes up a good white. Pkt., 10c; oz., 40c; ¼ lb., 75c.

Short Thick. 90 days. This little parsnip makes
a fine garden vegetable. The tops are only about half the size of Hollow Crown. The roots are short and thick, having a diameter of 2½ to 3½ inches and a length of only 6 or 8 inches at the thickened part. Pkt., 10c; oz., 45c; ¼ lb., 85c.

PEPPERS

Plants started eight weeks before are set out one week after frost proof date. Harvest continues until frost, if vines are picked clean.

Vitamin content increases as green pods turn red.

MAGNUM DULCE   RUBY KING   CALIFORNIA WONDER   HUNGARIAN

Sweet and Hot Varieties

LIKE egg plants and tomatoes, peppers should be started indoors. They are easy to grow, thrive in cool weather and will endure some frost. The plants should stand eight to eighteen inches apart in rows. They are constantly becoming more popular, both in salads and for use in cooking. A dozen plants will supply an average family. One packet produces 75 plants; one ounce, 1000 plants.

★Early California Wonder. Matures in about 60 days.
A quality giant is recommended for the home garden. Mild, sweet, midseason, it produces fruits 4 by 4½ inches, with thick flesh and bright crimson coloring. Pkt., 15c; ½ oz., 45c; oz., 85c.

★California Wonder. About 75 days. A mild,
sweet variety, very large. It resembles Chinese Giant in form, but has much thicker flesh. It has a crimson fruit. Pkt., 15c; ½ oz., 40c; oz., 70c.

"Windsor A." 70 days. Similar in structure
to California Wonder but more productive and earlier. Pkt., 10c; ½ oz., 35c; oz., 65c.

★Vaughan's Giant Magnum Dulce.
In 67 days. This mild pepper grows to immense size—7 inches long and 4 inches through—but when grown so large the yield is small. To get a large yield of medium sized peppers, pinch off the first buds. Pkt., 15c; ½ oz., 40c; oz., 70c.

Harris' Early Giant. 63 days. Heavy yielder
among the large peppers, also earlier. The plants are vigorous; peppers 4 by 4½ inches. Color, deep green turning to red; very sweet. Pkt., 10c; ½ oz., 35c; oz., 60c.

World Beater. About 75 days. Fruits 5 by 3½ in.
diameter; flesh thick and mild; very productive and a good shipper. Pkt., 10c; ½ oz., 35c; oz., 65c.

Crimson Giant. About 70 days. One of the earliest
large red. The peppers are green when young and a rich red when ripe; flesh thick, sweet and mild. Pkt., 10c; ½ oz., 45c; oz., 75c.

King of the North. In 64 days. A sweet medium
short and blocky. Not quite as early as Early Giant. Pkt., 10c; ½ oz., 40c; oz., 70c.

Chinese Giant. 80 days. Grows 4 to 5 inches
broad on top and of equal length, mild flavored and makes a very fine salad sliced and served like tomatoes. Pkt., 15c; ½ oz., 40c; oz., 75c.

★Hungarian or Banana (Hot). In 65 days. A
slender hot pepper much prized for canning. It is 1½ inches in diameter at the base and often 10 inches long. Yellow turning to red. Pkt., 15c; ½ oz., 40c; oz., 70c.

Hungarian or Banana (Sweet). In 65 days. Same as
above, but sweet. Pkt. 15c; ½ oz., 40c; oz., 70c.

Ruby King. In 68 days. One of the most popular,
growing 4½ to 6 inches long, 3½ to 4 inches thick. The peppers are a bright ruby-red and quite sharp in flavor. Pkt., 10c; ½ oz., 35c; oz., 60c.

Bull Nose, Hot. In 70 days. A pungent pepper.
Pkt., 10c; ½ oz., 35c; oz., 60c.

Pimento Perfection. In 73 days. Flesh thick and
very mild. Must be started early in the north to mature. Pkt., 10c; ½ oz., 30c; oz., 55c.

Large Bell. 70 days. Large, mild. Pkt., 10c; oz., 60c.

Cayenne. 70 days. Long, red, hot. Pkt., 10c; oz., 60c.

Vaughan's Sweet Mountain. In 70 days. Very
productive; the flesh mild and thick, 6x4 inches. Pkt., 10c; oz., 60c.

Oakview Wonder. In about 70 days. High
quality combined with earliness and high yield. Pkt., 10c; ½ oz., 40c; oz., 75c.

Oshkosh. 70 days. Small upright bush,
fruit 4"x3", deep green turning to orange-yellow. Pkt., 15c; ½ oz., 40c; oz., 75c.

Red Cherry. 70 days. Pkt., 10c; ½ oz.,
40c; oz., 75c.

Golden Queen. In 78 days. Pkt., 10c;
½ oz., 40c; oz., 70c.

Tabasco. About 95 days. Hottest of all.
Pkt., 15c; ½ oz., 40c; oz., 70c.

Red Chill. 75 days. Good hot pickling
Pkt., 10c; ½ oz., 40c; oz., 70c.

Chili Anaheim. In 80 days. Pkt., 10c.;
½ oz., 40c; oz., 70c.

Pimento Sunnybrook. About 73 days.
Pkt., 10c; ½ oz., 35c; oz., 65c.

PARSNIP VAUGHAN'S MARROWFAT. Pkt., 10c

Grow Your Own Mushrooms

TO GROW a crop of Mushrooms in your own basement cellar or well-built outbuilding—is a home gardening effort worth making. While these are quickly salable, we are sure most of our readers would insist on eating their own crops! The location of the beds must be one where a temperature of 55 degrees to 65 degrees can be kept during cold weather. A barrel may be used in which to confine the manure for growing. A leaflet, "How to Grow Mushrooms," FREE with orders for Mushroom Spawn.

PURE CULTURE BOTTLE SPAWN

This spawn is made in glass jars under absolutely sterile conditions, so that every mould, weed seed or insect is destroyed and each bottle contains nothing but pure spawn. One bottle equals 5 bricks of ordinary spawn and is sufficient for 40 square feet.

Per carton......	$ 0.90	25 cartons for...	$18.75
12 cartons for...	9.00	50 cartons for...	36.50

If wanted by Parcel Post allow for postage at zone rate, weight about 1 lb. per bottle.

PURE CULTURE BRICK SPAWN

One brick will spawn 8 to 10 square feet and comes in pure white.

Per brick.......	$ 0.35	Per 25 bricks....	$ 5.50
Per 5 bricks....	1.50	Per 50 bricks....	10.00
Per 10 bricks....	2.75	Per 100 bricks...	18.00

If wanted by Parcel Post add postage at zone rate, weight about 1 lb. per brick.

Okra

OKRA pods are used in soups, stews and salads. It is a hot weather plant, but can be grown in the North much like corn, the plants being started indoors in paper pots. The pods should be gathered each day while still tender and pulpy.

Quantity needed for 15 ft., 1 pkt.; 50 ft., 1 oz.

White Velvet. 70 days. Produces pods larger than any other. Pkt., 10c; oz., 15c; ¼ lb., 30c.

White Lightning. 65 days. Similar to White Velvet, 6 in. longer pod, remaining tender for a greater period of time, making it much more desirable. Pkt., 10c; oz., 15c; ¼ lb., 30c.

Tall or Perkins Mammoth. 68 days. The long pods, measuring 4 and 5 in., are produced in great quantities. Pkt., 10c; oz., 15c; ¼ lb., 30c.

Dwarf Long Pod. 65 days. Low, stocky and productive, with long pods. Pkt., 10c; oz., 15c; ¼ lb., 30c.

Clemson Spineless. 55 days. Similar to Dwarf Long Pod; a little taller bush, having longer and darker pod. Pkt., 10c; oz., 15c; ¼ lb., 30c.

OKRA DWARF LONG POD IN OUR TRIALS. Pkt., 10c.

ONION SETS

Use large sets planted 2 inches deep for green onions, smaller one inch deep for mature onions; space the first one-inch apart, the second 3 to 4 inches. Plant with the earliest crops.

WHITE RED YELLOW

VAUGHAN'S BOTTOM ONION SETS

The first home garden harvest in the spring is young onions from sets. Spring sets can be put into the ground as soon as it is able to be worked and in a few weeks the delicious young onions are ready to serve on the table. Plantings may be successively late into the summer, as long as the sets remain in good condition.

Quantity needed for 75 to 100 ft., 1-lb.

White Bottoms. Our sets of these are very choice, small, dry and unsprouted. Lb., 50c; 2 lbs., 95c; 5 lbs., $1.90; 10 lbs., $3.50.

White Sets being very scarce, when they are exhausted, we will substitute Yellow unless customer specifies otherwise.

Yellow Bottoms. Fine dry sets, medium in size and unsprouted. Lb., 50c; 2 lbs., 95c; 5 lbs., $1.90; 10 lbs., $3.50.

Red Bottoms. Bright, deep red in color, even and dry. Lb., 50c; 2 lbs., 95c; 5 lbs., $1.90; 10 lbs., $3.50.

Golden Globe. Sets. Large yellow globe. Very desirable as a large dry onion for the home gardener. A superior keeper. Lb., 50c; 2 lbs. 95c; 5 lbs. $1.90; 10 lbs., $3.50.

Pound and two pound prices for Onion Sets shown on this page include Parcel Post prepayment through first three zones. For further zones add 5c per pound. Onion Sets if ordered before March 1st, are 5c less per lb.

The largest onions may be grown from sets ½ to ¾ inches in diameter.

FOR FALL PLANTING

Yellow Multipliers. Especially valuable for the first early spring onions. They are very mild and sweet in flavor and far superior to the green onions from other sets. There are usually several stalks from a single bulb and in this way are very productive. Their most important quality is their extreme earliness being ready for eating ahead of any other kind. Lb., 50c; 2 lbs., 95c; 5 lbs., $1.90; 10 lbs., $3.50.

Egyptian or Red Perennial. For fall planting only. This variety never forms a large bulb; its value lies wholly in its special adaptability to produce green Onions for spring or fall use which are perfectly hardy and stay in the ground all the time. We sell in fall only, to be planted for early spring crop. Lb., 25c; 2 lbs., 45c; 5 lbs., $1.00; 10 lbs., $1.75.

BERMUDA ONION PLANTS

These are especially suitable for home gardens. Seed is sown early in Texas, and the plants are lifted, to be replanted in Northern gardens, to produce sweet, mature onions of Bermuda quality. Ready April 1st. Per bunch of approximately 100, 60c, postpaid. Ten bunches, approximately 1000, $4.00, postage extra; weight about 6 lbs. per 1000.

Close Cousins of the Onion

Garlic Sets

Selected Bavarian. In about 110 days. Garlic is grown by planting the small bulbs in rows, 4 inches apart in the row. Cover the bulbs with one inch of soil. When the tops turn yellow, lift the bulbs and dry in the shade. To keep for the winter, hang in strings in a dry basement. Lb., 40c; 10 lbs., $3.50. Postage extra. Write for latest market prices on quantities.

Chives

A perennial herb, a member of the onion family which every garden should grow. The slender, tubular leaves have a delicate onion flavor, just enough to season a green salad when the chopped-up leaves are used. The leaves are used for seasoning. The flowers are a beautiful lavender. Pkt., 25c; ½ oz., 90c; oz., $1.75.

Leeks

Leeks are better if transplanted. Use a dibber, set the plant deep in the hole and do not fill it up but let the soil wash in. Leeks are cousins of the onions and their flavor is subtly different when used in stews. All varieties mature in about 130 days.

★Elephant. Largest of all leeks. Pkt., 15c; ½ oz., 50c; oz., 95c.

Large Musselburg. Enormous broad leaves, mild flavor. Good exhibition sort. Pkt., 15c; ½ oz., 50c; oz., 95c.

Broad Scotch or London Flag. Hardy; a strong plant, with broad leaves. Pkt., 15c; ½ oz., 50c; oz., 95c.

Large Carentan. Pkt., 15c; ½ oz., 50c; oz., 95c.

LEEK ELEPHANT. Pkt., 15c.

VICTORY GARDEN MANUAL

By JAMES H. BURDETT

Fifty graphic illustrations. 4 full page color plates. 128 pages. $1.75. This intensely practical book embodies the experience of the fist Victory Garden year and gives complete instructions for planning, p an n and maintaining a Victory garden which will supply food in profusion but without waste and of maximum nutritive value. Tells how to apply in your garden the latest discoveries of science.

Sow with the earliest crops, in rich soil, in drills ½ inch deep. Thin to 4 inches apart, using discards in green stage. Water when needed. Harvest after tops shrivel and dry in the sun, store in a dry place.

VALENCIA SWEET SPANISH FROM A MIDWESTERN GARDEN. Pkt., 20c.

-LANT breeders select for parents, specimens which do well in their breeding grounds. If bred in Illinois, the progeny of these plants will be resistant to Illinois hazards, and will e a liking for similar soil and climate.

Breeding work in California necessarily develops strains that thrive under the unique ifornia conditions but which might not thrive so well elsewhere. Because of this we breed our onions in Illinois, so we can know that our strains are adapted to the conditions of soil weather which prevail in the great area lying east of the Rocky Mountains to the Atlantic an, where our seed is chiefly grown. Liking for this environment is bred into our onion strains.

Our strains are grown from mature onions which have been carefully inspected for con- ation to type, and excel in productiveness and uniform quality. The small additional t over ordinary seed is insignificant compared to the great improvement in your crop.

antity needed to sow: 25 ft., 1 pkt.; 125 ft., 1 oz.; acre, 6 lbs.

Onions for Winter Keeping

olden Globe 115 days. exceptionally fine ow globe onion of erior weight. When wn as a dry onion keeping quality is erior, making it y desirable for home and mar- gardener. Has ery deep globe, rying its great- diameter well from the root. s 3 skins for pro- tion and from d matures same e as Southport be. From sets matures much lier. It is a vy yielder and ne keeper. Pkt., ; ½ oz., 50c; oz., :; ¼ lb., $2.80.

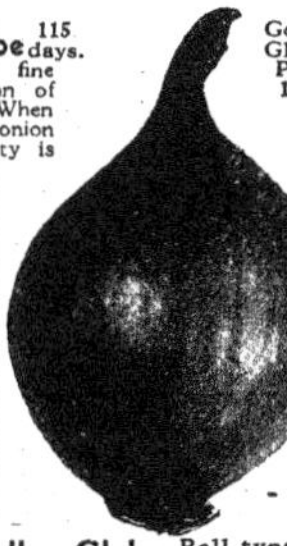

Golden Globe. Pkt., 15c.

Southport Yellow Globe. Ball type. In about 110 days. For growing on muck soil, this is the best keeping strain we have been able to develop in years of growing and selecting. This is the most uniform strain and will keep in storage longer than any other we know. It is preferred by large onion growers. Pkt., 15c; ½ oz., 50c; oz., 90c; ¼ lb., $2.60.

uthport Red Globe. About 110 days. A little deeper than Southport Yellow Globe, in color a rich dark red. A wonderful keeper with finely bred neck and a heavy yielder. Pkt., 15c; ½ oz., 40c; oz., 75c; ¼ lb., $2.35.

Vaughan's Special Yellow Globe. 100 days. ("MOUNTAIN" DANVERS.) Slightly smaller than Southport. When aphis damages the late onion crop it does not harm this variety, due to early maturity. Pkt., 15c; ½ oz., 50c; oz., 90c; ¼ lb., $2.60.

rge Red Wethersfield. About 100 days. An onion of very productive habit and a fine keeper. The skin is deep purplish red, which covers a round, somewhat flattened bulb of purplish white flesh. Moderately fine grain and mild flavor. In poor soil it does best, growing a thinner neck than in strong soil. It is standard in its class in the south and southwest Pkt., 15c; ½ oz., 40c; oz., 75c; ¼ lb., $2.30.

ncy Yellow Globe Danvers. About 110 days. This is early, almost true globe-shaped, beautiful yellow skin, pure white flesh, of very fine quality. It has a good size, and a fine thin neck. Vaughan's strain is so near to globe shape that it passes for globe on the market. The crop ripens uniformly at one time, and its keeping quality is excellent. Pkt., 20c; ½ oz., 50c; oz., 95c; ¼ lb., $2.80.

Brigham Yellow Globe Onion. 110 days. A strain of Southport Yellow Globe. While not as uniform in shape, it is among the best in production and keeping qualities. It may be grown successfully on either muck or heavy soil. Pkt., 15c; ½ oz., 50c; oz., 90c; ¼ lb., $2.60.

Ohio Yellow Globe. In 110 days. Of uniform shape, beautiful color and fine size, it out-classes the old type Yellow Globe Danvers. Its finely bred neck, large size, solid flesh of mild sweet quality, uniform growth, heavy yielding and superb keeping quality have made it a favorite. Pkt., 15c; ½ oz., 50c; oz., 95c; ¼ lb., $2.80.

Vaughan's Ideal White Globe. About 110 days. A strikingly handsome onion; very early, ripens evenly and is a fine keeper; the small, high-bred neck tells the story of quality; it is a true globe, pure white. Pkt., 20c; ½ oz., 70c; oz., $1.30; ¼ lb., $3.80.

SOUTHPORT YELLOW GLOBE. Pkt., 15c.

Spanish Type Onions

★Valencia Sweet Spanish. Matures in about 110 days. Here is a mild, sweet, giant onion of the true Spanish or Bermuda type, which you can grow from seed in your own garden. From seed it will produce onions weighing a pound; if started in the hot bed, two pound specimens can be grown. It takes two or three years for us to produce seed in Illinois, and the crop is always light, but the quality justifies the increased cost of seed. These onions are delicious at all stages of growth and will give you something to boast about. Pkt., 20c; ½ oz., 65c; oz., $1.20; ¼ lb., $3.65.

Riverside Sweet Spanish. 110 days. This is a California grown strain of the Spanish (Denia) onion. With us it grows larger than the American Prizetaker and does not produce the "stiff-necks" usual in the Spanish type. It is the most popular onion in Southern California and when grown as a specimen attains enormous size, 4 to 4½ pounds. In color it has a cream or pale yellow tint. Pkt., 15c; ½ oz., 55c; oz., $1.00; ¼ lb., $3.20.

Prizetaker—American Grown. 105 days. Among large onions this one is exceptional for size and beauty; it is of the same type as the large Spanish onions, imported and sold for high prices. Vaughan's American-grown seed has become thoroughly acclimated through many years of very careful, painstaking culture. Prizetaker is a yellow globe that matures to great size under right conditions; it requires a long season and should be started early in hotbed. When properly ripened it is a good keeper. Pkt., 15c; ½ oz., 45c; oz., 85c; ¼ lb., $2.70.

Onion Seed of Flat and Pickling Types

antity needed for 25 ft., 1 pkt.; 125 ft., 1 oz.

hite Portugal or Silverskin. About 100 days. This beautiful white onion is a splendid sort for growing white onion sets, pickles and for early bunching green onions. Vaughan's White Portugal or Silverskin is a medium size bulb, flat shape. It has fine mild flavor, and is best of the white onions for keeping. Pkt., 15c; ½ oz., 65c; oz., $1.25; ¼ lb., $3.60.

own Australian (Flat). About 100 days. A very desirable onion of medium size, with amber brown skin and solid white flesh. It is early, a heavy yielder and a long keeper; keeps well in warm climates. Pkt., 15c; ½ oz., 40c; oz., 75c; ¼ lb., $2.15.

Ebenezer. In 100 days. There has been a tremendous demand for this yellow skinned onion for the growing of Onion Sets. Ebenezer Onion Sets produce a much larger tonnage of marketable onions than does the old Strasburg or Danvers. Moreover, a smaller percent of the sets run to seed. Ebenezer is a fine keeper, mild and well flavored. Pkt., 15c; ½ oz., 40c; oz., 75c; ¼ lb., $2.15.

ITALIAN ONION SEED

Vaughan's Pickling. About 90 days. One of the best white onions for pickling; it is small, round, hard, crisp and tender, early and ripens uniformly. A very handsome sort with opaque white skin. Excellent for green onions. Pkt., 15c; ½ oz., 65c; oz., $1.25; ¼ lb., $3.60.

Bermuda Type

Crystal White Wax. In about 90 days. This is a pure white flat onion, very popular in the south, especially in Texas. Will make but small onions in the north. Very sweet. Teneriffe seed. Pkt., 15c; ½ oz., 35c; oz., 65c; ¼ lb., $2.00.

Bermuda Onion Plants started in Texas and sent North to grow on in your garden will give you backyard Bermudas with little trouble. See Page 80.

PEAS

Sow smooth seeded with earliest crops, wrinkled peas two weeks before fr proof date. Sow 2 inches deep, two inches apart in row, or in twin rows inches apart, with support between. Crop must mature before hot weath

Eat Your Own Peas Six Weeks for 25¢

EARLY GILBO. Pkt., 15c.

PEAS are rich in sugar, which begins to turn to starch when they are picked; thus home gardeners alone can enjoy this crop at its best.

Where hot dry summer weather cuts short the crop, the problem is to get the heavy yield, large size and sugar content of the late sorts into early yielding varieties which will bear a crop before the summer's drought arrives. Our strains are selected for these qualities. **Quantity needed for 100 ft., 1 lb.**

DWARF

★Little Marvel. 64 days. The most satisfactory pea in the average home garden. The big point in its favor is that it remains in prime picking condition a week longer than the older sorts. Very productive, hardy, luscious and sugary. Vines 18 inches, pod dark green, well filled. Pkt., 10c; ½ lb., 30c; lb., 50c; 2 lbs., 95c; 5 lbs., $2.00.

Giant Stride. 74 days. Pea blight is a wilt affecting peas when they are planted too often in the same ground. You will find the new Pea Giant Stride nearly 100% resistant, as well as of top quality and a heavy yielder. It makes a vine 16 to 18 inches tall, dark green, with pods longer than Laxton's Progress and better filled with peas of excellent flavor. Pkt., 10c; ½ lb., 30c; lb., 50c; 2 lbs., 95c; 5 lbs., $2.00.

★Early Gilbo. 72 days. A new pea from one of our oldest pea growers. Rogers Brothers have perfected what they consider one of their best market garden varieties and have named it after one of their oldest breeders. Vine 24-28 inches tall, very dark and heavy. Pod 4½-5 inches long by ½ to ⅝ inches wide, of the Dwarf Alderman type. Season 69 days. Pkt., 15c; ½ lb., 30c; lb., 50c; 2 lbs., 95c; 3 lbs., $2.00.

Nott's Excelsior. In 62 days. Almost as early as the round seeded varieties, but far superior to them in quality. Vines about 15 inches high, pods about 3 inches long, each containing 5 to 7 peas of good size, tender and delicious. Pkt., 10c; ½ lb., 25c; lb., 45c; 2 lbs., 80c; 5 lbs., $1.40.

LAXTON'S PROGRESS. Pkt., 10c.

★Century of Progress. Matures in about 76 days. This is a vigorous growing, heavy yielding variety which bears large, wrinkled peas of the very highest table quality in greater profusion than other varieties of equal quality. It grows 20 inches tall, with heavy foliage of a dark green, and dark green pods 4½ inches long. It is an excellent home garden variety. Pkt., 10c; ½ lb., 30c; lb., 50c; 2 lbs., 95c; 5 lbs., $2.00.

Laxton's Progress. 62 days. The earliest and by far the best of the large-podded, large-fruited wrinkled peas. Of all the varieties producing peas of equal quality, this is the heaviest yielding. It bears long pods, averaging one more pea to the pod than Hundredfold. Pkt., 10c; ½ lb., 30c; lb., 50c; 2 lbs., 95c; 5 lbs., $2.00.

Hundredfold. About 62 days. This is another of Vaughan's Specials that has proved itself a winner for gardeners. It is extra early, has large pods like "Telephone," which are filled with the finest flavored peas. Hundredfold is in season a few days later than the first earlies. It excels in size, appearance and productiveness. Pkt., 10c; ½ lb., 30c; lb., 50c; 2 lbs., 95c; 5 lbs., $2.00.

Sutton's Excelsior Improved. In about 63 days. It is a very fine first early dwarf pea, regarded by some as the best of the wrinkled sorts. Very hardy; can be planted early; vines are 18 inches high, very prolific; pods are almost square at lower end, larger and broader than the usual dwarf pea, dark green color. Pkt., 10c; ½ lb., 25c; lb., 45c; 2 lbs., 80c; 5 lbs., $1.40.

American Wonder. 61 days. Among the oldest of the home garden peas it is being superseded by Nott's Excelsior and Little Marvel. Pkt., 10c; ½ lb., 25c; lb., 45c; 2 lbs., 80c; 5 lbs., $1.40.

Premium Gem. 64 days. An extra early old type garden pea that could well be replaced by Nott's Excelsior or Little Marvel, as they are superior. Pkt., 10c; ½ lb., 25c; lb., 45c; 2 lbs., 80c; 5 lbs., $1.40.

Dwarf Telephone or Daisy. About 76 days. A mid-season maturing sort of merit; vines are dwarf and bear large, bright green pods, each containing 7 to 9 peas of finest quality. This is a splendid variety, of which we offer a high-class re-selected stock. Pkt., 10c; ½ lb., 25c; lb., 45c; 2 lbs., 80c; 5 lbs., $1.40.

Dwarf Defiance or Stratagem. About 79 days. Pea growers cannot afford to overlook this splendid main crop success; it is without a superior, a grand second early. The vines are vigorous, the pods dark green and immense in size and fullness, like "Telephone." The handsome pods are filled with peas that are sweet and rich flavored. Pkt., 10c; ½ lb., 25c; lb., 45c; 2 lbs., 80c; 5 lbs., $1.40.

Inoculate Seed Peas

To Stimulate growth, use culture of nitrogen secreting bacteria. Garden size, sufficient for 5 lbs. of seed of peas, beans and sweet peas. 10 cent.

Sow in Early Spring

LITTLE MARVEL—Dwarf, Early
EARLY GILBO—Dwarf, Main Crop
CENTURY OF PROGRESS—Dwarf, La

1 Pkt. of Each (3 pkts.),	25
½ lb. of each (1½ lbs.),	50
1 lb. of each (3 lbs.),	85

Tall Peas

THE gardener who takes pride in his p and whose space is unlimited will find tall-growing sorts unequaled for length of s son, heavy yielding and high quality. Supp should be given and they should be plan with plenty of room. Liberal fertilizing be well repaid.

★Vaughan's Improved Telepho 74 days. Of the tall-growing varieties of late p "Vaughan's Improved Telephone" is regarded experienced and successful growers as the best for general purposes. Uniformly large pods, 5 in or more long, filled with 8 to 9 delicious p Grows 4 feet high; is a main crop variety, ar heavy yielder. Pkt., 10c; ½ lb., 30c; lb., 50c; 2 l 95c; 5 lbs., $2.00.

Everbearing. About 74 days. For late summer autumn; very prolific variety. Pod about 3 in long, with large peas of good quality. Pkt., ½ lb., 25c; lb., 45c; 2 lbs., 80c; 5 lbs., $1.40.

EDIBLE POD PEAS

(Cooked like String Beans)

Dwarf Gray Sugar. About 65 days. Vines inches. Pkt., 10c; lb., 50c; 2 lbs., 95c.

MEDIUM HEIGHT

A HEAVIER yield without sacrificing quality is tained from the varieties of peas which req some support. The varieties listed below grow three feet high and should be given support chicken wire or brush between companion rows. smooth podded sorts may be sown first, and if allowed to mature too much, will be found to b good table quality.

World's Record or Improved Grad 60 days. Gradus is the greatest of the wrink peas; it is large, early, and in flavor equal to best wrinkled kinds. It is tender and should planted in the warmest spot in the garden. Vi 30 inches, pods 4 inches long, beautiful green co with 7 to 10 or more rich, tender peas in each. P 10c; ½ lb., 30c; lb., 50c; 2 lbs., 95c.

Thomas Laxton. About 62 days. This is a select of Gradus. The season is identical, but the pods square at the end and deeper green. Vines are 3½ feet high. A better yielder than Gradus. P 10c; ½ lb., 30c; lb., 50c; 2 lbs., 95c.

Alaska—Called Earliest of All. In about days. Alaska and "Maud S." are in all but co the same; Alaska seed is bluish in color; it is sta ard for market and canning. Pkt., 10c; lb., 4 2 lbs., 70c; 5 lbs., $1.25.

Pea Cultural Notes

Peas should be sown when the ground is ready work, without delay. It is important to have soil, somewhat light, and to give plenty of water full crop is to be produced. It will pay to us balanced commercial fertilizer in the row when seeds are sown. Do not crowd the seed. It is bet to sow in single rows, with two inches between seeds, or in double rows, the rows six inches ap and seeds two inches apart.

Two Pounds Prepaid

Catalogue prices of peas, beans and sweet corr include prepayment on lots up to and including 2 pounds. For postage charges on larger lots see page 120.

ertified Seed Potatoes

E offer certified stock only of Northern Grown Seed Potatoes that has been in-cted while growing and again at harvest. thing is certified but that which is 95% : of disease. These potatoes will be ready ship from Chicago on and after March 1, 4. Due to labor conditions we will fill no ers for less than 30 lb. and they will all shipped by express at the purchaser's ex-se. Prices are all F.O.B. Chicago. The chase price must be sent with every order 10 potatoes will be shipped C.O.D.

rices are all same, ½ bushel, (30 lbs.) $2.10; 1 hel, (60 lbs.) $4.20; 1½ bushels, (90 lbs.) 5. They do not exceed the ceilings in effect :he time this catalog went to press, and are ject to change.

ll potatoes will be sacked in ½ bushel, hel or 1½ bushel containers.

or the Home Garden—Early Ohio and Irish hier are the best early varieties, the former in the : and the latter in the west. One of the rural type :commended for the late crop.

irba Resistant. Warba is a new potato bred y the Minnesota Experiment Station, which is arly, highly productive, resistant to mosaic dis-ase, with upright compact vines. Tubers of excel-nt cooking quality and uniform size are round and locky, of white flesh and pale skin with pink eyes, en days earlier than Early Ohio. 30 lbs., $1.85; 0 lbs., $3.70; 90 lbs., $5.55.

h Cobbler—Early Heavy Cropper. An early f medium size, and in light soil maturing almost s soon as the smaller cropping earlies. Its size, hape, good quality and appearance commend it Our seed is grown in Red River Valley, Minnesota. 30 lbs., $1.85; 60 lbs., $3.70; 90 lbs., $5.55.

isset Rural. A mid-season late potato giving a heavy set of good sized potatoes, russet color out-side, but inside a good clear white. Preferred in many sections to the Rural New Yorker. 30 lbs., $1.85; 60 lbs., $3.70; 90 lbs., $5.55.

Field run pumpkins from our trials. Left to right: Top row: Mammoth French, Big Tom, Large Cheese, Mammoth Prize. Middle row: Colonial Pie, Golden Cushaw, Striped Cushaw, White Cushaw. Lower row: Bush or Everbearing, Sugar Pie, Winter Luxury, Kentucky Field.

Big and Small Pumpkins

SOW when the ground is warm and give the plants room to ramble. The partial shade of the sweet corn plot is ideal. A few hills will provide amply for pies and jack-o'-lanterns.

Autumn, Bush, or Everbearing. In 100 days. For the first time we offer a genuine bush form pumpkin, a boon for the home garden where space is limited. On a bush similar to that of Italian marrow, requiring a space 4 ft. square, it bears small pumpkins, excellent for pies. Pkt., 10c; oz., 20c; ¼ lb., 50c; lb., $1.50.

★Vaughan's Small Sugar Pie Pumpkin. 110 days. Well known as the best pie pumpkin. The fruit is small to medium size, with solid fine grained flesh, and a sweet, sugary, delicious flavor. Pkt., 10c; oz., 15c; ¼ lb., 45c; lb., $1.25.

★Large Field or "Big Tom." 110 days. The standard pumpkin grown in corn fields for a feeding crop. Pkt., 10c; oz., 20c; ¼ lb., 45c; lb., $1.25.

BIG TOM PUMPKIN. Pkt., 10c; oz., 20c; ¼ lb., 45c; lb., $1.25.

Cushaw. 110 days. We offer three strains. White, Striped and Golden. A favorite pumpkin for pies, having no seeds in the neck, all being con-fined in the enlarged portion near the blossom end. Pkt., 10c; oz., 20c; ¼ lb., 60c; lb., $1.75.

★Vaughan's Mammoth Prize. In about 120 days. Specimens have grown to 100 lbs; notwithstand-ing, it is among the best pie pumpkins. Flesh fine grained, sweet and tender. Requires a long season and plenty of room (one plant to a hill). Pkt., 10c; oz., 25c; ¼ lb., 65c; lb., $1.75.

Winter Queen or Winter Luxury. In about 100 days. A quality pie pumpkin and the best winter keeper. Nine or ten inches in diameter; its skin is a beautiful deep orange-yellow with a close netting. Pkt., 10c; oz., 25c; ¼ lb., 65c; lb., $1.75.

Colonial Pie. About 110 days. Fine quality, good keeper. Pkt., 10c; oz., 25c; ¼ lb., 65c; lb., $1.75.

Large Cheese. About 110 days. Large, flat like a cheese box. Pkt., 10c; oz., 15c; ¼ lb., 45c; lb., $1.25.

Kentucky Field. In 120 days. Medium size, oval shaped, lemon-yellow color. Pkt., 10c; oz., 15c; ¼ lb., 45c; 1 lb., $1.25.

SEMESAN BEL
DIP FOR LARGER POTATO CROPS

A one minute dip in Semesan Bel solution will re-duce scab and rot, even when used on clean seed potatoes. Increases in yield usually result. Directions for treatment are supplied. One pound treats 60 to 80 bushels. Prices of Improved Semesan Bel: ceiling prices, 2 oz., 30c; 1 lb., $1.65; 5 lbs., $7.15; 25 lbs., $33.25; 100 lbs., $125.00.

IRISH COBBLER. 30 lbs., $2.10.

VAUGHAN'S IMPROVED EARLY OHIO. 30 lbs., $2.10.

iughan's Improved Early Ohio (Red). A week to 10 days earlier than other strains of the same variety. The reason for this is not only in :he great care with which our seed is selected, grown and housed, but it is produced under condi-tions which are the most favorable in the Red River Valley of Minnesota, the natural home of high-class potato seed. 30 lbs., $1.85; 60 lbs., $3.70; 90 lbs., $5.55.

itahdin. Originated in Maine by the U. S. Dept. of Agriculture, it takes its name from Mt. Katahdin. The government spent $250,000 in pro-ducing this variety. It is a slightly oval white, very smooth, with shallow eyes. The vines are light green and vigorous. So far no trace of mosaic has been found on plants of Katahdin. It ripens about a week earlier than Rural New Yorker and has con-sistently out-yielded Rural New Yorker and Green Mountain, and grades out with a smaller percent of No. 2 grade and culls. The type is very uniform and in cooking and eating qualities it is unsur-passed. Katahdin does well on rich peat soils and on muck. 30 lbs., $1.85; 60 lbs., $3.70; 90 lbs., $5.55.

SWEET POTATOES

Sweet potatoes will be shipped either from 601 W. Jackson Blvd., Chicago, or from our farm in Southern Illinois, all by express at purchaser's expense. As they are very scarce we will ship Nancy Hall and Yellow Jersey only. Lb., 15c; 10 lb., $1.25; over 25 lbs., 12c per lb.

SWEET POTATO PLANTS

All orders for Sweet Potato plants will be shipped from our Southern Illinois farm, direct to the purchaser and no plants will be shipped C.O.D. Orders for 1000 or less will be sent by mail post paid, all orders for more than 1000 will be shipped express at purchaser's expense. Varie-ties Yellow Jersey and Nancy Hall only. 100, $1.25; 200, $2.00; 500, $3.50; 1,000, $5.75; By express per 1,000, $5.00.

Plants will be ready for shipment from April 15 to June 15. Our method of packing should insure safe arrival of plants in good condition. If larger quantities than quoted above are wanted, ask for special quotation.

RADISH

Sow with earliest crops, in ½-in. drill, 5 seeds to the in. Sow ea[ch]
types one week's supply at a time, at weekly intervals. Mix wi[th]
parsnips, parsley and carrots, to mark the row. Harvest when la[rge]
enough to eat. Summer and winter types have longer harve[st]

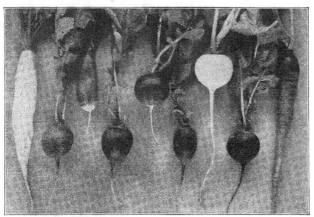

| Icicle | French Breakfast | Sparkler | White Box | | Cincinnati |
| | Crimson Globe | Scarlet Globe | Vick's Scarlet Globe | Saxa | Market |

RADISH, GIANT
BUTTER. PKT.,
10c; OZ., 20c.

RADISHES from April to December [is]
possible for the home gardener who [wants]
early, midseason, summer and winter ty[pes.]

Our strains are grown with the gre[atest]
care, which involves considerably incre[ased]
cost, but the additional cost is small c[om-]
pared with the great difference in your [garden.]

Quick growth is the secret of success[. A]
rich, light soil is required. The globe [and]
olive varieties grow faster than the long t[ypes]
and turn pithy sooner. The long types g[row]
more slowly and are slower to turn pith[y so]
they endure heat better. Winter radi[shes]
should be sown in June or later and allo[wed]
to develop in the cool, moist fall weat[her.]
Quantity needed for 15 to 20 ft., 1 p[kt.,]
75 ft., 1 oz.

Make Small, Frequent Sowings of These

★Early Scarlet Globe Select. (F.) 20 days. Vaughan's
Glasshouse Strain. For hotbed and greenhouse
forcing, and outdoor planting. Very early, crisp,
mild and tender; rich, bright scarlet in color, of
uniform globe shape. It is ready for the table in
25 days. For the home, plant every 10 days until
into June; again end of August.

Short Top—Pkt., 15c; oz., 25c; ¼ lb., 50c; lb., $1.50.
Medium Top—Pkt., 10c; oz., 20c; ¼ lb., 45c; lb.,
$1.25.

★Scarlet Turnip White Tip. 26 days. Vaughan's Selected Stock. This radish is a table dainty, crisp,
tender and sweet; it is turnip-shaped, bright scarlet
color with white tip, and is a high-class strain for
outdoor planting. It combines beautiful appearance with finest radish quality—appealing to the
eye and palate.

Vaughan's "Sparkler" Strain for Open Ground.
Pkt., 10c; oz., 20c; ¼ lb., 45c; lb., $1.25.

Icicle. 25 days. The finest white, which remains crisp and mild long after matur-
ity. It matures early with short top, which permits
close planting and forcing. Many of our customers
say it is the finest radish they have ever grown;
plant every 10 days for succession. Pkt., 10c;
oz., 20c; ¼ lb., 45c; lb., $1.25.

Saxa. (F.) 20 days. This is a European variety
which has become very popular in the United
States. It is one of the very earliest radishes and
slow to run to seed. The tops are very small, the
radishes are round and bright scarlet. We recommend it for the first planting in the garden, and
also for forcing in hotbed and greenhouse. Pkt.,
10c; oz., 20c; ¼ lb., 45c; 1 lb., $1.25.

Vick's Scarlet Globe. An olive shaped Scarlet
Globe Radish maturing in 20 days. Remains firm
and tender. Pkt., 15c; oz., 25c; ¼ lb., 50c; lb.,
$1.50.

★Giant Butter. 28 days. By far the largest of
the early turnip radishes. In
rich soil it will produce crisp, spicy, tender roots
of perfect globe shape two inches in diameter, only
a week later than the smaller globe types. It is
usable for a much longer season before it begins to
turn pithy, and by planting a succession of crops
it can be enjoyed throughout the summer. It is
seldom found in the market and will make your
friends talk. Pkt., 10c; oz., 20c; ¼ lb., 50c.

White Box—(Early White Turnip). 20 days. Our
earliest white radish. Turnip-shaped, short top and
a rapid grower—crisp. Pkt., 10c; oz., 20c; ¼ lb.,
50c; lb., $1.50.

Early Long Scarlet Short Top. 28 days. A long,
straight, smooth, red radish; it grows partly above
ground, developing a long, tender, crisp and sweet
root. Pkt., 10c; oz., 20c; ¼ lb., 50c; lb., $1.50.

Crimson Giant. (F.) 28 days. For forcing or outdoor planting. Although twice the size of other
forcing sorts this does not get pithy or hollow; the
skin is crimson, flesh is white; tender, crisp and
sweet-flavored. Sow thinly. Pkt., 10c; oz., 20c;
¼ lb., 50c; lb., $1.50.

Brightest Long Scarlet. 28 days. This is a home
garden favorite; the body is brightest scarlet color,
which blends downward to a long tip of pure white.
Matures in 25 days. Pkt., 10c; oz., 20c; ¼ lb., 50c;
lb., $1.50.

Improved French Breakfast. (F.) 25 days. Early
olive-shape 2 inches long, with slender tap root,
deep red skin, white tip. Flesh is solid, sweet, crisp
and tender, fine for the home garden. Pkt., 10c;
oz., 20c; ¼ lb., 50c; lb., $1.50.

Cincinnati Market. 30 days. A long red radish,
short top. If your market uses a long sort try this
one, Pkt., 10c; oz., 20c; ¼ lb., 50c; lb., $1.50.

Early Deep Scarlet Turnip. 26 days. An old stand-
by. Pkt., 10c; oz., 20c; ¼ lb., 50c; lb., $1.50.

Radishes supply, in a 2 oz., portion, 6 I.U. of Vitamin
B1, 11 milligrams of Vitamin C, 0.01 milligram of
Vitamin B2. Sow them thinly with slow germinating
seeds such as carrots, parsnips and parsley and harvest
the radishes before, the companion crop begins to
mature. Make frequent sowings of the early types
a week's supply at weekly intervals.

> **The Pocket Book of Vegetable Gardening**
> by Charles H. Nissley
>
> How, when, and what to plant. The latest
> practical, scientific advice on growing food for
> home use. Includes specially prepared charts
> showing Vitamin Contents and Nutritional
> Values as well as specific instruction for raising
> each vegetable. 244 pages illustrated; 30c by
> mail; 25c over the counter.

SUMMER RADISHES

When hot weather comes and spring varieties wi[ll]
turn pithy or run to seed, the varieties listed be[low]
will keep in good condition for a long time and fur[nish]
a most welcome tang to the salad course. Note [that]
they mature more slowly, so sow them early eno[ugh.]
All of the following:

Price, pkt., 10c; oz., 20c; ¼ lb., 50c; lb., $1.5[0.]

Long White Vienna. In 29 days. Snow wh[ite,]
very brittle and crisp.

White Stuttgart. About 45 days. A turnip sha[ped,]
large white radish.

White Strassburg. About 40 days. Larger size [and]
thicker than Vienna. Very solid.

> ### Long Season Radish Mixture.
> ½ oz. pkt., 15c.
>
> This is a mixture composed of equal parts
> of the following early midseason and late va-
> rieties: Scarlet Globe, Giant Butter, Icicle,
> Brightest Long Scarlet, and White Stuttgart.
> Sow thinly in the row, and harvest as they
> mature. This mixture will provide an in-
> teresting assortment of radishes for the table,
> spread over two months of harvest.

WINTER RADISHES

These should be sown from late in June to August [to]
produce the final radish crop. They grow largest [of]
all and can be stored for some time after the grou[nd]
is frozen. In spite of their size they are mild and [of]
fine texture.

Each of the following, pkt., 10c; oz., 20c; ¼ [lb.,]
50c; lb., $1.50.

California Mammoth Winter. About 60 da[ys.]
Long, very large size.

Rose or Scarlet China. In about 52 days. R[ed,]
medium size, fine keeper.

Chinese Mammoth or Celestial. About 60 da[ys.]
Immense size, flesh always crisp and mild.

Black Spanish, Long. In 58 days. Black skin [and]
white flesh.

Black Spanish, Round. In 56 days. Like L[ong,]
Black, only round.
(F.) Forcing Sorts.

★Varieties designated by a star as illustra[ted]
on this page are recommended as of especia[lly]
fine strains and suited to the home garden.

SQUASH

Sow 1 inch deep, in light soil, sunny location. Space bush types 3 feet apart in row, vine types in hills six feet apart, 3 plants to hill. Use summer squash at any size, delicious in baby stage.

JUMBO ACORN SQUASH, Pkt., 20c; ½ oz., 30c; oz., 50c.

★**Acorn, Table Queen, or "Des Moines."** Specify Green or Golden. Matures in about 88 days. In size equals a cocoanut, and a half, baked, serves one person amply. The shell is usually thin and it does not require over twenty minutes for baking or boiling. The color is dark green, even after picking and storing. The meat is dry and mealy. It yields enormously—a few hills furnishing an ample supply for a good sized family. Pkt., 10c; oz., 30c; ¼ lb., 75c; lb., $2.25.

Jumbo Acorn. Matures in about 65 days. Similar to the original Acorn, about ⅓ larger, having a rounded blossom end instead of pointed. Pkt., 20c; ½ oz., 30c; oz., 50c.

★**Buttercup.** 100 days. Its quality has no equal. The seeds are centered in blossom end and the rest of the interior is heavy flesh. A winter keeper. Pkt., 10c; oz., 30c; ¼ lb., 75c; lb., $2.25.

Butternut See novelty page. Pkt., 35c.

Sweet Potato. Improved. (Delicata Resistant.) 100 days. Its vigorous vine, resistant to mosaic disease, produces fruits averaging 8 to 9 inches, 3½ to 4 inches in diameter. Cream skin is marked by green stripes; flesh thick, orange and of unsurpassed sweetness. Pkt., 10c; oz., 35c; ¼ lb., $1.00; lb. $3.00.

"Sweet Potato." 100 days. It is an improved Delicata, as near as Table Queen. The fruit averages 6 to 8 inches long and it is thick fleshed. When baked and served with melted butter it is a table delicacy of the first order. Pkt., 10c; oz., 30c; ¼ lb., 75c; lb., $2.25.

"Kitchenette" (Hubbard). 110 days. Named "Kitchenette" because it is the smallest Hubbard. Pkt., 10c; oz., 35c; ¼ lb., 95c; lb., $2.75.

★**Vaughan's Chicago Warted Hubbard.** 110 days. Vaughan's Chicago Warted Hubbard Squash has been bred to the highest quality; fruits are large, skin, rough dark green, flesh, bright orange, fine grained, rich and dry. (Cucurbita Maxima.) Pkt., 10c; oz., 35c; ¼ lb., 95c.

New Brighton. 120 days. Of the Chicago Warted Hubbard type but twice the size. A very fine squash and well selected. This should be grown where the demand is for a large type. Pkt., 10c; oz., 35c; ¼ lb., 85c.

★**Blue Hubbard.** 110 days. A third larger than Chicago Warted and more prolific. We believe that it is superior in yield, quality, size and keeping. The blue-gray shell is more attractive and many prefer it. Pkt., 10c; oz., 35c; ¼ lb., 85c; lb., $2.75.

Original Hubbard. In 110 days. Not as large as Chicago Warted, but in shape and quality it is similar. Pkt., 10c; oz., 35c; ¼ lb., 85c; lb., $2.50.

Delicious. In 110 days. Specify Green or Golden. A fall and winter variety. Fine varies from 5 to 10 pounds each. (Cucurbita Maxima.) Pkt., 10c; oz., 35c; ¼ lb., 85c; lb., $2.50.

Prolific Straightneck. 55 days. Excels in tenderness, color, and productiveness. Served when about 6 in. long, it is delicious. Pkt., 10c; oz., 25c; ¼ lb., 65c; lb., $2.00.

Mammoth White Bush. About 60 days. An improved selection of "Early White Bush," much larger and deeper, has fewer scallops, and is a heavier producer. (Cucurbita Pepo.) Pkt., 10c; oz., 20c; ¼ lb., 50c; lb., $1.50.

Yellow Bush. About 52 days. (Cucurbita Pepo.) Pkt., 10c; oz., 20c; ¼ lb., 50c; lb., $1.50.

Early White Bush. About 55 days. Pkt., 10c; oz., 20c; ¼ lb., 50c; lb., $1.50.

Yellow Summer Straightneck. In about 60 days. This is a desirable improvement over the crookneck type. Pkt., 10c; oz., 20c; ¼ lb., 50c; lb., $1.50.

Giant Yellow Summer Crookneck. In about 55 days. Our strain produces fruit nearly double the size of the old "Crookneck." (Cucurbita Pepo.) Pkt., 10c; oz., 20c; ¼ lb., 50c; lb., $1.50.

BLUE HUBBARD SQUASH
Pkt., 10c; oz., 35c; ¼ lb., 85c; lb., $2.50.

Banana Squash. In 105 days. Of sweet potato quality. 12 inches long, 6 inches in diameter. Gray-green. Pkt., 10c; oz., 35c; ¼ lb., 85c; lb., $2.50.

Green Gold. Pkt., 25c; oz., 50c; ¼ lb., $1.50.

Boston Marrow. Pkt., 10c; oz., 20c; ¼ lb., 50c.

Fordhook. Pkt., 10c; oz., 25c; ¼ lb., 65c; lb., $2.00.

Yellow Summer Crookneck. Pkt., 10c; oz., 20c; ¼ lb., 50c; lb., $1.50.

PURPLE TOP WHITE GLOBE TURNIP

NEW ITALIAN MARROW, Dark Green Strain. Pkt., 10c; oz., 35c; ¼ lb., 85c; lb., $2.50.

Mammoth Chili. In 100 days. A popular exhibition sort. Specimens grow as large as 100 pounds. Rich orange yellow color. (Cucurbita Maxima.) Pkt., 10c; oz., 35c; ¼ lb., 75c; lb., $2.25.

VICTORY GARDEN WINNER.

★**New Italian Marrow or Zucchini.** 60 days. (Cucurbita Pepo.) When matured it is 18 in. long, 5 to 7 inches in diameter and an excellent keeper, very dark green. A bush type and very productive. There is nothing better for slicing and frying when small; if kept picked, it will continue to bear until frost. Delicious in the "baby" stage, 3 to 6 inches long. There are two strains, one light green with lighter markings, the other dark green or almost black. Both are the same shape and size.

Light Green Strain. Pkt., 10c; oz., 35c; ¼ lb., 85c; lb., $2.50.

Dark Green Strain. Pkt., 10c; oz., 35c; ¼ lb., 85c; lb., $2.50.

Cocozelle (Italian Vegetable Marrow). Ready in about 65 days. A bush variety. Fruits oblong, ribbed, 2 ft. in length. Color dark green with yellow and darker green stripes. Very fine flavor. Pkt., 10c; oz., 30c; ¼ lb., 75c; lb., $2.25.

Zucca de Pergola. About 110 days. (Cucurbita Pepo.) Grows 3 feet in length and 3 inches in diameter. Pale green in color. Used by Italians for slicing and frying like egg plant or baking, stuffed with meats. Pkt., 15c; oz., 35c; ¼ lb., $1.00.

Vegetable Marrow. About 100 days. (Cucurbita Pepo.) The fruit is generally eaten when less than half grown, as the flesh is then very tender. Also an excellent winter keeper when mature. Pkt., 10c; oz., 35c; ¼ lb., 85c; lb., $2.50.

Turnips

TURNIPS are cool weather plants and thrive best in Spring and Fall. For early use seed should be sown as soon as the ground can be prepared; it will give roots large enough for the table in six to ten weeks. For the Fall crop seed should be sown June to August and the plants will grow until freezing weather, when they should be harvested and stored.

★**Purple Top White Globe.** 57 days. Originated from "Purple Top Flat Turnip," is extensively planted and popular for its fine qualities. The flesh is firm, fine grained, sweet and mild flavored; it is of good size, globe-shaped, fine appearance, a good keeper. Pkt., 10c; oz., 20c; ¼ lb., 55c; lb., $1.50.

Purple Top Strap-Leaved. About 46 days. A table variety, fine, tender and deliciously flavored. It is broad shaped; medium size, white flesh, fine grain, splendid quality. Pkt., 10c; oz., 20c; ¼ lb., 55c; lb., $1.50.

Golden Ball or Orange Jelly. About 65 days. Medium size, globular table turnip. Flesh yellow, sweet. Pkt., 10c; oz., 25c; ¼ lb., 65c; lb. $1.75.

Early Snowball. In 40 days. Small, white, splendid quality. Pkt., 10c; oz., 25c; ¼ lb., 65c; lb. $1.75.

Early White Milan. In 42 days. Small, white, snowy white, has a polished appearance; medium size, white, tender, sweet. Pkt., 10c; oz., 25c; ¼ lb., 65c.

Shogoin. 30 days. A turnip used principally for greens. The root is small but the top is like mustard tops. Pkt., 10c; oz., 25c; ¼ lb., 65c; lb., $1.75.

Seven Top. 30 days. A variety much grown in the south for the tops, which are used as greens. Pkt., 10c; oz., 15c; ¼ lb., 30c; lb., $1.00.

Large Yellow or Amber Globe. In 76 days. Fine quality and sweet. Pkt., 10c; oz., 20c; ¼ lb., 55c; lb., $1.50.

Extra Early Purple Top Milan. About 42 days. An excellent medium size turnip; white flesh. Pkt., 10c; oz., 25c; ¼ lb., 70c; lb., $2.00.

White Egg. 60 days. Early, white skin, egg shape, tender. Pkt., 10c; oz., 25c; ¼ lb., 65c; lb., $1.75.

TURNIPS FOR STOCK

Cow Horn or Long White. In 70 days. Grows nearly half way out of the ground, carrot-shape, pure white. Oz., 20c; ¼ lb., 50c; lb., $1.40.

TOMATO

Plants started six to eight weeks before are set out two week after frost-proof date when all danger of chill is over. Pruned plants can be grown to stakes or fence 18 inches apart; space unpruned, 2 to 4 feet apart. Plants for late varieties can be grown from seed in open, preferably not transplanted.

Disease-Resistant Strains

★Break O'Day. 70 days. Developed by F. J. Pritchard, of Washington, D.C. A new wilt-resistant tomato that is nearly as early as Earliana and as productive as Marglobe. Its fruits are large, smooth, meaty, red and globular, very similar to Marglobe but usually larger. Used whole for salads or stuffed. Pkt., 10c; ½ oz., 35c; oz., 60c; ¼ lb., $1.75.

Early Baltimore. 73 days. Illinois University selection, thriving on all soils. Pkt., 15c; ½ oz., 30c; oz., 55c; ¼ lb., $1.60. Early Baltimore certified. Pkt., 20c; ½ oz., 40c; oz., 75c; ¼ lb., $2.50.

Illinois Baltimore. 84 days. A selection made by Huelsen of Urbana, Ill. Maturing same season as Indiana Baltimore. Deeper through and having additional feature of being resistant. Pkt., 15c; ½ oz., 30c; oz., 50c.

★Rutgers. In 86 days. New Jersey Experiment Station cross on Marglobe. One of heaviest croppers. Pkt., 15c; ½ oz., 35c; oz., 65c; ¼ lb., $2.00.
Rutgers certified. Pkt., 20c; ½ oz., 40c; oz., 75c; ¼ lb., $2.50.

★Pritchard (Scarlet Topper). 76 days. The fruit is solid, yield heavy and the color a brilliant red. It is a resistant second early of great merit. Pkt., 10c; ½ oz., 30c; oz., 50c. Pritchard certified. Pkt., 15c; ½ oz., 35c; oz., 60c.

★Marglobe. 77 days. A second-early, red-fruited variety equally suitable for trucking or canning. As early as Bonny Best, produces large, smooth, meaty, globular red fruits which ripen uniformly and are relatively free from cracks. They make a splendid canned product and first class pulp. Pkt., 10c; ½ oz., 30c; oz., 50c; ¼ lb., $1.50.
Marglobe certified. Pkt., 15c; ½ oz., 35c; oz., 60c; ¼ lb., $1.80.

Scarlet Dawn. In 70 days. Wilt and rust resistant, of deep red color, globe shape, heavy yielder. Pkt., 10c; ½ oz., 35c; oz., 60c.

TOMATO RUTGERS

THE LARGEST TOMATOES

Ponderosa—The Giant Tomato. Matures in about 88 days. Of the large fruited varieties, this one is most popular. The vines are strong in growth, and when planted in good soil and pruned to a single stem, the fruit reaches one pound in weight. Tomatoes grow in beautiful clusters. Pkt., 15c.

Oxheart. Matures in about 90 days. Popular because of its shape, large size, and excellent table qualities. Not a heavy yielder but often weighs 3 lbs. Skin pink, almost seedless, firm, sweet flesh, slices well. Pkt., 15c; ½ oz., 50c; oz., 90c.

Beauty (Purple). 82 days. Vines, vigorous and heavy bearers, fruit large, uniform; very smooth purplish pink skin; flesh light pink. Pkt., 10c; ½ oz., 35c; oz., 65c; ¼ lb., $2.60.

Crimson Cushion or Beefsteak. In about 96 days. Is very large, round and regular; bright scarlet skin, solid flesh of best quality, seed cells small. Plants are very prolific, fine appearance. Pkt., 10c.

New King. 100 days. Exceptionally large pink fruit. Pkt., 15c; ½ oz., 35c; oz., 60c; ¼ lb., $1.60

Prodigious. 100 days. Latest development by William E. Vail, of enormous size. We recommend this as being one of the largest tomatoes produced. Pkt., 25c; ¼ oz., 95c; oz., $1.75.

EARLY, SMALL VINES

Do Not Prune.

★Bounty. 60 days. Compact, small vine, not to be staked. Introduced by Dr. Harold Mattson. North Dakota Experiment Station. Excellent for the home garden, very productive. Pkt., 20c; ¼ oz., 40c; oz., 75c; ¼ lb., $2.25.

Bison. 60 days. Very early, small vine. Not good for staking. Pkt., 10c; ½ oz., 35c; oz., 60c.

★Firesteel. 62 days. A small vine, large fruited tomato that is early, smooth, red through, of semi-acid flavor. For dry seasons there is nothing equal to it. It will set fruit when other types are dropping their blossoms. Pkt., 15c; ½ oz., 35c; oz., 65c.

Pennheart. 74 days. Dr. C. E. Meyers of Penns lvania State College bred this large fruited, heavyyyielding, early variety of the determinate growth type. While not suitable for pruning and staking, its vine requires a space 2x4 feet for good results. Pkt., 35c; ½ oz., 65c; ¼ lb., $2.00.

Victor. 67 days. Compact vine, not suitable for staking. Pkt., 15c; ½ oz., 35c; oz., 65c.

EARLY, LARGE VINES

★Vaughan's Select Earliana. 66 days. Large, smooth bright red tomato. This variety is compact with stout jointed branches; the vines yield well and the fruit is of fine quality. Pkt., 10c; ½ oz., 35c; oz., 60c.

Nystate. In 68 days. From N.Y. Experiment Station. Pkt., 10c; ½ oz., 30c; oz., 50c.

John Baer. About 70 days. Extra early red. Not quite so early as Earliana, though there is only a few days' difference. John Baer yields a much heavier crop of larger, more uniform and more attractive fruits. Most profitable extra early sort. Pkt., 10c; ½ oz., 35c; oz., 60c.

EARLY, Large Vines—Continued.

Bonny Best. 74 days. A shade later than John Baer. Smooth, large and uniform fruit; yields well until frost. Pkt., 10c; ½ oz., 35c; oz., 65c; ¼ lb., $2.00.

June Pink. In 69 days. This is the earliest of the pink varieties and is similar in habit to the famous Earliana. Pkt., 10c; ½ oz., 35c; oz., 60c.

Chalk's Early Jewel. In 74 days. Pkt., 10c; ½ oz., 35c; oz., 65c; ¼ lb., $2.00.

Pan America. About 80 days. One of the latest Government developments for which they claim superiority in quality, firmness, and productivity. Pkt., 25c; ½ oz., 60c; oz., $1.00; ¼ lb., $3.00.

TOMATO Firesteel. Pkt., 15c; ½ oz., 35c; oz., 65c.

MAIN CROP

Early Detroit (Purple). In 80 days. Bears uniform, large, handsome, smooth fruit through the long season, yielding more market than Beauty. Pkt., 10c; ½ oz., 35c; oz., 65c; ¼ lb., $2.00.

Vaughan's New York. About 80 days. It is a second early red-skinned, firm-fleshed tomato of high quality, good size and attractive appearance. Pkt., 10c; ½ oz., 35c; oz., 60c; ¼ lb., $1.75.

Gulf State Market. About 80 days. This purplish pink tomato was developed from Early Detroit. Pkt., 10c; ½ oz., 35c; oz., 60c; ¼ lb., $1.75.

New Globe. Matures in about 82 days. This ball-shaped variety yields a heavy crop. The skin is a smooth, purplish pink. Uniform fruits. Pkt., 10c; ½ oz., 35c; oz., 65c; ¼ lb., $2.00.

Greater Baltimore (Indiana Strain). In about 83 days. Similar to Stone and very productive, fruits deep scarlet red often weighing 6 ounces; smooth and very solid. Pkt., 10c; ½ oz., 30c; oz., 50c; ¼ lb., $1.50
Greater Baltimore (Indiana Strain) certified. Pkt., 10c; ½ oz., 35c; oz., 60c; ¼ lb. $1.80.

MAIN CROP—Continued

Pepper. 80 days. This is purplish red, very smooth, medium sized, of excellent quality, with few seeds, and a sub acid flavor. The plants are dwarf but prolific. The fruits do not crack. Pkt., 25c; ¼ oz., 35c; ½ oz., 65c; oz., $1.00.

Dwarf Champion. About 86 days. Of dwarf habit and upright tree-like growth. It is of medium size, very smooth, purplish pink. Pkt., 10c; ½ oz., 35c; oz., 65c.

Improved New Stone. 86 days. Smooth skin, small core, fine-grained flesh with little acidity. Pkt., 10c; ½ oz., 25c; oz., 35c.

Dwarf Stone—The Largest Dwarf Tomato. 92 days. It resembles "Dwarf Champion," but is of stronger growth and more erect. Pkt., 10c; ½ oz., 35c; oz., 65c; ¼ lb., $2.00.

YELLOW TOMATOES

Orange King. 66 days. A small vine variety of true orange flesh and skin, not suitable for staking. It bears smooth fruits of medium size, thick flesh and mild flavor. Seed scarce. Pkt., 15c; ½ oz., 30; oz., 50c.

Jubilee. 90 days. Won bronze medal, 1943. All America trials. Pkt., 25c.

Golden Queen. 84 days. Golden yellow. Pkt. 10c; ½ oz., 40c; oz., 70c.

Golden Oxheart. Pkt., 20c; ½ oz., 55c; oz., $1.00.

Golden Ponderosa. Pkt., 15c; ½ oz., 50c; oz., 95c.

SMALL FRUITED TOMATOES

Very Desirable for Pickles and Preserves. Mature in about 73 days.

Dwarf Pear. 73 days. Improved type. Pkt., 15c; ½ oz., 40c; oz., 75c.
Any of the following, pkt., 10c; ½ oz., 40c; oz., 75c.

Red Currant. Very small.

Red Cherry. Small fruit, bright scarlet.

Two Peach Tomatoes. Red or yellow.

Yellow Plum and Red Plum. Fruit 2 inches.

Yellow Pear and Red Pear. Distinct shape.

Ground Cherry, Husk or Strawberry. The small yellow fruit is enclosed in a husk. It is very sweet; prized for eating, preserving and making pies.

Italian Canner. 75 days. A very productive, long plum-shaped tomato. It is firm, not having any hollow parts, and the walls are exceptionally thick. Pkt., 15c; ½ oz., 60c; oz. $1.00.

GREENHOUSE TOMATOES

Bonny Best. Red. The most popular American variety, for forcing. Forcing strain.

Long Calyx. Red.

Michigan State Forcing. Red.

New Globe. Pink.

Any of above, pkt., 25c.

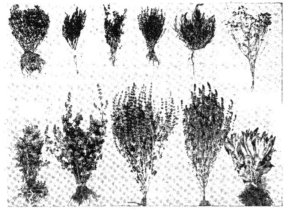

| Sweet Marjoram | Caraway | Coriander | Thyme | Rosemary | | Anise |
| Rue | | Catnip | Sweet Basil | Summer Savory | | Sage |

Plants for Your Herb Garden

Ten Annual Herb Plants, Your Choice, by Express, at Buyer's Expense, for $2.00.
Ten Perennial Herb Plants, Your Choice, by Express, at Buyer's Expense, for $2.50.

MIXTURE OF ANNUAL HERB SEEDS FOR 15c.

This is intended to meet the needs of those who want to grow a row or bed of herbs without sowing a full packet of each variety. It will contain all available varities of useful annual herbs. Sow in a nursery row, or seed box and transplant to a row or border in the Victory garden.

MIXTURE OF PERENNIAL HERB SEEDS FOR 15c.

For small gardens, this will give enough plants of assorted varieties to supply the family needs, without the expense of purchasing a packet of each. Sow in a nursery row and transplant in the fall to a permanent location.

Anise. Used for garnishing, seasoning and for cordials. Pkt., 10c; ½ oz., 50c.

Basil, Sweet. The leaves are used for flavoring soups and stews. Pkt., 10c; ½ oz., 35c; oz., 65c.

Borage. Flowers excellent for bees. Leaves used in salads. The flower spikes can be used in cooling drinks. Pkt., 10c; ½ oz., 35c; oz., 60c.

Caraway. Seeds are used for flavoring bread, pastry, meats, etc. Pkt., 10c; ½ oz., 30c; oz., 50c.

*Catnip. Grown for bee pasture. The leaves and young shoots are used for seasoning. Pkt., 10c; ½ oz., 50c; oz., 90c.

*Chamomile (Anthemis Nobilis). The dried flowers possess medicinal value. Pkt., 20c.

*Chives. Member of the onion family used for flavoring. Pkt, 25c; ½ oz., $1 10; oz., $2.00.

Coriander. The seeds are used for flavoring. Pkt., 10c; ½ oz., 30c; oz., 50c.

Dill. Leaves are used in pickles and for flavoring soups and sauces. Pkt, 10c; oz., 25c; ½ lb., 65; lb., $2.00.

*Fennel. The leaves boiled are used in fish sauces and are excellent for garnishing. The seeds are used for flavoring. Pkt., 10c; ½ oz., 20c; oz., 35c; ½ lb., $1.00.

*Horehound. The leaves are used for flavoring and also in the manufacture of cough remedies. Pkt. 25c.

*Lavender. The leaves are sometimes used for seasoning, but the plant is chiefly grown for its flowers, which are fragrant. There are two kinds.

*Lavender Vera or True. The best. Pkt., 25c. ¼ oz., $1.00.

*Lavender Spica. Not quite so strong as Vera. Pkt., 10c; ½ oz., 35c.

Marjoram (Sweet). The leaves and ends of shoots are used for flavoring in summer and dried for winter use. Plants only.

*Mint, Old Fashioned. For mint sauce and juleps. Plants only.

*Pennyroyal. Leaves are used for seasoning puddings. Plants only.

*Peppermint. The leaves and stems are used for flavoring and for oils. Plants only.

*Rosemary. The leaves are used for seasoning. Plants only.

*Rue. For medicinal purposes; good for fowls, for the roup. Plants only.

Saffron. Used for coloring dishes, also flavoring. Pkt., 10c; ½ oz., 30c.

Summer Savory. The leaves and young shoots are used for flavoring. Pkt., 10c; ½ oz., 60c; oz., $1.00.

Sage, English Broad Leaf. Pkt., 25c; ½ oz., $1.00; oz., $1.90.

*Thyme. Used for seasoning; a tea is also made for nervous headache. Pkt., 25c.

Wormwood. Beneficial for poultry. Plants only.

Varities marked (*) are perennials.

TISANES OR HERBAL TEAS

Herb Teas in general are made by pouring boiling water over the dried herb (about one teaspoonful to each cup of water), allow to steep about ten minutes, strain. Serve plain or with lemon or honey. Milk and cream are taboo. A porcelain container, and not metal, is used as in making other teas.

Chamomile—Well known for its delightfully soothing quality.

Peppermint and Lemon Verbena—Delightful lemon flavor.

Mint—Very refreshing with slice of lemon, served hot or cold.

Alfalfa and Peppermint.

Linden Blossom

Sage

Each of the above, per jar, 40c.

DRIED HERBS FOR SEASONING.

Magic Box of 4 jars for $1.25; or 6 for $1.75; also "Sampler" Box of 12 put up in glassine envelopes for $1.25, including: Basil, Lovage, Mint, Sage, Tarragon, Thyme, Poultry Seasoning, Fish Herbs, Omelet Herbs, Salad Herbs, Savory, Meat Herbs and Tomato Herbs.

Vaughan's Seed Store 87

New and Standard Giant Dahlias

SEMI-CACTUS TYPE

Outstanding Dahlias

The following can be supplied in tubers only.

Adolf Mayer. Very dark red, almost black. A real sensation. Price, $1.00; 3 for $2.70.

American Purity. (S. C.) Color a large full and glistening white with petals beautifully quilled at the tips. Excellent stems carry the flowers well above the healthy foliage. An ideal exhibition Dahlia. Price, each, $1.00; 3 for $2.70.

American Victory. (F. D.) An even tone of rich oxblood red that does not fade. Plant is strong and easy to grow. Clean medium-sized foliage and good stem. Has two Achievement Medals to its record. Price, each, $2.00; 3 for $5.40.

Cheer Leader. (F. D.) Self-color of rose pink with long strong stems. Unexcelled as a cut flower. Large and deep flower. Price, $1.50; 3 for $4.00.

Cherokee Brave. (I. D.) Ox-blood red that holds its color in the sun. Long stiff stems. Strong grower with heavy foliage. Price, $1.00; 3 for $2.70.

Darcy Sainsbury. (F. D.) Its large size and pure white color make it a standout in the Dahlia. A good grower, free bloomer and fairly tall bushes. Price, each, $1.00; 3 for $2.70.

Eventide. (I.D.) True purplish shadings. Its unusual production of big blooms, most excellent stem and vigorous habit of growth, good substance of bloom make it one of the best of the new varieties. Price, $1.50; 3 for $4.00.

Flash. (S. C.) A crimson red tipped pure white. Petals are serrated and they curl and twist. An early and prolific bloomer throughout the entire season. Price, each, $2.00; 3 for $5.40.

Gertrude Lawrence. (I. D.) Color is best described as a currant red. Blooms are very large. Long jointed stems hold the bright flowers well above the foliage. Perfect stems and rugged plant growth. Price, each, $1.00; 3 for $2.70.

Ginger Rogers. (I. D.) The color of this fine variety is a citron yellow. A large, many-petalled flower with very great depth, being nearly "ball shaped" when matured. A free bloomer and strong grower. Price each, $3.50.

Katie K. A clear pink of large size on long stem. Price, $1.00; 3 for $2.70.

Kentucky Sportsman. (I. D.) Color, gold, shading to apricot-yellow and then to a distinct orange, ending with white tips. Price, $1.00; 3 for $2.70.

Lois Walcher. (F. D.) Color, deep amaranth purple that breaks sharply into pure white. The stems are ideal. The healthy bush is an early and prolific bloomer. Price, $1.25; 3 for $3.35.

Maffie. (S. C.) Massive blooms of an intense red that does not fade or burn. A clean, strong-growing plant with insect-resistant foliage. The giant blooms are held erect on long and strong stems. Winner of many honors as the "biggest and best" variety. Price, each, $3.50.

Mary Taylor. (Inc. C.) Color is grenadine pink with lemon yellow center. A bright, clear flower with perfect form and unusually good stems. Achievement Medal winner and an Honor Roll dahlia. Price, each, $1.50; 3 for $4.00.

88 INDEX ON FINAL PAGES

IN THE following we offer what we consider the best of the Foreign and American Dahlias. We will supply Tubers of proper planting size on all varieties listed.

KEY TO ABBREVIATIONS: F. D., Formal Decorative; I. D., Informal Decorative; S. C., Semi-Cactus; Str. C., Straight Cactus; Inc. C., Incurved Cactus.

KEEPING CUT DAHLIAS

After cutting, strip the foliage except at the top; recut the stem and immerse in water as hot as the hand can bear, being sure that none of the foliage gets in the water. When the water cools the Dahlias are transferred to a pail of cold water and left in the cellar over night. We have found that they keep several days and increase in size.

Margie Parrella. (F. D.) Pure white. Blooms will open full in the hottest weather without being bruised or burnt. One of the best white cut flower varieties. Price, $1.50; 3 for $4.00.

Mayor Frank Otis. Soft, rich golden yellow with just a touch of copper shading. A vigorous grower, free bloomer and has a fine stem. Large blooms unusually broad and deep with artistic petal formations. Price, $1.00; 3 for $2.70.

Miss Oakland. Pure white. Perfect habit of growth, free flowering; unexcelled for cut flower or exhibition. Price, each, $1.00; 3 for $2.70.

Mrs. James Albin. (F.D.) A soft pleasing yellow with fine formal blooms carried on straight stiff stems. The plant is 4 to 5 feet high, has a clean sturdy growth and branches freely, making it easy to cut the blooms with long stems. It also has exceptional keeping qualities. Received the Certificate of Merit of the American Dahlia Society. Price $1.00; 3 for $2.70

Monarch of the East. It is a big, bold bloom, a real giant in the Dahlia world. Its color is a golden bronze with a coral red reverse. Price, each, $1.00; 3 for $2.70.

Murphy's Masterpiece. (I. D.) A dark red shading toward garnet, it will withstand sun without fading. The plant is a strong grower and producer of large blooms. Price, $1.00; 3 for $2.70.

Premier's Winsome. (I. D.) White suffused with mallow pink. A Dahlia of merit, with all the good qualities a Dahlia should have. A massive bloomer. Price, $1.25; 3 for $3.35.

Rita Wells. (I.D.) Color is buff and gold with tints of grenadine pink. Producing large blooms with great depth gives the blooms a massiveness which never failed to stop visitors. Good grower with long strong stems. Price, $1.50; 3 for $4.00.

Snowcrest. (Inc. C.) A pure white of medium size blooms with fine form. A free bloomer and good keeper. Good clean grower and exceptionally fine foliage. Winner of many prizes and Achievement Medals. Price, $3.50.

Son of Satan. (S. C.) One of the largest and brightest of its type. Bright scarlet blooms on excellent stems. Blooms up to 12 inches in diameter. A sensation in any garden, and a winner in any show. Each $1.00; 3 for $2.70.

Sunrays. (I. D.) Clear buff with apricot suffusion, with a distinct peach-red reverse, strong sturdy grower. A great prize winner. Price, $1.50; 3 for $4.00.

The Governor. (F. D.) A large bright sulphur yellow which is definitely a formal. Early to bloom, it gives a wealth of flowers until frost. One of the leading winners in its class. Strong grower with good stems. Each $1.50; 3 for $4.00.

Thunderbolt. (Inc. C.) A large vivid scarlet. An early and free bloomer. The huge blooms are held on strong stems well above the foliage. A strong grower. On the House Beautiful Honor Roll. Price, each, $1.25; 3 for $3.35.

Victory. (F. D.) Color rose-pink with a golden suffusion. Excellent keeping qualities. Fine stems and insect proof foliage. Bush is vigorous and free branching. Winner of many Blue Ribbons at leading shows. Each $2.00; 3 for $5.40.

Your Lucky Star. (S. C.) The centers are white and the outer half is a distinct clear lavender. Very large well-formed flowers of unusual beauty. Good grower with fine stem. Price, $1.25; 3 for $3.35.

SPECIAL OFFER. (88) One tuber each Cheer Leader, Eventide, Mary Taylor, and The Governor, for $5.70. Postpaid to 8th Zone.

SPECIAL OFFER. (88 A) One tuber each Lois Walcher, Monarch of the East, Premier's Winsome, Son of Satan, and Your Lucky Star, for $4.60. Postpaid to 5th Zone.

SPECIAL OFFER. (88 B) One tuber each Cherokee Brave, Darcy Sainsbury, Katie K., Mayor Frank Otis, and Mrs. James Albin, for $3.90. Postpaid to 5th Zone.

FORMAL DECORATIVE
TUBERS ONLY

Avalon. Pure, clear yellow with large flower. Price, each, 35c; 3 for 85c.

Buckeye Bride. A geranium-pink, a rare and beautiful shade. The flower is large, held at a correct angle on the stem. Price, each, 75c; 3 for $2.00

Cavalcade. A beautiful new shade of old-rose. Flowers on long stiff stems. Each, 50c; 3 for $1.25.

Clara Carder. A large cyclamen pink with a flush of yellow at the base. In a color class by itself. Price, each, 50c; 3 for $1.25.

Florist White. Pure white, fine shaped flowers with long, stiff stems. Good grower. Price, each, 50 3 for $1.25.

Gallant Fox. A brilliant red. Its keeping qualities, sturdy stem and fine color make it a valuable sort. Price, each, 35c; 3 for 85c.

Jersey's Beauty. It is still in a class by itself, perfect bloom of eosine pink, carried high on white stem. Price, each, 35c; 3 for 85c.

Kentucky Sun. A large clear yellow producing quantities of uniform flowers. A fine exhibition and commercial dahlia. Price, 50c; 3 for $1.25.

King of the Blacks. Darkest rich velvet red, almost black. Compact, vigorous. Each, 75c; 3 for $2.00

Long Island Red. Color geranium red. Medium size, well shaped flowers, carried on wiry stem well above the foliage. Price, each, 75c; 3 for $2.00

Mrs. Ide Ver Warner A refined, mauve-pink, beautifully formed. Large blooms carried on long, strong wiry stems. Price, each, 35c; 3 for 85c.

Negus. Oxblood red to almost black in center. Good size blooms held erect on strong stems. A strong robust plant with fine insect-resisting foliage. Price each, 75c; 3 for $2.00.

Oakleigh Monarch. A clear, brilliant cerise red. Very large blooms of great depth which keep well when cut. Strong, rugged grower. Each, 75c; 3 for $2.00.

Omar Khayyam. A Chinese red at the base of petals, shading to a bright orange with paler tips, giving a soft effect. Price, each, 35c; 3 for 85c.

Rose Fallon Color dark orange tinted with amber and salmon. Price, each, 35c; 3 for 85c.

Rose Glory. Pure deep rose-pink. Free and early bloomer. Strong grower with long straight stems Medium height. Price, each, 35c; 3 for 85c.

Sultan of Hillcrest. Color, strontian yellow with sunrise yellow reverse. The bush habits and foliage are perfect. Price, each, 75c; 3 for $2.00.

Thomas A. Edison. A royal purple with a brilliant rich finish. Price, each, 75c; 3 for $2.00.

Queen City. Scarlet pink or light cherry red. A cut flower variety outstanding in color, and is very attractive, keeping well when cut. From July it produces flowers until frost. Strong grower with good stems. Price, each, 50c; 3 for $1.25.

White King. A pure white, large flowering. Free flowering on long stems. Price, each, 35c; 3 for 85c

White Wonder. The giant blooms are pure white with long twisted and curled petals. Foliage thick leather-like. Price, each, 50c; 3 for $1.25.

SPECIAL OFFER. (88 C) One tuber each Clara Carder, Florist White, Negus, Queen City, and Sultan of Hillcrest, for $2.60. Postpaid to 5th Zone.

SPECIAL OFFER. (88 D) One tuber each Avalon, Gallant Fox, Jersey's Beauty, Mrs. Ide Ver Warner, Omar Khayyam, Rose Glory, and White Wonder, for $1.95. Postpaid to 8th Zone.

Disbudding   **Technique**

The Diagram shows a Typical Dahlia Plant which has been pinched back after making the first four leaves, and thereafter disbranched and disbudded to produce 10 exhibition flowers.

POMPON DAHLIAS

Under this head come those small Bouquet Dahlias that are so popular for cut flowers.

Price except where noted: Each, 35c; 3 for 85c; 6 for $1.60.

Amber Queen. Solid amber color and a beautiful shade. Prolific bloomer.

Bacchus. Clear, bright red, rounded and full.

Bronze Beauty. Gold apricot. Fine cut flower variety.

Catherine. Bright yellow. Good form and stem.

Edith Mueller. A bright soft apricot suffused peach red.

Little Dorothy. A variation of white and yellow on long wiry stems, making it a fine pompon. Price, each, 50c; 3 for $1.25.

Little Herman. Deep red, tipped white; very free.

Mary Munns. Fuchsia with dark orchid sheen.

Morning Mist. A pale lavender. Very free bloomer with fine long stems.

Rosa Wilmoth. Small, fine formed rose-pink.

Sherry. A deep purple which is nearly round and very attractive.

Snowclad. The best pure white pompon.

SPECIAL OFFER. (89 B)

One tuber each Bacchus, Catherine, Edith Mueller, Mary Munns, Morning Mist, and Snowclad, for $1.50. Postpaid to 5th Zone.

SPECIAL OFFER. (89 C)

One tuber each Amber Queen, Bronze Beauty, Little Herman, Rosa Wilmoth, and Sherry, for $1.35. Postpaid to 5th Zone.

SHOW OR BALL SHAPED

A. D. Livoni. A beautiful soft pink flower with quilled petals. Price, each 35c; 3 for 85c.

Bonnie Blue. Lavender blue. A popular variety of its type and color. A good cutflower and good keeper when cut. Price, each 35c; 3 for 85c.

Charlotte Caldwell. Bright, orange, very free blooming. Sturdy plants. Price, each 50c; 3 for $1.25.

Mary Helen. A primrose colored ball. One of the best ball types. Price, each 35c; 3 for 85c.

Rosy Dawn. Color a beautiful shade of yellow shading to a strawberry red at the tips of petals. A strong grower, insect-resistant foliage. A good keeper when cut. Price, each, 50c; 3 for $1.25.

SPECIAL OFFER. (89 D)

One tuber each of the above 5 Dahlias for $1.55. Postpaid to 5th Zone.

MINIATURE DAHLIA

TUBERS ONLY

These small type Dahlias have become popular owing to their usefulness. Can be planted in garden, border or beds fairly close, about 20 to 24 inches apart. Their freedom of bloom and keeping a long time when cut make them ideal for arrangements.

Audries Orange. (S. C.) A bright orange. One of the finest miniatures. Very neat in appearance and excellent for exhibition. Price, each, 50c; 3 for $1.25.

Baby Royal. (S. C.) One of the finest miniatures of salmon-pink shaded apricot. A good cut flower. Price, each, 35c; 3 for 85c.

Bishop of Llandoff. (Duplex.) Brilliant rich red blooms, in contrast to the dark bronze-black foliage, make it outstanding. Each, 50c; 3 for $1.25.

Fairy. (F. D.) Described as a miniature Jersey's Beauty, but lighter in color. A violet-rose shading mauve at tips. Price, each, 35c; 3 for 85c.

Little Dream. (S. C.) Color lavender pink with white center. Dwarf grower and free bloomer. Price, each, 50c; 3 for $1.25.

Little Duke. (F. D.) Color a deep rich burgundy. The very dark green, insect-resistant foliage forms a pleasing contrast with the richly colored blooms. Strong grower and good stems. Price, each, 50c; 3 for $1.25.

McKay's Purity. (F. D.) Pure white with uniform blooms carried on long, strong stems. Strong growing plant. Price, each, 75c; 3 for $2.00.

Princess Alba. (F. D.) A miniature that sets a new high standard in the white class. The plants are tall and of excellent growing habit producing quantities of perfectly formed blooms on fine stems. Price, each, 75c; 3 for $2.00.

Ranger. (F. D.) A clear orange-red, blooms on long stiff stems. The tall growing plants are of perfect habit and produce an abundance of blooms. Price, each, 75c; 3 for $2.00.

Snowsprite. (S. C.) Glistening snow white in color with perfect stems and artistic form. Good, dependable variety. Price, each, 75c; 3 for $2.00.

Sylvia. Rich deep carmine. A dahlia that grows well, blooms profusely and keeps well. Price, 35c; 3 for 85c.

SPECIAL OFFER. (89E)

One tuber each Bishop of Llandoff, Little Duke, Princess Alba, and Ranger, for $1.80. Postpaid to 5th Zone.

SPECIAL OFFER. (89 F)

One tuber each Audries Orange, Baby Royal, Fairy, Little Dream, and Sylvia, for $1.50. Postpaid to 5th Zone.

INIATURE AND POMPON DAHLIAS

INFORMAL DECORATIVE

TUBERS ONLY

...rnia Idol. A giant clear yellow that can win ...ny class in which it may be entered. It is a ...olid grower. This Dahlia will be a popular ...ety for years. Price, each, 75c; 3 for $2.00.

...kee Rose. Lavender rose. Plant is vigorous ... long, erect stems and uniform full-centered ...ers. Recommended as an exhibition or cut ...er variety. Price, each, 50c; 3 for $1.25.

...s Velvet Wonder. Color is a rich violet ...ole. The huge blooms can be grown to im-...se size. A strong grower with striking foliage. ...ood exhibition variety. Each, 75c; 3 for $2.00.

...Cowl. A large flower of warm buff and old ..., blending to a bright salmon at the center. ...ce, each, 35c; 3 for 85c.

...y's Beacon. The color is Chinese-scarlet with ...aler reverse, giving a two-toned effect. Price, ...h, 35c; 3 for 85c.

...Baker. A deep butter Yellow Free Bloomer ... good grower. Price each, 50c; 3 for $1.25.

Geo. Le Boutillier. A rich velvety carmine, ...nt in size and outstanding in all respects. A ...lthy, vigorous grower. Each, 50c; 3 for $1.25.

...rt Emmett. Clear cardinal red inclining to ...nson. A dependable grower with good stems and ...t keeping qualities. Price, 75c; 3 for $2.00.

CIAL OFFER. (89) One tuber each

California Idol, ...nt's Velvet Wonder, Jane Cowl, Jersey's ...con, and Mrs. George LeBoutillier, for ...00. Postpaid to 5th Zone.

SEMI-CACTUS

TUBERS ONLY

...l. Bright glowing henna red. A tight petaled ...m of fine form and good stem. Price, 50c; ...r $1.25.

Trimbee. Color of richest deep petunia violet. ...mmense size, borne well above the foliage on ...f rigid stems. Price, each, 50c; 3 for $1.25.

...y's Dainty. A fine formed white of medium ... with fine stems. A good exhibition and cut ...er. Price, each, 50c; 3 for $1.25.

...shine G. A beautiful, true rose-pink flower ...h petals tipped yellow. Each, 35c; 3 for 85c.

...i. A flaming red with a slight touch of gold at ... center. Strong grower with heavy foliage. ...ce, each, 50c; 3 for $1.25.

...of Bethlehem. Flowers are pure white with ... pointed petals with large tight center. Free ...omer and needs disbudding. Each, 50c; 3 for ...25.

IAL OFFER.(89 A) One tuber each of

the above 6 Dahlias for $2.15. Postpaid to 5th Zone.

...hlia Tubers. To color. In white, pink, ...yellow, red, variegated and lavender. Price, ...each, 20c; doz., $2.00, postpaid.

DOROTHY S.

Cannas are becoming more popular. The new varieties with large flowers in new colors are unequalled for creating a colorful show from July till frost. They do best in full sun and respond quickly to feeding.

Number of Cannas required for round beds planted eighteen inches apart each way: Seven feet—19 plants, one for center; six for first row, twelve for second row. Ten feet—37 plants, one for center; six for first row, twelve for second row, eighteen for third row.

New and Popular Cannas

Ambassador. 3½ to 4 ft. Bronze foliage; color, poppy red; very brilliant flowers.

Hungaria. 3½ ft. Best pink Canna. Leaves bluish green, never burn. Flowers large, with big petals.

King Humbert. 4 ft. Scarlet flowers, bronze leaves. This remarkable "Gold Medal" Canna has been the sensation of the past fifteen years.

The President. 4 ft. A rich glowing scarlet on strong stalks; green foliage.

Yellow King Humbert. 4 ft. Foliage a very dark green, flowers a deep rich yellow, softly spotted and blotched with bright red.

PRICES OF ABOVE
DORMANT 2-3 EYE ROOTS. Available March 1 to April 15; 3 for 50c; $1.75 per doz.; $12.00 per 100.

CHOICE CANNAS

Copper Giant. 4 ft. The finest variety we know. Its giant flowers borne on strong stalks with green foliage are of a vivid hue, with great carrying power, of madder red and old rose with a suggestion of burnished copper in the mass effect. It blooms continuously throughout the season.

Dorothy S. 4 ft. A beautiful salmon red. Green foliage. Produces large flowers on very vigorous plants.

Eureka. 4 ft. Free-flowering variety with striking white flowers which first appear cream. Green foliage.

Improved Florence Vaughan. 4 ft. Rated finest of all yellows. Large lemon-yellow flowers, red red dots, luxuriant green foliage.

PRICES OF ABOVE
DORMANT 2-3 EYE ROOTS. Available March 1 to April 15; 3 for 65c; $2.25 per doz.; $15.00 per 100.

Available April 20 - June 5.

PENNISETUM CUPREUM

A fine bronze Ornamental Grass. Needs rich soil and sunny location. Plants, 3 for $1.00; doz., $3.00; 100, $20.00.

Early Flowering Chrysanthemums

GARDEN TYPE

COLORFUL GARDEN TYPES

Achievement. New early light bronze, dwarf bushy plant. Blooms early September.

Autumn Lights. Unusual coppery orange disc-shaped. Blooms about Sept. 20. Erect growth. Medium height and large blooms.

Dean Kay. New. The first of a new hardy strain from Iowa. Extremely prolific and free blooming. Single plants run 4 feet in diameter with hundreds of 2-inch semi-double bright pink flowers.

Geronimo. An early double dark bronze. Free flowering and of bushy habit.

King Midas. Hardy, vigorous type with immense golden yellow flowers tinged bronze when opening. Blooms Oct. 12.

Lady Lavender. 1939 Introduction, Large double silvery lavenders blooms by Oct. 10.

Mrs. Sam P. Rotan. Big fluffy double golden yellow shaded to deep orange. Blooms Oct. 15.

Muskogee. Semi-double purplish-rose, slight yellow central disk. A good U. S. Department of Agriculture variety.

Seminole. The earliest good white. Full double. U. S. Department of Agriculture origin.

Symphony. Very large flowers, 3 in. diameter, in mauve, rose, lilac and coppery shading. Blooms Oct. 12.

Tasiva. A fine double white. Blooms Oct. 7.

The Moor. Double maroon. Blooms Oct. 7.
Any of above, 40c each; 3 for $1.00.

COLLECTION 90A: ONE EACH OF ABOVE $3.25 (Postage Extra).

COLLECTION 90D: ONE EACH OF Autumn Lights, Dean Kay, Lady Lavender, Mrs. Rotan, Seminole, and The Moor, (Postage Extra)........ $1.55

SPOON CHRYSANTHEMUMS

Silver Spoon. White Tubular petals.

Orchid Spoon. Large double light pinkish lilac.

Jasper Spoon. Yellow and jasper red.

Golden Spoon. Semi-double golden apricot-yellow.

Rose Spoon. Large single old rose.
Any of above, 40c each; 3 for $1.00.

COLLECTION 90S: ONE EACH FOR $1.55 (Postage Extra) ....

6 Outstanding Chrysanthemum Collection, for . . (Postage Extra) $2.00

See Inside Back Cover for Color Illustration.

Success With Chrysanthemums
Divide plants every spring. Plant in sunny but sheltered spot. During dry spells water heavily once weekly.
Mulch with ½ inch straw litter about July 1st to promote early growth

CHICAGO CHRYSANTHEMUMS
Originated by Dr. Kraus (U. of C.)

Barbara Small. Clear rose pink, 3-inch double. Flowers well spaced. Late September.

Flavita. Nearly double lemon yellow, flat flowers, 2 inches diameter. Low grower and free blooming from late September on. Excellent for borders.

Goldridge. Double, deep golden yellow, 3 inches. Free flowering. Mid-September.

Harbinger. Deep primrose yellow. 2½ inch double flowers. Well branched, making excellent plants. Blooms September on.

M. J. Costello. Double flat flowers, golden yellow, reddish gold center in the bud. 2½ inches. Blooms early September.

Polar Ice. Glistening blue white with no trace of cream color. 2½ to 3 inches double. Very free flowering. Early September on.

Redbank. Bright red, single yellow center. 2-ins. Blooming in mid-September.

Robt. Brydon. Dark garnet red. Low, bushy, free flowering, about 2½ to 3 inches in diameter. Sept.

Wm. Longland. Double, clear bronze, diameter 2½ inches, tall and upright. Long season, from mid-September on.
Any of above, 60c each; 3 for $1.50.

COLLECTION 90U: ONE OF EACH. Express $3.90 or Postage Extra. ....

NEW KOREAN MUMS

Hardy, single Daisy Chrysanthemums first introduced in 1914. Numerous new varieties have added to the charm, coloring and abundant flowering of this new race of hardy mums.

Pysche. Large shell pink. 4 in. in diameter.

Saladin. Heavily petalled Daisy-like blossoms. 3 in. diameter. Oriental red with coppery tones.

Sappho. Bright lemon-yellow. Dwarf type. Blooms earliest of all.

Saturn. Sparkling orange bronze, thin halo of light orange.
Any of above, 40c each; 3 for $1.00.

COLLECTION 90K: THE SET OF ABOVE $1.25 PLANTS FOR (Postage Extra). ....

JOAN HELEN: An unusually brilliant new chrysanthemum. Large semi-double flowers with petals of Garnet lake shading to Rhododendron purple surrounding a brilliant yellow disc. Flowers are borne in such profusion that the plant becomes a veritable mound of sparkling color. Plant is dwarf and comes into full bloom early. Be sure to order this outstanding variety. Each, 75c; 3 for $2.00.

Mrs. Du Pont: A distinctive and lovely chrysanthemum with a soft peach tint dominating. It has a luminous sheen giving it an outstanding and unusual color. 3 for $1.25; doz., $3.75; each, 50c.

Eugene A. Wander: A very large flowered early variety with a glistening golden yellow color, occasionally showing a slight bronze tint. An excellent recent introduction. 3 for $1.25; doz., $3.75; each, 50c.

COLLECTION 90X: ONE EACH OF THE $1.50 ABOVE (Postage Extra). ....

Gail S. A beautiful peach bronze with an apricot sheen overlay. Is a fine addition to the early blooming group. Each $1.00. 3 for $2.75.

POMPON TYPE

BUTTON OR POMPON TYPE

Jewell. Stout full button. Dark orchid pink. great favorite.

Pygmy Gold. Dwarf growth, covered with round golden pompons. 1 in. diameter. Blooms in Sept.

September Bronze. Early medium bronze pompon One of the best.

White Gull. Entire plant covered with soft balls pure white.
Any of above, 40c each; any 3 for $1.00.

COLLECTION 908: ONE EACH OF THE $1 ABOVE (Postage Extra). ....

CUSHION OR AZALEA-LIKE MUMS

Amelia. Known as Azalea-like mum. Very dw and early. Forms large mound covered with ma medium size double light pink blooms.

King Cushion. Habit of growth same as Amel Very dwarf and early with light bronze flowe

Queen Cushion. True Azalea type. Very dwarf a early. Medium size double white flowers.

Santa Claus. Striking introduction with big, bus growth covered by brilliant red flowers fr September on. Height is medium and bloo average 2-inch diameter.

Yellow Cushion. A yellow form of the cushi type which is a perfect match for the other colo Foliage, flowers, growth and hardiness are the tr Azalea type. Color a dark lemon-yellow.
Any of above, each, 40c; 3 for $1.00.

COLLECTION 90C: ONE EACH OF ABOVE $1 (Postage Extra). ....

FALL BLOOMING PINK DAISY

Chrysanthemum Clara Curtis. New late bloomi pink Daisy, perfectly hardy. Hundreds of salmo pink flowers, 3 inches diameter, in late August fro plants two years old. Each, 50c; 3 for $1.25.

PINCH BACK YOUR MUMS
To make garden Chrysanthemums bushy, covered with flowers, pinch off the tops of all stems twice before they attain the height of 10 inches. After the ground freezes give a liberal covering of hay, straw or leaves, to prevent premature thawing out during the winter and early spring.

Vaughan's *New and Standard* Gladioli

PEARL HARBOR   RANGER (Commando)   MARGUERITE   CORINNE VAUGHAN

Best of the New Introductions

ng of Hearts (Salbach). Ex. (Picardy X Grand Opera.) Sold under protection of U. S. Patent No. 160. The individual florets consistently measure from 8 to 8½ inches in diameter. The flower stems are not thick, but are strong and wiry, adding to the grace of this fine new variety. The plants are tall, make a vigorous growth, with deep green foliage, and carry a flower spike 2½ feet long. The blooms are of heavy substance and are always perfectly placed. Six to 7 well spaced blooms open at one time with 10 to 11 unopened buds. Light coral-ed with light carmine red line in throat. The whole color effect is more on the salmon, but distinctly on the coral red tones. Each, 30c; doz., $3.00.

arguerite (Pommer). Ex. Makes a massive spike of deep watermelon pink, with cream throat. Tall spike with unusually long flower-head. Its exceptional lasting qualities make it a good cut flower. Each, 40c; doz., $4.00.

egon State (Bones). Ex. Salmon-pink with cream throat. Remarkably good substance, standing in good condition two days longer than Picardy. Florets face one way, which makes it a good cut flower variety. Each, 20c; doz., $2.00.

arl Harbor (Kenyon). Dec. A color of purest white, no markings, which make this variety of valuable commercial importance as a cut flower. Unusual lasting qualities, straight grower, vigorous and a rapid propagator. Tall spike carrying 20 to 12 buds, opening 10 to 12 lovely large florets of pure white at one time. Balance of spike showing buds shows. Each, 50c; 5 for $2.25.

nger (Vaughan). Formerly Commando. One of the rarest of gladiolus colors is dark red. Few varieties of this color have been bred which meet all round requirements, including exhibition size and quality, vigor of growth in the field, and ease of propagation. Perhaps the best to this time has been the Pfitzer creation, Commander Koehl, and our 1943 introduction Ranger is in every respect an improvement over this.

In color, Ranger is much the same deep red as Commander Koehl, possibly half a tone darker. Its florets are larger, more evenly arranged on the stalk, and face better. The even self-color continues in the throat, without markings. The stalk is among the tallest, and grows with exceptional vigor. All red gladioli are known as poor propagators, and more than one new red has looked fine when first introduced; only to deteriorate in a few years. Ranger is one of the best propagators we have seen among the reds, and having it under observation for several years we are confident it will take a permanent place as leader in its color. Each, 50c; doz., $5.00.

Sir Galahad (Salbach). Ex. Sold under protection of U. S. Patent No. 356. A study in contrast, for the purity of its soft creamy yellow is enhanced by its diamond shaped blotch of rich crimson in the deep cream colored throat. A pure and perfect flower, well named for Galahad, the perfect knight. Florets are large and wide open—long flower spike with at least 6 of the 18 flowers open at once. Blooms are perfectly placed, and are of heavy substance. Stems always straight. For a clean, soft flower that is at the same time bright, Sir Galahad is supreme. Each, 30c; doz., $3.00.

Snow Princess (Pfitzer) Ex. A very fine new white ★of good size and form. Tall, with long flower spike and many open blooms that are always perfectly placed. Stems never crook. Snow Princess is one of the very best whites. Mid-season. Each, 25c; doz., $2.50.

Vredenburgh (Pfitzer). Ex. A very vigorous new ★white that should be of great value, particularly because of its earliness, size of blooms and placement of florets. Each, 20c; doz., $1.75; per 100, $12.00.

California (Salbach). Ex. Sold under protection of U. S. Patent No. 359. An immense deep geranium pink that is simply breath taking. Almost a self color, except for a slightly deeper pink blotch in throat. Blooms are well expanded, are of heavy substance and are slightly ruffled. Plants make vigorous growth and are tall with long flower spikes. As many as six to eight blooms open at one time. Each, 30c; doz., $3.00.

Chamouny (Baerman). Ex. An outstanding decorative variety. Rich, light cerise rose with the faintest edging of light rose; perfectly placed florets on tall slender spike, eight or more open at same time. Each, 25c; doz., $2.50.

Coral Glow (Ellis). Ex. A rather unusual shade of ★rich coral orange; will open six or more extra large blooms of perfect placement and heavy substance; a particularly strong growing variety. Each, 20c; doz., $2.00.

Corinne Vaughan. (Vaughan). An orchid self, ★with the tallest spike and largest florets yet produced in this color. It is definitely earlier than Minuet, which in our opinion, it surpasses in size and beauty. It has exceptionally large florets, well placed and facing properly. Each, 35c; doz., $3.50.

(★) This mark indicates the variety is of outstanding merit.

Double Victory (Kundred). Dec. Double Flower-★ed — blooms in 65 days. At last a fully double Gladiolus. Fully double blush white, light pink and cream in throat. Shapely flower uniformly spaced and placed on a good stem. First time shown on display in Detroit, Michigan, this past year. Awarded a Certificate of Merit for a new achievement in the Gladiolus World. Each, $1.00; 3 for $2.50

Glen Lake (Vaughan). Ex. In effect it is a lavender self paler than Minuet, with markings negligible and only in the deep throat. Stem is tall and strong florets faced well and overlapping, six to eight open at once. It is earlier than Minuet, opens better, is a far better propagator. This is a fine, tall growing variety for the garden, but of exceptional value for cut flower arrangements, both for room decoration and for the costume. Each, 30c; doz., $3.00.

Helen of Troy (Salbach). (Patented) Ex. A truly magnificent flower; in color a lively peach-toned apricot with soft carmine throat markings; seven or more giant sized blooms on strong stiff spikes. A real 'champion.' Each, 30c; doz., $3.00.

Jalna (Palmer). Ex. Irridescent salmon and ★ashes of roses. A very unusual and beautiful smoky. 10 or more large wide open well placed blooms open at a time. Fine exhibition variety and indispensable for the home garden. Fine propagator. If you like the smokies, by all means get Jalna. Each, 20c; doz., $1.75; per 100, $12.00.

General List

PINK AND ROSE

Aladdin (Palmer) Ex. Grenadine to grenadine ★pink or in common language bright beautiful salmon with large cream blotch. 8-10 very large beautifully ruffled blooms open at a time on a long straight spike. Plant very strong and robust. Each, 15c; doz., $1.50; 100, $10.00.

Betty Nuthall (Salbach). Ex. One of the outstanding gladioli of recent introduction. Light coral with pale orange throat and light feathering of carmine. Ea., 10c; doz., 65c; 100, $4.50.

Bingo (Canine). Ex. Immense cream-buff, pink ★flecking and soft Picardy blotch in throat. Each, 15c; doz., $1.50; 100, $10.00.

Debonair (Palmer). Ex. La France pink to shrimp ★pink in throat with creamy throatpmark, lightly peppered crimson. Each, 10c; doz., 75c; 100, $5.00.

Edith Mason (Vaughan). Ex. Delicate geranium ★pink, exquisite. Each, 10c; doz., 80c; 100, $5.90.

Heritage (Ristow). Ex. Very large warm pink, ★throat lighter, with white midribs on lower petals. Each, 15c; doz., $1.50; 150, $10.00.

Hillsdale (Vaughan). Ex. True Tyrian rose, shading darker toward outer edge of petals, lighter toward throat; back of petals delicately traced with minute white lines. Darker feather on two lower petals. Tall. strong spikes. Blooms in early midseason. A valuable addition to a color class with few outstanding varieties. Each, 35c; doz., $3.50.

Michigan (Vaughan). Ex. Grows uniformly 4-5 ft. tall, with a strong spike which stands upright without staking. Its magnificent flower plumes are composed of florets 5 inches across, overlapping and facing perfectly, with 10 to 13 open before the lowest floret fades. It is without superior in size and perfection of form. Outside of petals, a strong salmon-red; inside, an orange salmon; the whole effect being a vivid salmon, many tones deeper than Picardy. Throat and small blotch on lower petal are lemon-yellow, blending with and softening the general effect. An exhibition variety of the first rank. Each, 35c; doz., $3.50.

Johannes Sebastian Bach (Pfitzer). Ex. Salmon, shading, bit lighter in throat. Tall and strong. Well arranged flower-head. 10 to 12 open at once. Each, 15c; doz., $1.50; 100, $10.00.

Margaret Fulton (Palmer). Dec. Early salmon-pink. Each, 10c; doz., 75c; 100, $5.00.

Mrs. E. J. Heaton (Heaton). Ex. Glowing strawberry pink blended with some cream in throat. Each. 10c; doz., 75c; 100, $5.00.

New Era (Ellis). Ex. Beautifully ruffled rich pink, cream throat. Tall spike, many florets open at one time. Each, 20c; doz., $1.75; 100, $12.00.

Peggy Lou (Wilson-Evans). Ex. Smooth, deep shrimp pink with a slight rosy cast and a slight peppering of deeper rose in the throat. Each, 20c; doz., $1.75; 100, $12.00.

Phyllis McQuiston (Stewart). Dec. A gorgeous pure pink. Each, 15c; doz., $1.50; 100, $10.00.

Picardy (Palmer). Ex. A most sensational flower of delicate apricot-pink. The individual florets are all extremely large, slightly ruffled and of heavy wax-like substance. Each, 10c; doz., 80c; 100, $5.50.

Queen Helen II (Salbach). Ex. Grenadine pink with prominent pinard-yellow blotch and carmine feathering deep in throat. Each; 10c; doz., 80c; 100, $5.50.

Reverie (Palmer). Dec. Light sufrano pink shading to cream throat. Each, 20c; doz., $1.75, 100, $12.00.

Rosa Van Lima (Pfitzer). Dec. Pure self-colored light pink. Many flowers open at one time. Strong grower. Each, 15c; doz., $1.50; 100, $10.00.

Rapture (Palmer). Dec. Tall late salmon with creamy throat. Each, 10c; doz., $1.00; 100, $7.00.

Sensation (Marshall). Ex. Large Dec. Bright but soft rose salmon shading lighter in upper throat with darker feather on the lip. 6-9 heavily ruffled massive blooms on a spike of 17-20 or more buds. Very tall grower and massive often reaching 6 feet in height. A good propagator and one that everyone should have in his garden. Each, 25c; doz., $2.50.

Sonatine (Pfitzer). Dec. Tall light pink, flaked darker. Large blooms on stiff stems. Each, 10c; doz., $1.00; 100, $7.00.

W. H. Phipps (Diener). Ex. Enormous flowers of ★La France pink, overlaid with salmon-rose, lighter towards the center. Each, 10c; doz., 80c; 100, $5.50.

PINK AND ROSE MIXED

Made up by ourselves from varieties listed and others. Doz., 75c; 100, $5.00.

RED

Algonquin (Palmer). Dec. Early, brilliant glowing ★scarlet, on 8-10 wide open ruffled needlepoint blooms open on a tall straight spike. Many people consider this the best scarlet on the market. Each, 20c; doz., $2.00; 100, $15.00.

CARRIE JACOBS BOND. Each, 50c.

FRAGRANT GLADIOLUS

Carrie Jacobs Bond

A rose-red, with white veins on lower two petals; throat stippled white. Florets 4 inches across, borne on slender, wiry stem. It grows 3½ feet tall, blossoms in 65 days, is a vigorous grower and a good propagator. The fragrance suggests that of violets and is the strongest of any large flowered Gladiolus we have seen. The fragrance from a bouquet of this variety will delicately perfume a room.

Each, 50c; doz., $5.00

DEBONAIR

RED—Continued.

Beacon (Palmer). Ex. Salmon-scarlet with cre ★throat. Tall spike, eight florets open at Each, 15c; doz., $1.50; 100, $10.00.

Bill Sowden (Fallu). Dec. Immense, ma ★ruffled, deep blood-red, usually flaked da Each, 10c; doz., $1.00; 100, $7.00.

Commander Koehl (Pfitzer). Ex. An outstan ★variety in form and color. Gigantic flowers of scarlet, well formed, no blotches. Each, 10c; $1.00; 100, $7.00.

Communist (Vaughan). Ex. Flaming red, lit ★than Commander Koehl, more vivid than Bennett, with a better spike than either. color is even except for deep crimson in the th Flowers in 100 days. Each, 35c; doz., $3.50.

Dr. F. E. Bennett (Diener). Ex. Scarlet th ★stippled with ruby and white. Big, vigoroi ribbon winner. Each, 10c; doz., 85c; 100, $6

Dream of Beauty (Zimmer). Ex. Large rose Good color, strong grower. Each, 10c; doz., $ 100, $7.00.

Red Lory (Errey). Ex. Red with purplish bl ★Fine for exhibitions. Each, 10c; doz., $1.00; $7.00.

Red Phipps (Briggs). Ex. Really a pink ove ★scarlet. Each, 10c; doz., 85c; 100, $6.00.

Rewi Fallu (Fallu). Ex. Early deep blood Very large blooms on a tall straight spike. E 15c; doz., $1.50; 100, $10.00.

Scarlet Bedder (Salbach). Dec. Fine early sca Each, 10c; doz., $1.00; 100, $7.00.

Southern Cross (New Zealand). Ex. Large, ★red. Very good color. Each, 10c; doz., $1 100, $7.00.

Valeria (Pruitt). Ex. A very soft red with a row mark of light cream in the throat. Stand. well. Five to seven large ruffled flowers open time. Each, 15c; doz., $1.50; per 100, $10.00.

Van Tienhoven Ex. Beautiful bright poppy Long straight spikes with many flowers open at time. Each, 10c; doz., $1.00; 100, $7.00.

Wurtembergia (Pfitzer). Ex. Large scarlet v ★bread soft cream blotch. Each, 10c; doz., $1 100, $7.00.

RED MIXED

Made up by ourselves from varieties listed others. Doz., 85c; 100, $6.00.

LAVENDER

Dr. Moody (Kenyon). Ex. Light lavender. Ea 10c; doz., $1.00; 100, $7.00.

King Arthur (Arenius). Ex. Grand deep r lavender, florets large and fluted. Each, 15c; d $1.25; 100, $8.00.

Milford (New Zealand). Ex. One of the b Clear azure-blue, slightly darker at edges of pet Very large, nine open. Spike and placement go Each, 10c; doz., $1.00; 100, $7.00.

Minuet (Coleman). Ex. Large light lavender. ★recommend it. Each, 10c; doz., 95c; 100, $6.

LAVENDER MIXED

Made up by ourselves from varieties listed others. Doz., $1.00; 100, $7.00.

SMOKY

Bagdad (Palmer). Ex. Very large smoky old-r ★Each, 10c; doz., 75c; 100, $5.00.

Mother Machree (Stevens). Ex. Soft smoky lav ★der. Large flower and plant with beautiful color of lavender and orange, subdued with neutral gr Each, 15c; doz., $1.50; 100, $10.00.

Vagabond Prince (Palmer). Ex. Iridescent, g ★net brown, lighter in upper throat, small flar scarlet blotch below. The color combination is v attractive. Each, 15c; doz., $1.50; 100, $10.00.

SMOKY MIXED

Made up by ourselves from varieties listed a others. Each, 10c; doz., $1.00; 100, $7.00.

THRIPS TREATMENT

Vaughan's bulb farms in Michigan and the mountains of Tennessee are free from thrips. This insect pest is prevalent in many sections, however, and your planting may become infested from some neighboring focus. If thrips are known to be near you, prevention is advisable. Rotenone sprays and dusts are effective. (See page 106.)

The U. S. department of agriculture recommends, after plants have reached 6 inches in height, weekly spraying with the following formula: ¼ lb. Tartar emetic, 1 lb. brown sugar, 6 gallons of water.

We will ship Tartar Emetic, ceiling prices, postpaid for ¼ lb., 35c; ½ lb., 60c; 1 lb., $1.00.

| PICARDY | PALM SPRINGS | MAID OF ORLEANS |

YELLOW

Cadillac (Vaughan). Ex. Tall spike, flowers well ★placed and of good form. Seven open at one time. 5 to 7 buds. Color, golden apricot fading to apricot-rose toward edge of petals, no throat markings, stamens and pistils creamy white. A very warm and pleasing shade. Each, 15c; doz., $1.50; 100, $10.00.

Golden Chimes (Ellis). Ex. Highly ruffled light yellow. Each, 10c; doz., $1.00; 100, $7.00.

Golden Dream (Groff). Dec. Clear deep yellow. ★Each, 10c; doz., 80c; 100, $5.50.

Golden Goddess (Salbach). Ex. The first patent-★ed Gladiolus. Ten to sixteen florets open at once, deep rich golden yellow. Introduced only last season, but we have arranged with the patentee for the right to sell this outstanding new Gladiolus. Each, 15c; doz., $1.50; 100, $10.00.

Mary Shary (Vaughan). Dec. Clear soft primrose-★yellow with a deeper yellow in throat, faint marking in throat. Spike tall, straight and strong. Flowers well placed, 6 to 8 open. By artificial light remains a beautiful yellow for evening decorations. Each, 15c; doz., $1.50; 100, $10.00.

Miss Bloomington (Kunderd). Dec. Tall, light yellow, flowers well placed. Each, 10c; doz., $1.00; 100, $7.00.

Royal Oak (Vaughan). Ex. Primrose yellow, lightly suffused with pink, the lower petals showing a single fine line of red in the center. 5-7 well placed flowers open at a time. The spike carries 16 to 20 buds. Exceptionally early, blooms in 60 days. Strictly a commercial variety. Each, 10c; doz., $1.00; 100, $7.00.

YELLOW MIXED

Made up by ourselves from varieties listed and others. Doz., 75c; 100, $5.00.

BLUE AND PURPLE

Ave Maria (Pfitzer). Dec. Extremely good blue-purple. Strong grower, flowers well arranged. Each, 15c; doz., $1.50; 100, $10.00.

Blue Beauty (Pfitzer). Ex. Light blue; shading ★darker toward the edge. Large wide open flowers. Strong grower. Each, 20c; doz., $1.75; 100, $12.00.

Chas. Dickens (Pfitzer). Dec. Purple-violet. Each, ★10c; doz., $1.00; 100, $7.00.

BLUE AND PURPLE—Continued.

Hopi (Vaughan). Dec. A shapely flower of medium ★size, with florets of velvety substance exceptionally well placed, five to six open at once. In color a bright maroon, with slightly darker harmonizing blotch in the throat. Each, 10c; doz., 85c; 100, $6.00.

Kalamazoo (Vaughan). Ex. Large, compact flowers ★of beautiful violet-purple, with a creamy white throat. Each, 10c; doz., $1.00; 100, $7.00.

King Lear. (Palmer). Ex. Very early. Clear deep purple with silver line on edge of all petals. Very large heavily waved and ruffled. 5-6 open. Each, 15c; doz., $1.50; 100, $10.00.

Paul Pfitzer (Pfitzer). Dec. Fine reddish purple. Many flowers open at a time. Each, 10c; doz., $1.00; 100, $7.00.

Pelegrina (Pfitzer). Dec. Deep blue. Each, 15c ★doz.; $1.25; 100, $8.00.

BLUE AND PURPLE MIXED

Made up by ourselves from varieties listed and others. Doz., $1.00; 100, $7.00.

ORANGE

Barcarole. (Palmer). Dec. mid-season. Large clear orange of an unusual but most exquisite clear clean shade. 6-7 heavily ruffled blooms open. A gorgeous variety that must be seen to be appreciated. Each, 15c; doz., $1.50; 100, $10.00.

Bit of Heaven (Crow). Ex. Flaming orange with yellow throat. Each, 10c; doz., $1.00; 100, $7.00.

Dearborn (Vaughan). Dec. Immense florets of ★deep flesh color, light coral reflex, lip amber yellow, blending to flesh, marked with a feathering of deep crimson. Tall, straight spike with twenty or more florets, four to six open at a time, measuring five to six in. in diameter. A giant gladiolus that blooms early. Each, 10c; doz., 85c; 100, $6.00.

(★) This mark indicates the variety is of outstanding merit.
For Type Classification which is used in all Flower shows, we are marking each variety as follows: Ex.—Exhibition. Dec.—Decorative. S. D.—Small Decorative.

ORANGE—Continued.

Duna (Palmer). Ex. Clear, soft, light pinky buff, bit yellow at base. Back of petals a shade darker. 5-6 open on medium tall spike. High in color values and we like it better than Wasaga. Each, 10c; doz., 85c; 100, $6.00.

Orange Queen (Pfitzer). Dec. A large flowered primulinus of wonderful glowing orange, with red stripes on lower petals. Each, 10c; doz., 75c; 100, $5.00.

Palm Springs. (Vaughan). Ex. A clear soft lumi-★nous orange-buff self color, marked only by lighter toning in the throat. Each, 10c; doz., 85c; 100, $6.00.

Wasaga (Palmer). Dec. Clear apricot, buff throat. ★Large flowers and beautiful for basket work. Trifle darker than Duna. Each, 10c; doz., 85c; 100, $6.00.

ORANGE MIXED

Made up by ourselves from varieties listed and others. Doz., 80c; 100, $5.50.

WHITE

Albatross (Pfitzer). Ex. Pure white. Each, 10c; ★doz., $1.00; 100, $7.00.

Corona. (Palmer). Dec. Creamy white shading more creamy toward the throat with wide rose picotee edge on all petals. Very distinctive and beautiful. 6-8 very large wide open blooms on a head of about 18 buds. Tall, strong grower and a fine propagator. Corona takes very well in the cut flower market. Each, 30c; doz., $3.00.

Maid of Orleans (Pfitzer). Ex. Milky white, cream ★throat. Each, 10c; doz., 85c; 100, $6.00.

Margaret Beaton (Twomey). Ex. New immense ★white with orange-scarlet blotch. Each, 20c; doz., $2.00; 100, $15.00.

Myrma (Pruitt). Ex. An excellent white, sister to ★Shirley Temple, ruffled and strong grower. Each, 30c; doz., $3.00.

Shirley Temple (Pruitt). Ex. Color rich cream, ★almost white, with richer cream throat mark. Six to eight very large, most beautifully ruffled flowers open at one time. A maximum spike is equal in size to Picardy or Miss New Zealand. Despite its enormous size it carries not the least bit of coarse-ness. As a cut flower it will stand up with the best of them, the last bud on the spike blooming out perfectly. Makes beautiful foliage and large, high crown bulbs. Makes ample bulblets that grow readily, without pregermination. It blooms some-what later than Picardy. Each, 10c; doz., $1.00; 100, $7.00.

Star of Bethlehem (Pfitzer). Ex. Enormous snow-★white. Good exhibition variety. Each, 15c; doz., $1.50; 100, $10.00.

White Triumphator (Pfitzer). Dec. Pure white, good for cutting. Each, 10c; doz., $1.00; 100, $7.00.

WHITE MIXED

Made up by ourselves from varieties listed and others. Doz., 80c; 100, $5.50.

Vaughan's "Standard" Mixture $2.25 50 Bulbs. First Size

We do not send out any mixtures that will not make a brilliant showing in the gardens of our customers. This one will be found satisfactory everywhere, for mixed beds, borders and masses. These are first-size bulbs. Where wanted by mail add for postage at zone rates, 100 bulbs packed, 6 lbs.

Price, doz., 60c, postpaid; by express, not prepaid, 50 for $2.25; 100 for $4.25; 250 for $10.00; 500 for $18.00; per 1,000, $35.00.

Primulinus Hybrids Mixed $5.00 100 Bulbs

The range of colors is from the purest and lightest of yellows to deepest orange and from the softest shade of salmon pink to rich crimson. On account of their slender and graceful habit, delicate colors and shape of the flowers, they are ideal for vases. Doz., 75c; 100, $5.00.

Prices for single bulbs and the doz., as above, include free parcel post delivery through 8th zone. For prepayment to further zones, add 5c doz.

Bulbs Shipped Separately from Seed

Because of weather conditions during January, February and early March, we prefer to send out bulbs after March 20th except to customers in the south or California, to whom we ship at once, packed against freezing. Customers should open the package upon arrival, and if bulbs can not be planted at once, they should be placed in a dry and frostproof cellar until ready to plant.

Amaryllis

AMARYLLIS

Largest of flowers which are easily forced indoors, our new hybrids are gorgeous in size and coloring.

Vaughan's New Hybrids. Mixed. Flowers are immense, in an amazing range of color blends, splashed and striped in a manner not seen in other strains.

	Each	Doz.	100
2-2½ in. Dia.	$0.35	$3.50	$25.00
2½-3 in. Dia.	.50	5.00	37.50

APIOS Tuberosa

Splendid hardy climber. Color chocolate brown, fragrant. 2-4 bulbs should be planted together at a depth of 3-4 inches. Grows best in loose rich soil.

Price, each, 15c; doz., $1.50; 25 for $2.50, prepaid.

Begonias

DOUBLE BEGONIA

Tuberous Rooted—Unexcelled for summer bedding. When fully exposed to the sun the beds must be kept moist. All prepaid.

Crispa Single—Red, orange, yellow, rose, white. Large flowered.

Medium Size. Each, 30c; doz., $3.00; 100, $22.50.
LargeSize. Ea.,35c;doz.,$3.50;100,$27.00.

Camellia Flowered Double—Red, yellow, rose, white, orange.
Medium Size. Each, 35c; doz., $3.50; 100, $27.00.
Large Size. Each, 45c; doz., $4.50; 100, $32.00.

94 **INDEX ON FINAL PAGES**

Summer Flowering Bulbs

BEGONIAS—Continued

Carnation Flowered or Frilled—Same colors as above.
Medium Size. Each, 35c; doz., $3.50; 100, $27.00.
Large Size. Ea., 45c; doz., $4.50; 100, $32.00.
Fragrance—A fragrant Begonia. Single flowers of deep pink. The fragrance is distinctive and pleasing. Each, 35c; doz., $3.50.
Pendula—Used in hanging baskets. Each, 30c; doz., $3.00; 25 for $5.50. Double blooming, many fine pinks.
Narcissus-Flowered in Mixture. Inner petals joined into a large semi-double or single corona with petals elegantly crimped at margin. Each, 30c; doz., $3.00; 25 for $5.50.

NEW BEGONIAS

Multiflora Hybrids—In a shady place, where they can be well watered, these compact plants will bear double flowers of gorgeous coloring, measuring 2 to 3 inches across. They will blossom until killing frost. Each, 35c; doz., $3.50; per 100, $25.00.

Golden Yellow CALLA LILY

Calla Elliottiana. Flower rich golden yellow; foliage dark green with creamy spots. Makes a good pot plant for indoor culture. Does well outside even in full shade. Besides blooms it will act as a foliage plant all summer. Price, each, 30c; doz., $3.00; 100, $22.50.

CALLA LILY
(Richardia Maculata)

Spotted leaf, white flower. Can be planted out of doors after danger of frost is over. Take up in fall before freezing. Each, 25c; doz., $2.50; 100, $18.00.

CHLIDANTHUS Fragrans

Chlidanthus Fragrans (The Gold Flower). Produces clusters of from two to four golden yellow, trumpet-shaped flowers that are delicately fragrant. Handle in the same manner as gladiolus.
Price, each, 15c; doz., $1.50; 100, $10.00, prepaid.

CINNAMON VINE
(Dioscorea Batatas)

Well-known hardy climber; quick grower. Large Roots, 3 for 40c; doz., $1.50; 25 for $2.50, prepaid.

Gloxinias

GLOXINIAS

These showy plants are easily grown in pots and transplanted to a garden bed, preferably in a semi-shaded place.

Mixed Colors. Each, 40c; 3 for $1.10, doz., $4.00.

Hyacinthus Candicans

HYACINTHUS CANDICANS

(Galtonias) Summer Hyacinth—Perfectly hardy and of vigorous growth. Flowers are pure white and pendulous, 4 feet high.

Price, First Size, each, 20c; doz., $2.00, prepaid; Selected Size, each, 25c; doz., $2.50, prepaid.

CALADIUM Esculentum

Elephant's Ear—Good effect as a border for tall-growing Cannas when edged with Coleus or other low-growing foliage plants.
First Size—5 to 7-inch circumference. Mailing weight, 4 lbs. per doz.
Price, 3 for 25c, prepaid; doz., $1.00; 25 for $1.50; not prepaid.
Select Size—7 to 9-inch circumference. Mailing weight, 6 lbs. per doz.
Price, 3 for 55c, prepaid; doz., $2.00; 25 for $3.50, not prepaid.
Extra Large—9 to 11-inch circumference. Mailing weight, 10 lbs. per doz.
Price, 3 for 85c, prepaid; doz., $3.00; 25 for $5.75, not prepaid.

Ismene Calathina

ISMENE CALATHINA

(Peruvian Daffodil) Flowers are pure white, borne three or four on a stem, and are very fragrant. Not hardy. Price, each, 25c; doz., $2.50, prepaid.

LILY OF THE VALLEY

Large Clumps—For outdoor planting, clumps are best. Plant clumps in a shady moist place. Each, 65c; doz., $5.00; prepaid.

MADEIRA VINE

One of the best and most popular climbers for foliage effect. Price, 3 for 30c; doz., $1.00; 25 for $2.00, prepaid.

OXALIS

Summer-Flowering—Useful little plants, very effective in masses or beds and particularly valuable for edgings. They produce an unbroken row of foliage about one foot high in continuous bloom. Very fine to grow in hanging baskets indoors. The colors are white, red, pink. Price, any color, doz., 45c; 25 for 85c; 100 for $3.00; prepaid.

Milla Biflora

New introduction from Mexico, where it is called Estrellitas, or Little Stars. Showy white flowers, two inches in diameter, with six petals not quite separated. The stems are wiry, 12 to 18 inches tall. Very free blooming from July to September.

MILLA BIFLORA

Flowers cut well and have a pleasant Lily-like fragrance. Should be dug in fall, except in milder climates.

Each, 20c; doz., $2.00; 100, $15.00.

Montbretias

MONTBRETIAS

Plant Early Montbretias are easily grown and their graceful flower-stems add much to any garden. They are highly valued for cut flowers. Our mixture contains many bright shades of yellow, salmon, orange, and scarlet.

They do best in a light loamy soil enriched with leaf mould and a little lime, no manure. Where the ground freezes deeply in the winter, they can be treated as gladioli. But in localities where the ground does not freeze deeply, the usual winter protection may be given, and they will multiply.

Special Mixed. Price, 3 for 30c; doz., $1.10; 100, $7.50, prepaid.

Earlham Large Flowered Hybrids
They are a completely new race, being generally much taller and more robust in growth, and having flowers of great size and beauty, some measuring 3 to 4 inches.

Special Mixed. 3 for 50c; doz., $1.80; 100, $13.00, prepaid.

RANUNCULUS

Set 3 or 4 inches apart, pressing firmly into the soil, claws downward, and cover them with sand, then with soil; keep the crown of the tubers four inches under the surface. Water them well.

First Size—Doz., 95c; 100, $6.50; 1000, $60.00.

Second Size—Doz., 65c; 100, $4.50; 1000, $40.00.

Summer Flowering Bulbs

SPREKELIA

Formosissima (Jacobean Lily)
Closely allied to the Amaryllis, bearing showy brilliant crimson flowers. Dormant bulbs planted in the border early in May will flower within 3 or 4 weeks after planting, or they may be flowered as pot plants in the house during the early spring months.
Large Size—Each, 30c; doz., $3.00; 100, $25.00.

Tuberoses Double
(Polianthes Tuberosa)

TUBEROSES

Excelsior Dwarf Pearl Double Easily recognized by its exquisite fragrance and beautiful flower-spikes, which are borne on long stems, making it an admirable cut flower. If started in pots, and at the end of May moved to open ground, can be flowered much earlier.

Mammoth Bulbs—Each, 20c; doz., $1.75; 25 for $3.00, prepaid.
First Size—Each, 15c; doz., $1.10; 25 for $1.75, prepaid.
Second Size—Price, doz., 75c; 25 for $1.25, prepaid.
Mexican (Single)—They have tall, stiff stems, flowers pure white, single; true tuberose fragrance.
Price, doz., 75c; 25 for $1.25, prepaid.

Tigridia

(Shell-Flower of Mexico)
Few flowers are more gorgeously colored or so beautiful. Plant in sunny positions in a flower border in well-drained soil. Put a little sand under the bulb. Can also be used in beds. They bloom from July until frost. Height, 3 ft.

TIGRIDIA

	Each	Doz.	100
Scarlet	$0.15	$1.35	$9.00
Yellow	.15	1.35	9.00
Orange	.20	1.80	13.00
Light Pink	.20	1.80	13.00
Rose	.20	1.80	13.00
Creamy white	.20	1.80	13.00

Mixed. Price, 3 for 40c; doz., $1.35; 100, $9.00, prepaid.

Fairy Lily

Zephyranthus, Zephyr Lily
One of the prettiest and most easily grown bulbs. Plant in open ground like gladiolus bulbs.
Candida—Pure white and the most profuse bloomer of all.
Price, doz., 60c; 25 for $1.05; 100, $4.00, prepaid.

ZEPHYRANTHUS

Rosea—Beautiful clear rose; flowers large and very handsome.
Price, each, 15c; doz., $1.25; 100, $8.00, prepaid.

THREE ITEMS BELOW
Ready for delivery after June 20.
Order NOW.

Resurrection Lily

(Amaryllis Hallii) (Lycoris Squamigera)
For Outdoor Planting
Produces in early spring attractive green foliage which grows until May, when it ripens off and disappears, and one not familiar with its habits would think the bulb had died, but about a month later, as if by magic, the flower stalks spring from the ground to a height of two or three feet, developing an umbel of large and beautiful lily-shaped flowers three to four inches across and from eight to twelve in number, of a delicate lilac-pink shaded with clear blue.
Culture—The bulb is perfectly hardy without any protection. The proper time to plant is in the summer when the bulb is dormant. Cover the crown about four inches. Each, 75c; doz., $7.50.

Lycoris Radiata

A coral red Spider Lily. Bulbs planted 5 inches deep July 15th bloomed September 4th. This is not hardy, but has been known to survive freezing in pots. It sends up foliage in March. After

LYCORIS RADIATA

the foliage dies down the bulb is dormant and sends its blossom up in August or September. Lily-shaped flowers of orange-red.
Each, 30c; doz., $3.00; 100, $20.00.

STERNBERGIA LUTEA

These bulbs planted about 4 inches deep July 15th bloomed from August 7th to September 7th. The flower is yellow and looks very much like a Crocus. They have a thin Hyacinth-like foliage. Hardy with some protection.
Each, 25c; doz., $2.50; 100, $15.00.

| LILIUM SUPERBUM | LILIUM REGALE | LILIUM CANADENSE | LILIUM UMBELLATUM |

Hardy Lilies for Spring Planting

HARDY lily bulbs, of 1943 crop, carried over the winter in cold storage, may be planted in the spring, and will blossom in midsummer, when the garden needs their glory.

Lilies are truly among the most beautiful of all bulbous plants. They are especially suitable for planting in herbaceous borders, and enjoy a position where they are protected by the shade of surrounding plants. Light, well-drained soil is recommended. Bulbs should be planted 5 to 6 inches below the surface, and to prevent the accumulation of excessive moisture, surround the bulb with coarse sand and fill in with a mixture of fibrous loam and leaf-mold.

Many varieties are termed "stem-rooters"—that is, they develop roots on the stem up to two or three inches from the ground. These roots are voracious feeders, and on them depend greatly the number and size of flowers. When they appear, the plant should receive a top dressing of good rich soil on which they can feed freely.

For the smaller varieties, plant in clumps, the bulbs about 6 inches apart, leaving more space for the strong and larger species. The most striking mode of planting is in groups of 3 to 9 bulbs in a mass.

Lilium Canadense
(Meadow Lily)

The whole plant has a downward, graceful movement and looks like a slender, tiered green belfry ringing golden bells. The flowers are nodding, bell-shaped, with petals flaring out and turning back slightly. They are heavily dotted on the inside with purplish brown dots. Blooms the end of June to July. Should be planted five inches deep. It is an excellent lily for naturalizing. Height, 3 to 5 ft.
Canadense Mixed—Each, 25c; dozen, $2.50; 100, $15.00.

Lilium Pardalinum

(Leopard or Panther Lily)—A late June flowering lily of rich scarlet and yellow, spotted rich brown from the Sierra Nevada Mountains of California. Ten to thirty flowers on a 5-6 foot stem.
Each, 35c; doz., $3.50; 100, $25.00.

Lilium Phillipinense Formosanum

A refined and graceful Lily with long grassy foliage, and long wide-mouthed trumpet flowers of the purest white, slightly marked externally with reddish brown. The plants grow to a height of 2-3 feet, are very robust and offer great resistance to wind and weather. It is hardy, very fragrant and one of the loveliest of the new varieties.
Each, 40c; doz.; 100, $30.00.

Lilium Regale

The large, trumpet-shaped flowers are snowy white, with a pure yellow center, while the exterior of the petals is slightly tinged pink. It is a strong grower, attaining the height of three or four feet. The flowers are beautiful, possessing a delightful fragrance. The bulb, which should be given good, sharp drainage (as should all lilies), is perfectly hardy, usually presenting a dried, shriveled appearance.
6-7 inch. Each, 40c; doz., $4.00; 100, $25.00.

Lilium Superbum

(American Turk's Cap, Swamp Lily)—The most magnificent and showy of the native North American species, well worthy of extensive culture. This splendid lily produces from ten to forty flowers of brilliant orange-scarlet, shaded yellow and spotted purplish brown at the base, with red anthers, in late July and August. This lily requires an acid condition and should be planted at least 8 inches deep. Height, 3-8 feet. Each, 30c; dozen, $3.00; 100, $20.00.

Lilium Tigrinum
(Tiger Lily)

Plant this lily at least 500 feet from where you have other Lilies planted to prevent spreading mosaic disease.

Because it is so widely cultivated in this country this lily has come to be looked upon as native. The flowers are orange, spotted purple, opening in August and September on 2-4 foot stems.
Double. Each, 35c; doz.; 100, $25.00.

Lilium Testaceum
(The Nankeen Lily, Excelsum, Isabellum)

A cross of the Madonna lily with the scarlet turks-cap, Chalcedonicum. It grows as high as six feet. There are three to ten flowers, three to four inches across. They are nodding, with reflexed, waxy, glistening petals, rounded at the tips, and of a creamy peach color popularly known as Nankeen yellow.
Each, $2.25; doz., $22.50.

Lilium Tenuifolium

The lovely Coral Lily of Siberia. A great beauty. The brightest of all lilies. Grows 20 inches high, with finely cut foliage, slender stems and beautifully shaded coral-red flowers. One ought to grow them by the dozen, they are so fine for cutting and making clumps for the lawn. Blooms very early. Each, 20c; dozen, $2.00; 100, $15.00.

Lilium Umbellatum
(Subspecies of Davurieum)

This group of lilies is of hybrid origin, and thrives in American garden borders, multiplying and enduring. They are early flowering, blooming during the first part of June. Usually attaining the height of two to three feet, they carry four to six flowers of cup-shape.
Mixed. Each, 35c; doz., $3.50; 100, $25.00.

Lilium Candidum for July and August Shipment
The ideal time to plant this lily is in mid-summer.

18-20 Centimeters each	35c; doz.,	$3.50
20-22 Centimeters each	55c; doz.,	5.50
22-24 Centimeters each	65c; doz.,	6.50
24-26 Centimeters each	80c; doz.,	8.00

LILIUM TESTACEUM

ew Hardy Everblooming Roses

the following five varieties:
s, $1.50; 3 of one kind for $3.75

AARS 1940. (Pat. 443.) "The Rose
· of Roses in shades of gold." Its un-
1g, ruddy· orange toned with saffron
a dual tone effect of indescribable
beauty. Buds long and pointed. flowers
size, often five inches in diameter.
rous, with healthy, glossy green foliage.
t.

¡chesse Charlotte. AARS 1943.
(Patent Ap-
or.) This rose is truly an Aristocrat which
provides a new shade of red or claret never before
seen in the rose world. The long streamlined buds
of magnificent Morocco-red open to firm-petaled
blooms of dusky coral-red which do not fade but
gradually merge to a lovely coral-pink. When un-
folding the petals recurve and make artistic informal blooms with a hint of carnation fragrance.

★Heart's Desire. (Patent 501.) AARS 1942.
This is the No. 1 Rose of
the 1942 "All-America Rose Selections," and what
a Rose, for it really has everything that your heart
could desire. It has color, a pure, even shade of
luminous red which does not blue or burn, even in
the hottest weather. It has fragrance, a small vase
of flowers will sweetly perfume a whole room. It
has rich foliage and produces quantities of flowers
on long cutting stems all season. It has vigor,
being a strong grower like Radiance and Crimson
Glory, its parents.

★Mary Margaret McBride. (Patent 537.)
AARS 1943.
This deliciously fragrant rose is indeed a new
triumph. Its long-pointed, salmon-pink buds gradually unfold, petal by petal, holding its radiant
beauty at all stages. The full double blooms are
large, high centered and a lovely coral-pink color
fused with a shimmering gold at the base. It is
excellent for cutting and is noted for its generous
blooms, even in the hottest summers. Foliage is
luxuriant.

★Pearl Harbor—"The Memory Rose."
This name was chosen to commemorate in some
degree the deeds of our fellow Americans, many of
whom gave their lives that we may live. It is a
plant of tremendous vigor that will grow and bloom
freely under most adverse conditions and there is
scarcely a period during the season when magnificent buds and flowers are not available. The flowers are borne on vigorous canes and the bud is
exceptionally long and pointed. The upper surface
of the petals is a delicate shade of shell-pink, shaded
golden-bronze at the base. The outer, or reverse
side of the petals is vivid Tyrian-rose. Last, but
not least, the plants of Pearl Harbor are practically
thornless.

> **★ Indicates outstanding garden
> varieties.**

HEART'S DESIRE

MME. CHIANG KAI-SHEK
"The First Lady of China"
Dormant Roses, each $2.00; 3 for $5.00.

AARS 1944. (Patent Applied For). The
"Honor Rose" for 1944. It has
long pointed buds of light yellow which open full
to beautifully formed, creamy yellow, long stemmed
flowers over dark green, large and leathery, disease
resistant foliage. The divine form, alluring perfume, sheer elegance and fine growth, combined
with those indefinable qualities that breeding alone
can convey, truly depict the patrician in this, the
loveliest of all yellow Roses.

AARS ROSE COLLECTION
One each Grand Duchess Charlotte, Heart's Desire,
Mary Margaret McBride and Mme. Chiang Kai-
Shek, dormant (value $6.50) for $5.50.

Price of the following five varieties:
Dormant Roses, $1.25; 3 of one kind for $3.15

★Charlotte Armstrong. AARS 1941. (Pat.
455.) An amazingly
beautiful new Rose that is said to outbloom most
varieties three to one throughout the season. The
long, slender, blood-red buds open into magnificent,
brilliantly colored flowers, spectrum-red in cool
weather, cerise in hot weather. Blooms are on long
stems and are very lasting when cut; plants are
strong and vigorous with good foliage.

★Crimson Glory. (Patent No.105.) We consider
this the finest of the new red
Garden Roses. It gives a quantity of fine blooms
all summer and fall. Its large, urn-shaped buds
open to deliciously fragrant flowers of intense, deep
vivid crimson shaded ox-blood red and mellowed
by a soft velvety nap. Vigorous growth.

★Eclipse. (Patent No. 172.) Introduced in 1936,
this Rose is internationally famous and is
of sensationally new form. Long, streamlined buds
of clear, bright yellow, freely produced. Semi-
double blooms, lasting well. A fine garden Rose.

★President Macia. A superb variety that really
performs. Extra long,
pointed buds of rich carmine-pink, opening into
great big blooms, often 5 inches across, of soft
flesh-pink, brightened by a yellow flush at the base.
Vigorous grower with long stems.

★Signora. (Patent No. 201.) There is no other
Rose quite like this one, which is
one of the finest of the new varieties that have
come to America. A warm symphony of color,
mostly in shades of brownish orange and salmon.
It is a vigorous, tall and free blooming plant with
long buds opening double and fragrant.

FOUR GREAT ROSES
One each Signora, Crimson Glory, Eclipse,
and Sterling, dormant (value $4.75) for
$4.00. Shipped express collect.

Price of the following varieties:
Dormant Roses, $1.00; 3 of one kind for $2.50

★Christopher Stone. One of the three finest
red Roses. Produces
quantities of brilliant, glowing velvety scarlet
blooms of good form all season. Delicious fragrance.

★Duquesa de Penaranda. This glorious Rose
produces two dis-
tinct types of flowers. In summer they are coppery
apricot, in autumn a luscious cinnamon-peach color.

★Girona. Here is one of the most fragrant Roses
in existence and one of the best of all
garden Roses for cutting. Very strong growing,
with good foliage, and superb blooms of a beautiful red and yellow combination.

★Mme. Joseph Perraud. Nasturtium orange
buds, open to
fragrant flowers of a charming Nasturtium buff.

★McGredy's Ivory. "The perfect white Rose."
Perfect buds open into
magnificent perfect blooms of ivory-white.

★McGredy's Yellow. Beautifully formed
buds of pure, light
butter-cup yellow; open flowers cup-shaped.

★Picture. This is one of the loveliest of all pink
Roses, every flower being a perfect pic-
ture in color and form. The nicely formed buds
open into medium-sized flowers of velvety rose-pink
with a warm salmon undertone. A splendid cutting
Rose that produces quantities of fragrant bloom.

See Page 62 for "Pixie" and "Tom Thumb,"
miniature Everblooming Roses.

STERLING

★Poinsettia. Here is the Rose that will be the
sensation of your garden for it is
the most dazzling red Rose we have ever seen. The
buds are ideal in form, long and pointed, and open
into large, semi-double, beautiful Poinsettia-scarlet
blooms, with large well-shaped petals. The plants
are good and the blooms are produced profusely
during the whole season.

Sister Therese. One of the most dependable of
the yellow roses. The long
pointed buds, streaked with a rich carmine, are
perfectly shaped. The full blooms are a beautiful
clear chrome yellow and are borne on the plants
in candelabras. Excellent for cut flowers; sweet-
brier fragrance. Strong grower with good foliage.

★Southport. Very showy, probably the most
brilliant of all scarlet Roses. Fine
buds of lovely form on long stems. Prolific bloomer.

★Sterling. (Patent No. 21.) Here is a new Rose
that is just about perfect. The flowers
are a beautiful clear pink with orange base; bud
pointed and very lasting when cut. It is a vigorous
grower, has disease-resistant foliage; and it blooms
and blooms.

★The Doctor. The most glorious pink Rose we
have ever seen. The buds are long
and pointed and expand to simply enormous blooms
of beautiful, glowing rosy pink with satiny pink
edges. Intensely fragrant; excellent for cutting.

Treasure Island. A beautiful blend of flaming
coppery-pink, inside of petals
light salmon, orange at base. Buds long and pointed
on stiff stems, flowers large and fragrant; excellent
for cutting. It is considered superior to the famous
Countess Vandal which it resembles.

Will Rogers. (Patent No. 256.) This Rose is
one of the finest of velvety reds.
In color it is a black crimson-maroon and holds
well. Very vigorous and has a really intense old
rose fragrance. It is ideal for cutting and bears
quantities of flowers throughout the season. Does
best in semi-shade.

DELUXE ROSE COLLECTION
One each of McGredy's Ivory, Picture Sister Therese,
Treasure Island and Will Rogers, dormant, (value
$5.00) for $4.25. Shipped express collect.

NEW PERPETUAL FLOWERING
DOORYARD ROSE

Dormant Roses, 3 for $3.75; each, $1.50

Mabelle Stearns. (Patent No. 297.) A Rosa
Setigera Hybrid that
is hardy without protection in the Temperate Zone.
Very hardy plants growing 2 feet high and spreading 6 to 8 feet or more if permitted. The full double
delightfully fragrant flowers of peachblossom-pink
are produced in panicles from June until frost, and
are excellent for cutting. Rich, green, healthy
foliage. Excellent for embankment and memorial
plantings.

McGREDY'S SCARLET

CHOICE EVERBLOOMING HYBRID TEA ROSES

Dormant Roses, 90c; 3, $2.40; 12, $8.50

★Autumn. Unique coloring, a gorgeous burnt orange, streaked and marked with red. Large handsome buds developing to full double, fragrant blooms.

★Betty Uprichard. "If I had room for only one Rose in my garden, it would be Betty Uprichard"—such is the enthusiasm of one great Rose lover for this vigorous, very fragrant Rose. Pointed copper-red buds, opening, reveal petals of soft salmon-pink which, in full bloom, contrast prettily with a reverse of orange-carmine.

Caledonia. Has beautifully shaped, long snow-white buds which open to fine double flowers on long stems for cutting. It has a delicious fragrance and is profuse in its habit of bloom.

★Condesa de Sastago. Everyone likes this spectacular Rose with its cupped flowers of orange-scarlet on the inside and yellow on the reverse. Strong grower with heavy foliage; fragrant, free flowering.

★Cynthia. A Superb variety that we know will please every rose lover. The exceptionally well-formed buds are on stiff stems and open into full double flowers of a rich glowing oriental red or brilliant carmine. A vigorous grower and an outstanding cut flower variety.

★Dainty Bess. We consider these exquisite flowers of delicate rose-pink, with contrasting center of wine-red stamens, the finest of all the single Roses. The flowers are 3 to 4 inches across, come continuously in clusters on long spikes, and are very lasting when cut.

Dame Edith Helen. Though there are many fine pink Roses, this one remains a leader. Blooms are of magnificent size and substance on the reverse of vigorous upright growth. It is extremely double and high centered with broad petals that curl back luxuriously.

★Editor McFarland. Perfectly formed lasting, brilliant rose-pink flowers, excellent for cutting. Its vigorous growth, healthy foliage and abundance of fragrant bloom make it most dependable.

☆Etoile de Hollande. A brilliant dark red Rose of magnificent size and perfect form. Vigorous grower, heavy bloomer; flowers deliciously fragrant and beautiful in all stages of development.

★Golden Dawn. Noted for its quantity of bloom and considered the finest light yellow garden Rose. Buds lemon yellow, splashed with carmine, open to great big fragrant blooms of pale straw yellow. Bushy, vigorous grower, bronzy green foliage.

Gruss an Teplitz. Rich scarlet shading to crimson, very fragrant. A vigorous grower and in bloom all the time. One of the best outdoor bedding varieties. Very hardy.

★Joanna Hill. One of our most popular Roses and the best of its color. Rich cream and ivory with a yellow-orange heart. A long-lasting cut flower of fine form, whether in graceful bud or full blown flower.

Kaiserin Auguste Viktoria. Creamy buds developing slowly to snowy white blooms of perfect form.

Leonard Barron. A very hardy Rose. Its immense blooms, over 5 inches across, are probably the largest of any everblooming rose. They are a lovely salmon-pink with an amber glow. Vigorous, bushy growth.

★Margaret McGredy. Comparatively new and is a striking variety. Large Oriental red blooms, rich color and vigorous, bushy growth. Blooms continuously.

★McGredy's Scarlet. A Rose with the McGredy name is always a top-notcher and this one is no exception. Its perfectly formed flowers of vivid rose-red come on long stems and are excellent for cutting.

★Mme. Butterfly. This Rose should be in every collection, large or small. Time has proved its dependability and endeared it to the hearts of all. Light pink petals with deep shadings of apricot and gold at its heart and petal lips of ivory white.

★Mme. Jules Bouche. Long pointed, shapely buds, excellent for cutting, opening into superb white flowers, slightly shaded at times with blush pink; fragrant. Plant exceptionally strong and continuously in bloom.

★Mrs. Charles Bell (Shell-Pink Radiance). An exquisite shade of salmon-shell-pink that is not found in any other Rose. Has all the excellent qualities of Radiance.

★Mrs. Erskine Pembroke Thom. An unfading yellow with dark healthy foliage. Slender buds open to perfectly shaped flowers of canary yellow.

Mrs. Pierre S. DuPont. One of the most continuously blooming Roses grown and winner of more medals than any other outdoor Rose. Long pointed, reddish gold buds opening into exquisitely formed flowers of dark golden yellow that holds well. Compact bushes with glossy, healthy foliage.

Mrs. Sam McGredy. Exceptionally good all-purpose variety with elegant, shapely buds produced singly on strong slender stems. Well-shaped blooms of coppery scarlet-orange, outside of petals heavily flushed with red. Beautiful plants, bronzy foliage and spreading habit.

President Herbert Hoover. Its deep copper-red buds open slowly to a wonderful blend which can only be described as multi-colored, with a dominance of cerise-pink and rich cream veined with scarlet. Superb buds; large flowers, lasting well; long stems—in fact every detail of this excellent rose adds to the beauty that has made it so popular.

★Pink Dawn. Full, double flowers o glistening rose-pink, changing to soft pink with a gold base. Buds are extra long; excellent for cutting. Very popular as it blooms freely and grows vigorously like the Radiance Roses.

★Radiance. Large, full, deliciously fragrant blooms of brilliant rosy carmine, shaded with pink. Constant bloomer and excellent keeper in hot weather. Easy to grow and one of the most popular Roses in America.

★Red Radiance. Flowers clear cerise-red. Size, as in the parent Radiance. Hardy; strong grower.

Talisman. A remarkable blending of gold, apricot, yellow, deep pink, and old rose. The Rose of many Gold Medals.

POLYANTHA EVERBLOOMING ROSES

Dormant Roses, 90c; 3, $2.40; 12, $8.50

These, like the Floribundas, are very hardy and continuous blooming, producing their small flowers in large, showy clusters on neat, compact bushes.

Ideal. A rich lustrous garnet. The flowers are produced in large trusses and are very effective.

Gloria Mundi. Double flowers of glowing orange-scarlet, in large clusters.

★Orange Triumph. One of the best of all Polyanthas, producing huge clusters of magnificent salmon-red blooms all season. Strong grower with good glossy green foliage.

FLORIBUNDA ROSES

These Roses are among the hardiest and most continuous blooming hybrids offered, giving a spectacular and permanent display from June until frost. Their flowers are almost as large as those of the Hybric Teas, but are borne in clusters which are very showy in the garden and provide excellent bouquets for the house. Wonderful for planting in groups in the border, for bedding or for everblooming hedges. A dozen plants should give you hundreds of blooms this summer. Price, except where noted.

Dormant Roses, 90c; 3 of one kind for $2.40;
12 for $8.50; 25 for $15.65

★Dagmar Spath (White Lafayette). Large trusses of pure white semi-double flowers, produced freely all summer. Excellent for cutting.

★Improved LaFayette. An unusually prolific large flowering variety; very showy and fine for mass plantings. Flowers deep brilliant red, richly suffused crimson, almost as large as a Hybrid Tea Rose.

★Mrs. R. M. Finch. Double soft rosy-pink flowers, 2 inches in diameter, in large showy, fragrant clusters. One of the finest pink Floribundas. Vigorous grower.

★Pink Gruss an Aachen. Large, very double, deep salmon-pink blooms like a hybrid tea rose. Ideal for bedding; produces a constant mass of bloom.

★Rosenelfe. Unusually beautiful, silvery rose-pink flowers of Gardenia-like form. They are very double, about 2½ inches across, and are produced freely all summer.

World's Fair. (Patent No. 362.) Large clusters of velvety, black-scarlet flowers, nearly 4 inches across, with 18 to 20 petals. Blooms continuously; fragrant. Luxuriant foliage. **Dormant, $1.00; 3 for $2.50.**

THREE NEW FLORIBUNDAS

Cheerio. Superb variety with brilliant double flowers of clear mallow pink shading to Tyrian rose at the base of the petals with reverse or outside a luminous rose-madder. $1.00; 3 for $2.50.

Red Velvet. A spectacular double Rose, covered with urn-shaped buds opening to well-rounded flowers of an intensely vivid crimson lake. The velvety finish of the flowers adds to the beauty and richness of the color. $1.25.

Sunmist. Graceful, pointed buds opening into large, well-rounded flowers of a clear light sulphur yellow shading to mellow canary yellow toward the base of the petals. Forms large flower clusters that give a glorious effect. $1.00; 3 for $2.50.

RED VELVET, SUNMIST, CHEERIO

bing Roses

PATENTED ROSE DOUBLOONS

Vaughan's Fruit Trees

All trees, except where noted, are 4 to 6 ft. in height, ⅝ inch caliper and up. They are shipped via express (charges collect) from our Nurseries, Western Springs, Illinois.

APPLE TREES

Each, $1.50; 3 for $3.90.

Summer Varieties

Anoka. Fruit striped red; excellent for cooking. Tree is naturally dwarf; bears very young.

Beacon. Fruit bright red. Similar to the old favorite, Duchess, but better in every way.

Yellow Transparent. Very early pale yellow.

Fall Varieties

McIntosh Red. Popular bright red apple; flesh white, juicy and of excellent flavor. Very hardy.

Snow (Fameuse). Has fine flavor and snow white flesh.

Wealthy. The best and most satisfactory fall apple. Large fruit, heavily streaked red, juicy and of good flavor. Trees bear when young and have enormous crops.

Winter Varieties

Cortland. Large red of good flavor. Keeps well.

Jonathan. Medium sized bright red; white flesh; juicy and of extra fine flavor; never disappoints.

Northwestern Greening. Large green; good keeper.

Red Delicious. Large dark red of highest quality and flavor. Splendid keeper.

Rome Beauty. Large cooking apple. Keeps late.

Roxbury Russet. A good russet; excellent keeper.

Stayman's Winesap. Large dark red, keeps well.

Tolman Sweet. Very sweet pale yellow; productive.

Yellow Delicious. Golden color, delicious flavor.

Crab Apple Varieties

Dolga. Large, flaming red fruit; white flesh. Excellent for jelly. Very hardy; bears abundantly.

Whitney. Bright red, striped fruit of good size.

QUINTUPLET APPLE TREE

5 Kinds of Apples on One Tree

Anoka, Delicious, Jonathan, Grimes Golden, and Yellow Transparent. This is the ideal tree for the small yard, 5 different varieties of apples are grafted on the main stock of one tree, which will give you good apples for summer, fall, and winter. $2.95 each.

HANSEN'S HARDY APRICOTS

You are sure of a crop with these new drought resistant, extremely hardy varieties. The fruit is good for eating and excellent for sauce. Each, $2.00; 3 for $5.70.

CHERRIES (SOUR)

Each, $2.50; 3 for $6.75.

Early Richmond. Very popular early red, sour cherry that ripens in June.

Montmorency. Large fruits of deep, cherry red; ripens after Early Richmond.

PEARS

Each, $2.00; 3 for $5.70.

Bartlett. Very popular large summer pear.

B. Bosc. Extra long, russet colored. Oct.

Gorham. Similar to Bartlett, but blight resistant and keeps a month longer.

Kieffer. Large late pear for canning.

Seckel. Small, deliciously sweet pears.

PEACHES

4 to 5 ft., ⅝ to ¹¹⁄₁₆ inch caliper, each, $1.50; 3 for $3.90.

Elberta. Large yellow; very popular. Sept.

J. H. Hale. Extra large; fine flavor.

Polly. Extremely hardy variety; flesh white.

PLUMS

Each, $2.50; 3 for $6.75.

Burbank. Large fruit, cherry-red with lilac bloom.

Reine Claude (Green Gage). Yellowish green.

Shropshire Damson. Small purplish black.

Stanley Prune. Popular purple plum.

Terry. Fine mottled red.

Underwood. Good early red.

DWARF FRUIT TREES

These dwarf trees have low broad heads so that fruit can easily be picked and they take up little room in the garden or on the lawn. They usually bear good crops within 3 or 4 years and the fruit is of extra high quality. Plant 8 feet apart, and each spring trim off one-third to one-half of the previous season's growth.

Dwarf Apples. Delicious, Yellow Delicious, 2 yr., 3 to 5 ft., $2.50.

Dwarf Pears. Bartlett, Kieffer or Seckel, 2 yr., 3 to 5 ft., $2.50; 3, $6.75.

See Page 105 for Small Fruits

Vaughan's Seed Store   99

Flowering Trees and Shrubs

HEATHERMINT

ALMOND (Prunus)

Flowering Almond (Prunus Glandulosa). *4 to
6 ft.* These bushy shrubs never fail to produce in
early spring, before the leaves appear, a profusion
or small very double white or pink, rose-like flowers
that are closely set along the branches.
Double Pink. 2 to 3 ft., $1.00; 3, $2.50; 10, $8.00;
3 to 4 ft., $1.25.

Siberian Flowering Almond (Prunus Nana). *3 ft.*
Bright rose pink flowers on dwarf bushes, bloom in
early spring. Small almond fruits add interest in
summer to this hardy shrub. The slender, dark
green leaves change to bright orange and red in
fall. It is ideal for low hedges. 18 to 24 in., 85c;
3 for $2.40.

BARBERRY (Berberis)

Green Leaved Barberry (B. Thunbergi). *4 ft.*
Popular hedge plant. Scarlet berries in fall and
winter. 18 to 24 in., 65c; 3, $1.35; 10, $4.00; 100,
$45.00.

Mentor Barberry (B. Mentorensis). (Patent No.
99) *3 ft.* It is extremely hardy and is able to withstand intense heat and drought without wilting or
burning. Its foliage is heavy and thick and remains
green until after the holidays. 18 to 24 in., 75c;
3, $2.00; 10, $5.00; 100, $45.00.

Red-Leaved Barberry (B. Thun. Atro Purpurea).
4 ft. The foliage is a rich, bronzy red all summer.
Plant in full sun to develop its coloring. 15 to 18;
in., 70c; 3, $1.85; 10, $6.00.

Truehedge Columnberry (B. Thun. Erecta).
(Patent No. 110) *4 to 5 ft.* Of distinct pyramidal
habit, it may be used for formal hedge or individual
specimens without pruning. 18 to 24 in., 65c 3,;
$1.80; 10, $5.30; 25, $11.50; 100, $42.00.

Korean Barberry (B. Koreana). *6 ft.* Its large
leaves turn red orange and purple in the autumn.
Has bright red berries that hang on late into winter. 3 to 4 ft., 90c; 3, $2.50; 10, $7.50; 4 to 5 ft.,
$1.00; 3, $2.75; 10, $8.50.

BEAUTY BUSH (Kolkwitzia Amabilis)

Its trumpet-shaped pink flowers make a wonderful
showing in June. Grows from 6 to 8 ft. tall and
fully that wide. 2 to 3 ft., $1.00; 3, $2.70.

BIRCH (Betula)

European White Birch (B. Alba). *30-40 ft.* Of
very upright habit with beautiful white bark. Foliage small and finely toothed. 8 to 10 ft., $3.75;
6 to 7 ft. clumps, $5.50; 3 for $9.00.

Cut-Leaved Weeping Birch (B. Pendula Gracilis).
30–40 ft. An unusually graceful drooping tree, with
deeply cut foliage and silvery white bark at maturity. 8 to 10 ft., $4.75.

BUCKTHORN (Rhamnus)

Cathartica. *10 to 12 ft.* A fine, robust shrub, with
handsome dark green foliage and green fragrant
flowers that are followed by showy black berries.
It is extremely hardy and will thrive in dry soils
or partial shade. Makes a fine hedge, either informal or clipped. 3 to 4 ft., 75c; 3, $1.65; 10,
$5.00; 4 to 5 ft., 75c; 3, $1.95; 10, $6.00.

HYBRID BLUEBERRIES

Highly Ornamental Plants—Delicious Fruits.
3 to 5 ft. Beautiful all year. The foliage is a deep,
rich green in summer, turning to a beautiful crimson in fall, and all winter the twigs are bright red.
Excellent for planting with Evergreen or Broad-
leaved Evergreens, as they require an acid soil.
Large clusters of beautiful blue fruits, plump,
meaty, tender and practically seedless. Flowers
are not self-fertile and therefore we only sell 3 or
more plants to a customer so that we can supply
more than one variety. Price, 2-year clumps, B & B
3 for $3.90; 5 for $6.25.

BRIDALWREATH (Spiraea)

5 to 6 ft. One of the most beautiful and useful shrubs.
2 to 3 ft., 65c; 3, $1.50; 10, $4.50; 100, $40.00;
3 to 4 ft., 75c; 3, $1.95; 10, $5.50; 100, $45.00.

BURNING BUSH (Euonymus)

Winged Burning Bush (E. Alatus). *6 to 8 ft.* Bark
cork-like and curiously winged; leaves small; fruit
red; in autumn, foliage bright red. One of our best
shrubs for specimen plantings and for growing in
shady locations. 2 to 3 ft., $1.50; 3, $4.00; 3 to
4 ft., $2.00; 3, $5.00; 4 to 5 ft., $2.50.

Dwarf Burning Bush (E. Alatus Compacta). *4 to
6 ft.* A compact form of the above. 18 to 24 in.,
$1.25; 3, $3.25; 2 to 2½ ft., $2.00; 2½ to 3 ft.,
$2.50; 3 to 3½ ft., $3.00.

**European Burning Bush or Spindletree (E. Euro-
paeus).** *12 to 14 ft.* Very handsome in autumn
and winter when it is loaded with rose-colored and
orange berries. 3 to 4 ft., 75c; 3, $2.00; 4 to 5 ft.,
90c; 3, $2.50.

FOUR NEW BUDDLEIAS
(Butterflybushes or Summer Lilacs) $2.50

One each of those listed below.

The long tapering spikes thickly covered with
minute tubular flowers of pleasing fragrance bloom
during July and continue until frost. Excellent for
cut-flowers. The stalks die to the ground each winter
but come up vigorously again in the spring.

Charming. *4 ft.* A glorious variety, bearing elegant
long sprays of lavender-pink blooms. Is decidedly
pink in color as compared with other varieties.

Dubonnet. *4 ft.* A splendid new color, matching
that of the French Dubonnet wine, glowing red in
the sun or under artificial light.

Orchid Beauty. *3 to 4 ft.* A fine Buddleia having
flower heads up to 24 inches in length, broad at
the base. Individual florets fringed; color soft
cattleya-lilac with brilliant orange eye.

Royal Purple. (New). *3 to 4 ft.* One of the loveliest
of all the Buddleias, with very shapely, extra long,
full spikes of bloom that are a brilliant, glowing
red-purple in color.

Prices of above, field grown, each, 75c; 3 for $2.00.

HARDY BUTTERFLY BUSH

Buddleia Alternifolia. *4 to 6 ft.* Does not freeze
to the ground in winter. Its flowers are lavender-
purple with a reddish crimson eye and are borne
many together in compact rounded clusters from
the axils of the leaves in early summer. Forms a
beautiful bush. 18 to 24 in., 75c; 3, $1.95.

HANSEN BUSH CHERRY

Prunus Besseyi. *4 to 5 ft.* Hardy, quick-bearing
cherry. Fruit resembles a small plum, massed in
clusters from the ground up; good to eat fresh and
makes delicious preserves. Have striking ornamental value, dwarf, bushy nature, fragrant white
flowers in spring and beautiful silvery green foliage
which turns rich red and gold color in fall. 2 to 3
ft., 65c; 3, $1.75; 10, $6.00.

BRILLIANT CHOKEBERRY

Aronia Brilliantissima. *6 to 8 ft.* Brilliant red berries in August that remain until winter and bright
crimson foliage in fall. 3 to 4 ft., 75c; 3, $2.00.

CORALBERRY

Symphoricarpos Vulgaris. *3 to 4 ft.* Has coral-red
berries in fall. Succeeds in shade. 3 to 4 ft., 65c;
3, $1.80; 10, $5.00.

COTONEASTER

Peking Cotoneaster (Acutifolia) *5 to 10 ft.* Small
leathery leaves of rich glossy green, jet black berries
in fall. Extremely hardy, it makes one of our finest
hedges. Can be trimmed like Privet. 3 to 4 ft., 70c;
3, $1.80; 10, $6.00; 100, $50.00.

CRAB, FLOWERING (Malus)

Eleyi Crab (M. Eleyi). *10 to 15 ft.* Red foliage
spring later turning to bronze green. Produc
clusters of wine red flowers and fruits of a da:
red color. 4 to 5 ft., 5 to 6 ft., 6 to 8 ft.

**Carmine Floribunda Flowering Crab (M. Atr
sanguinea).** *10 to 15 ft.* Its spreading branch
are covered in May with carmine flowers succeed
by small, yellowish fruit. 4 to 5 ft., 5 to 6 ft., 6 to 8 [
Price of above, except where noted, 4 to 5 ft
$1.75; 3, $4.65; 5 to 6 ft., $2.25; 3, $6.25; 6
8 ft., 1 to 1¼ in. caliper, $2.75. For oth
varieties and larger sizes, write for prices.

**Bechtel's Double-Flowering Crab (M. Ioens
Bechteli).** *10 to 15 ft.* Trees of medium size a
covered in early spring with large, beautiful, doub
fragrant flowers resembling small roses of a delica
pink. 3 to 4 ft., $1.75; 4 to 5 ft., $2.25.

Sargent Crab (M. Sargenti). *5 to 6 ft.* Dwa
spreading variety. Flowers pure white; dark r
fruits. 4 to 5 ft., 1¼ to 1½ in. caliper, $5.25; 5
6 ft., 1½ to 1¾ in. caliper, $7.50.

CRANBERRYBUSH (Viburnum)

American Cranberrybush (V. Americana). *10*
Showy, edible, cranberry-like berries in fall an
early winter. 3 to 4 ft., $1.00; 3, $2.50.

DEUTZIA

Gracilis (Slender D.). *3 ft.* Its slender, gracei
branches bear a profusion of pure white flowers
May. 15 to 18 in., 75c; 3, $2.00.

Lemoine. *3 to 4 ft.* Pure white flowers borne
in fall with its red foliage and clusters in late May. 18
24 in., 75c; 3 for $2.00.

DOGWOOD (Cornus)

Coral Dogwood (C. Alba Sibirica). *6 to 10*
Bright coral-red branches. 3 to 4 ft., 75c; 3, $2.0
10, $6.00; 4 to 5 ft., 90c; 3, $2.50.

**Goldentwig Dogwood (C. Stol. Flaviramea
6 to 10 ft. Attractive golden yellow bark. 2 to
ft., 65c; 3, $1.65; 10, $5.00; 3 to 4 ft., 75c;
$2.00; 10, $6.00.

Gray Dogwood (C. Paniculata). Very attracti
in fall with red foliage and clusters of white
berries; bark gray. 3 to 4 ft., 70c; 3, $1.75; 1
$5.00; 4 to 5 ft., 80c; 3, $2.00; 10, $6.00.

**Pink Flowering Dogwood (C. Florida Rubra
15 ft. A small, upright tree that produces larg
deep rose-colored flowers in early spring. Ve
showy. 3 to 4 ft., B. & B., $5.00. 4 to 5 ft., B
B., $6.00.

Silky Dogwood (C. Amomum). *8 to 10 ft.* Pur
stems in winter. 3 to 4 ft., 65c; 3, $1.65; 10, $5.
4 to 5 ft., 70c; 3, $1.80; 10, $6.00.

White-flowering Dogwood (C. Florida). *15 to
ft.* Masses of large, single white flowers in Ma
3 to 4 ft., B. & B., $3.00.

ELM (Ulmus)
3 Quick Growing Varieties

American Elm, Moline Type. *80 to 100 ft.* E
ceedingly large foliage. Of upright habit. Splenc
tree for the street or for small yards.

American Elm, Vase Type. *80 to 100 ft.* A tr
vase-shaped tree.

Chinese or Siberian Elm (U. Pumila). *75 ft.* (
account of its rapid growth, resistance to disea
and ability to thrive in almost any situation, t
is one of the most popular trees in America.
(Prices of the above 3 Elm Trees as follows:)

Height	Caliper	Each	10
8 to 10 ft.	1 to 1¼ inch	$2.50	$22.
8 to 10 ft.	1¼ to 1½ inch	3.00	27.
10 to 12 ft.	1½ to 1¾ inch	3.60	32.
10 to 12 ft.	1¾ to 2 inch	4.00	37.
12 to 14 ft.	2 to 2¼ inch	4.75	45.

Larger sizes, prices on application.

CHINESE ELM HEDGING

Ulmus Pumila. It forms a beautiful, dense, imper
trable hedge with small dark green foliage. It c
be kept low-growing and clipped, or can be us
where immediate screening effects are desired. F
hedge purposes, plant seedlings 12 to 18 inct
apart: 2 to 3 ft. seedlings, not transplanted, |
$1.50; 50, $6.00; 100, $10.00.

for the Home Landscape

FIREBUSH OR FLOWERING QUINCE
Cydonia Japonica. *4 to 5 ft.* Brilliant orange-scarlet flowers in April, followed by yellowish green, quince-shaped, fragrant fruits. 18 to 24 in., 60c; 3, $1.50; 2 to 3 ft., 75c; 3, $1.95.

FRINGETREE
White Fringetree (Chionanthus Virginica). *9 to 15 ft.* In late May or early June a thick white mist of pendent fringe-like flowers, mixing with large leathery leaves, present a unique sight. Valued as a lawn specimen. 3 to 4 ft., $1.25.

GOLDEN BELL (Forsythia)
Border Forsythia (F. Intermedia). *6 to 8 ft.* Bright golden yellow flowers in early s r n . 3 to 4 ft., 65c; 3, $1.75; 4 to 5 ft., 75c; 3, $1.95; 10, $6.00.
Korean Golden Bell (F. Ovata). *5 to 8 ft.* Extremely hardy and very early. The flowers are pale primrose-yellow. 2 to 3 ft., 75c; 3, $2.00.
Showy Border Golden Bell (Forsythia Intermedia Spectabilis). *6 to 8 ft.* Its large, rich, yellow blossoms completely cover the wide spreading branches in early spring. 2 to 3 ft., 65c; 3, $1.65; 3 to 4 ft., 70c; 3, $1.85; 4 to 5 ft., 80c.

HAWTHORN (Crataegus)
Paul's Double Scarlet Hawthorn (C. Oxyacantha Splendens. *12 to 15 ft.* Very showy blossoms of bright scarlet color, large, full and very double. 4 to 5 ft., $3.00; 5 to 6 ft., $3.75.

HEATHERMINT (Elsholtzia Stauntoni)
3 to 4 ft. Produces attractive spikes of reddish purple flowers, resembling heather; September and October. The leaves of the plant, when bruised, emit a mint fragrance. Plant in a sunny location. 18 to 24 in., 75c; 3 for $2.00; 10, $6.50.

HONEYLOCUST (Gleditsia)
Thornless Honeylocust (G. Triacanthos Inermis). *50 to 70 ft.* A large, vigorous tree with spreading branches, thornless or nearly so, and handsome feathery fern-like leaves. Good for yard or street planting and will withstand the dust and smoke of a city well. Thrives in any soil and will endure drought. 6 to 8 ft., $2.25; 8 to 10 ft., 1 to 1¼ in. caliper, $3.50.

HYDRANGEA
Peegee Hydrangea (H. Paniculata Grandiflora). *8 to 10 ft.* Immense panicles of bloom a foot long, white turning to rose, commencing to bloom in August, 18 to 24 in., 65c; 3, $1.75; 10, $5.00; 2 to 3 ft., 75c; 3, $2.00; 10, $6.50.
Snowball Hydrangea (H. Arborescens Grandiflora). *4 ft.* Large, flat heads of snow-white flowers in June and July. Thrives in shade. 2 to 3 ft., 75c; 3, $2.00; 10, $6.50.
Blue Hydrangea. *2 ft.* Blooms of deep and intense blue last for a long time in late summer. Will grow in sun or light shade. Protect during winter in colder climates. Use a little alum when planting to assure the best color. $1.50.

KOREAN GOLDEN BELL

HONEYSUCKLE (Lonicera)
White Belle H. (L. Bella Albida). *8 to 10 ft.* Upright in growth, excellent for hedges. White flowers, red fruits. 4 to 5 ft., 70c; 3, $1.75; 10, $5.00.
Tatarian Honeysuckle. *9 to 10 ft.* One of our best shrubs for screen and border plantings.
Pink, Red or White. 3 to 4 ft., 75c; 3, $2.00; 10, $6.50; 4 to 5 ft., 90c; 3, $2.25; 10, $7.50.
Zabel Red H. (L. Korolkowi Zabeli). *10 ft.* A dense upright growing shrub. This variety produces a grand display of red flowers in spring followed by red fruits in summer. It is probably the darkest colored bush honeysuckle. 2 to 3 ft., 75c; 3, $1.95.

KERRIA (Corchorus)
Japonica Flore Pleno (Double Kerria). *4 to 5 ft.* Showy, bright double yellow flowers from June to September. g 2 to 3 ft., 90c; 3, $2.50.

LILAC SPECIES
Lilac (Syringa Japonica). *15 to 20 ft.* The last of the Lilacs to bloom, bearing its small creamy-white flowers in upright clusters from 12 to 18 inches long in June and July. 3 to 4 ft., $1.00; 3, $2.75.
Late Lilac (Syringa Villosa). *7 to 8 ft.* An attractive round topped shrub with bright green foliage. Flowers flesh-colored and borne in clusters. Blooms after the common Lilacs are gone. 3 to 4 ft., 90c; 3, $2.40; 4 to 5 ft., $1.00; 3, $2.75.
Persian Purple (Syringa Persica). *8 to 10 ft.* The most graceful and freely flowering of the Lilacs, with purple-lavender flowers, in loose panicles. 2 to 3 ft., 75c; 3, $1.95; 10, $6.00; 3 to 4 ft., 85c; 3, $2.25; 10, $7.00.

LINDEN (Tilia)
Pyramidal European Linden (Tilia Platyphyllos Pyramidalis). *60-80 ft.* New Linden of true pyramidal form: It does not attain the extreme narrow effect of the Lombardy Poplar, but will fill its place in many landscapes where a narrow tree of long life is needed. 8 to 10 ft., $4.50.

MAGNOLIA
Saucer Magnolia (M. Soulangeana). *20 ft.* Flowers come before the long glossy leaves, and are 3 to 5 inches across, cup-shaped, rosy pink when in bud. A full-sized tree is a bouquet of thousands of showy flowers, not surpassed by any other tree in effectiveness. 2 to 3 ft., B. & B., $6.50; 3 to 4 ft., B. & B., $9.50; 4 to 5 ft., B. & B., $12.00; 5 to 6 ft., B. & B., $15.00.
Star Magnolia (M. Stellata). *12 ft.* The first Magnolia to blossom. No plant flowers more freely; and in early spring its semi-double, snow-white flowers of starry form appear in countless numbers and attract attention on all sides. 18 to 24 in., B. & B., $6.00; 2 to 2½ ft., B. & B., $7.50.

MOUNTAIN ASH
Sorbus Aucuparia. *25 to 30 ft.* A handsome tree with compound leaves of dark green turning to a golden yellow in autumn. The white flowers are followed in fall by large clusters of bright red berries. 6 to 8 ft., $2.75; 8 to 10 ft., $3.50.

HYBRID LILAC

MAPLE (Acer)
Columnar Norway Maple (Acer Platanoides Columnare). *50-60 ft.* Compact columnar form of the Norway Maple. 6 to 7 ft., $3.25; 10, $30.00; 7 to 8 ft., $3.75; 10, $35.00.
Norway Maple (Acer Platanoides). *50 to 75 ft.* A large and handsome tree with spreading branches, and compact, round head. Broad, dark green foliage, fading with tones of yellow and gold in autumn.

Height	Caliper	Each	10 for
8 to 10 ft.	1¼ to 1½ inch	$4.00	$37.50
8 to 10 ft.	1½ to 1¾ inch	4.50	42.50

Larger sizes, prices on application.

Schwedler Maple (Acer Platanoides Schwedleri). *40 to 60 ft.* Gleaming red and purple leaves in spring, changing to dark green during summer. 6 to 8 ft., $3.25; 8 to 10 ft., 1 to 1¼ in. caliper, $4.50.
Sugar Maple (Acer Saccharum). *50 to 75 ft.* The dark green foliage changes in autumn to brilliant tones of orange and lemon. 8 to 10 ft. 1¼ to 1½ in. caliper, $4.00; 10 for $37.50.

MOCK ORANGE (Philadelphus)
Common Mock Orange. *7 to 10 ft.* The free flowering single white found in the old-fashioned gardens. Of rapid growth, forming a large bush. 3 to 4 ft., 65c; 3, $1.65; 10, $6.00; 4 to 5 ft., 75c; 3, $1.75; 10, $6.00.
Innocence. *5 ft.* Long arched branches carrying a wealth of large single flowers of the purest white assuming the appearance of snowy sheaves of bloom. 3 to 4 ft., $1.75; 3 for $5.00.
Norma. *7 to 8 ft.* Unusually large, glossy white, single flowers in good sized sprays. An upright grower with light green leaves. 3 to 4 ft., 75c; 3, $2.00; 10, $6.00; 4 to 5 ft., 90c; 3, $2.50.
Virginalis. *7 to 8 ft.* One of the most beautiful shrubs grown. In June the plants appear as a huge bouquet, being completely covered with extra large, single and semi-double flowers that are pure white and sweet-scented. It has a long blooming season, the new wood producing large individual flowers often 3 inches across; throughout the summer. 2 to 3 ft., 90c; 3 or $2.50; 3 to 4 ft., $1.25.

OCEAN SPRAY
Holodiscus Discolor. *3 to 5 ft.* This shrub is appropriately named, as the graceful large clusters of drooping, creamy white flowers in July remind one of breaking, small white caps of waves. 7 to 3 ft., $1.00; 3 for $2.50.

PRIVET HEDGE (Ligustrum)
Amur Privet (L. Amurense). *12 ft.* One of the best hardy hedge plants. May be sheared to any extent. 18 to 24 in., 10, $1.75; 100, $15.00; 2 to 3 ft., 35c; 10, $3.00; 100, $20.00; 3 to 4 ft., heavy 50c; 10, $3.50; 100, $25.00.
Regal Privet (L. Ibota Regelianum). *8 to 10 ft.* Dark, glossy green leaves; spreading, graceful habit. Grows well in sun or shade. 2 to 3 ft., 65c; 3 for $1.75; 10, $5.50; 3 to 4 ft., 80c; 10, $7.00.

PLUM (Prunus)

Nanking Cherry (Prunus Tomentosa). *4 to 6 ft.* An extremely hardy shrub with pale pink flowers followed by brilliant scarlet, edible fruits that ripen in June. 3 to 4 ft., 75c; 3 for $2.00; 10, $6.00; 4 to 5 ft., $1.00; 3, $2.70; 10, $8.50.

Newport Purple-Leaf Plum (Prunus Cerasifera Newport). *12 to 15 ft.* A small tree shrub. The leaves, when young, are lustrous crimson, changing to a dark purple and retain this beautiful tint until they drop, late in autumn. The tree is covered early in spring with small, single pink flowers, which appear before the leaves. 3 to 4 ft., 85c; 3, $2.40; 10, $7.50.

ROSE OF SHARON

Hibiscus or Shrub Althaea. *6 to 12 ft.* An upright shrub, blooming in August and September. The flowers resemble those of the hollyhock, and are very showy. Double pink, purple, red, or white. 3 to 4 ft., 75c; 3, $2.00.

HYBRID RUGOSA ROSES

Prices, 2 year, 85c; 3, $2.40; 10 $7.50.

Belle Poitevine. *5 to 6 ft.* Very large, full double, loosely formed flowers of bright pink all summer.

Hansa. *5 to 6 ft.* Double, reddish-violet flowers of large size, freely produced. Very sweet scented.

F. J. Grootendorst. *5 to 6 ft.* The flowers are bright red, beautifully fringed, and produced in clusters. It blooms from early summer until frost.

Pink Grootendorst. *5 to 6 ft.* A variety similar in every way to the F. J. Grootendorst except that the flowers are a clear pink.

GOLDEN ROSE OF CHINA

Rosa Hugonis. *6 ft.* Excellent hardy rose that makes a spectacular show when its long arching branches are thickly set with lovely single yellow flowers in May. 2 yr., 85c; 3, $2.40.

SNOWBALL

Clove-scented Snowball (Viburnum Carlesi). *4 ft.* This dwarf, compact shrub, bearing large corymbs of delicate pale rose blossoms, tinted white, has a delicious clove-scented fragrance. Hardy, but best planted in a somewhat sheltered position. 18 to 24 in., $2.25.

Old-Fashioned Snowball (V. Opulus Sterile). *8 to 10 ft.* Large balls of white flowers in May. 2 to 3 ft., 75c; 3, $2.00; 3 to 4 ft., $1.00; 3, $2.50.

SNOWBERRY (Symphoricarpos)

S. Racemosus. *3 to 5 ft.* Waxy white berries in fall. Does well in shade. 3 to 4 ft., 65c; 3, $1.80; 10, $5.00; 4 to 5 ft., 75c; 3, $2.00.

SNOWGARLAND

Spiraea Arguta Multiflora. *4 to 5 ft.* Showy shrub with leaves of narrow, bright green, fading with tones of yellow and orange in fall. Flowers are small, pure white, and are borne in early spring in such profusion that the whole shrub appears laden with snow. 2 to 3 ft., 65c; 3, $1.65; 10, $5.00; 3 to 4 ft., 75c; 3, $2.00; 10, $6.00.

EVERBLOOMING SPIRAEA

Spiraea Froebeli. *3 ft.* Round, flat clusters of rosy-pink flowers from June to October. Beautiful foliage all season. One of our best low growing shrubs for general use and for flowering hedges. 18 to 24 in., 65c; 3, $1.65; 10, $5.00; 24 to 30 in., 75c; 3, $2.00; 10, $6.00.

Spiraea Anthony Waterer. *2½ ft.* Flat clusters of rosy-crimson flowers throughout the summer and fall. 15 to 18 in., 65c; 3, $1.65; 10, $5.00; 18 to 24 in., 75c; 3, $2.00; 10, $6.00.

TAMARIX SUMMER GLOW

Hispida Aestivalis Rubra. *8 to 10 ft.* Magnificent new variety with wine-red flower spikes that appear all during the summer. Feathery gray-green foliage. To get the best results, Tamarix should be cut to the ground when planted. 2 yr., No. 1, 85c; 3, $2.25.

VIBURNUM

Beautiful Autumn Fruits and Foliage.

Arrow Wood (V. Dentatum). *10 to 12 ft.* Of upright habit; dark green foliage which changes to purple and red in autumn. White flowers in flat clusters in June; dark blue fruits in autumn. Succeeds in shade. 3 to 4 ft., 75c; 3, $2.00; 4 to 5 ft., 90c; 3, $2.50.

Wayfaring Tree (V. Lantana). *15 ft.* Large robust shrub with soft, heavy leaves, silvery beneath. Clusters of white flowers in May succeeded by red fruit, turning black in autumn; retains its foliage very late. 3 to 4 ft., 75c; 3, $2.00; 4 to 5 ft., 90c; 3, $2.25; 10, $7.50.

VAUGHAN'S EVERGREENS

All Prices Are F. O. B. Our Nurseries, Western Springs, Ill.

PFITZER JUNIPER. Best of all Evergreens

ARBORVITAE (Thuja)

Globe Arborvitae (T. Occidentalis Globosa). A round, compact form with deep green foliage. 12 in., $2.25; 15 in., $2.75; 18 in., $3.50.

Pyramidal Arborvitae (T. Occidentalis Pyramidalis). A compact, narrow pyramidal tree. 2½ to 3 ft., $2.75; 3 to 3½ ft., $3.50; 3½ to 4 ft., $4.00; 4 to 4½ ft., $4.50; 4½ to 5 ft., $5.00.

CEDAR (Juniperus)

Redcedar (J. Virginiana). Tall growing, one of the best known evergreens. 2 to 2½ ft., $3.00; 2½ to 3 ft., $3.50; 3 to 3½ ft., $4.00; 3½ to 4 ft., $4.50.

Burk Redcedar (J. Virg. Burki). An improved form of Silver Redcedar. 2½ to 3 ft., $4.50; 3 to 3½ ft., $5.50; 5 to 5½ ft., $10.50.

Cannart Redcedar (J. Virg. Cannarti). Fine Pyramidal form with heavily tufted deep green foliage. 3 to 3½ ft., $6.50; 3½ to 4 ft., $7.00; 4 to 4½ ft., $8.00; 4½ to 5 ft., $9.00.

Silver Redcedar (J. Virg. Glauca). One of our choicest evergreens with attractive blue tinged foliage. 2½ to 3 ft., $4.50; 3 to 3½ ft., $5.50; 3½ to 4 ft., $6.50; 4 to 4½ ft., $7.75; 4½ to 5 ft., $9.00; 5 to 5½ ft., $10.00.

Dundee Juniper (J. Virg. Pyramidiformia Hilli). Dense conical form; bluish gray-green foliage, plum colored in winter. 3 to 3½ ft., $6.50; 3½ to 4 ft., $7.00; 4 to 4½ ft., $8.00; 4½ to 5 ft., $9.00;

EVERGREEN SPURGE

Pachysandra Terminalis. A low growing ground cover. The thick leathery green leaves hold on all winter. Excellent for a shady location, especially under trees where grass will not do well. It is well suited for growing between Evergreens. Pot plants, 3 for 85c; 12 for $2.50; 100 for $15.00.

FIR (Abies)

White Fir (A. Concolor). Tall, pyramidal tree; with foliage of varying shades of dark green and blue. 2 to 2½ ft., $4.50; 2½ to 3 ft., $5.50; 3 to 3½ ft., $6.50; 3½ to 4 ft., $8.00.

JUNIPER (Juniperus)

Canadian Juniper (J. Canadensis). Dwarf evergreen of erect habit; grayish green foliage. 15 to 18 in., $1.90; 18 to 24 in., $2.75; 2 to 2½ ft., $3.50.

Keteleer Juniper (J. Chin. Keteleeri). Similar to Cannart Redcedar, but of more open growth and pyramidal habit. 2½ to 4 ft., $4.25; 3 to 3½ ft., $5.00; 3½ to 4 ft., $6.25; 4 to 4½ ft., $7.25.

Pfitzer Juniper (J. Chin. Pfitzeriana). One of the best Junipers. Of broad, bushy growth, with thick, rich green foliage. 12 to 15 in., $2.00; 15 to 18 in., $2.50; 18 to 24 in., $3.50; 2 to 2½ ft., $5.00.

Andorra Juniper (J. Communis Depressa Plumosa). Of prostrate habit; foliage bright green in summer, rich reddish purple in winter. $3.50; 18 to 24 in., $4.00; 2 to 2½ ft., $4.50; 2½ to 3 ft., $5.00; 3 to 3½ ft., $6.00.

Savin Juniper (J. Sabina). A dwarf evergreen with semi-erect spreading branches. 18 to 24 in., $3.00; 2 to 2½ ft., $3.75; 2½ to 3 ft., $4.50.

Von Ehron Savin Juniper (J. Sabina Von Ehron). Semi-spreading; very dark green foliage. 18 to 24 in., $3.50; 2 to 2½ ft., $4.50; 2½ to 3 ft., $5.50.

Upright Von Ehron Savin Juniper. An upright form of the above. 2 to 2½ ft., $4.50; 2½ to 3 ft., $5.50.

SPRUCE (Picea)

Black Hill Spruce (P. Canadensis Albertiana). A very dense, compact growing spruce with green or bluish foliage. 18 to 24 in., $3.00; 2 to 2½ ft., $4.00; 2½ to 3 ft., $4.75; 3 to 3½ ft., $5.50; 3½ to 4 ft., $6.50; 4 to 4½ ft., $7.50.

Colorado Blue Spruce (P. Pungens Glauca). Very showy, rich silvery blue foliage. 2 to 2½ in., $5.50; 2½ to 3 ft., $6.50; 3 to 3½ ft., $7.50.

Colorado Green Spruce (P. Pungens). A very popular variety with heavy, light green foliage. 2 to 2½ ft., $3.50; 2½ to 3 ft., $4.00; 3 to 3½ ft., $4.75; 3½ to 4 ft., $5.75.

Moerheim Blue Spruce (P. Pungens Moerheimi). "The Aristocrat" of all evergreens. Foliage bright, intense steel blue. 3 ft., $10.50; 3½ ft., $12.50; 4 ft., $16.00; 4½ ft., $20.00.

PINE (Pinus)

Austrian Pine (P. Nigra). A good tree for city planting. A distinctive variety with stout spreading branches and long rich green needles. 2 to 2½ ft., $3.00.

Mugho Pine (P. Mont. Mughus). Good low growing evergreen. 12 in., $2.00; 15 in., $3.50; 18 in., $4.25; 2 ft., $5.00.

Scotch Pine (P. Sylvestris). A picturesque evergreen of rapid growth; valuable for windbreaks. 2 to 2½ ft., $2.75; 2½ to 3 ft., $3.75.

YEW (Taxus)

Spreading Yew (T. Cuspidata). Of dense, spreading growth, with heavy, dark green foliage. 15 to 18 in., $5.00; 18 to 24 in., $6.50; 2 to 2½ ft., $8.00; 2½ to 3 ft., $10.00.

Upright Yew (T. Cusp. Capitata). An upright or pyramidal form with glossy, deep green foliage. 18 to 24 in., $4.50; 2 ft., $6.00; 2½ ft., $8.00; 3½ ft., $12.00.

Hick's Yew (T. Media Hicksi). A distinct columnar form with rich, deep green foliage. 2 to 2½ ft., $4.75; 2½ to 3 ft., $6.50; 3 to 3½ ft., $8.50; 3½ to 4 ft., $10.50.

Write for prices on larger sizes of Evergreens.

FRENCH PUSSY WILLOW

Salix Caprea. *10 to 15 ft.* Small tree or large shrub with handsome fur-like catkins which appear in early spring before the leaves. 3 to 4 ft., 90c; 3 for $2.25.

WINTERCREEPER (Euonymus)

These trailing Euonymus are valued for their dense evergreen foliage and hardiness. They can be used for ground covers on terraces or under trees; very effective when planted with Evergreens.

Bronze Wintercreeper (E. Radicans Colorata). A fine new variety introduced by the Arnold Arboretum, with bright red foliage in winter 12 to 15 in., pot-grown, 60c; 3, $1.50; 10, $4.50.

Bigleaf Wintercreeper (E. Radicans Vegetus). Sometimes called "Evergreen Bittersweet" on account of its gorgeous red berries which are resplendent all winter against a rich deep evergreen foliage. Makes a useful ground cover or will climb on brick or stone. 3 year, 12 to 15 inch, in 6 in. pots, $1.25.

WEIGELA (Diervilla)

Abel Carrieri. *6 ft.* Very floriferous, producing quantities of large, showy, trumpet-shaped pink and carmine flowers in June. 3 to 4 ft., 90c; 3, $2.25.

Bristol Ruby. (Plant Patent No. 492.) *6 ft.* Splendid new variety that blooms profusely in June and early July and occasionally later in the season. Color in effect is a soft ruby-red shading to garnet-crimson. 2 to 3 ft.; $1.25; 3 to 4 ft., $1.75.

Crimson Weigela (Floribunda). *6 ft.* Crimson flowers in June and July. 3 to 4 ft., 90c; 3, $2.25.

Pink Weigela (Rosea). *5 to 6 ft.* Large, rosy-pink flowers in June. 2 to 3 ft., 75c; 3, $2.00.

WITCH HAZEL (Winter-Blooming)

Hamamelis Vernalis. *5 to 6 ft.* Blossoms as early as January and will continue to bloom for a long time. The profusion of flowers have a spicy fragranee and vary from bright yellow to shades of old gold, reddish brown and maroon. Best results when planted in sheltered place well open to winter sun. 2 to 3 ft., $1.00.

Vaughan's Hardy Climbing Vines

CLEMATIS Belle of Woking

TRUMPET CREEPER

Bignonia Radicans. A robust, tall climber with great leathery trumpet-shaped flowers of brilliant orange-scarlet which last a long time in the summer. Useful wherever a showy flowering vine is desired. Will cling to wood. 2 yr., 60c; 3 for $1.60.

Bignonia Mme. Galen. A more dwarf form of the above with immense flower clusters, often exceeding 15 inches in length. 2 yr., grafted, $1.00; 3 for $2.75.

BITTERSWEET (Celastrus Scandens)

A native climbing or twining plant with handsome large leaves; yellow flowers in May and June and clusters of ornamental orange-capsuled fruit in autumn. Succeeds well in shade. We recommend planting 2 or more in a group. 2 yr., 75c; 3 for $1.95; doz., $7.50.

CREEPER (Ampelopsis)

Boston Ivy (Ampelopsis Tricuspidata or Veitchei). The grandest hardy climbing vine in existence for covering houses, churches, schools, etc. Its glossy, ivy leaves overlap each other, and its long delicate young shoots stretch up the walls with free and rapid growth. The tendrils at nearly every point cling firmly to the smoothest surface of rock or brick. 2 year, 75c; 3 for $1.95; doz., $6.00; 3 year, 90c; 3 for $2.25.

Engelman's Creeper (Ampelopsis Engelmani). One of the hardiest, best and quickest growing climbers for the north and northwest. Leaves color beautifully in the fall. Has a tendency to cling to brick or stucco. 2 yr., 60c; 3 for $1.50; doz. $5.00.

DUTCHMAN'S PIPE

Aristolochia Sipho. A vigorous and rapid-growing climber, bearing striking brownish colored flowers, resembling a miniature pipe in shape. Its large, rich glossy, dark green heart-shaped leaves give a tropical foliage effect and produce a splendid shade. It is very hardy and will thrive in sun or shade. 2 yr., grafted, $1.25.

LARGE-FLOWERING CLEMATIS

The Large-Flowering Clematis are the most beautiful of flowering vines. All except the variety Belle of Woking should be pruned in spring, as they produce their finest flowers from wood made during the current year. We supply own-root plants which are the best.

Henryi. Pure white flowers, usually eight-petaled, and often 6 to 8 inches in diameter.

Jackmani. This variety, with its strong, healthy growth, hardy nature and rich, deep velvety purple flowers, is the most satisfactory of its class. Blooms with astonishing profusion.

Mme. Edward Andre. Very beautiful bright velvety red, free-flowering and continuous bloomer.

Ramona. An extra good variety that gives plenty of bloom of a distinct shade of light lavender blue.

Prices of the above 4 varieties: 2-year, each, $1.00; 3-year, each, $1.25.

Gold Medal Collection. One each Jackmani, Henryi and Mme Edward Andre. 2-year for $2.75; 3-year for $3.45.

FIVE FINE NEW VARIETIES

Belle of Woking. Handsome double flowers of silvery blue. Profuse bloomer in July and again just before frost. 2 yr., $1.25; 3 for $3.25.

Comtesse de Bouchaud. Beautiful flowers with gracefully curved petals of satiny rose. Blooms from July to Sept. Very distinct. 2 yr., $1.25.

Crimson King. Truly spectacular, bright red flowers that are often 6 to 7 inches in diameter. Blooms from June to September. $1.50.

Lord Neville. Very dark, velvety blue-purple. Exquisite in color, with petals rich in texture. Has a long blooming season. 2 yr., $1.25.

Prins Hendrik. Of rare orchid-like beauty, with georgeous azure-blue, ruffled petals, often 7 inches in diameter. Blooms from June until frost. $1.75.

Deluxe Collection: One each of Belle of Woking, Crimson King, and Lord Neville. 2-year, for $3.50.

VARIOUS SPECIES OF CLEMATIS

Duchess of Albany (New). Vigorous sprays of gorgeous pink trumpet-shaped flowers about 3½ to 4 inches long. Blooms from July to September. Flowers will last two weeks when cut. 2 yr., $1.50.

Sweet Autumn Clematis (Clematis Paniculata). The flowers are pure white, deliciously fragrant and produced with the greatest freedom in September when few other vines are in bloom. The most popular of all the small-flowered vines. 2 yr., 75c; 3 for $2.00.

HARDY ENGLISH IVY

Hedera Helix Gracilis. A graceful evergreen vine that has dark green foliage and is identical in habit with the well-known English Ivy, except that it is hardy and has smaller leaves. Succeeds well in shady places and makes an excellent ground cover. 2½ in. pots, each, 50c; 3 for 85c; doz., $2.75; 100, $15.00.

HONEYSUCKLE (Lonicera)

Excellent vines for covering arbors, fences, pergolas, verandas, etc., and for ground planting under trees. If used on terraces or embankments will prevent washing. All are hardy and improve in beauty yearly.

Everblooming Honeysuckle (Lonicera Heckrotti). Remarkable for large size and distinct appearance of its flowers, crimson-carmine without and golden apricot inside. They are very beautiful and fragrant and are in bloom from the middle of June until the coming of frost. 2 yr., 75c; 3 for $2.00.

Hall's Honeysuckle (Lonicera Japonica Halleana). One of the finest of all vines. Almost evergreen, with very fragrant, pure white flowers, changing to yellow, in late summer and fall. 2 yr., 65c; 3 for $1.75; doz., $5.00.

CLIMBING HYDRANGEA

Hydrangea Petiolaris. A worth - while hardy climber with white, four-petaled flowers in 6 to 8 inch loose clusters in July. Will cling to brick or stone walls. Slow growing when young, but once established, makes a rapid growth. Grows best on north or east sides of buildings. Strong pot-grown plants, 2 yr.; 3 for $3.25.

SILVER LACE VINE

Polygonum Auberti. Of strong, vigorous growth, attaining a height of 25 feet or more, producing through the summer and fall great foamy sprays of white flowers that turn rose-colored as they begin to fade, and the combination of white and rose makes an exceedingly pretty picture. 2 yr., 75c; 3 for $2.00; doz., $7.50.

KUDZU or Jack-and-the-Bean-Stalk Vine

The most remarkable climber extant. In rich soil will grow 70 feet in one season. Starts into growth slowly, but after three or four weeks grows almost beyond belief. Leaves in shape like Lima Bean; dark green; texture soft and woolly. Fine for porches, arbors, old trees, etc. 60c; 3 for $1.35.

WISTARIA

Very strong growing vines that climb high and twine tightly. To get the best bloom, do not over-water or over-fertilize, but prune regularly, cutting back all superfluous growth in August and again in September.

Chinese Wistaria (Wistaria Sinensis). Blooms very profusely early in summer; flowers violet-blue, in long pendulous clusters. Our plants are propagated from blooming wood. 2 yr., grafted, $1.00.

Pink Wistaria (Wistaria Multijuga Rosea). The queen of the Wistarias. Vigorous growing, with extremely long, full clusters of beautiful pink flowers. 1 yr., grafted, $1.25.

White Chinese Wistaria (Wistaria Sinensis Alba). Pure white, very fragrant, 2 yr., grafted, $1.00.

All prices f. o. b. our nurseries, Western Springs, Ill.

If wanted by Parcel Post, add 10c for 1 plant, 20c for 3 plants for postage.

WISTARIA

Vaughan's Irises

OUTSTANDING VARIETIES

★Cheerio. 40 in. Considered the most brilliant of all the red toned Irises. S. golden tan flushed rose; F. rich glowing velvety red. Produces an abundance of finely formed flowers. A "must have" for your garden. 35c; 3 for $1.00.

E. B. Williamson. 36 in. An excellent new Iris of rich, glowing coppery-red, almost a self, with a silky, lustrous finish. Unusual in color, perfect in form, and strong in growth, it is one of the finest of all Irises. 75c.

Golden Treasure. 38 in. An exquisite new creamy yellow Iris with a glowing golden heart and rich yellow beard. Huge flowers and perfectly branched stems. 50c.

Golden Majesty. 42 in. A truly superb Iris which is "tops" in its color class. It is a gleaming, deep rich, pure yellow self which does not fade. The flowers are large and of thick substance, have beautifully rounded domes and flaring falls. $1.50.

★Los Angeles. 40 in. Giant, snowy-white flowers of satin texture; the standards faintly edged lavender blue. One of the finest of all white Irises. 35c; 3 for 90c.

★Junaluska. 40 in. One of the most beautiful Iris in existence. S. rosy copper threaded with gold; F. brilliant copper-red. Huge flowers of perfect form and heavy substance. Fine garden variety. 50c; 3 for $1.25.

★Frieda Mohr. 42 in. A gigantic lilac-pink bicolor 6½ inches from the top of the standards to the tip of the falls and 6 inches horizontally. 35c; 3 for 75c.

Ming Yellow. 50 in. The perfect yellow Iris. The gigantic blooms remind one of a smooth, rich flawless carpeting of deep, yellow velvet. Vigorous in growth, it has strong foliage and stout, well branched stems. $2.00; 3 for $5.00.

Missouri. 36 in. Dykes Medal, 1937. Of sensational size and unquestionably one of the best of all blue Irises. S. clear vivid blue; F. slightly darker; semi-flaring. 50c; 3 for $1.25.

★Naranja. 40 in. One of the most talked of Iris originations. A large flowered yellow with a distinct orangy overcast on the falls. Decidedly and delightfully different. 40c.

★No-we-ta. 35 in. A beautiful, true pink self in effect with yellow flushes at the center. The whole flower is softly frilled. An exquisite Iris and a fine garden variety. 35c.

Prairie Sunset. 37 in. A gorgeous new blend of gold that captures and holds within itself all the warm, glowing colors of the western sunset. It has one of the highest ratings of Irises. $5.00.

★Sierra Blue. 48 in. Dykes Medal 1935. Enormous flowers of soft clear, enamel-like blue, reminding one of the blue of the Sierra mountains. It has widely flaring falls, good substance, and a refined finish and graceful form that is really exceptional. 35c.

Snowking. King of the white Irises. Giant snow-white flowers of fine form and heavy substance. Bold and strong in growing habits; very hardy. 50c; 3 for $1.25.

Seven Iris Aristocrats $2.00

Catalogue Value $2.60 (If wanted by mail, add 15c)

These are among the fifty finest Irises in cultivation. Each is rated close to perfection and not long ago not one could have been purchased for the price of the collection. Your Iris display is lacking if you have not these varieties; and our low prices make it possible to own them for less than the cost of ordinary plants.

★Buechly Giant. 40 in. This new variety has the largest flowers of any Iris we grow. It is a clear lavender blue bicolor that has the perfect form of Frieda Mohr. Will create a sensation in any garden. 35c; 3 for 90c.

★California Gold. 36 in. A super novelty with magnificent, large flowers of dazzling, deep golden yellow. Good garden variety as it does not fade. Late. 35c; 3 for 90c.

★Copper Lustre. 36 in. Dykes Medal, 1938. Considered "the Iris of the Century." Its flowers are of huge size and its color a blend of glowing copper and gold with iridescent sheen. Nothing quite like it. 50c; 3 for $1.25.

★Crystal Beauty. 40 in. Large, perfectly shaped flowers of pure snow white on well branched stalks. 35c; 3 for 90c.

★Depute Nomblot. 50 in. This Dykes Medal Winner of 1930 is a magnificent Iris of greatest vigor; has strong foliage and stout, nicely branched stems. Flowers are of enormous size. S. coppery-red, flushed golden bronze; F. rich claret crimson. The entire flowers seem lightly dusted with gold which sparkles in the sun. 35c; 3 for 90c.

★The Black Douglas. 48 in. S. dark violet; F. blackish violet. Very fine, richly colored Iris of good form. 35c.

Wm. Mohr. 26 in. One of the most remarkable Irises ever raised. The ground color is pale lilac, the standard flushed darker, and the whole flower is beautifully veined manganese-violet. The plants are small, but the blooms are simply immense. 35c; 3 for 90c.

OUTSTANDING VARIETIES—Continued

Tiffany. 36 in. A sensational plicata creation in creamy yellow gaily stitched in a burnished rosy bronze. Hardy, free blooming plants that will create a refreshing atmosphere in your garden. 75c.

★Wabash. 39 in. Dykes Medal 1940. S. snowy white; delightfully ruffled at the edges; F. wide and flaring, deep hyacinth violet with a definite white edge. Has wonderful substance and orchid-like beauty. Voted by the Iris experts in 1940, 1941 and again in 1942 as the best Iris in commerce. $1.00.

FALL BLOOMING IRISES

These varieties bloom in the Spring with the Early flowering varieties and have a habit of blooming again in the Autumn.

Price, except where noted, 35c each; 3 for 75c.

Autumn Queen. 18 in. Pure white flowers of good size and quality.

★Eleanor Roosevelt. 28 in. An outstanding variety of very fine deep velvety purple. Profuse bloomer twice a year.

October Blaze. 34 in. Big, glowing red-purple, somewhat on the order of Indian Chief. Late. 50c; 3 for $1.25.

Southland. 28 in. Clear deep chrome yellow of large size and heavy substance. Lovely planted with Eleanor Roosevelt.

SIBERIAN IRISES

Price, except where noted, 25c; 3 of one kind for 50c; 12 of one kind for $1.75; large clumps, 75c; 10 for $5.00.

Butterfly. 36 in. Lovely porcelain blue flowers; vigorous grower.

★Emperor. 48 in. Large flowers of a deep, rich violet-blue. Very fine.

Orientalis. 24 in. Rich purple. Fine for naturalized plantings.

★Perry's Blue. 48 in. Large, well formed flowers of a beautiful shade of sky-blue.
One of the most popular and finest of Siberian Iris.

Mixed Seedlings. 3 for 40c; 12 for $1.50.

IRIS AS A CUT FLOWER

Iris picked from your own garden make excellent cut-flowers, lasting for a week or more if cut with plenty of buds.

Try shortening the stems and use the tips, as is done so effectively with Glads in a bowl or low vase. Try the tips in a corsage too, and many of your friends will think you are wearing Orchids which the Iris so closely resemble.

DWARF IRISES

Dwarf varieties, growing from 6 to 8 inches high, that bloom two weeks in advance of the tall bearded Iris. Suitable for rock gardens or borders.

Price, any of the following except where noted, 25c each; 3 of one kind for 50c; 12 for $1.75.

Cristata (Crested Iris). Early. A dainty dwarf creeping variety with large blue flowers. Fine for use in the rock garden.

Cyanea. Very dwarf, rich crimson purple; fragrant.

Orange Queen. Clear deep yellow with orange beard.

Spring Skies. Lovely light blue, the shade of the Belladonna Larkspur.

IRIS KAEMPFERI

The last of the Iris species to bloom and the most beautiful, their remarkable flowers, generally rather flat and wide, appearing in June and July. Plant in a sunny and moist location, but not where water will stand.

Price, each 50c; 3 for $1.25.

★Gold Bound. Double. White with gold-banded center. Earliest to bloom.

Kumochi-Guma. A very full double of dark purplish indigo. Mid-season.

★Mahogany. Large double flowers of velvety-mahogany red. Late.

★Momigi-No-Taki. (Maple Waterfall). Bright rosy crimson feathered in white. Double.

★Purple and Gold. An enormous double of rich violet-purple with gold center.

Seacrest. Six large wavy white petals with blue haft.

Special Offer No. 104-A. One each of above 6 named Kaempferi Irises (Value $3.00) for $1.95. (Postage 15c additional.)

Peonies

Peonies may be planted in Spring with good results, but they should be put in early. Orders should be sent at once so that we can forward when weather permits.

Edulis Superba. (7.6) Usually blooms for Decoration Day. The large flowers are a beautiful deep, vivid pink, and are borne profusely on tall, strong stems. Very fragrant. 60c.

Felix Crousse. (8.4) Its large, globular flowers are a brilliant, dazzling ruby-red. Late mid-season. 60c.

Mad. de Verneville. (7.9) Very full and double, pure white, center tinted blush. Exquisite rose fragrance. Very beautiful reliable flower; early. 60c.

Special Offer No. 104B. One each of the above 3 Peonies (value $1.80) for $1.35. (Postage and Packing, 15c additional.)

Baroness Schroeder. (9.0) Immense flowers of great substance. Delicate flesh-white, excellent cut. Rose fragrance; late. 90c.

Festiva Maxima. (9.3) Large flowers, often 7 to 8 inches in diameter. Flowers pure white, dotted carmine. Fragrant; early. 60c.

Karl Rosefield. (8.8) Mammoth blooms of rich velvety crimson; early midseason. 75c.

Mary Brand. (8.7) Full double flowers of vivid crimson. Free blooming.

Sarah Bernhardt. (9.0) One of the best pink peonies in the world. A prolific bloomer of perfectly formed, dark rose-pink flowers in late midseason. $1.00.

Venus. (8.3) Delicate shell-pink; excellent cut. Midseason. 75c.

Special Offer No. 104C. One each of Baroness Schroeder, Karl Rosefield, Sarah Bernhardt and Venus, (value $3.40) for $2.00. (Postage and Packing, 15c additional.)

Two Hardy Water Lilies, $2.75
Prepaid 600 Miles Value $3.70

One each of Paul Hariot (Sunset Coloring) and Pink Opal (deepest pure pink). The most satisfactory varieties among the hardies.

For all its beauty, no plant is less exacting than the Water Lily. Full sun—warm water—d a bushel of soil per plant (even less for the tub varieties) are all these exotic beauties mand to produce flowers through the entire summer.

A pool can be built to harmonize with either natural or formal garden designs. It will rnish a home for goldfish and other aquatic animal life. Besides lillies, other interesting bog nd water plants can be grown.

Hardy Water Lilies

his group requires less heat and will bloom earlier spring. Can be carried over winter by the amateur ith some protection. While flowers are smaller, they e borne over a longer season than the Tropicals. ost satisfactory for the average gardener.

HARDY WATER LILIES

ttraction. Garnet red with ruby shading. Finest red. $3.00.

iromatella. Pure canary yellow. Very vigorous and free flowering. $1.75.

carboucle. Brightest crimson and scarlet. Very striking. $2.50.

loriosa. Deep carmine rose. Free and vigorous. $2.50.

onnere. A pure white snowball with over 80 petals. $2.50.

ermine. A star-shaped white of clear, luminous texture. $1.85.

ames Brydon. Rosy crimson, small growth. Good for tubs. $2.25.

aul Hariot. Opens soft, clear yellow, deepens to apricot. $1.85.

'ink Opal. Although new, so vigorous that the price is low. Deepest pink of great beauty. $1.00.

iioux. LARGEST of the sunset tints. Opens brassy yellow, deepens to blood red. $1.95.

iunrise. Huge yellow borne above water like a tropical. $3.00.

WATER LILY, MRS. W. R. JAMES

Two Tropical Water Lilies $3.85
Prepaid 600 miles. Catalogue Value $5.00
One each Blue Beauty and Pink Pearl

Tropical Water Lilies

Although these cannot be set out until after June 1st in the vicinity of Chicago, by August 1st hey have produced dozens of huge flowers. Must have warm water with full exposure to sun. All listed are day bloomers.

TROPICAL WATER LILIES

iet out after June 1st in vicinity of Chicago. By \ugust 1st will be in full bloom. Must have warm water nd full exposure to sun. All are day bloomers xcept Missouri.

\ugust Koch. Medium sized lovely lavender flowers. Free flowering. $2.25.

'rances Griffith. Outstanding royal purple. Best of its color. $2.50.

Mrs. W. R. James. A finer pink than Pershing Huge flowers. $2.50.

Blue Beauty. Huge sky-blue. Most vigorous of all. $2.50.

Mrs. George Pring. Star-shaped white flowers free-blooming. $2.50.

Missouri. Huge white flowers that open at night. $3.75.

Pink Pearl. Freest, brightest pink of lovely form. $2.50.

For prepaid delivery, add 10c each to hardy varieties. Tropicals can only be shipped via express collect.

Four Choice New Grapes $1.75
One each of 4 varieties listed. (Postage and packing, 15c additional.)

:ACO (Red). This is the most beautiful of the hardy grapes. The bunches are large and compact, of good size and form, color wine-red with abundant bloom. Fruit is sweet and palatable weeks before fully ripe.

FREDONIA (Black). The earliest good black grape, ripening about three weeks before most varieties. Clusters of medium size and compact; the berries large, with firm tender flesh of very good quality.

POR LAN (White). This is the earliest of all Grape large in bunch and berry; flesh sweet, juicy and of fine color. Hardy, vigorous, productive.

SHERIDAN (Black). Probably the most valuable grape sent out by the New York Experiment Station, as it is expected to replace Concord, which it surpasses in many regions. Large in bunch and berry; keeps and ships well. Good quality

Price of above 4 varieties, 2 yr. No. 1., 60c each; 3 for $1.50; 10 for $4.50.

---

100 Strawberry Plants, $1.75

Special Offer No. 106S. A Strawberry collection, 100 fine strong plants (spring delivery only) in four good sorts, our selection, postpaid, for $1.75.

Strong Field Grown Plants, Shipped from Early Spring up to May 15

STANDARD VARIETIES

SENATOR DUNLAP. Midseason. The fruit is dark red with glossy finish. The meat is a bright red all through and exceedingly juicy. It succeeds everywhere and with everybody—the beginner as well as the veteran grower.

PRICE, on the above varieties, 25 for 75c; 50 for $1.10; 100 for $1.65, postpaid to 4th zone; 250 for $3.20; 500 for $5.00; 1000 for $8.00 by express at buyer's expense.

CATSKILL. Midseason. Produces large crops of big scarlet berries of fine flavor.

CLERMONT. An unusually fine flavored berry, producing large crops of firm large fruit.

DORSETT. Early. Will undoubtedly be a leader among early, heavy cropping varieties.

FAIRFAX. Medium early. Rich in flavor, uniformly large fruit in abundance.

PREMIER. Early. Berries are. large, beautifully formed, red through and through; flavor delicious. A splendid shipper.

PRICE, on the above varieties, 25 for 95c; 50 for $1.55; 100 for $2.50, postpaid to 4th zone; 250 for $5.00; 500 for $7.80; 1000 for $12.50, by express at buyer's expense.

EVERBEARING VARIETIES

'GEM. A good medium size, heavier producing everbearing berry. Fine quality and firm everbearer. Produces during late summer months large size berries of fine appearance and flavor.

MASTODON. Most widely planted everbearer.

PRICE, on the above varieties, 25 for $1.35; 50 for $2.25; 100 for $3.60, postpaid to 4th zone; 250 for $7.50; 500 for $12.00; 1000 for $18.00, by express at buyer's expense.

SMALL FRUITS

All Prices F.O.B. Western Springs, Ill. (If wanted by mail, add 10c per 10, 15c per 25 or 25c per 50 for postage and packing.)

BLACKBERRIES—Price, 3 for 75c; 10 for $2.00; 25 for $4.50; 50 for $7.50.

Alfred. Mammoth, jet black berries, almost coreless.

Eldorado. Enormous yielder of large berries.

BOYSENBERRY (Thornless). Sensational new fruit. Huge berries of rich purplish maroon. Very sweet; delicious flavor; few seeds. Price, 3 for 75c; 10 for $1.80; 25 for $6.60.

RASPBERRIES—Price, except where noted, 3 for 75c; 10 for $2.00; 25 for $4.50; 50 for $7.50.

Cumberland (Black). Extra large, oval, rich and juicy. Good quality; very productive.

Indian Summer—The Best Everbearing Red Raspberry. Large berries of high quality ripen early and then produce a second crop in Sept. and Oct. Price, 3 for 90c; 10, $2.25; 25, $5.00.

New Logan (Black). Heavy yielder; early.

Latham (Red). The most widely planted Red Raspberry. Berries are immense, dark red in color and well flavored. Extremely hardy.

Morrison (New Black). An extra large berry of high quality; not as seedy as most blackcaps Price, 3 for 90c; 10, $2.25; 25, $5.00.

Sodus (New Purple). Very heavy yielder of fine berries for home use. Large fruit; distinct flavor. Price, 3 for 90c; 10, $2.25; 25, $5.00.

Sunrise (New Red). Extra early variety of large size and fine flavor. Very hardy and disease resistant. Price, 3 for 90c; 10 for $2.25; 25 for $5.00; 50 for $9.00.

RHUBARB—See page 76 for Varieties and Prices

GRAPES—Price, each, 50c; 3 for $1.35; 10 for $4.00.

Catawba (Red). Large bunches of coppery-red fruit. Late bearing; excellent for grape juice.

Concord (Black). The most popular grape in America. Large, handsome bunches of large, luscious berries; juicy, sweet and tender. Very hardy and productive.

Niagara (White). Large, handsome, very sweet.

Newest Improved Spray

Add Postage According to Weight and Zone (Page 8).   Shipping w

ACME RED RIVER POTATO MIX (Special Formula for Potatoes). A new patented copper fungicide with quick-killing arsenic. Drives off Flea Beetle and Leafhopper and prevents Blight from gaining a foothold. Stimulates foliage, making more and better potatoes. Complete control in one operation. Can be used as a dust or spray. Ceiling prices, 1 lb. bag, 35c; 4 lb. bag, 85c.

ACME WETTABLE DUSTING SULPHUR. An improved dusting sulphur recommended to control Mildew, Leaf Spot, Black Spot, and Rust on rose bushes, chrysanthemums, snapdragons and other foliage, also Red Spiders on Evergreens. Will control chiggers in the lawn. Ceiling prices, 2 lb. Shaker top package; 35c; 4 lb. bag, 60c.

ACME COPPER QUEEN. A strong liquid copper spray for control of mildew, leaf spot, and black spot on roses, flowers, and plants. Ceiling prices. 8-oz. can, 35c; pt., 60c; qt., 95c; gal., $2.25.

ACME COPPER SHIELD PRUNING PAINT. Prepared liquid paint containing copper, for treating wounds to prevent hard rot fungus and other fungi. Ceiling prices, pt., 45c; qt., 75c; gal., $2.35.

ACME GARDEN GUARD. A strong, safe rotenone dust in 1-lb. shaker top cans. Ceiling price, each, 40c; postpaid, 50c. 6 lb. Pkg., $1.10.

ACME SCIENTIFIC ROSE SPRAY. Consists of three elements A. B. C. for complete protection from sucking and chewing insects, black spot and other fungus diseases. The number indicates number of gallons of spray each set will make. Ceiling prices, No. 3 set, 95c; No. 6 set, $1.50; No. 24 set, $4.00; No. 48 set, $6.00; No. 96-set, $9.75.

ACME STOP. A tree-banding compound which prevents insects from crawling up trees. Ceiling prices, 6-oz. can, 35c; 1 lb., 65c; 5 lbs., $3.00; 10 lbs., $5.00.

ANTROL. Sets containing 4 jars and 4-oz. bottle of syrup. Ceiling price, 60c; extra jars each, 10c. 4-oz. bottle syrup, 25c. Pint bottle of syrup, 50c; gal., $2.75.

ANTROL ANT POWDER. Kills ants, roaches, silverfish and other pests. Packed in handy shaker twist-top can. Ceiling price, 4½-oz. can, 25c.

ANTROL ANT TRAPS. Kill both sweet and grease eating ants. Ceiling prices, each; 10c; 6 for 50c.

ANTROL READY FILLED SETS. Consisting of four patented glass "feeders" filled with regular antrol syrup. Ceiling price, per set, 40c.

APEX ANT KILLER. Thallium sulphate kills ants in their nests. Ceiling price, each, 25c; 5 for $1.00.

APHIS SPRAY. Improved Nicotine Spray. Combining a soft fish-oil soap with black leaf 40. Ceiling prices, per 3-oz. tube, 35c; 12-oz. tube, $1.00.

ARSENATE OF LEAD (Dry). For dusting and spraying. Solves the problem of controlling practically all leaf-eating insects in an efficient manner. Ceiling prices, 1 lb. carton, 35c; 4 lbs., 95c; case of 24 lbs., $4.85; 100 lbs., $16.00.

BLACK ARROW DUST. A non-poisonous pyrethrum dust, effective against many insects. Ceiling prices 2 lb., bag 50c.

BLACK LEAF 40 is a solution of Nicotine Sulphate. It is highly recommended by Experiment Stations throughout the United States as a spray for soft bodied sucking insects. For spraying only. Directions must be followed carefully. Ceiling prices, 1-oz. bottle, 36c; 5-oz. can, $1.05, makes 40 to 100 gallons; 1-lb. bottle, $2.50, makes 40 to 200 gallons; 2-lb. can, $3.70, makes 200 to 500 gallons; 5-lb. can, $6.90, makes 400 to 1000 gallons; 10-lb. can, $11.65, makes 840 to 2100 gallons.

BORDEAUX MIXTURE (Dry). The best fungicide for curing and preventing black rot, mildew, blight, leaf curl, scab or other fungoid diseases on fruits and plants. 1 lb. will make 5 gallons liquid. Ceiling prices, lb., 35c; 4 lbs., 95c; case of 24 lbs., $4.85.

BUG GUN. A practical self-dusting package, consisting of Rotenone, all ready to use. Complete with dust. Ceiling prices, each, 35c, postpaid, 50c.

CALCIUM, ARSENATE (Dry). Ceiling prices, lb., 35c; 4 lbs., 85c.

CARBON DISULPHIDE. For ants and cut worms. (By express only.) Ceiling prices, 1 lb., 60c; ¼ lb., 30c.

CYANOGAS CALCIUM CYANIDE "G." Greenhouse fumigant. For aphis, white fly, thrips, soft scale, and mealy bug and control for crop-destroying insects. Ceiling prices, 5 lbs., $3.00; 25 lbs., $10.00; 100 lbs., $30.00. (By express only.) Write for leaflet.

CYANOGAS-A DUST. Kills ants, moles, mice, rats, groundhogs and prairie dogs. (By express only.) Ceiling prices, 4-oz. tin, 30c; ½ lb., 45c; 1 lb., 75c; 5 lbs., $3.00; 25 lbs., $10.00; 100 lbs., $30.00.

DENDROL. A dormant spray oil. Ceiling price, $1.25; 5-gal. drum, $5.00; 13-gal. drum, $9.00.

DOG-SHOO. Keeps dogs and cats away from evergreens, shrubs, posts, walls or any place where they are not wanted. Leaves an odor scarcely noticeable by humans but very offensive to animals. Ceiling prices, qt., 85c; gal., $1.95.

ROTOTEC

The ideal Victory Garden Spray. Contains full amount of Rotenone necessary for good insect control. The toxic principles of Rotenone bearing roots are carefully extracted and dissolved in the mild vegetable type oil that protects and amplifies the effectiveness of the Rotenone. Safe to use on practically all vegetables. Can be used in combination with other insecticides and fungicides. Particularly effective in the control of many types of beetles such as, Mexican Bean Beetle, and Potato Flea Beetle, Cabbage Worms, Plant Lice, Aphids and Thrip, etc. Ceiling price, 4-oz. bottle, $1.00; pint, $2.75. Ounce makes 4 to 6 gallons spraying solution.

DOGZOFF. Breaks dogs of bad habits. Spray underneath your evergreens, and guard them completely against the depredation of dogs. Non-poisonous. Ceiling price, per bottle, 60c; by mail, 70c.

DRY LIME SULPHUR. For dormant spray use 12 to 15 lbs. to each 50 gals. of water. For summer spray, 3 to 4 lbs. to each 50 gals. of water. Ceiling prices, lb., 35c; 5-lbs., $1.50; 25 lbs., $4.50; 100 lbs., $12.50.

DX PYRETHRUM. Liquid spray. Ceiling prices, 1½ oz. bottle, 35c; 1½ quint bottle, $1.25.

FISH-OIL SOAP. Standard wash for trees and plants where insects and eggs affect the bark. Ceiling prices, lb., 35c; 5 lbs., $1.50; 10 lbs., $2.50.

FLOWERS OF SULPHUR. For dusting. Ceiling prices, lb., 15c; 10 lbs., $1.00; 50 lbs., $3.00; 100 lbs., $5.50.

FORMACIDE FORMALDEHYDE DUST. Control "damping off" of flower and vegetable seedlings. Ceiling prices, 1 lb., 85c; 5 lbs., $2.50; 25-lbs., $10.00; 50 lbs., $12.50.

FUNGINE. New remedy for mildew, rust and other fungus diseases; for greenhouse and outdoor use. Ceiling prices, pt., 65c; qt., $1.10; gal., $3.00.

FUNGTROGEN. A preventive and remedy for mildew, black spot, and many fungus diseases of roses and other plants. Ceiling prices, ½ pt., 75c; pt., $1.25; qt., $2.00; gal., $6.00.

GRAPE AND ROSE DUST. Excellent for the prevention and destruction of mildew on plants. Ceiling prices, lb., 35c; 5 lbs., $1.25; 25 lbs., $6.25.

KALITE. Rotenone impregnated dust for Victory Gardens. Ceiling prices, 1-lb. pkg., 35c; 4 lb. bag, $1.00; 25 lb. bag, $3.75.

KRYOCIDE. Can be used as a spray or dust, highly effective in controlling many chewing insects. Ceiling price, 1 lb., 35c.

KRYOCIDE D50 with sulphur. A combination insecticide and fungicide for chewing insects. Contains natural cryolite. Ceiling price, 1 lb., 50c; 3 lbs., 85c.

LEMON OIL. Destroys mealy bug, scale, red spider. Ceiling prices, ½ pt., 35c; pt., 60c; qt., $1.00; ½ gal., $1.75; gal., $3.00, 5 gals., $12.00.

LIME SULPHUR. (Solution.) The best remedy for San Jose scale. One gallon makes twelve. Ceiling prices, per qt. can, 50c; 1 gal., $1.35; 5-gal. can, $4.50. Write for prices in barrel lots.

MAGNETIC SPRAY Wettable Sulphur. Can be used as a combination spray with other insecticides. Ceiling prices, 4-lb. bag, 60c; 24 lbs., $2.75.

NAPTHALENE FLAKES. Ceiling prices, 1 lb., 40c; 5 lbs., $1.50; 10 lbs., $2.75; 25 lbs., $6.25; 100 lbs., $22.00.

NEW EVERGREEN SPRAY. Non-poisonous insecticide. No spreader required; retains its strength. Ceiling prices, oz. bottle, 35c; 6-oz. bottle, $1.00; 16-oz. bottle, $2.40; gal., $12.20.

NICO-FUME POWDER FUMIGATOR. Lights quickly, burns evenly and will not go out. No waste; every particle is consumed. It retains its strength indefinitely. Ceiling prices, 5-lb. tin, $4.25; 10-lb. tin, $7.35.

NICO-FUME POWDER PRESSURE FUMIGATOR. Is now burned under pressure in the can in which it is packed. Ceiling prices, ½-lb. can, 60c; doz. $6.00; 1-lb. can, $1.00; doz., $9.00.

NICO-FUME LIQUID. For fumigating or spraying; contains 40 per cent nicotine. Ceiling prices, 1 lb., $2.50; 4 lbs., $7.10; 8 lbs., $13.00.

NICOTINE PYROX. For chewing and sucking insects. Ceiling prices, 20 oz. jar, 60c; 5 lbs., $2.00.

NIKOTEEN. 30% grade. For spraying and fumigating. Ceiling prices, oz. bottle, 35c; ½ pt., $1.25; pt., $2.25; 5 pts., $6.00; original case, 10 pts., $18.50. 40% grade, 4 lbs., $7.10; 8 lbs., $13.00.

PARIS GREEN. A poisonous insecticide in powder form; for insects which chew. Ceiling prices, ¼ lb., 20c; per lb., 35c; 5 lbs., $2.50; 14 lbs., $6.00.

PENETROL. An activator for nicotine spraying solutions. Ceiling prices, qt., 85c; gal., $2.00; 5 gals., $7.50.

PINE TAR. For tree surgery. Stops bleeding of the sap. Ceiling prices, pint, 40c; qt., 75c; gal., $1.75.

POMO GREEN. Without nicotine. The new green fungicide for roses and other flowers and ornamentals; will control black spot, mildew and chewing insects. Ceiling prices, lb., 50c; 5 lbs., $1.75; 25 lbs., $8.00.

POMO GREEN. With nicotine. Ceiling prices, lb., 75c; 5 lbs., $3.00.

Sprayers and Dusters for Insecticides

WHEELBARROW SPRAYER

Ask for Prices on insecticide nozzles.

New Streamlined No. 60SG

Goes anywhere like a wheelbarrow, through narrow openings. For spray solutions, disinfectants or whitewash. With extra long handle and large air chamber, fittings, steel extension; develops 250 lbs. pressure with minimum of effort. Made of best materials, all working parts of brass or bronze. Cart is strong, all steel and cross braced. Tank holds 18 gallons. Fully equipped with hose, nozzle, etc. $27.50.
Shipping weight, 80 lbs.
No. 60 S.P.G. Same as above, but with pressure tank and gauge and iron wheel. Price, $41.50.

SINGLE CYLINDER BRASS BUCKET PUMP

SMITH STURDY NO. 82 BRASS BUCKET PUMP, develops high pressure on up and down stroke. A handy sprayer for spraying insecticides, whitewashing, etc. Price each $6.25.

Garden Hose Sprayer

WITH CRYSTAL CLEAR CARTRIDGE CHAMBER

AND

INSECTICIDE CARTRIDGES

A special mixing and spraying nozzle which attaches to your garden hose. Insert insecticide cartridge and spray—as easy as watering your lawn. Standard, each, $4.00.
36 inch extension, straight or angle, $1.75.
We can supply a complete line of cartridges, Rotenone, Nicotine, Pyrethrum, Sulphur, Bordo or Arsenate of Lead. Price, each, 35c; doz., $4.00.

PNEUMATIC SPRAYER

Compressed air hand sprayer. Operator sprays with one-half labor ordinary sprayer requires. Throws a fine mist and can be used to apply insecticides, etc. One quart size has extra nozzle for underleaf spraying. Galv. tank, $1.50; tin $1.25.

ARNOLD VICTORY SPRAYER, price each $1.00, postpaid $1.10. This sprayer will handle standard cartridges same as the Garden Hose Sprayer. Price of cartridges $.35 each, three for $1.00, dozen $3.60.
Write for Price on Power Sprayers.

DOBBIN'S BIGHEAD SPRAYER

5¾" diameter opening. Easy to fill, drain and clean Positive quick sealing device. Equipped with patented self-lubricating pressure seal valve plunger. More air per stroke. Brass shut-off with trigger quick spray lock. Universal nozzle, sprays at any angle. Will handle all spray solutions, 4 gallon capacity.
No. 44G Galvanized tank. Each $8.00.

HAND SPRAYER 60c
Full qt. size, Pint Size, ea., 35c.

SMITH'S SPECIAL SPRAYER

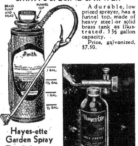

A durable, low priced sprayer, has a funnel top, made of heavy steel or solid brass tank as illustrated. 3½ gallon capacity.
Price, galvanized, $7.50.

Hayes-ette Garden Spray

This little sprayer does the work of the larger type sprayer. Weight a little over a pound filled. Simply attach to your garden hose. Operates on 20 to 150 lb. water pressure. Capacity 1½ gal. of mixed spray material. Can also be used for spraying shrubs and vines. $2.95.

Hayes Jr. Spray Gun

All Purpose Sprayer. Makes 3 gals. of mixed spray material at a time. Sprays liquid and most wettable powders, up, down and sideways. Attach to your garden hose. Gives you the efficient performance of heavy, expensive equipment. Operates on water pressure from 30 to 75 lbs. No moving parts to wear out or break. Each, $5.95.

NEW STREAMLINED HARCO SPRAYER

Get Penetrating Spray quickly, easily with this brand new, efficient, easy-to-use Harco sprayer. Harco, plus good liquid insecticide means quick, certain death to garden-blighting insects and destructive fungus pests. Harco's conveniently long extension rod sends a penetrating spray right where it is most needed for effective garden pest control. Each, $2.35.

Dusters and Blowers
The American Beauty Dust Sprayer

The most powerful hand duster made. Has a large, powerful bellows that throws dust to the top of twenty-five foot trees. A man will average eight acres per day on trees. Dusts truck crops at an average walking speed, and dusts under side of leaves. Has a spiral agitator that crushes and grinds the dust and feeds directly into the moving air blast; does not choke or clog. Has an efficient regulator for discharge control. It is considered the standard of efficiency by all authorities. Price, $25.00.

BLUE BEAUTY DUSTER

A fitting companion for the American Beauty Duster—each, $22.50.

CALIFORNIA LITTLE BEAUTY DUSTER

For those growers operating two to three acres of vegetables, grapes or berries—price, each, $10.00.

SUPERBUILT UNIVERSAL DUSTERS No. 200

A powerful duster for field, garden or orchard use. Gears contained in duster proof gear case run in oil—easy running. Powerful air blast breaks up powder into uniform size dust. Complete with attachments for dusting one or two rows, including return bends which are adjustable for forward or rear dusting.
No. 200, capacity 5 to 10 pounds, with return bends for dusting in rear of operator.........Each $15.00

CHALLENGE DUST GUN No. C3

For Dusting Rotenone, Pyrethrum Dust, etc. Adjustable to all conditions. Made so the discharge nozzle may be swung from front to rear of operator and can be raised or lowered for high or low plants. Operator can always work in upright comfortable position. Each, $19.80.

For Smaller Dusters, See Page 108

Dusters—Miscellaneous Garden Aids

FEENEY MODEL B DUSTER

Splendid Hand Duster. Each, $1.00. Postpaid, $1.10.

POWDER GUNS

CYCLONE Small size, 30c. Jumbo size, 50c. Postage, extra, each, 5c. JUMBO

DOBBIN'S IMPROVED HAND DUSTER

Recommended for applying Pyrethrum, Rotenone, Derris Root. A uniform discharge down to the last particle of dust. For all garden and field crops. Self-lubricating pressure seal valve plunger. Capacity 1 lb. equipped with two-way dust cap.
No. 432. Duster........Each $1.50. Postpaid, $1.75

CENTROBELLOW—V.
Powder Bellows

A handy bellows for victory gardens—easily filled by removing the nozzle; suitable for all garden powders. Price, 6 oz. capacity, each, $1.10, postpaid, $1.25; 12 oz. capacity, $1.35, postpaid, $1.50.

ACME TOMATO DUST PUMP GUN

Contains basic copper arsenate. The latest improvement in the insecticide field containing a safe arsenical for controling the tomato worm and the tomato fruit worm as well as the early and late blight and other fungus diseases which infest the tomato plant. Will not cause worm wilt. A full pound in a pump gun duster package ready to use. 89c each.

ROTENONE GARDEN GUARD PUMP GUN

The old proven Rotenone insecticide which controls both sucking and eating insects. A full pound in a pump gun duster ready to use. 59c each.

ACME BAIT-M
(With Metaldehyde)

A double action insect bait. Proven for years, to control Cut Worms, Sow Bugs, Grasshoppers and Earwigs. Also contains the marvelous new ingredient Metaldehyde which is so effective in destroying Slugs and Snails. Packed in new modern packages equipped with special pour-out spouts. 1 lb. cartons, 25c; 2½ lb. cartons, 50c; 10 lb. bag, $1.75.

Victory Garden Rabbit Repellent

With safety to all including the rabbits. This 200 mesh fine snuff-like product is impregnated with rain resistant repelling "naturals" so that an application should last several weeks. 5 lb. package will treat 100 to 150 individual plants or 200 to 250 running feet of plant row. Price 1 lb. pkg. 45c, 5 lb. bag $1.75.

HAVAHART ANIMAL TRAPS

No. 1—5x5x18 in. For weasles, rats and chipmunks, each $2.50.
No. 2—7x7x24 in. For muskrats, minks, squirrels and rabbits, each $3.50.

Rodent Rockets

DESTROY GOPHERS & MOLES

...THE EASY WAY

Novel, effective destroyers; strike like a match and blitz out whole families of gophers, moles, rats, field mice, ants, etc., at one "shot". Safe, sure, efficient aids to hunters in "un-treeing" holed-up woodchucks, raccoons, etc. 3 for 25c; dozen, 95c.

Chaperone Powder Dog Repellent

A new household dog repellent for keeping dogs off rugs and furniture. Odorless to humans and does not stain, but is very repulsive to dogs. ⅓ oz., tin, 25c; large size, $1.00.

Chaperone Liquid Dog Repellent

For 'outdoor' and garden use. Keeps dogs away longer from trees, shrubs and plants than most liquid repellents. 4 oz., bottle 50c; 12 oz., can, $1.00.

PUSSY SCAT

Powder repellent for household use keeps cats away from furniture, curtains, drapes, clothing, etc. Trial size can 25c; large size can, $1.00. Postpaid, $1.10.

U-MIX-IT

Pulverized Asphalt—A new, low-cost, water-proof compound. Has a multitude of uses. No waste; you mix it as you need it. Can be used for tree surgery, roofing, cellar windows and walls, cracks in concrete in fish pools; a handy material for sealing cracks in tanks, dams, silos etc. You can make your own water-proof plastic putty with U-Mix-It. One gallon costs about 25c and will putty 300 lineal feet of glass ¼" x ¾". Packaged in 1-lb. boxes at 25c; 5 lbs. for 75c; 15 lbs. for $1.50; and 100 lbs. for $8.00.

SEAL-A-SEME

A specially prepared material for repairing leaky metal containers such as cans, vases, buckets, etc.; easily applied; brine proof. 1 lb. can, $1.00; 5 lbs., $3.50.

HOTKAPS

These plant protectors mean larger, earlier, premium crops.

Protects plants from frost and other elements, matures crops earlier, keeps insects out, keeps soil soft. They are made of a specially prepared waxed paper and are cone-like in shape, measuring about 11 inches in diameter at the base and coming to a point at the top. When placed over the plants and held firmly in place by the soil around them, Hotkaps become individual miniature hothouses.

Hotkap Setter. Will prove very helpful. This is a small steel cone, the exact shape of the Hotkap itself, with a handle at the top. The cost of the Hotkap setter is nominal and it can be used a lifetime.

Prices: 1,000 lots, $11.00; 5,000 lots, $10.75 per M; 10,000 lots, $10.50 per M; 250 Trial Package including Fibreboard Setter with Tamper, $3.50; 100 Home Package, including Fibreboard Setter with Tamper, $1.95. Wt.: 1,000 package HOTKAPS, 28 lbs.; 250 package, 9 lbs.; 100 package, 5 lbs.; Fibre-board Hotkap Setter, 3 lbs.; Fibreboard Setter alone, 25c.

SPECIAL VICTORY GARDEN PACKAGES HOTKAPS

Including setter. Package of 25 Hotkaps and cardboard fibreboard setter, 50c, postpaid 63c; package of 100, including fibreboard setter, $1.95, postpaid, $2.25.

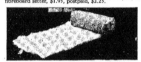

Glass Wool Mulch.

Protection and perfect mulch for your prized Plants and Shrubs; has been proved superior to all other mulches for the winter protection of plants. A snowy white blanket composed of extremely fine glass fibres; put up in bats; 24" x 96" in size and approximately 1½ inches thick at 1¾ lbs. per cubic foot density. Price, bat, 98c; three for $2.65; carton of 12, $8.95.

CAMCOX CREMEGLOVE

Protects hands from oils, paints, grease, grime, and dirt —a protection for your hands in the garden, housework, etc., gives you the freedom of bare hands with the protection gloves afford. Price, 8 oz. jar, 35c; postpaid, 45c; 16 oz. jar, 60c; postpaid, 75c.

handoo
PROTECTIVE, LIQUID

FILM GLOVE

The new amazing lotion, greaseless, non-alcholic, to protect your hands in the garden; for housework, factory, garage, etc. Apply liberally on hands and nails, allow to dry for an invisible stain; washes off with soap and water. Price, 3 oz. bottle, 46c; 8 oz., 80c; 16 oz., $1.40.

ant Stakes, Supports, Labels and Boxes

Adjusto Plant Support

Has a unique self-locking adjustable feature causing the hoop to positively stay where put, yet it can be instantly adjusted to any height desired. The heavy green painted wood stake ⅝ inch square will stand firmly in the ground. The hoop is of 8 gauge galvanized wire, 13 inches in diameter, and may be opened up to put around large plants. 3 ft.; doz., $3.00; 4 ft., doz., $3.50; 5 ft., doz., $3.85;-extra wire hoops, doz., $1.65.

UTILITY VICTORY GARDEN STAKE

VICTORY GARDEN
UTILITY STAKE

MADE OF RUGGED HARDWOOD PAINTED GREEN

Clothes line size hole

A sturdy hard wood stake 3 ft. long, over 1" diameter with pointed end. Has 2 holes to support rows of white ordinary clothes line or wire over ¼" diameter. Handy for circling trees and ornamental shrubs to repel dogs and prevent trespassing. Painted green to harmonize with lawn and garden. Can be used as a plant stake and can also be used on newly seeded lawns and flower beds. Price, per pkg. of 4, 60c; 3 pkgs. for $1.75.

JUMBO SIX FT.—3 TIE DAHLIA STAKE

For Dahlias, Gladiolas, Young Fruit Trees, Vines, Pole Beans, Giant Peas, and a score of other needs. Purposely made for any Garden purpose. Made of rugged hardwood with 3 (¼") holes to regulate respective heights of tall growing flowers, vegetables, plants and shrubs. Price, per doz., $3.60; 3 doz. $10.50.

TWISTEMS
Perfect Plant Ties

Made in two utility sizes, 7 in. and 16 in., put up 250 to a bundle. A very handy tie for tomatoes and other vegetable plants. Just a single twist of the wrist and the plant is tied. Price 7 in. per bundle of 250, 50c; 16 in. per bundle of 250, $1.00.

STAKES—HEAVY TONKIN Natural Color

Heavy weight bamboo, entire stake same weight; not taper. Ideal for roses, dahlias, young trees, etc. Will last a lifetime. F.O.B. N. Y. F.O.B. Chicago.

Length	Diameter	Doz.	100	Doz.	100
2 ft.	¼ to ⅜ inch	$1.40	$7.50	$1.50	$8.50
3 ft.	⅜ inch	1.65	9.25	1.85	9.50
4 ft.	¼ to ½ inch	2.00	10.25	2.25	11.00
5 ft.	¼ to ½ inch	2.25	12.00	2.45	12.50
6 ft.	½ to ⅝ inch	1.30	13.30	2.73	14.50

STAKES, WOODEN. Painted green.

Heavy Grade (for Dahlias)

	Per doz.	Per 100
3 ft.	$1.60	$10.50
4 ft.	1.95	13.50
5 ft.	2.50	16.50
6 ft.	2.95	20.50

Light Grade (for smaller plants)

	Per doz.	100		Per doz.	100
2½ ft.	$0.40	$2.20	3½ ft.	$1.25	$ 8.75
3 ft.	.60	3.65	4 ft.	1.60	10.50
3½ ft.	.95	4.95	5 ft.	2.25	13.95
	1.10	6.95			

STAKES—BAMBOO Painted Green.

	100	1000		100	1000
2 ft.	$1.25	$5.00	3 ft.	$1.75	$ 9.50
2½ ft.	1.40	7.00	3½ ft.	2.00	11.00
2 ft.	1.60	8.00	4 ft.	2.25	12.50
Bamboo not painted, 6 ft.				2.95	26.50

STAKES—Galvanized Wire.

	100	1000		100	1000
No. 9 Wire			No. 8 Wire		
2½ ft.	$0.40	$1.40	3½ ft.	$0.75	$2.85
3 ft.	.45	1.75	6 ft.	1.25	4.75
4 ft.	.50	2.25			

WAYWARD VINE GUIDE AND SUPPORT

PATENTED

For Training and Supporting Ivy, Small Fruiting Trees and all other Vines, etc. on Brick, Stucco, Stone and Cement Walls without Defacing. No Nails—No Holes. Price, box of 25, including cement, $1.00; postpaid, $1.10.

LABELS

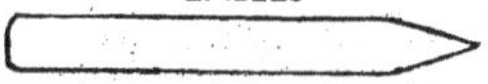

Wooden. For pots, painted.

	100	1000		100	1000
4-inch	$0.45	$7.25	12-inch	$4.60	$12.95
6-inch	.60	3.50			

Tree, Labels Wired. 3 ½ in. 100, 60c; 1000, $3.50.

LABELS. Zinc, Tree. Wired 3 ¾ inches long, ⅞ inch wide. Price per doz., 30c; 100, $1.95.

Simplex Weatherproof Plant Labels. White celluloid with transparent cover of genuine mica, including copper wires for attaching. No. 1, 3 x ½ inches. Doz., 50c; 100, $3.00.

A New Weatherproof
METAL PLANT MARKER

USE A PENCIL • No fade-out of your markings

Beauty, Strength, Permanence. Made of metal; green baked enamel finish.

Slip-over fool-proof metal cap with non-shatterable transparent window.

Stake 1" long; ample white marking space 2 ½" x 1⅛"

12 markers	$1.00
25 markers	2.00
50 markers	3.75
100 markers	7.00

Rose-Los Angeles

No. 31 SIMPLEX Green Weather-Proof Plant Labels. Price includes copper wires for attaching and steel stylus for marking. No. 31, size 3 x ½ inch, per doz., 40c; per 100, $2.50.

Copper. Indestructible. Tree and shrubbery, copper wired. Small, 30c doz.; 100, $1.95; large, 40c doz.; 100 for $2.65.

"GARDEN CHIEF MARKER"

Treated with a preservative that protects against decay.

Undercut groove contains white chemically treated waterproof name card, covered by a dirt-proof transparent window. Just use ordinary pencil, and the name will remain for years.

12-inch size, doz., 50c; 3 doz., $1.35.
18-inch size, doz., 65c; 3 doz., $1.75.

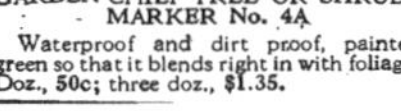

GARDEN CHIEF TREE OR SHRUBS MARKER No. 4A

Waterproof and dirt proof, painted green so that it blends right in with foliage. Doz., 50c; three doz., $1.35.

PERMA LABEL
(New Improved Type)

Made of Sorex. Since metal labels cannot be had any more, this is a very good substitute. This label should last at least a few seasons. It can be tied around a branch or shrub and tied with one loop. Ordinary pencil marking will not wash off. Price, per 100; 500 for $2.50; 1000 for $4.50.

EVERLASTING LEAD PERMANENT LABELS

Same as illustrated above. These labels do not have hole. They can be tied around twig or limb with one loop. Made of soft lead should last permanently. Price, per 100, $1.25; 500 for $5.50.

GARDEN LINE REEL. (Weight, 2 lbs.) Each, $1.65.
GARDEN LINE. Each heavy braided. Per 90 feet, $1.10; by mail, $1.20.
GRAFTING WAX. Per ¼ lb. bar, 25c; ½ lb. bar, 40c; 1 lb. bar, 65c.

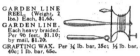

CANNING LABELS

LABELS
MARKING CANNING PRESERVING

No. 72—General. Size 5 in. x 5 in. Printed green cover with red lettering. Contains ready printed labels. 10 each of 20 popular home-canned fruits and vegetables and 20 blank, fancy border labels, total 220 labels. Size 2-5/16 in. x 1 in. Printed in red on white gummed paper, perforations between labels. A place for date of canning provided on each label. Book of 220 labels 10c.

LABELS
MARKING CANNING PRESERVING

No. 73—Cosmopolitan. Size 5 in. x 5 in. Printed red cover with green lettering contains 220 blank, fancy border decorative labels with ample writing space for those who wish to make up their own canning labels. Designed to give a uniform appearance to canning shelves. Label size 2-5/16 in. x 1 in. Printed on red on white gummed paper, perforations between labels. Packed 3 doz. to box. Weight 3-¾ lbs. Book of 220 labels 10c.

BOXES

BOXES—Cut Flower.—Vaughan's "White" Grade, green lined, moisture-proof board. Very popular. Packed 25 complete boxes per bundle.

Size, Inches	Weight Per 100	Size, Inches	Weight Per 100
3 x21x5	45 lb.	$12.00	3½x30x5	75 lb.	$15.50
3⅓x24x5	60 lb.	14.00	4 x24x8	85 lb.	18.50
5 x36x8	135 lb.	27.50	5 x28x8	105 lb.	21.50
5 x42x8	170 lb.	28.00			

Hormones, Inoculators and Test Kits

ROOTONE

A hormone powder easy to use, anyone can apply safely, no skill is needed to apply Rootone, no measurements, no vials, no elaborate charts to follow, just dip and plant. Price, ¼ oz. pkg., 25c; 2 oz. jar, enough to treat 3,000 cuttings, $1.00; 1 lb. jar will treat up to 30,000 cuttings, $5.00.

Rootone No. 10

1 lb. can, $10.00. Write for leaflet; all postpaid.

HORMODIN ROOT FORMING CHEMICAL

Hormodin is a hormone-like plant growth substance. Its principal use is to stimulate rapid root growth on cuttings. Makes it possible for growers to reproduce plants from cuttings with high percentages of successful results. 240 unit size, $2.50; 480 unit size, $4.50; 960 unit size, $8.00.

HORMODIN POWDERS

POWDER NO. 1: Designed primarily for use on Carnations, Chrysanthemums, Poinsettias, Roses, and similar types. Many house, garden, and greenhouse plants are included in the complete list. Price, 1¾ oz. pkg., each, 50c; 1 lb., $3.00.

POWDER NO. 2. Designed for use on less sensitive species, which comprise many of the semi-woody types and many of the common shrubs. Price, 1¾ oz., 75c; 1 lb., $4.50.

POWDER NO. 3. Designed for use with the more resistant species which comprise most of the evergreens and dormant leafless cuttings. Price, 1 oz., $1.00; ½ lb., $4.50.

The three Hormodin Powders are designed to cover the full propagating range with a one-dip treatment. Complete directions for each powder are included with the package.

Combination package of No. 1-2-3 in one carton, each, 75c.

FRUITONE

Hormone spray for preventing preharvest drop of apples. Holds apples on the tree longer. Fruitone sprays on flowers produce better set of seed and fruit, such as tomatoes, and beans. 2/5 oz. pkg. 25c; 2 oz. can, $1.00, makes 25 gals. of spray; 12 oz. can, $5.00, makes 150 gals. of spray.

TRANSPLANTONE

The most effective form of vitamin B_1, contains plant hormone: Vitamins B and C and other growth substances: One level teaspoon makes 10 gallons of solution, water your plants with Transplantone to get better roots, more vigorous growth and quality flowers. ½ oz., pkt., 25c; 3 ounce can, $1.00; 1 lb. can, $4.00.

Zoom B-1

The only liquid vitamin B-1 plant growth stimulant with added chemicals to keep its strength indefinitely. 2-oz. dropper top bottle, enough to make 250 gallons of solution. Price, $1.00.

GRAIN-O

Bigger yield at amazing low cost. Just dust Graino powder on all your garden and field seed. It inoculates it with hormones and vitamins; makes bigger rooted, drouth resistant plants; encourages healthier growth, increases yield. For corn, costs only ½c to 4c an acre. Packet sufficient for average garden, 25c. Popular 20-in-one size for market garden and small farm, contains 20 individual treatment packets, $1.00; pound size, $3.00.

BACTO

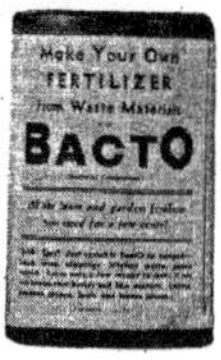

Make your own fertilizer, easy, quick—often in little as three weeks. Just sprinkle Bacto on kitchen waste, leaves, garden rubbish, sewage sludge, etc. 5 lb. bag makes up to a ton of rich, soil-building organic humus, better than manure. Sprinkle in outdoor toilets, reduces odors, makes easily-handled ash of waste. 5 lb. bag, $1.65; 25 lbs., $5.25; trial 4 oz. carton, 35c.

THE SUDBURY HOME GARDENER SOIL TEST KIT

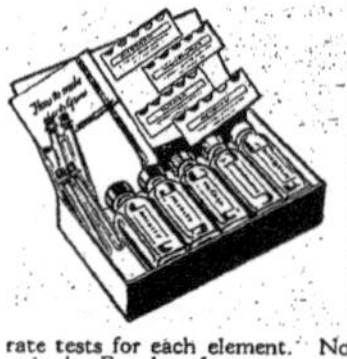

This simple, practical, easy-to-use kit is your best insurance of garden success. Made by the maker of professional field kits used by nurserymen, growers and greenkeepers throughout the country. Tests nitrogen, phosphorus, potash and acidity. It will make at least three separate tests for each element. No technical skill required. Results of tests are apparent immediately. The Sudbury Home Gardener's Soil Test Kit, complete with instructions and data on plant needs, $2

Testing Fluid for Refill—Specify whether for nitrogen, phosphorus, potash, or acidity. When ordering the above, it requires No. 2 and No. 3 to make Nitrogen Tests, No. 4 and No. 5 for Phosphorus Tests, No. 6 and No. 7 to make Potash Tests, therefore when ordering, please order two numbers as tests cannot be made unless they are used in combination as specified above. 2 oz., 75c; 6 oz., $1.50.

NEW CLUB MODEL KIT

(Suitable Gift Suggestion)

An inexspensive kit for garden clubs, 4-H clubs, etc. A very good value for amateurs. Cased in attractive imitation leather, makes a wonderful gift. Each, $4.75.

FLORALIFE

Makes your cut flowers live longer. Pkt. to make 1 qt. solution, each 10c, three pkts. for 25c. Home size tin makes 30 qts., each $1.00; 100 qt. size, each, $3.00; gift pkg., $1.00.

MACKWIN, LIQUID VITAMIN B1

One-half oz. bottle makes 120 gallons solution. E 35c, postpaid, 40c; 2 oz. bottle, $1.00. Vitamin Crystals, hundred milligram bottle makes 2000 gall each, $1.00.

BASKET-MAKING MATERIALS

Add postage to your order if to go by mail.

The Raffia which we import is the finest grade to be obtained. Besides the natural shade, we have it in 12 different colors: dark red, Irish-green, olive-green, pea-green, navy-blue, seal-brown, orange, black, old gold, pink, purple, and bright red.

Raffia Fibre for Baskets, Etc.

	Bunch	Lb.	5-lb. Lots Per Lb.
Natural, Best Grade, about 2 oz.	$0.20	$0.95	$0.90
Colored, about 1 oz.	.20	1.30	1.25

Reeds White Prime the Best Quality

Nos. 1 to 7 are the common sizes, 6 and 7 being used for the coarser work.

	½-lb.	Lb.	5-lb. Lots, Per Lb.
No. 1	$0.65	$1.10	$1.00
No. 2	.60	1.15	.95
No. 3	.55	.95	.90
No. 4	.50	.85	.80
No. 5	.45	.80	.75
No. 6	.40	.75	.70
No. 7	.37	.70	.65
Flat Reed, ⅜-inch	.45	.80	.75
Split Reed, No. 6	.45	.80	.75

All numbers above per bunch, 20c.

GLAZING MATERIALS

GARLANITE. The original white glazing compound, remains soft and pliable, easy to apply and remove. Gal., $2.85; safety model, glazing gun, $4.95.

PUTTY. Twemlow's Old English. Semi-liquid. Same as Mastica. Per gallon, $2.95.

PUTTY KNIFE. Each, 35c.

Flower Pots and Tubs

POTS (Flower)

F. O. B. Chicago. Write for New York Prices.

RED CLAY POTS. We pack these carefully, but will not be responsible for breakage.

	Doz.	100		Doz.	100	Each
2 in.	$0.40	$1.60	6 in.	$1.40	$ 8.50	....
2½ in.	.45	1.85	7 in.	1.85	13.00	....
3 in.	.55	2.75	8 in.	2.50	18.00	....
4 in.	.75	3.30	10 in.	...	....	$0.65
5 in.	.95	6.10	12 in.	...	....	.95

GREEN NEPONSET PAPER POT. Especially adapted for growing.

	Doz.	100	1000
2½-inch	$0.35	$1.30	$ 9.50
3-inch	.40	1.60	10.75
4-inch	.50	2.10	14.50
5-inch	.75	2.65	22.00

POTS (Azalea, Cyclamen or Fern). ¾ size, in height of standard flower pot.

	Each	Doz.		Each	Doz.
6-in.	$0.20	$1.40	9-in.	$0.35	$3.60
7-in.	.25	1.85	10-in.	.65	....
8-in.	.30	2.50	12-in.	.95	....

BULB POTS. ½ size in height of standard flower pot.

	Each	Doz.		Each	Doz.
6-in.	$0.20	$1.40	8-in.	$0.30	$2.50
7-in.	.25	1.85	10-in.	.65	6.25

SAUCERS—Clay

	Doz.	100		Doz.	100
5-inch	$0.65	$4.40	9-inch	$2.20	$14.85
6-inch	.95	6.60	10-inch	3.20	....
7-inch	1.20	8.25	12-inch	4.65	....
8-inch	1.60	10.50			

SAUCERS—Green Rubber

Size A, 5-inch, takes up to 6-inch pot. Ea., 30c

Size B, 6⅝-inch, takes up to 8-inch pot. Ea., 50c.

Size C, 9¾-inch, takes up to 12-inch pot. Ea., 75c.

NEPONSET PAPER POTS (RED). Made of water-proof paper, light, clean and unbreakable.

	Doz.	100	1000
2 -in.	$0.18	$0.75	$ 4.50
2¼-in.	.20	.85	5.25
2½-in.	.23	1.00	5.75
3 -in.	.28	1.25	6.85
3½-in.	.35	1.45	8.00
4 -in.	.40	1.65	9.45
5 -in.	.45	2.35	13.75
6 -in.	.50	2.60	17.00

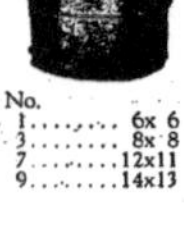

TUBS (Flower) Richmond. These are made of best seaso White Virginia Cedar, secu bound with welded wire ho Painted green with durable paint. Prices F. O. B. Chicag New York. If handles are requi add 45c per tub. First figure lowing number of tub gives di eter in inches at top of tub; sec figure, depth in inches.

No.		Each	No.		E
1	6x 6	$0.85	11	16x15	$
3	8x 8	.95	13	18x17	
7	12x11	1.75	14	19x18	
9	14x13	2.35			

Garden Hose, Sprinklers and Irrigators

WATER NON-KINKABLE HOSE

This is the finest grade of hose obtainable at this time. This is a two braid hose and is suitable for garden and greenhouse use. ¾ inch smooth cover. ¾ ft. lengths. Coupled, $14.95.

A Good Grade Garden Hose, ¾-inch, fitted with ¾-inch couplings, 50 feet length, $5.95.

MIST-IC Fanshaped Flat Spray

Made of plastic—light in weight and easy to handle, this slotted nozzle throws a perfect spray, and even fine fan-shaped flat spray that is just what gardeners want and need. Each, 50c; postpaid, 60c.

LINCOLN PARK OR BUTTERFLY

Cheapest and best sprinkler made. Each, 65c.
Mounted on stand: 2-foot, $1.75; 4-foot, $2.00; 6-foot, $2.35.

GARDEN CLUB PLASTIC ADJUSTABLE HOSE NOZZLE

Dark red finish. Adjustable for sprays, streams and shut-off, leak proof. It is a satisfactory wartime substitute standard brass nozzle. Each, 75c; postpaid, 85c.

PLASTIC CLINCHER HOSE COUPLING

Tight grip, will not leak, easily applied. Made with dark green plastic body. The heavily plated steel fingers grip the hose tightly and make a leak-proof connection. The couplings have large octagon shaped swivel. They are easily attached. Each, 40c; doz., $4.40.

PLASTIC CLINCHER HOSE MENDER

Price each, 15c; doz., $1.30.

SOIL SOAKER

Soil Soaker for deep soaking, the water method approved by agricultural colleges and nurseries, now available for home use. Equipped with regular hose connection for attaching to hose or pipe. No. 0, 12 ft., Price, $1.40; No. 1, 18 ft., $1.90; No. 2, 30 ft., $2.90; No. 3, 50 ft., $4.75.

FERTILIZER APPLICATOR
(Fertilizes as you Sprinkle)

Make fertilizing as easy as sprinkling your lawn. Fertilize through your hose. Mixes the right amount of ammonium sulphate; nitrate of soda; potash or any soluble fertilizer with the water with which you sprinkle your lawn. One end screws into the faucet, the other end takes the hose, the small tube drops into the bucket of fertilizer. Made of die cast metal. Price, $1.95; postpaid, $2.10.

WATER WAND

Watering shrubs, flowers and trees is a simple job with Water-wand; no danger of washing away the rich top soil. Each, $2.50.

VITAMIST FOR LAWN VIGOR

Vitamize as you sprinkle. No special nozzle or attachment necessary. Fits any garden hose or sprinkler. Just insert Vitamist cartridge in hose or sprinkler, turn on water, adjust nozzle to fine spray and sprinkle any part of lawn or garden. A cartridge requires about five or six minutes to dissolve. Packed 30 cartridges in a box. Thirty weeks supply for average lawn and garden. Price: $1.00 per box.

KNIVES

Budding. Aluminum handle. Each, $2.50; by mail, $2.60.
Budding and Prop. Two blades; white handle; brass caps. Each, $1.75; by mail, $1.85.
Propagating. "The Vaughan," best of all. Each, $1.75; by mail, $1.85.
Pruning. Stag handle. Each, $2.50; by mail, $2.60.

Potato Knife. "The Humphrey." Will cut to one or more eyes without injuring the vital tissues. Each; postpaid, 35c; 3 for $1.00.

CARBORUNDUM BRAND. Home and garden sharpening stone. For sharpening knives, shears, edgers, etc. 10¼ inches long over all. Fitted with a durable wood handle finished in red. Each, 85c; by mail, 95c.

KNEE PADS

All rubber cushion pads constructed of solid and sponge rubber with adjustable straps; fit any knee, will not slip down when walking. Price, $1.95; postpaid, $2.10.

Bird Houses and Feeders

AUTOMATIC BIRD FEEDERS
(Patented)

An economical feeder for all kinds of seeds, cracked corn or other small food.

If filled with sunflower seeds, it unfailingly attracts Cardinals rose-breasted Grosbeaks, Finches and many other large as well as small pretty birds all year around.

Birds enjoy swinging with the feeder. Each, $2.00; 3 for $5.75.

WREN HOUSE No. 16

This time-tested stepkut house is designed to meet the needs of birds, the steps help nestlings to reach the exit, bottom removable for cleaning. Price, stained brown, each, $1.50; white and green, each $1.75.
Blue Bird House No. 5 similar to the above, stained brown, $1.25.

MARTIN HOUSE No. X315

Twenty compartment house, two stories high, unpainted, $15.00. Painted two coats in white and green, $18.00. Twenty-eight compartment house, three stories high, unpainted, $18.00. Painted two coats white and green, $21.00. Crating charge $1.00 extra.

ROBIN ROOST No. 4

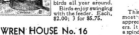

Robins will not occupy a nesting box, but insist on a covered sheltered shelf, which allows them to see on at least three sides. Stained brown — each $1.50; 3 for $4.25.

No. FS 21. Garden Craft Feeding Station

This is one of the most successful and appreciated bird feeders. It is equipped with a spindle for mounting, and the double weather vane keeps the sheltered end headed into the wind, thus keeping the food dry in rainy or snowy weather.
Size 24x12x12. Shipping weight 16 lbs.
Price stained brown $6.00
Price painted green and white 8.25
Price stained with glass back 8.25
Erection Post bored for mounting rod.....1.50

No. FS. 10. Garden Craft Bird Feeder

This cleverly constructed feeder will provide endless pleasure and satisfaction for bird lovers. You will be more than repaid for your generosity in providing food for your feathered friends during the early spring, late fall and winter, by their appreciation. Size 8x3x10 in. Shipping weight 3 lbs.
Price.....................$1.75
Erection pole with arm...............$1.25

Lawn Making Equipment

USE EROSIONET

For New Lawns, Weak Lawns, and Stubborn Terraces

Made of strong open mesh fabric, will hold your seed and sod firmly in place; prevents washouts, does not present an unsightly appearance, grass and clover soon rendering it almost invisible. Can be removed when grass becomes 2½ in. high. Width 45 inches. Price per yd., 12½c; 25 yd. lots, 11½c per yd.; 100 yd. lots, 10½c per yd.; rolls of 250 yds., 9½c per yd.

Flame Shooter Gun

General utility torch indispensable on the farm, garden, barn, etc., handy for cleaning out irrigation ditches, removing weed and destroying insect pests. 4 gal. heavy all-welded (not riveted or soldered) corrugated fuel and air tank tested to 100 lbs.; burns kerosene, range oil, stove or light furnace oil. Price complete, $18.95 (weight 17 lbs.).

ORNAMENTAL LAWN FANS

Most popular and inexpensive. Are most substantially built in natural wood finish.
No. 106—Height 72 in. Spread 42½. Price each, $2.00.
No. 108—Height 96 in. Spread 60 in. Price each, $2.65. (No. 106 may be shipped parcel post.)

Saxolin Duplex Crinkled Waterproof Tree Wrap

For covering the trunks of transplanted and newly set fruit and shade trees. Helps your stock to get off to a healthy start. Rolls, 4 inch wide, about 155 ft. to a roll. Weight, about 2½ lbs. Ea., 75c; doz., $7.20.

NEW HANDY SEEDER

This little handy seeder will sow seeds up to size of sweet peas, scatters seed individually, prevents crowding and choking of seedlings, eliminates guess 'work because you can see each seed drop, no matter how fine. Saves time because you can sow seeds twice as fast. Price each, 65c, postpaid.

MOSS

MOSS Sphagnum. Burlapped bales. Ea., $3.50.
SHEET MOSS (Green). Freshly gathered; for windows, boxes, etc. Per sack, $2.75.

HAMMOND WEED KILLER

One gallon will make forty gallons of solution. This is enough to treat about 2000 square feet. Easy to handle, simply mix with water and apply with a sprinkling can and all vegetation withers and dies. A few rains wash the ground all clean, then it is ready for cultivation so you can start reseeding. Price, per quart, 60c; gallon, $1.75; 5 gallons, $7.00.

Greenlee Earth Auger

A handy auger for drilling holes to feed plant food to trees and shrubs. 2-inch size with 6-inch twist; length 40 inches overall. Each, $4.00.

KEEP OFF THE GRASS

METAL LAWN SIGNS

These attractive signs have raised letters, baked enamel finish for long attractive service. Have center holes for attaching to stakes. Size 3¾x12 inches. Colors, green on white and black on white. Sign wordings—Please-Seeded—Keep off Grass.
Signs with stakes, each, 35c; six for $1.80.

HANDY ADJUSTABLE LAWN RAKE

An all-purpose lawn rake. Depth gauges adjustable, ADJUSTABLE makes rake pull easily over oil without pulling up sod; made of high carbon steel. 5 ft. ash handle. Ceiling price, each $1.75.

HANDY CRAB GRASS RAKE

This rake is formed so that the teeth pull flat on the sod; thus they get under the branches of the Crab Grass, shear off the entire head of the plants and keep them from further seeding. You can eliminate crab grass with this rake and not harm the other grasses; it will also pull out any weed that clings close to the ground. Each, $1.50.

O. K. ELECTRIC GRASS CUTTER

Trimmer and Edger

For formal gardens, terraces and small steep lawns. Completely finishes, no other implements needed. Will also trim hedge, cuts any way, moved or held. Weight 5 lbs. A real implement; has a 9-inch revolving blade and long handle. Price, $27.50.

O. K. ELECTRIC HEDGE TRIMMER

No gears, no bottom to choke up, does not disturb, cut after made. It is a quality, practical trimmer. Heavy duty hedge trimmer has oilless bearings and more power than the Home Jr. Price, $22.00.

For ordinary grass and weeds, each part of Herbicidol may be diluted with forty to fifty parts of water. One gallon will cover app. 2,500 sq. ft. Herbicidol is a poison. Live stock should be kept off the treated ground until the dead leaves wither away. Qt., 75c; gal., $2.00; 5 gals., $7.50; 10 gals., $12.50; 55 gals., $44.00.
A $5.00 deposit is required on drums. Drums returnable prepaid for credit in good condition within 30 days.

HERBICIDOL

THE WEED EXTERMINATOR

For Paths, Cobble Gutters, Drives, Tennis Courts etc.

MEO-181. Destroys Dandelions, Crab grass, and other common weeds. Any spraying apparatus which spreads a fine atomized mist is suitable for applying MEO-181. Price, gal., $1.55.

ZOTOX
CRAB GRASS KILLER

Kills both the plant and seeds of Crab Grass and checks reinfestation. It does not destroy lawn grasses and is not injurious to soil. Simply mix with water and spray. When used as an over all spray, it kills dandelion, plantain, buckhorn, etc.—The 8 oz. bot. ($1.00 size) makes 5 gallons and treats 1,000 sq. ft. For spot treatment of small patches it goes much further. 8 oz. bottle $1.00; 16 oz. bottle, $1.50; 32 oz. bottle, $2.50; 5 lb. bottle $4.50.

GETZUM WEED GUN

Kills dandelions and other weeds without injury to lawn. Does not sterilize the soil. Does not corrode or rust metals. Insures easy and economic application. No stooping or back breaking. Place cane on crown of dandelion or weed and press handle lightly. A small amount of chemical is released and does all the work. Price complete with liquid, $1.75. Killer Kemical, pint, 30c.

Bergman Lawn Mower Sharpener

A high-grade, durable lawn mower sharpener easy to use and adjustable to all types of machines. No danger of making low spots in the blade. Price, $1.00.

MOLE TRAP

Improved with patented setting attachment. One of the best mole and gopher traps. Each, $2.00.

Mole Trap

Tool Supply Limited

Our stocks of garden tools are not large, and replacements are uncertain, because of war restriction. Customers are advised to place their orders as early as possible, to insure delivery.

Garden Tools, Pruners and Seeders

TELEPHONE THREE PRUNER

A strong rugged pruner with operating mechanism entirely in the pruner head. Can be fitted to any pole. Price, $2.00.

THE PORTER POINTCUT PRUNER

Designed for the fruit grower. Light in weight, 2½ lbs., 20 inches long. Easy to use in close places. $6.00.

BUCKEYE PRUNER

A strong rugged pruner handles reinforced by strap iron. 20 inch, each, $2.50; 26 inch, $3.00.

Snap Cut Pruner. No. 906B. Heavy duty, full polished. $2.35.

SPADE. Razor Back. Rolled in backbone extending full length through blade frog and socket. Ceiling price, ea., $2.00.

SHOVEL. Razor Back. Same construction as spade. Ceiling price, each, $2.00.

California Pole Trimmer curved draw cut saw with crook for removing branches. Ceiling price, each, $3.00.

18-inch Double Edge Pruning Saw. Highest quality. Ceiling price, each, $2.25.

Hand Curved Pruning Saw of highest quality. Ceiling price, each, $2.25.

PRUNING SHEAR—9 In.

With ratchet, high quality, each, $2.25; postpaid, $2.35.

GARDEN TROWEL

A sturdy durable trowel made from heavy gauge pressed metal. Price, 40c each, postpaid, 50c.

STANDARD TREE PRUNERS

A popular tree pruner operated by lever connected to the blade by a strong wire. Practical service cable made of high quality material throughout, easily cuts 1 inch branches. 6 ft. each, $3.25; 8 ft. each, $3.50; 10 ft. each, $3.75; 12 ft. each, $3.95.

No. 110 GARDEX PULL HOE WEEDER

This improved tool will do your weeding even in hard, dry and heavy soil. It will enter hard soil just as easily as light soil, cutting the roots of the weeds 2 to 3 inches deep. Made of specially rolled steel. The shares and cutting blades are sharp and resharpen while in use. Price: 5" width, $1.75; 8½" width, $2.25.

No. 1523 GARDEX CULTIVATOR WITH WEEDER

Cultivate and weed with one tool. Important for every gardener. The 3-prong cultivator loosens the soil thoroughly while the weeding blade cuts off all weeds quickly. One tool for two purposes. Painted red, 3 prongs 4½" wide. Weeding blade 4" wide—withouthandle, $1.40.

No. 1605 GARDEX INTERCHANGEABLE GARDEN CULTIVATOR

The ideal tool, and the friend of many gardeners. A faithful helper for every woman who tends her own flower and vegetable garden. Loosens and air-conditions the soil in flower and vegetable gardens. The position and construction of the tines cause them to penetrate any soil easily, and they loosen and aerate the ground thoroughly with an easy pulling motion. No chopping hoe can do this job so evenly and neatly. No backaches and blisters—it's a favorite tool with every gardener. Attractive low price.
No. 1605—5 prongs adjustable width ¾" to 7"—with 5 ft. normal length Gardex handle.........$1.75

ASBESTOS TORCH

Practical for burning caterpillars, worms and other tree pests. It it a black lined ball, filled with asbestos fibre, so constructed that it can easily be attached to any pole. Dip the torch in kerosene and light. Ea. 50c; 3 for $1.35.

SEED SOWER

Cyclone. (New Improved Model.) An accurate portable seeder, for all broadcast sowing or fertilizing. Fits comfortably over shoulder; provided with automatic adjustment for stopping flow of contents when required. A great time and labor saver. Each, $3.25.

E. Z. FERTILIZER SPREADER

Fertilize your lawn, sow your seed the new E.Z. way. Simply fill container, push like a vacuum cleaner and your lawn is covered quickly. Comes knocked down. Each, $1.25.

HEAVY DUTY FERTILIZER DISTRIBUTOR

Spreads any kind of commercial fertilizer, grass seed and top dressing. It has a shut-off control and adjusting device right on handle. 24-in., $17.50; 36-in., $24.00.

No. 751 GARDEX DIBBLE

For garden and field. Made out of steel, hollow. Light as a feather, with a pistol grip that makes it easy to handle, does not tire your hand when planting. Equally well liked by gardener and farmer. Painted red; half polished. Size overall 11¾". Price, 90c; postpaid, $1.00.

DIBBER. For transplanting vegetable plants, steel point (weight, 10 oz.). Each, $1.00.

WIRE FRUIT PICKER

A mechanical apple and fruit picker, so simple children can pick fruit with no danger. Without pole, price, 90c each; postpaid, $1.00.

EVER-READY

Vaughan's Wick-fed

WOOD SEED STARTER

View of Wick-fed Starter with Plant Bands. Size, 12x18 inches, 4 inches high.

How wick is placed in bottom of starter.

End view showing water pan below.

COMPLETE, WITH FIBRE GLASS WICK, 60 PLANT BANDS, AND SPHAGNUM MOSS, FOR (Weight 4½ lbs.) $2.50

This seed starter must not be confused with the fragile, impractical pasteboard devices which have disappointed so many customers. This is a full size "flat," made of heavy wood to last for years, stained pale green, which you will be glad to have in your sun parlor or living room window.

It makes use of two of the most recent scientific developments in seed starting: 1. Wick-feeding of water, which keeps the soil at just the right moisture, never drying out, never too wet, and never dripping dirty water from an overflow. 2. The use of sphagnum moss to prevent damping off of seedlings, highly recommended by the U. S. D. A.

As shown in the illustrations, water is supplied to the soil from a pan placed underneath the starter, by the agency of capillary attraction, through a fibre glass wick, the top of which is frayed and embedded in the soil, the lower end being immersed in water in the pan below. Any suitable pan, saucer, or dish can be used.

Fill this container with water daily, and the wick will do the rest. This method of watering leaves nothing to chance or judgment, and solves in the easiest imaginable way one of the most serious problems of seed-box management. It has been thoroughly tested by Cornell University. The wick will last indefinitely.

Seeds may be sown in the starter in rows, broadcast or, as shown in the illustration, in plant bands. If started in plant bands, and grown one plant to a band, sturdy full size pot plants will be produced without transplanting. Seedlings may be easily transplanted into plant bands, if preferred. Start the seedlings in a small box, or get two seed starters, using one in which to start seeds, the other in which to transplant. Complete instructions for the management of tne starter with detailed directions for a long list of subjects with each starter.

DE LUXE SEED STARTER AND POT COMBINATION

Finished in attractive green color waterproof with same sub-irrigation device as No. RG. 33 comes in two models.

No. R. G. 50 with 50—2¼ inch pots large enough to grow medium size plants, price 79c postpaid 80c.

No. R. G. 24 with 50—3 inch pots for growing larger plants for early maturity, price 89c, postpaid $1.00.

GREEN THUMB WINDOW GARDEN

For use in the house to start seed and grow strong. Plants there are two seed starters with a total capacity of five to ten dozen seedlings the strongest plants are selected for transplanting into the three transplant boxes with a total capacity of 33 potted plants; have slender shape which fits even narrow window sills. They are finished in an attractive green color and look well in any room of the house. A self watering feature consisting of a sub-irrigation device simplifies growing. Watering is reduced to adding measured quantities once or twice a week as definite conditions develop. Strong sturdy (Waterproof) No. R. G. 33 price, 79c, postpaid, 90c.

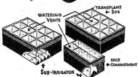

HOTBED MATS for protecting hotbeds. Made of poplin materials, vat dyed and Sanforized to make them damp proof. 76x40 inches—$5.25 each, dozen $59.00; 76x76 inch—$8.00 each; dozen $95.00.

PUTTIROPE. A great new improvement for glazing, and caulking. Easy to apply, won't deteriorate, run or get brittle. Price per box, 100 ft., $1.35; 1000 ft., $6.75.

HOTBED SASH

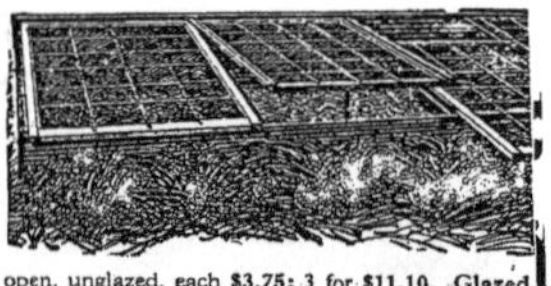

HOTBED SASH. 3x6 feet. 1⅜ inches thick, made from sap-free cypress or sap-free cypress and redwood, for three rows 10 inches wide glass, lapped, nailed together with white-leaded joints, reinforced across the center with galvanized flat steel bar; open, unglazed, each $3.75; 3 for $11.10. Glazed, painted one coat, 10x14 inches double strength flat drawn greenhouse glass, each, $6.95; 3 for $20.25. When less than three glazed sash are ordered, there will be an extra charge of $1.00 for crating.

VITAPANE

A flexible glass substitute; transparent all purpose window material, withstands wind, snow and rain, allows more light, permits easy inspection. Put up in rolls 36 inches wide. Price per 50 ft. roll, $9.25. ½ roll, $5.00; per yd., 75c.

CEL-O-GLASS

Will take the place of glass in hotbed sash, garage and barn windows, storm doors, and for many other purposes, at a great saving. Unbreakable and very light in weight. No glazing. Hammer and tacks are the only tools you need. Put up in rolls 3 feet wide up to 100 feet long. Per square yard, $1.35; 25 ft. roll 3 ft. wide, $9. 75; 100 ft. roll, $35.00.

GLAZING POINTS. Vaughan's Perfection. No rights or lefts; No. 2, small, for single thick glass; No. 2½, double thick, for greenhouses and skylights. Price per box of 1 lb., 75c; by mail, 80c. Siebert's Improved. Easy to drive, and will not wedge or crack glass, 2 sizes, ⅝ and ⅞ inch long. Price per lb., 70c; by mail, 80c.

SEED FLATS. Made from genuine Red Cypress, knocked down, bundled in bundles of 10 flats each, with nails.

	Inside Dimensions	Per Bundle of 10
No. 2.	22⅜x15x2¾ inches	$3.40
No. 1.	20 x14x2¾ inches	3.00
No. 2-A.	22⅜x15x3¾ inches	3.60
No. 1-A.	20 x14x3¾ inches	3.40

We do not break bundles.

WINDOW FABRIC VIO-RAY. A strong fabric treated by a patented process to make it transparent, weather-proof and water-proof. It costs much less than glass and for many purposes is superior. Anyone can put it up. It comes in rolls 36 inches wide and any length. Per yd., 48c; 10 yd. roll, $4.50; 25 yds., $11.00.

Standard Grade Tested

Hotbed

THERMOMETERS. Tin Case. 8-in. 50c.

Hotbed. Brass point, wooden frame, $3.75.

Self-Registering. With magnet to set it, 8-inch, each, $9.00; registers highest and lowest temperature.

Tin Case. Standard grade, tested. 8-inch, each, $1.50.

Thermometers shipped by parcel post at purchaser's risk only.

PEST EXTERMINATORS

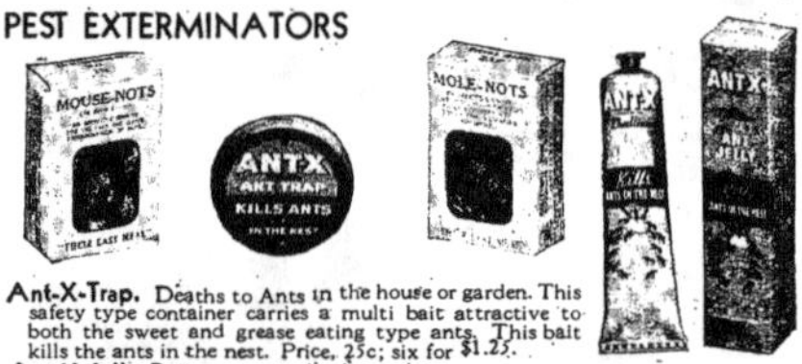

Ant-X-Trap. Deaths to Ants in the house or garden. This safety type container carries a multi bait attractive to both the sweet and grease eating type ants. This bait kills the ants in the nest. Price, 25c; six for $1.25.

Ant-X Jelly Bait. Kills quickly. This jelly controls sweet and grease eating ants. It will also kill ants in the nest. 1 oz., 35c; 4 oz., tube, $1.00; Industrial size, 5-lb. pail, $15.

Dog-Check. The ideal repellent as a means of checking doggie habits. Safe and harmless to use. New formula will permit spraying on new growth. Unaffected by rain, one spraying lasts from two to three weeks. 3-oz. size, complete with sprayer, 60c; 8-oz. size, with sprayer, $1.00; 32-oz., size, $3.00; gallon, $11.50.

Rat-Nots. Safe way to exterminate rats. Prepared Bait, containing Squill. Can be used without fear of harming humans, dogs, live stock, etc. Trial size package of 9 Nots, 25c; Estate size, 60 Nots, $1.00.

Mouse-Nots. Impregnated seed bait kills mice. Trial size package, 9 Nots, 25c; Estate size, 60 Nots, $1.00.

Mole-Nots. Life saver for lawns, bulb and seed beds. Trial size, 8 Nots, 35c; Estate size, 50 Nots $1.00; Jumbo size, 125 Nots, $2.00; Gardener size, 400 Nots, $5.00; Giant size, 1,000 Nots, $10.00.

Roach-Nots. Semi-toxic insecticide in prepared bait form. Very effective in controlling Roaches. Trial size, 9 Nots, 25c; Estate size, 60 Nots, $1.00.

...ces include delivery within 25 miles of Chicago on 25, 50 and 100 lb. quantities delivered with orders of seeds, bulbs and supplies ...re. On larger quantities than 100 pounds, owing to close quantity ...mer pays all freight or express charges.

N'S BALANCED PLANT RATION (3-10-6)

...cent nitrogen; ten percent phosphoric acid; six per-...—This is a balanced fertilizer, chiefly composed of organic ...blood and potash), which has been used for 50 years with excel-...y florists, truck gardeners and amateurs, and which we recommend ...ertilizer for all around use in the home garden.

...use 20 to 40 lbs. per 1,000 square feet; and for cultivated gardens, ...r 100 square feet. As liquid manure, use 1 part to 30 parts of water. ...ces, 5 lbs., 50c; 10 lbs., 95c; 100 lbs., $4.00.

...HAN'S "ROSE GROWER" BONE MEAL

...ecial brand we have put up for our trade. It is ground fine, hence ...Free from acid, and a superb article. It is made from bone accu-...rge slaughter houses, and should not be compared with the Bone ...om cattle heads and feet gathered upon the western prairies. Our ...r" Bone has been slightly steamed to soften it and is thus quicker ...Analysis: Nitrogen, 3¾ percent; total phosphoric acid, 22 per-...g prices, 5 lbs., 50c; 10 lbs., 95c; 25 lbs., $1.65; 50 lbs., $2.65; ...0; 100 lbs., $21.00.

...D BONE MEAL. Ceiling prices, 25 lbs., $1.50; 50 lbs., $2.50; 100 ...00 lbs., $18.50; 1,000 lbs., $35.00; 2,000 lbs., $69.00.

VAUGHAN'S SHEEP MANURE

...ure, natural manure, and its effect is immediate; it is excellent for ...the soil for greenhouse plants—one part manure and six parts ...over and dug into the vegetable garden or placed directly in drills ...omotes a rapid, steady growth until maturity. It makes the richest, ...uickest liquid manure. For use in liquid form, one pound to five ...ter will make a liquid which can be used with safety daily if neces-...b lbs., 75c; 25 lbs., $1.35; 50 lbs., $1.95; 100 lbs., $2.75; ...00.

Cattle Manure. Manufactured by special process from selected fresh cleanings from cattle ...is no offensive odor, and when spread on lawn and garden it ...into the soil so that there is no refuse to blow about or be raked ...growing season begins. 25 lbs., $1.35; 50 lbs., $2.40; 100; $3.25; ...50; 1,000 lbs., $24.00.

...ificial Stable Manure. Make it yourself, in your own garden. To each ton ...y, cornstalks or dried leaves add 150 lbs. of Adco to make four tons ...hree tons of rotted manure. Adco contains nothing injurious to ...irmful to animal or plant life. Shipments accompanied by full ...eiling prices, 7¾ lb. bag, $1.00; 25 lbs., $2.50; 150 lbs., $11.50. ...okiet.

...m Sulphate. For creating acid condition in the soil. Ceiling prices, 1 lb., 35c; 5 lbs., 60c; 10 lbs., ..., $2.00; 100 lbs., $4.75.

...um Nitrate. Nitragin content 34%. Since it is almost im-...possible to secure Sulphate of Ammonia and ...oda, this is a good substitute and runs much higher in Nitragin ...ling price 5 lbs., 60c; 10 lbs., $1.00; 25 lbs., $1.60; 50 lbs., $2.75; 100

...ake your own fertilizer easy, quick—often in as little as three ...cks. Just sprinkle Baeto on kitchen waste, leaves, garden rub-...sludge, etc. 5-pound bag makes up to a ton of rich, soil-building ...us, better than manure. Sprinkle in outdoor toilets; reduces odors, ...handled ash of waste. ...65; 25 lbs., $5.25; Trial 4-oz. carton, 35c.

e Improved. Fertilizer with a peat-moss base impregnated with a high grade manure. Per 50 lb bag, ...gs for $12.50; 10 bags for $24.00.

Fertilizer (4–9–3). A high organic all around plant food for feed-...ing, forcing and finishing. The best substitute for Clay's fertilizer, ...orted from England. Ceiling prices, 25 lbs., $4.25; 50 lbs., $6.50; ...00.

Fulton's Plantabb. Odorless plant food in tablet form, supplies a completely balanced plant food including vitamin B-1. Ceiling prices, per box of 30 tablets, 25c; box of 75 tablets, 50c; box of 240 tablets, $1.00; postpaid. Large size approximately 1,000 tablets, $2.75.

Hardwood Ashes. Rich in potash and con-taining all of the fertiliz-ing elements except nitrogen. Is used on the lawn at the rate of a ton or more per acre as a first appli-cation, an annual dressing of three hundred pounds afterwards.
...ices, 25 lbs., $1.25; 50 lbs., $1.95; 100 lbs., $3.45; 500 lbs., $13.50; ...5.00; 2,000 lbs., $48.00.

Plant Food. Can be used in dry or liquid form; teaspoon-ful makes 1 gallon. Contains vitamin B-1. percent nitrogen; 6 percent phosphoric acid; nineteen per-... Ceiling prices, 3 oz. tin, 25c; 1 lb., $1.00; 10 lbs., $8.00; 25 lbs., ...s., $25.00; 100 lbs., $40.00.

...uid Plant Food. For summer use. A complete, balanced ration for lawns, plants and trees. A ...ition containing all essential elements; nitrogen, phosphate, potash, ...lcium baron, sulphur, etc. Merely dilute Kem solution with hy-...Directions on container. Ceiling prices, house plant size, 25c; qt. ...l size, $1.25.

Lime, Hydrated. A neutralizer for soil acidity. Ceiling prices, 10 lbs., 35c; 50 lbs., $1.25.

Leaf Mold. For correction of clayey and sandy soil conditions. Per bushel, $1.40; per bag of two bushels, $2.50.

Limestone, Pulverized. Is a neutralizer for soil acidity, also im-proves the texture of the soil and liberates ni-trogen and other plant food and stimulates bacterial action. Apply after the land is plowed or dug for a crop, scattering with a lime distributor, 2 tons or more per acre, or by hand in small gardens—about a large handful to a square yard. Ceiling prices, 100 lbs., $1.45; 500 lbs., $5.50; 1,000 lbs., $8.00; 2,000 lbs. $14.50.

Lime Phosphate, Ruhm's. Nature's source of phosphorus. The most phosphate at lowest unit cost. Ceiling prices, 100 lbs., $2.45; 500 lbs., $9.00; 1,000 lbs., $16.00; 2,000 lbs. $29.00.

Liqua Vita. A liquid plant food contains all the necessary elements. ½ oz. will make 1 gal. of solution. Ceiling prices, 12 oz., 50c; qt., $1.00; gal., $3.50.

Milorganite. Activated sludge fertilizer, free of weed seeds. Feeds over a long period. Ceiling prices, 25 lbs., $1.00; 50 lbs., $1.65; 100 lbs., $2.75; 500 lbs., $12.00; 1,000 lbs., $23.00.

Muriate of Potash. Should be used liberally; especially for all root crops. Ceiling prices, 25 lbs., $1.50; 50 lbs., $2.45; 100 lbs., $3.85.

Nitragin. The Original Legume Inoculation.
Culture A. For alfalfa, sweet clover, burr clover and hubam clover. Ceiling prices, 1 bu. size, 50c; 2½ bu. size, $1.00.
Culture B. For clovers, medium and mammoth red, alsike, crimson and white. Ceiling prices, 1 bu. size, 50c; 2½ bu. size, $1.00.
Culture C. For all vetches. Peas, Austrian, Can-adian, golden and sweet peas, broad beans and lentils. Ceiling prices, medium size will inoculate up to 100 lbs. seed; 50c large size will inoculate up to 1200 lbs. seed; $5.70.
Culture D. For Beans. String, snap, wax, navy, kidney and scarlet runner. Ceiling prices, 1 bu. size, 50c.
Culture E. For peanuts, cow peas, velvet beans and lima beans. Ceiling prices, small bu. size, 30c; 5 bu. size, 55c; 25 bu. size, $2.50; 30 bu. size, $3.25.
Culture L. For all Lespedeza, small size inoculates up to 50 lbs. Ceiling prices, 35c; large size up to 100 lbs. price, 50c.
Culture S. For Soy Beans, all varieties. Ceiling prices, small size inoculates up to 120 lbs. seeds, 30c; 5-bushel size, 55c; 25 bushel size, $2.50; 30 bushel size, $3.25.
Garden Size. For garden peas, sweet peas, beans, lima beans and lupines. Ceiling prices, pkt., 10c; three for 25c; each packet will treat up to 6 lbs. of seed.
Lupines, all varieties. Per can, 50c. Will inoculate up to 100 lbs. seed.

Peat, Orchid. Very useful for orchids and azaleas. Ceiling price, $3.75 per sack, of about two bushels

Special Lawn and Ornamental Fertilizer. 6% nitrogen. 12% phos-phate, 4% potash for lawns, trees, shrubs, etc. Ceiling prices per 100 lbs., $4.00.

Super Phosphate. Twenty percent available. Ceiling prices, 25 lbs., $1.15; 50 lbs., $1.75; 100 lbs., $2.75; 500 lbs., $9.75; 1,000 lbs., $18.00; 2,000 lbs., $33.00.

Stim U Plant Tablets Plus Vitamin B1. For potted plants. Well balanced plant food. Ceiling prices, per pkg., 30c, postpaid; large pkg., 100 tablets, 75c, by mail, 85c.

Mackwins Vitamin B-1. The only liquid vitamin B-1 plant growth stimulant with added chemicals to keep its strength indefinitely. 2-oz. dropper top bottle, enough to make 230 gallons of solution. Ceiling price, 39c.

NOTE: Cannot supply Scotch Soot and Clay's Fertilizer during present emergency. Electra is a good substitute for Clay's.

Loma Victory Garden Fertilizer. A balanced fertilizer con-taining 4% nitrogen, 12% phosphate, 4% potash, for food production only. Ceiling prices, 10 lbs., 80c; 25 lbs., $1.45; 50 lbs., $2.35; 100 lbs., $3.70; 500 lbs., $17.75; 1,000 lbs., $34.50; 2,000 lbs., $64.00.

Vigoro Victory Garden Fertilizer. For food production only. 4–12–4 analysis. Ceiling prices, 5 lb. pkg., 50c; 10 lb. carton, 80c; 25 lbs., $1.45; 50 lbs., $2.35; 100 lbs., $3.70; 500 lbs., $17.75; 1,000 lbs., $34.50.

Vaughan's Fancy Grasses and Field Seeds

For Lawn Seed Mixtures, See Page 5. All Prices Prepaid, Except where Specifically Noted.
All Grasses and Field Seed Prices Are Subject to Change Without Notice.

Fancy Kentucky Blue Grass
POA PRATENSIS

Extra Heavy Sun-Cured Seed. Specially recleaned. Price, ½ lb., 35c; 1 lb., 55c; 2 lbs., $1.10; 3 lbs., $1.60; 5 lbs., $2.60; 10 lbs., $5.00; 15 lbs., $7.40; 20 lbs., $9.70; 25 lbs., $12.00; 50 lbs., $22.00.

Fancy Seed, actual weight, 21 lbs. per bu. (Standard grade of recleaned blue grass.) Price, ½ lb., 30c; 1 lb., 45c; 2 lbs., 90c; 3 lbs., $1.30; 5 lbs., $2.10; 10 lbs., $4.00; 15 lbs., $5.90; 20 lbs., $7.70; 25 lbs., $9.60; 50 lbs., $19.00.

CANADA BLUE GRASS (Poa compressa)
Valuable on poor soils and clay. It does not make so dense a growth as the Kentucky Blue Grass, and color is not so pleasing. Used particularly for pastures. Sow 40 to 60 lbs. per acre for pasture; in Fall or Spring. Price, 1 lb., 55c; 2 lbs., $1.10; 3 lbs., $1.60; 5 lbs., $2.60; 10 lbs., $5.00; 15 lbs., $7.40; 20 lbs., $9.70; 25 lbs., $11.50; 50 lbs., $21.00.

WHITE CLOVER
Extra Fancy Seed. Price, ¼ lb., 35c; ½ lb., 65c; 1 lb., $1.15; 2 lbs., $2.30; 3 lbs., $3.40; 5 lbs., $5.50; 10 lbs., $10.75; 15 lbs., $15.75; 20 lbs., $20.40; 25 lbs., $24.50.

Choice. Price, ¼ lb., 30c; ½ lb., 60c; 1 lb., $1.05; 2 lbs., $2.10; 3 lbs., $3.10; 5 lbs., $5.00; 10 lbs., $9.75; 15 lbs., $14.25; 20 lbs., $18.40; 25 lbs., $22.00.

RED TOP GRASS (Agrostis alba)
Extra Fancy, recleaned solid seed. Price, ½ lb., 25c; 1 lb., 40c; 2 lbs., 80c; 3 lbs., $1.15; 5 lbs., $1.85; 10 lbs., $3.50; 15 lbs., $4.85; 20 lbs., $6.25; 25 lbs., $7.25; 50 lbs., $13.50.

Rye Grasses
Use all rye grasses at the rate of 30 to 40 lbs. per acre for pastures and 5 to 7 lbs. per 1000 sq. ft. for lawns. Sow either fall or spring.

English or Perennial Rye Grass (Lolium perenne). A lawn grass where quick results are wanted. Price, 1 lb., 45c; 2 lbs., 90c; 3 lbs., $1.30; 5 lbs., $2.10; 10 lbs., $4.00; 15 lbs., $5.90; 20 lbs., $7.70; 25 lbs., $9.50; 50 lbs., $18.25; 100 lbs., $35.00.

Common Rye Grass. The Italian type of rye grass, grown in this country. An annual, generally lasting a second year. Develops rapidly. Used in the south for Winter lawn grass. Sow in October in the south, Spring or Fall in the north. Price, 1 lb., 30c; 2 lbs., 60c; 3 lbs., 85c; 5 lbs., $1.35; 10 lbs., $2.50; 15 lbs., $3.65; 25 lbs., $5.75; 50 lbs., $10.00.

Fescues
★**CHEWING'S FESCUE (NEW ZEALAND GROWN).** This grass is valuable on sandy soils and in shade. Chewing's Fescue is a perennial with a fine blade and a spreading root system. Sow either Spring or Fall (last week in August or the first week in September) at the rate of 5 lbs. to 1,000 sq. ft. Price, 1 lb., 95c; 2 lbs., $1.90; 3 lbs., $2.80; 5 lbs., $4.55; 10 lbs., $8.90; 15 lbs., $13.00; 20 lbs., $17.00; 25 lbs., $20.75; 50 lbs., $40.00.

★**CREEPING RED FESCUE.** One of the best fescues obtainable, it spreads from the roots, making a dense turf which tends to crowd out weeds. Does well in shade and is good on sandy soil. Price, 1 lb., $1.00; 2 lbs., $2.00; 3 lbs., $2.95; 5 lbs., $4.80; 10 lbs., $9.40; 15 lbs., $13.75; 20 lbs., $18.00; 25 lbs., $22.00; 50 lbs., $42.50.

BIRD SEED
Rape. Large—sweet (not bitter like the small black). 1 lb., 30c; 5 lbs., $1.40; 10 lbs., $2.70; 25 lbs., $6.25.

Sunflower. 1 lb., 35c; 5 lbs., $1.70; 10 lbs., $3.30; 25 lbs., $7.50.

Vaughan's Canary Mixture. 1 lb., 35c; 5 lbs., $1.70.

Finch Seed. 1 lb., 25c; 5 lbs., $1.15; 10 lbs., $2.25.

Parrakeet Seed. 1 lb., 30c; 5 lbs., $1.40; 10 lbs., $2.70.

Vaughan's Wild Bird feeding Mixture (as recommended by the Illinois Audubon Society). 1 lb., 15c; 2 lbs., 25c; 5 lbs., 60c; 10 lbs., $1.15; 25 lbs., $2.75; 100 lbs., $10.00.

Prices do not include Postage. See table at the back of book for rates.

Let us help you solve your lawn and golf grass problems. Advice gladly given on handling fertilizer problems, and combating insect and disease attacks.

116 INDEX ON FINAL PAGES

CERTIFIED VICLAND OATS
This strain, developed by the Wisconsin Agricultural Experiment Station, has created a sensation among farmers. It is highly resistant to smuts and early rusts, early maturing, produces strong straw and is slow to sprout in the shock. The grain is heavier than the average and yield superior.

We offer Wisconsin certified seed, produced directly from foundation stocks supplied by the Wisconsin College of Agriculture, grown under careful field supervision and laboratory tests to insure a high degree of purity and germination.

1 bu., $2.25; 10 bu., $2.10 each, freight collect. Bags included.

CLOVERS AND ALFALFA
(Northern Grown)

Medium Red. (Purity 99.00 or better). Sow at the rate of 8-10 lbs. per acre. Price, 1 lb., 60c; 5 lbs., $2.75—Postpaid. By Freight collect, 1 pk., $7.00; ½ bu., $13.90; 1 bu., $26.70; 100 lbs., $44.50. Bags included.

Alsike Clover. (Fancy). Sow at the rate of 5 to 6 lbs. per acre. Price, 1 lb., 55c; 5 lbs., $2.60—Postpaid. By Freight collect, 1 pk., $6.40; ½ bu., $12.75; 1 bu., $24.40; 100 lbs., $40.70. Bags included.

Alfalfa Seed. (Northern). 1 lb., 70c; 5 lbs., $3.25—Postpaid. By Freight collect, 1 pk., $7.95; ½ bu., $15.80; 1 bu., $30.55; 100 lbs., $50.90. Bags included.

Write for Complete Price List of Field Seeds or let us know your requirements and we will be glad to quote special quantity prices. Purity and Germ. tests made in our own laboratories.

Miscellaneous
Awnless Brome Grass (Bromus inermis). Very strong, quick growth, making two crops of very abundant pasture. Has proven very valuable for pasture when sown with alfalfa. Good in very sandy soils because of its strong spreading root system. Not a lawn grass. Sow in the Spring. 2 bushels per acre (14 lbs. per bushel). Postpaid. By Freight collect, 1 lb., 40c; 3 lbs., $1.15; 5 lbs., $1.65; 10 lbs., $3.00; 25 lbs., $6.25; 50 lbs., $11.75; 100 lbs., $22.00.

Timothy (Phleum pratense). Most popular of all hay grasses. Vaughan's Fancy seed (99.5% pure or better). Price, 1 lb., 30c; 2 lbs., 55c; 3 lbs., 75c; 5 lbs., $1.10—Postpaid. By Freight collect, ½ bu., $3.10; 1 bu., $6.10 (45 lbs.); 100 lbs., $13.50. Grain bags included.

Reed Canary Grass. A fine perennial for hay or pasture on low marshy land. Use 5 to 8 lbs. per acre broadcast, and 3 to 5 lbs. with drill. Sow early in Spring or August. September. Lb., 50c; 3 lbs., $1.45; 5 lbs., $2.25—Postpaid. By Freight collect, 10 lbs., $4.00; 25 lbs., $9.00; 50 lbs., $17.00; 100 lbs., $33.00.

Sudan Grass. Sow 35 lbs. per acre. Makes an excellent emergency hay crop. Can be sown any time from May 20th to June 20th. It withstands long periods of drought. Lb., 35c; 5 lbs., $1.50—Postpaid. By Freight collect, 10 lbs., $2.75; 25 lbs., $5.00; 50 lbs., $9.00; 100 lbs., $16.00; sacks included.

Dwarf Essex Rape. Makes a quick pasture and is very valuable feed. Ideal for sheep, hogs and cattle. Sow in early spring. 5 to 10 lbs. per acre, or with spring grain. 2 lbs. per acre. 1 lb., 35c; 5 lbs., $1.50—Postpaid. By Freight collect, 10 lbs., $2.50; 100 lbs., $18.00.

Winter Vetch. A very valuable leguminous plant, especially for lighter soils. Can be sown spring or fall. Sow 15 to 20 lbs. of Vetch and ½ bushel grain, per acre. Makes splendid hay. Lb., 35c; 3 lbs., $1.00; 5 lbs., $1.40—Postpaid. By Freight, collect, 10 lbs., $2.50; 25 lbs., $5.85; 100 lbs., $20.00.

HYBRID FIELD CORN
We offer State Certified Hybrids—

For many years breeders at the University of Wisconsin have been constantly at work developing and improving hybrids adapted to Northern Illinois, Wisconsin, Michigan, Iowa and Indiana.

Through arrangements with the University we are able to offer these proven hybrids at the following prices:

Flat kernels (Edge Drop). Peck, $2.75; ½ bu., $4.75 Bu., $8.50.

Above Prices Freight Paid.

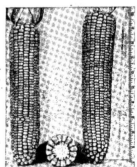

ven before France fell and while her finest perfumes were still available, invited direct comparison with these, regardless of price.

oday, imported perfumes are no more. Vaughan's fine floral perfumes are available, can still be compared with the finest, regardless of price.

While unusual demand has exhausted stocks of some odors, we have been tunate in replacing most of these from small lots of fine essential oils im- ted before war destroyed contact with Europe's great producing centers.

f you can no longer find your favorite imported odor, you will find the owing blends of the same individual character as the best Parisian uquets: Bouquet S, Bouquet X, Hawaiian Lei, Zanzibar, Calcutta, Victoria gina and Song of the Heart.

The Following Odors Are Available in Either Cologne or Perfume

Cologne is about one-eighth the strength of perfumes (about double the ength of ordinary toilet water). It is used wherever a perfumed lotion is inted—in the bath, on linens, or as a refreshing lotion.

Appleblossom: Soft, yet fresh and clean.

Bouquet S: A delicately feminine blend h floral oils that in France and America is cepted as the leading type of odor in the etter shops.

Bouquet X: Another blend, slightly drier" and less sweet. An exotic fragrance referred by women accustomed to the better rench perfumes.

Carnation: Many acknowledge it as the est recreation of this beloved old favorite.

Forest Breeze: A smoky, piney fragrance —the scent of a pine forest on an autumn day.

Freesia: We are proud to have captured he elusive scent of this delicate flower.

Gardenia: Not sweet like so many "Gar- lenia" perfumes—a rich, intense odor.

Geranium: Like a crushed leaf of the green lant.

Vaughan's Sampler: To prove to our cus- tomers the high quality of our perfumes, we have assembled a "Sampler" collection, featuring our ten leading fragrances, a full one-eighth dram of each, enough for several applications. All ten fragrances, $1.00 plus 10c tax. $1.10 postpaid.

Hawaiian Lei: A lovely blend of exotic tropical flowers.

Heather: A rich "smoky" or "peaty" fra- grance that goes well with sport clothes.

Lavender: The well-known English type, not sweet or "musky" like so many near-lavenders.

Lilac: Lilacs wet with morning dew. Fresh and leafy—our largest selling odor.

Lily of the Valley: At last, a satisfactory reproduction of this elusive scent.

Magnolia: The veritable fragrance o the Southern Magnolia—rich and lush.

Red Rose: The Damask Rose type.

Sweet Pea: The true fragrance of the origi- nal Spencer sweet pea.

Violet: The English violet, softer than the Parma type.

Wild Rose: Like the breeze through a Sweet Briar hedge in June.

Zanzibar: Like a clipper ship laden with rare oriental woods and the spices of the Indies.

"Personalized Perfumes"

	Cost of Perfume	Federal Tax	Total Price
Dram	$ 1.50	$0.15	$ 1.65
Ounce	10.00	1.00	11.00

We take pleasure in offering this group of highly individual, specially blended odors, which while not ex- actly matching the perfume of par- ticular flowers, do express the enchanting fragrance of gardens and woodlands.

Calcutta: The oil from which this perfume was made was intended origi- nally for introduction at $75.00 an ounce by a famous French house. Escaping the fall of Paris, the perfumer brought this oil to America as his only remaining asset. We contracted for the entire stock. This is perhaps the last great perfume that will come from Paris until Germany falls.

The fragrance is that of the rich, opu- lent bouquets for which the French are famous, yet it is so dry and woodsy that it is not cloying. Outstanding.

Victoria Regina: Based on the formula for the consecrated oil used in anointing Queen Victoria at her corona- tion. Rich and fragrant. Not for the ingenue.

Song of the Heart: A dry, woodsy fragrance with no trace of sweetness, yet definitely not heavy. A perfume of un- usual distinction.

PERFUME PRICES			
Size	Cost of Perfume	Federal Tax	Total Price
1 dram	$0.65	$0.07	$0.72
2 drams	1.25	.13	1.38
½ oz.	2.25	.23	2.48
1 oz.	4.00	.40	4.40

COLOGNE PRICES			
Size	Cost of Perfume	Federal Tax	Total Price
1 oz.	$0.50	$0.05	$0.55
4 oz.	1.25	.13	1.38
½ pint	2.35	.24	2.59
1 pint	4.50	.45	4.95

American Soaps of Imported Quality

Six 3-Ounce Cakes, Your Choice of Fragrances, in Black and Gold Gift Box, $1.10. Three 6-Ounce Cakes, Your Choice of Fragrances, n Black and Gold Gift Box, $1.00. Either Mailed to Your Order For 5 Cents Extra.

War and embargo which have stopped all mports need not deprive you of the pleasure f using quality soaps today,

Made in the best European tradition, as high a quality as the pre-war imported soaps of iirty years ago, Vaughan's Floral Scented oaps can be used with confidence by those ccustomed to these luxury products. Yet the ost is less than one-third that of soaps of qual quality.

Made from the same fine oils used in our Perfumes and Colognes. Fragrances available include the following (see descriptions under Perfume list above.)

Carnation, Lilac, Lavender, Geranium, Vio- let.

Following Prices on Soaps are Prepaid: 3 oz. cake, 23c; 6 oz. cake 41c. THESE ARE CEILING PRICES

Leonard Holden Vaughan

Born March 8, 1880.   Died September 11, 1943.

Leonard Holden Vaughan, President of Vaughan's Seed Store, died on September 11, 1943. He had been President since 1924, when he succeeded his father, John Charles Vaughan, who founded the business in 1876.

Born in Chicago in 1880, Mr. Vaughan was educated in the Chicago public schools, and in Armour Institute Academy, from which he graduated in 1899. After six months in the University of Chicago, he was enrolled in the department of horticulture of Cornell University, during the period of Prof. Liberty H. Bailey's active teaching. He was graduated in 1903 and at once entered the business.

After a training period he was placed in charge of the vegetable seed and greenhouse departments, and soon instituted and managed extensive seed and bulb growing operations, in which he took great interest, and which were constantly expanded during his life.

When he became President, he was thus equipped with thorough scientific training and twenty-one years' active participation in the business.

from the horticultural department of Cornell University, and passed several years in acquiring experience in seed an bulb production in various countries of Europe, and sections of this country. He assumed charge of the New York branch in 1930, since when he has acquired familiarity with all departments of the business.

Other officers are:

Carl Cropp, Vice President
Carl V. Cropp, Secretary
Leonard H. Vaughan, Jr., Assistant Secretary
Dr. Roger T. Vaughan, Treasurer
Gager T. Vaughan, Ass't Treasurer

Leonard H. Vaughan, Jr., a graduate of Cornell, after working in various departments for five years, was made sales manager of the company in 1938, and continues to perform those duties in addition to assuming charge of the seed and bulb farms.

Gager T. Vaughan, also trained in the horticultural department of Cornell University, entered the business in 1937, as manager of the grass seed department, in which he continues, with added duties in the supervision of other departments.

Following the example of his father, he devoted much time to furthering the interests of horticulture. He was President of the American Seed Trade Association in 1911, of the Society of American Florists in 1929, and of the Illinois State Florists' Association in 1941 and 1942. He was constantly active on committees of many organizations and just before his death, had been appointed a member of a committee of the seed trade to work with the O.P.A. on price ceilings. He was also interested in outside community activities, having been a member of the Lyons Township High School Board for nineteen years and president of that School Board for four years.

His interest in bulb growing, first concentrated on Gladioli, led him to undertake extensive experiments in commercial production of Tulip and Lily bulbs, which had never been successful in this country. When war interrupted imports from Holland and Japan, he had built up the largest tulip production in this country which thereupon became available for American use. Our Lily bulb production was also well under way in Louisiana and Oregon.

In 1904 Mr. Vaughan married Anita Wilkens, who survives with six sons and one daughter. His sons are John Charles Vaughan; Leonard H. Vaughan, Jr.; Gager Throop Vaughan; Lieut. Alan W. Vaughan, U. S. Army; Ensign Warren L. Vaughan of the U.S. Coast Guard; and Ensign Edward H. Vaughan, U. S. N. His daughter is Mrs. G. Raymond Donnersberger.

Mr. Vaughan was succeeded as President of the company by his eldest son, John Charles Vaughan, who, for several years has been manager of the New York branch. The new President was graduated

Carl Cropp, Vice-President, who has been head of the flower seed department of the company for nearly sixty years, continues to be active in that position. He is known internationally as a specialist in annual and perennial flower seeds, and for several years he has been assisted by his son, Carl V. Cropp.

Under these directing heads the organization includes the following, who perform duties in which they were trained during the life either of J. C. Vaughan, the founder, or of Leonard H. Vaughan.

Edward H. Goldenstein, Manager of Bulb Department.
R. C. Becker, Manager of Nurseries.
Scott J. Redfern, Manager of Vegetable Seed Department.
E. A. Hesket, Credit Manager.
James H. Burdett, Advertising Manager.
John F. Tomczak, Head of Supply and Fertilizer Departments.
William Stallman, Head of Mail Order Division.
R. M. Carleton, Manager of Retail Store, Chicago.
Charles Keegan, Manager New York Branch.
M. Watson, Flower Seed Manager at New York.
M. Pettet, Manager Market Gardener Sales.
L. Thurlimann, Head Seed Analyst.
Frank E. McFarland, Manager of Greenhouses.

Vaughan's Seed Store, Inc., operates a retail store at 10 W. Randolph St., one of the largest retail seed stores in the United States; offices and warehouse which fill the seven story building at 601 W. Jackson Blvd., Chicago; Nursery and Greenhouse Departments at Western Springs, Illinois, a retail store and wholesale branch at 47-49 Barclay St., New York City; and farms for the production of seeds and bulbs in various sections of the United States.

J. C. VAUGHAN, PRES.

Presenting for Our Sixty-eighth Year

CARL CROPP, V. PRES.

CABLE ADDRESS
VAUGHAN, CHICAGO
CAROTIDA, NEW YORK

Vaughan's SeedStore

NEW YORK.
47-49 BARCLAY ST.

GREENHOUSES AND NURSERIES,
WESTERN SPRINGS, ILL.

GENERAL OFFICES AND WAREHOUSES
601-609 WEST JACKSON BLVD., CHICAGO 6, ILL.

CHICAGO LOOP STORE
10-12 W. RANDOLPH ST.

How to Order

How to Order: Please follow these instructions, and fill out order sheets carefully. Give correct address, with Delivery Zone, if you are in a large city.

Seed and Bulb Orders: Write quantities distinctly in the column provided and attach prices.

Plant and Tree Orders: State quantity, size or age of each variety, with prices attached.

C. O. D. Orders: Because the post office fee for collection on a C.O.D. order which the customer must pay, is out of proportion on small orders, we must decline to accept any C.O.D. order for less than $5.00. We make no C.O.D. shipments unless one-third of amount is paid in cash with order. No trees, plants or other perishable stock, are sent C.O.D.

Remittance: Please remit by money order or certified check. Do not send currency unless registered.

Mistakes: If there is any error in filling your order, write us at once with correct copy of order, for quick investigation.

Express Shipments: General orders for garden seeds with heavy weights of corn, beans, fertilizers, etc., should go by express, also all shipments containing breakables. Orders over 5 lbs. going to 5th Zone travel cheaper by express than parcel post.

All Trees, Shrubs, Bulbs and Hardy Plants are shipped as soon as weather permits. Tender plants from Greenhouses for bedding, etc., are shipped usually after May 15th. (Southern shipments any time after February.) State plainly date and manner of shipping you wish.

Parcel Post: Fourth Class Mail Matter, which includes seeds, plants, bulbs, roots, books, tools, insecticides, odorless fertilizers and requisites, may be forwarded by domestic parcel post within the United States.

DELIVERY

All flower seeds prepaid.

All vegetable seeds up to 2 lbs. prepaid. Over 2 lbs., by express or freight at buyer's expense.

All bulbs and Dahlias, bought at single and dozen prices, are prepaid to fifth zone from Chicago or New York. Larger quantities by express at buyer's expense. Exceptions to this rule are specifically noted in the offers.

All Water Lilies by mail or express at buyer's expense, except where otherwise specifically stated.

All Roses, Trees, Shrubs, Perennial and Annual Plants are shipped from Western Springs at buyer's expense.

All tools and supplies, including insecticides and fertilizers (except as specified on page 108), are F. O. B. Chicago or New York and shipped at buyer's expense.

All lawn seed is prepaid to any part of the U. S. A.

Purchases for $2.00 or more made at our loop store 10 W. Randolph St. delivered free within a 25 mile radius. This offer is subject to change with out notice, owing to war restrictions.

☛ These special Free Deliveries do not include C. O. D. shipments which travel at buyer's expense.

Our Responsibility: It is so manifestly impossible for a seller of any per ishable article to be responsible for what may happen to it after it leaves his hands, especially for seeds, which are planted in the ground under varying conditions of soil and climate, that we, in common with all American seed houses, disclaim responsibility as to the crop which may be raised from seeds which we sell.

We wish it understood that all our stocks are sold under the following conditions: VAUGHAN'S SEED STORE gives no warranty, express or implied, as to the productiveness of any seeds, bulbs or plants it sells; nor does it warrant fertilizer other than in respect to data required of the seller by statutes. It is expressly agreed that the limit of liability for all claims for loss or damages due to any cause shall be in a sum no greater than the invoice price of the goods and in no case shall it be responsible for loss or damage of the crop.

DOMESTIC PARCEL POST RATES . On Seeds, Plants, Bulbs, Roots, Books, Tools, etc. within the U. S. and Possessions.	First pound or fraction	Each additional pound or fraction
Local—Chicago or New York City	7c	1c (2 lbs.)
First and Second Zone within 150 miles of either	8c	1.1c
Third Zone within 150 to 300 miles	9c	2.9c
Fourth Zone within 300 to 600 miles	10c	3.5c
Fifth Zone within 600 to 1000 miles	11c	5.3c
Sixth Zone within 1000 to 1400 miles	12c	7c
Seventh Zone within 1400 to 1800 miles	14c	9c
Eighth Zone all over 1800 miles	15c	11c
Canada	14c	14c

Parcel Post Rates By Zones

Vaughan's Seed Store at Chicago and New York covers the United States in a remarkable way to secure cheap postal rates for its many mail order customers.

All parcels under 8 ounces are prepaid everywhere in the United States FREE. BUT seeds ordered at peck, bushel or five-pound rates, or bought in even larger quantities at cheaper prices, should go by freight, when possible, at buyer's expense.

To liberal orders from distant points WE ADD FREE, SPECIAL NEW VARIETIES of value to partly cover postage or express charges.

Aster Harrington's Pink

Asters

ardy Asters, flowering in the fall, have made
markable advances. Many of the new var-
es are All-American flowers, having been
ed from native types that grow on our road-
es. The first true pink, an American pro-
ction, is now available. For complete list of
ardy Aster Seeds and Plants, see Index.

eechwood Challenger. (New). 2½ ft.
Darkest red of all. 3 for $1.50; each, 60c.

rikarti (Wonder of Stafa). 2 ft. Amellus
type. Large sky-blue flowers in profusion
from September till late October. A famous
and valuable variety. 3 for $1.75; each, 65c.

arrington's Pink. First true pink hardy
Aster. Large flowers of luminous true pink,
first of this color on bushy plant. 3 for $1.50;
doz., $4.75; each, 60c.

Blue Gown. 4 ft. Very large flowers of a
delightful china blue color. Pyramidal
growth. 3 for $1.50; doz., $4.50.

Mount Everest. 3 ft. Best white variety.
Large flowers. 3 for $1.50; each, 60c.

Palmyra. Very hardy semi-double pink.
Medium height. Novelty. 3 for $1.50;
each, 60c.

Shasta Daisy

Chiffon. 2 ft. The flowers, 2 inches across,
have fringed and laciniated petals, interlaced, see picture. Long flowering period.
Needs winter protection. 3 for $1.25; doz.,
$4.00; each, 50c.

Hardy Carnation

Beatrix. 16 in. Has large, double, pale salmon-pink blooms, very fragrant and giving
an abundance of bloom all summer. 3 for
$1.25; doz., $4.00; each 50c.

Crimson King. 2 ft. Closely resembling a
Carnation in size and habit of growth. Large,
fragrant, bright crimson blooms of velvety
appearance borne in profusion in June and
continuing until heavy frost. 3 for $1.25;
doz., $4.00; each, 50c.

Silver Mine. Produces pure white flower on 8
to 10 inch stem. Deep green foliage; it is
a prolific bloomer. One of the most striking
recent introductions. 3 for $1.35; doz.,
$4.25; each, 55c.

Carnation Crimson King

Chrys. Pohatcong. 3 for $1.25	Chrys. Roberta Copeland. 3 for $1.25	Chrys. Algonquin. 3 for $1.25

Chrys. Sept. Bronze. 3 for $1.00	Chrys. Glomero. 3 for $1.25	Chrys. Redbank. (U. of C.) 3 for $1.50

Six Outstanding Chrysanthemums,
Catalogue Value $2.65, **$2.00** •
By Express Collect

ne Each of the Varieties Illustrated above, as follows: Pohatcong, lavender rose; Roberta Copeland, Tomato red; Algonquin, deep yellow; Glomero,
bronze yellow, 3 for $1.25; Sept. Bronze, large bronze button, 3 for $1.00; Redbank, bright red, 3 for $1.50. For complete list of Chrysanthemums, see index.

1944